Keep this book. You will
need it and use it throughout
your career.

HOSPITALITY INDUSTRY COMPUTER SYSTEMS

Educational Institute Courses

Introductory

INTRODUCTION TO THE HOSPITALITY INDUSTRY
Third Edition
Gerald W. Lattin

AN INTRODUCTION TO HOSPITALITY TODAY
Second Edition
Rocco M. Angelo, Andrew N. Vladimir

TOURISM AND THE HOSPITALITY INDUSTRY
Joseph D. Fridgen

Rooms Division

FRONT OFFICE PROCEDURES
Fourth Edition
Michael L. Kasavana, Richard M. Brooks

HOUSEKEEPING MANAGEMENT
Margaret M. Kappa, Aleta Nitschke, Patricia B. Schappert

Human Resources

HOSPITALITY SUPERVISION
Second Edition
Raphael R. Kavanaugh, Jack D. Ninemeier

HOSPITALITY INDUSTRY TRAINING
Second Edition
Lewis C. Forrest, Jr.

HUMAN RESOURCES MANAGEMENT
Robert H. Woods

Marketing and Sales

MARKETING OF HOSPITALITY SERVICES
Revised Edition
Christopher W. L. Hart, David A. Troy

HOSPITALITY SALES AND MARKETING
Second Edition
James R. Abbey

CONVENTION MANAGEMENT AND SERVICE
Leonard H. Hoyle, David C. Dorf, Thomas J. A. Jones

MARKETING IN THE HOSPITALITY INDUSTRY
Third Edition
Ronald A. Nykiel

Accounting

UNDERSTANDING HOSPITALITY ACCOUNTING I
Third Edition
Raymond Cote

BASIC FINANCIAL ACCOUNTING FOR THE HOSPITALITY INDUSTRY
Raymond S. Schmidgall, James W. Damitio

FINANCIAL ACCOUNTING FOR THE HOSPITALITY INDUSTRY II
Second Edition
Raymond Cote

MANAGERIAL ACCOUNTING FOR THE HOSPITALITY INDUSTRY
Third Edition
Raymond S. Schmidgall

Food and Beverage

FOOD AND BEVERAGE MANAGEMENT
Second Edition
Jack D. Ninemeier

QUALITY SANITATION MANAGEMENT
Ronald F. Cichy

FOOD PRODUCTION PRINCIPLES
Jerald W. Chesser

FOOD AND BEVERAGE SERVICE
Anthony M. Rey, Ferdinand Wieland

HOSPITALITY PURCHASING MANAGEMENT
William P. Virts

BAR AND BEVERAGE MANAGEMENT
Lendal H. Kotschevar, Mary L. Tanke

FOOD AND BEVERAGE CONTROLS
Third Edition
Jack D. Ninemeier

General Hospitality Management

HOTEL/MOTEL SECURITY MANAGEMENT
Raymond C. Ellis, Jr., Security Committee of AH&MA

HOSPITALITY LAW
Third Edition
Jack P. Jefferies

RESORT MANAGEMENT
Second Edition
Chuck Y. Gee

INTERNATIONAL HOTEL MANAGEMENT
Chuck Y. Gee

HOSPITALITY INDUSTRY COMPUTER SYSTEMS
Second Edition
Michael L. Kasavana, John J. Cahill

MANAGING FOR QUALITY IN THE HOSPITALITY INDUSTRY
Robert H. Woods, Judy Z. King

Engineering and Facilities Management

FACILITIES MANAGEMENT
David M. Stipanuk, Harold Roffman

HOSPITALITY INDUSTRY ENGINEERING SYSTEMS
Michael H. Redlin, David M. Stipanuk

HOSPITALITY ENERGY AND WATER MANAGEMENT
Robert E. Aulbach

HOSPITALITY INDUSTRY COMPUTER SYSTEMS

Second Edition

Michael L. Kasavana, Ph.D.
John J. Cahill, CHA

EDUCATIONAL INSTITUTE
of the American Hotel & Motel Association

Disclaimer

...ccurate and authoritative information in regard to the subject matter covered. It is sold with the understanding that the publisher is not engaged in rendering legal, accounting, or other professional service. If legal advice or other expert assistance is required, the services of a competent professional person should be sought.
—*From the Declaration of Principles jointly adopted by the American Bar Association and a Committee of Publishers and Associations*

The authors, Michael L. Kasavana and John J. Cahill, are solely responsible for the contents of this publication. All views expressed herein are solely those of the authors and do not necessarily reflect the views of the Educational Institute of the American Hotel & Motel Association (the Institute) or the American Hotel & Motel Association (AH&MA).

Nothing contained in this publication shall constitute a standard, an endorsement, or a recommendation of the Institute or AH&MA. The Institute and AH&MA disclaim any liability with respect to the use of any information, procedure, or product, or reliance thereon by any member of the hospitality industry.

©Copyright 1992, 1996
By the EDUCATIONAL INSTITUTE of the
AMERICAN HOTEL & MOTEL ASSOCIATION
1407 South Harrison Road
P.O. Box 1240
East Lansing, Michigan 48826

The Educational Institute of the American
Hotel & Motel Association is a nonprofit
educational foundation.

Printed in the United States of America
 2 3 4 5 6 7 8 9 10 00 99 98 97 96

 ISBN 0-86612-064-5
 ISBN 0-86612-125-0 (pbk.)

Editors: George Glazer
            Priscilla J. Wood

Contents

Congratulations   ix

Preface   xi

Study Tips   xiii

Part I   Introduction to Computer Systems   1

1   Automation in the Hospitality Industry   3

   Data Processing   4
   Electronic Data Processing   5
   Types of Computers   8
   Computers in the Hospitality Industry   10
   Hotel Property Management Systems   11
   Computerized Restaurant Management Systems   16
   Sales and Catering Applications   17
   Hospitality Accounting Applications   18
   Summary   20
   Key Terms   21
   Discussion Questions   22

2   Essentials of Computer Systems   25

   Input/Output Units   25
   The Central Processing Unit   31
   External Storage Devices   34
   Anatomy of a Microcomputer   36
   Software   41
   The Operating System   41
   Summary   46
   Key Terms   47
   Discussion Questions   48

3   Generic Applications Software   51

   Word Processing Software   51
   Electronic Spreadsheet Software   58
   Database Management Software   64
   Electronic Communications   71
   Summary   76
   Key Terms   78
   Discussion Questions   79

Part II   Computer-Based Hotel Property Management Systems **81**

4 Computer-Based Reservation Systems **83**

Central Reservation Systems 83
Property-Level Reservation Module 89
New Developments 94
Summary 97
Key Terms 97
Discussion Questions 98

5 Rooms Management and Guest Accounting Applications **101**

Rooms Management Module 101
Guest Accounting Module 108
Summary 114
Key Terms 115
Discussion Questions 115

6 Property Management System Interfaces **119**

Point-of-Sale Systems 119
Call Accounting Systems 123
Electronic Locking Systems 129
Energy Management Systems 131
Auxiliary Guest Services 132
Guest-Operated Devices 133
Summary 140
Key Terms 141
Discussion Questions 142

**Part III   Computer-Based Food and Beverage Management
Systems** **143**

7 Food and Beverage Applications—Service **145**

ECR/POS Hardware Components 145
Computer-Based Guest Checks 156
ECR/POS Software 157
Automation Advances 162
Automated Beverage Control Systems 169
Summary 174
Key Terms 175
Discussion Questions 176

8 Food and Beverage Management Applications **179**

Recipe Management 179
Sales Analysis 184
Menu Management 185

Integrated Food Service Software 191
Management Reports from Automated Beverage Systems 194
Summary 199
Key Terms 202
Discussion Questions 202

Part IV   Other Hospitality Applications **203**

9   Hotel Sales and Food Service Catering Applications **205**

Automation and the Hotel Sales Office 205
Yield Management 219
Food Service Catering Software Packages 226
Summary 231
Endnotes 232
Key Terms 233
Discussion Questions 233

10   Accounting Applications **235**

Accounts Receivable Module 235
Accounts Payable Module 238
Payroll Module 242
Inventory Module 246
Purchasing Module 250
Financial Reporting Module 253
Summary 258
Endnotes 259
Key Terms 259
Discussion Questions 260

Part V   Management Responsibilities **263**

11   Selecting and Implementing Computer Systems **265**

Analyzing Current Information Needs 265
Collecting Relevant Sales Information 269
Establishing Computer System Requirements 270
Determining the Hardware Configuration 273
Requesting Proposals from Vendors 277
Site Surveys by Vendors 279
Evaluating Vendor Proposals 280
Contract Negotiations 283
Installation Factors 285
Summary 291
Key Terms 292
Discussion Questions 292

12   Managing Information Systems **295**

MIS Design and Function 295

Managing Multi-Processor Environments 297
MIS Security Issues 299
Summary 306
Key Terms 306
Discussion Questions 307

Glossary 309

Index 349

Review Quiz Answer Key 353

The Educational Institute Board of Trustees 357

Congratulations. . .

You have a running start on a fast-track career!

Developed through the input of industry and academic experts, this course gives you the know-how hospitality employers demand. Upon course completion, you will earn the respected American Hotel & Motel Association certificate that ensures instant recognition worldwide. It is your link with the global hospitality industry.

You can use your AH&MA certificate to show that your learning experiences have bridged the gap between industry and academia. You will have proof that you have met industry-driven learning objectives and that you know how to apply your knowledge to actual hospitality work situations.

By earning your course certificate, you also take a step toward completing the highly respected learning programs—Certificates of Specialization, the Hospitality Operations Certificate, and the Hospitality Management Diploma—that raise your professional development to a higher level. Certificates from these programs greatly enhance your credentials, and a permanent record of your course and program completion is maintained by the Educational Institute.

We commend you for taking this important step. Turn to the Educational Institute for additional resources that will help you stay ahead of your competition.

Preface

Automation is one of the fastest changing aspects of the hospitality industry. Advances in the areas of reservation systems, guest services, food and beverage management, hotel sales, food service catering, and hospitality accounting have placed computer systems technology in virtually every area of hospitality operations. Today, more than ever before, hospitality managers must understand the fundamental features of computer systems and manage the information systems within their organizations.

This second edition of *Hospitality Industry Computer Systems* begins by examining the essentials of computer systems. Part I lays the foundation for future chapters by defining basic terms, describing hardware and software components, and presenting examples of how generic software applications (word processing, electronic spreadsheets, database management, and electronic communications) are used in the hospitality industry.

Part II focuses on some of the components of a computerized hotel property management system. Computerized front office applications consist of a series of software programs (or modules), including reservations, rooms management, and guest accounting functions. A variety of stand-alone applications may also be interfaced with an installed property management system. Popular interfaces include microcomputers, point-of-sale systems, call accounting systems, electronic locking systems, energy management systems, auxiliary guest service devices, and guest-operated devices.

Part III examines features of computerized restaurant management systems. These chapters describe service-oriented computer applications that rely upon electronic cash register (ECR) and point-of-sale (POS) technology to monitor service area transactions through cashier terminals, precheck terminals, remote work station printers, and network controllers. Also presented are management applications that cover a broad range of functions, including recipe management, sales analysis, and menu management.

Part IV features other hospitality applications. Chapter 9 describes computer applications in relation to hotel sales office functions and yield management strategies, as well as off-premises and home-delivery food service catering operations. Chapter 10 examines hospitality accounting applications for both lodging and food service operations. Accounting applications are designed to monitor and process accounts receivable and accounts payable transactions, payroll accounting, and financial reporting. Other accounting applications are described in relation to inventory control and valuation, purchasing, and budgeting.

Part V focuses on managing the information systems in lodging and food service operations. Selecting and implementing computer systems technology is discussed with specific emphasis on assessing information needs, establishing computer system requirements, and vendor contracting. Managing multi-processor environments and information security issues are also addressed.

A debt of gratitude is owed to the following people who devoted the time and effort to make this text a valuable resource for the hospitality industry: Richard M. Brooks, CHA, Vice President of Rooms Management, Stouffer Hotel Company; John S. Chasel, Certified Public Accountant, Daytona Beach, Florida; Galen Collins, Assistant Professor, Northern Arizona University; G. C. (Mike) Fleming, Director of Research and Development, Opryland Hotel; Robert Grimes, President, Strategic Technology Services; Mark Nemtzow, Manager of Education and Consulting Services, Strategic Technology Services; and Bill Sullivan, Manager, Finance and Information Systems, E. I. du Pont Company. Also, a special note of thanks goes to Robert Horgan, President, Newmarket Software Systems, Inc., for contributing materials and reviewing the chapter on hotel sales and food service catering applications.

Michael L. Kasavana, Ph.D.
Professor
School of Hotel, Restaurant, and Institutional Management
Michigan State University

John J. Cahill, CHA
Senior Vice President, Management Information Systems
InterContinental Hotel Corporation

Study Tips for Users of
Educational Institute Courses

Learning is a skill, like many other activities. Although you may be familiar with many of the following study tips, we want to reinforce their usefulness.

Your Attitude Makes a Difference

If you want to learn, you will: it's as simple as that. Your attitude will go a long way in determining whether or not you do well in this course. We want to help you succeed.

Plan and Organize to Learn

- Set up a regular time and place for study. Make sure you won't be disturbed or distracted.

- Decide ahead of time how much you want to accomplish during each study session. Remember to keep your study sessions brief; don't try to do too much at one time.

Read the Course Text to Learn

- *Before* you read each chapter, read the chapter outline and the learning objectives. If there is a summary at the end of the chapter, you should read it to get a feel for what the chapter is about.

- Then, go back to the beginning of the chapter and *carefully* read, focusing on the material included in the learning objectives and asking yourself such questions as:

  —Do I understand the material?

  —How can I use this information now or in the future?

- Make notes in margins and highlight or underline important sections to help you as you study. Read a section first, then go back over it to mark important points.

- Keep a dictionary handy. If you come across an unfamiliar word that is not included in the textbook glossary, look it up in the dictionary.

- Read as much as you can. The more you read, the better you read.

Testing Your Knowledge

- Test questions developed by the Educational Institute for this course are designed to measure your knowledge of the material.

- End-of-the-chapter Review Quizzes help you find out how well you have studied the material. They indicate where additional study may be needed. Review Quizzes are also helpful in studying for other tests.

- Prepare for tests by reviewing:

  —learning objectives

  —notes

  —outlines

  —questions at the end of each assignment

- As you begin to take any test, read the test instructions *carefully* and look over the questions.

We hope your experiences in this course will prompt you to undertake other training and educational activities in a planned, career-long program of professional growth and development.

Part I

Introduction to Computer Systems

Chapter Outline

Data Processing
Electronic Data Processing
    Advantages of Electronic Data
      Processing
    Types of Data
    Binary Coding
Types of Computers
    Mainframe Computers
    Minicomputers
    Microcomputers
    Portable Computers
Computers in the Hospitality Industry
Hotel Property Management Systems
    Front Office Applications
    Property Management System
      Interfaces
Computerized Restaurant Management
    Systems
Sales and Catering Applications
Hospitality Accounting Applications
Summary

Learning Objectives

1. Describe the functions performed in each of the three phases of the data processing cycle.

2. Identify the ways in which electronic data processing differs from non-automated data processing.

3. Describe the three different types of data, and explain the importance of classifying data by type.

4. Explain what the term "binary code" means.

5. Distinguish bits from bytes.

6. Describe four types of computers.

7. Identify the most common front office components of a property management system.

8. Identify some of the computer systems that can interface with a hotel's property management system.

9. Compare electronic cash registers and point-of-sale terminals.

10. Describe the benefits of hotel sales and food service catering software applications.

11. Describe some of the applications typically included in hospitality accounting and back office modules.

1

Automation in the Hospitality Industry

EVERY BUSINESS collects and analyzes data about its operations. **Data** are facts and/ or figures to be processed into useful information. While all businesses use some type of information system, a computerized system enables management to achieve its goals more easily.

A **computer** is a managerial tool capable of processing large quantities of data more quickly and accurately than any other data processing method. Computers can perform arithmetic operations such as addition, subtraction, multiplication, and division, and they can perform logical functions as well, such as ranking, sorting, and assembling operations. In addition, computers can store and retrieve tremendous amounts of information and thereby allow managers to exercise control over procedures that they might otherwise overlook.

A computer system also streamlines the process of collecting and recording data and expands the ways in which information is organized and reported. In addition, a computer system enables management to speed up the process by which useful information is made available to those who make decisions.

How much does a manager need to know about a computer to operate one? About as much as a motorist needs to know about auto mechanics to drive a car.

A motorist does not need to master the mechanical wonders of the internal combustion engine to drive a car. A driver simply needs to learn how to instruct the machine. He or she only needs to learn how to turn the ignition key, push the gas pedal, apply the brake, and so on. Sparks jump, cylinders explode, pistons pump, and gears turn, regardless of the driver's knowledge of mechanical engineering. However, if a motorist has some understanding of auto mechanics as well as basic auto maintenance skills, the car should perform even better and meet his or her transportation needs for a longer period of time.

Similarly, in order to use a computer as an effective means of operating an information system, a manager does not need to learn the intricacies of electronic circuitry etched on silicon chips. The manager simply needs to learn the commands by which to instruct the computer to carry out the desired functions. However, if a manager also has some basic knowledge about the essential operations of a computer system, he or she will be better equipped to use a computer as an effective tool in managing information needs. A basic knowledge of the way computer systems operate enables managers to select computer systems which best meet the information needs of their operations, or to expand the data processing functions of their present computer systems. Some knowledge of computer jargon

3

(frequently termed "computerese") can be extremely helpful in identifying the functions desired from a computer system and in understanding the functioning of the system itself.

This chapter introduces many basic computer terms while explaining the nature of electronic data processing. The chapter also identifies the basic information needs of lodging and food service operations and examines how computerized information systems meet these needs.

Data Processing

Data processing involves transforming raw facts and isolated figures into timely, accurate, and useful information. Every day, hospitality managers are bombarded with facts and figures about the results of operations. However, these individual pieces of data are relatively meaningless until they undergo a process that organizes or manipulates them into useful information.

Information, the result of data processing, is clearly one of the most valuable resources of a hospitality business. Information can increase a manager's knowledge regarding guests, service, labor, finance, and other areas of concern. Also, information may reduce the uncertainty that managers may experience in decision-making situations. And, after decisions have been made, information can provide managers with important feedback on the effectiveness of their decisions and may even indicate new areas of concern that call for corrective action.

Data processing is not unique to the world of business; it is an important function that occurs in everyday life as well. Everyone processes data. For example, consider what may happen on a typical payday.

After receiving a paycheck, a person may consider all of the items he or she would like to purchase, the cost of those items, and the difference between the amount of the paycheck and the total amount of the planned purchases. If the amount of the paycheck is greater than the amount of planned purchases, the person may decide to place the surplus amount in a savings account. If, on the other hand, the total amount of planned purchases is greater than the amount of the paycheck, the person may reconsider the purchase options, or, perhaps, consider taking out a loan.

In this example of data processing, a collection of data (the amount of the paycheck and the purchase options) is processed (totaled and compared) and, thus, transformed into information (surplus or deficit) useful in making decisions (what to buy, how much to save, or how much to borrow).

The conversion of data into information is accomplished through a cycle of events identified as input, process, and output. Using the terms of our previous example of data processing in everyday life, the paycheck and the purchase options are inputs; totaling the planned purchases and comparing that total with the amount of the paycheck is the processing; and the resulting surplus or deficit is the output. The sequence of input, process, and output is the basic **data processing cycle** as illustrated in Exhibit 1.

During input, data are collected and organized to simplify subsequent processing functions. During processing, input data are mathematically manipulated

Exhibit 1   The Data Processing Cycle

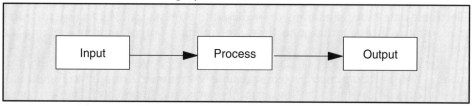

Exhibit 2   The Electronic Data Processing Cycle

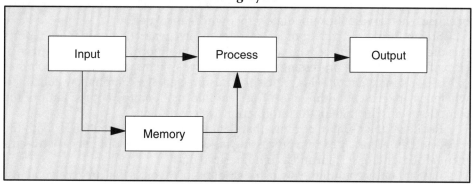

or logically arranged to generate meaningful output. The output can be reported for immediate use or saved for future reference.

The data processing cycle is not new, nor is it limited to computer applications. For example, standard recipes can be viewed as data processing techniques that food service operations have used for a long time to convert raw ingredients into finished menu items. Viewed from the perspective of the data processing cycle, ingredients and their corresponding quantities are the inputs to recipe production; following the recipe's instructions is the process by which the desired recipe output (the number of standard portions) is produced.

Electronic Data Processing

The speed, accuracy, and efficiency required for an effective information system are often best achieved through electronic data processing. The difference between data processing (DP) and electronic data processing (EDP) lies in the automation of the process and the addition of a memory unit. Exhibit 2 illustrates the electronic data processing cycle.

Electronic data processing employs a computer system. The automation of input, process, and output events within the basic data processing cycle results in faster and more efficient operation. Also, the addition of a memory unit allows for the storage of data or instructions for more reliable and thorough processing.

Advantages of Electronic Data Processing

Electronic data processing transforms data into timely, accurate, and useful information by reducing turnaround time, streamlining output, and minimizing the handling of data.

Turnaround time refers to the time that elapses between data input and information output. Computer systems are able to minimize turnaround time for almost all data processing tasks. Inquiry and search procedures should be performed within an acceptable response time. For example, if a front desk employee needs to find out in which room a guest is registered, the information should be generated quickly. Also, a busy food and beverage manager would appreciate the speed and accuracy of an effective computer system when spot-checking the inventory level of expensive ingredients immediately following a meal period.

Streamlining the output of a computer means generating only those reports that are requested by those who will actually use the information. A frequent criticism of electronic data processing is that computer systems produce large volumes of irrelevant information. This criticism is misdirected. If a computer system overwhelms management with reams of useless information, it is not the fault of the computer—it is the fault of the information system design.

Reducing the number of times that data must be handled enhances both the speed and the accuracy of data processing tasks. Consider the difference between a manual accounting system and a computerized one.

In a manual accounting system, the amounts of invoices that are received must first be recorded in a journal. The amounts are carried over to a ledger. Amounts recorded in the ledger are then used to prepare financial statements. During each of these steps it is possible for a bookkeeper to make any number of mistakes such as recording the wrong number, writing a number's digits in the wrong order (transposing them), calculating a total incorrectly, and so on. The greater the number of times data must be handled, the greater the possibility for error.

In a computerized data processing system, the invoice amount is entered only once. The amount can then be accessed by the programs which prepare the journal, ledger, and financial statements. Therefore, when the amount of the invoice is entered correctly, all of the subsequent financial statements will be mathematically correct. If the amount is entered incorrectly, but the mistake identified and corrected, the correction automatically flows from the journal through to the financial statements. With electronic data processing, there are fewer opportunities for error, because it is not necessary to rehandle the same data at each step in the accounting process.

Types of Data

There are three distinct types of data. One type is called **alpha data** because it consists only of letters of the alphabet. For example, the names of menu items, servers, and hotel guests are all types of alpha data. A second kind of data is called **numeric data** because it consists only of numbers. Menu prices, room numbers, guest check serial numbers, and occupancy percentages are all forms of numeric data. The third type of data is termed **alphanumeric data** because it is made up of both letters and numbers. A hotel's street address, a menu item's description, and personnel records are all examples of alphanumeric data used in the hospitality industry.

Classifying data by type can be very helpful when users are operating in a computerized environment. When a data processing system is programmed, each data element must be "introduced" to the computer so that the computer is aware of the type of data and the maximum number of characters (i.e., letters, numbers, or symbols) it may have. Once the computer is programmed with this information, the system will not allow users to input data which does not meet precise specifications. For example, if a reservation system expects the telephone number of a guest to have ten numeric characters, and a user mistakenly enters nine numbers and a single letter, the computer will refuse the data entry and inform the user that he or she has made a mistake. This feature reduces the potential number of data entry errors and enhances the reliability of the data entered into the electronic data processing system.

Binary Coding

Regardless of whether alpha, numeric, or alphanumeric data are to be entered into an electronic data processing system, in order for the computer to process it, the data must be translated into a binary code. The **binary code** is a counting system based on two digits, zero and one. This is the easiest way for a computer to handle data because electronic circuits have two natural states: "on," usually represented by binary digit one; and "off," represented by binary digit zero.

A **bit** is the smallest unit of electronic data. The term bit is short for a *BI*nary digi*T* (which is either zero or one). All characters (letters, numbers, and symbols) are represented by a special sequence of binary digits. For example, the characters "A," "B," and "C" may be converted into binary code as follows:

$$A = 01000001$$

$$B = 01000010$$

$$C = 01000011$$

A special sequence of bits representing a single character is called a **byte**. A byte is a group of adjacent bits that work, or are operated on, as a unit. Theoretically, a byte may be any length, but the most common length for a byte is eight bits, with some computers using seven.

Bytes take up memory space and are typically measured as kilobytes. A **kilobyte** represents approximately one thousand bytes (1,024 bytes). Kilobyte is often abbreviated as "K" or "KB" and is used to describe computer memory capacity. A **megabyte**, abbreviated as "MB," represents approximately one million bytes (1,048,576 bytes). A **gigabyte**, abbreviated as "GB," represents approximately one billion bytes (1,073,741,834 bytes).

The memory capacity of computers has increased dramatically. Only a few years ago, small personal computers were typically advertised as having 256 K memory. Many standard personal computer units soon increased to 640 K memory. Today, personal computers can store 20 to 40 megabytes of data.

Types of Computers

Advances in computer technology have made it difficult to classify computers in terms of variables other than memory capacity. In the past, computers were relatively easy to classify in relation to such variables as:

- Speed of operation

- Size of components

- Number of peripheral devices supported

- Number of simultaneous users

- Extent of software library

- Complexity of operation

- Cost

However, recent advancements in computer design and technology have made it increasingly difficult to differentiate computers by any single variable. Given this situation, it is best to discuss the different types of computers from a historical perspective and define mainframe computers, minicomputers, and microcomputers in terms of their places in the evolution of computer technology.

Mainframe Computers

The term "mainframe computer" was originally used to describe the *MAIN FRAME*work of the central processor within a computer system. The first mainframe business computers appeared in the early 1950s and were made up of vacuum tubes for electronic circuitry. Punched cards were the main source of input, and magnetic drums were used for internal storage. First generation computers were slow and bulky, and generated extraordinary amounts of heat.

A second generation of mainframe computers evolved in the early 1960s as transistors and diodes became the main circuit components. Transistors were smaller, faster, and more reliable than the vacuum tubes that they replaced. Magnetic cores replaced magnetic drums as main storage and magnetic tape and disks became available for external data storage.

In the mid-1960s, transistor technology was replaced by solid-state logic in the form of silicon chips with integrated circuitry. **Silicon chips** are pieces of semiconductor material onto which electronic circuitry is etched. These chips are no larger than one's fingernail and can hold as much information as did hundreds of electronic tubes connected to the original mainframe computers. Along with the installation of silicon chips, computer storage shifted from magnetic cores to integrated circuit boards that provided expandable storage.

Today, there are mainframe computers as large as the early machines; however, they are capable of processing more data than all of the original mainframe computers combined. In fact, today's hand-held calculators offer virtually the same level of sophistication as the first mainframe computers.

Minicomputer. (Courtesy of MAI Basic Four, Inc.)

The use of silicon chips produced gains in efficiency and also reduced the size and cost of computers. Many businesses soon found that their data processing needs could be met by a minicomputer.

Minicomputers

The third generation of computers (in the early 1970s) produced the **minicomputer**—a slower, less powerful, but smaller and cheaper alternative to the mainframe computer. The computer's commercial potential began with the appearance of the minicomputer. These systems possess the same components as larger mainframe computers but typically have reduced memory capability and slower processing abilities. Minicomputers also allow fewer users to simultaneously interact, and support fewer peripheral devices (such as printers and display screens). Although the minicomputer is less powerful than a mainframe computer, it is generally more powerful than a microcomputer.

Microcomputers

The fourth generation of computers (mid-1970s) introduced the **microcomputer,** or "personal computer." Despite their small size, they contain the same types of components as the larger machines and may have options such as hard disks, color monitors, graphics capability, and others. Many hospitality businesses find that their data processing needs can be met by microcomputers.

A microcomputer is so compact that its central processing unit (CPU) is contained on a single silicon chip that is less than one quarter of an inch square and uses less energy than a 100-watt light bulb. The CPU of a microcomputer is also known as a **microprocessor.** The microprocessor is an integrated circuit package containing a complete electronic circuit or group of circuits. Its circuits make up a

Microcomputer. (Courtesy of Sanyo Business Systems Corporation)

central processing unit that controls the computer, carries out calculations, directs the flow of data, and performs many other functions as well. Businesses that in the past exclusively used mainframes and minicomputers are currently using powerful microcomputers.

Portable Computers

Portable computers offer many complete system features, approximate microcomputer performance, and provide unmatched convenience. Initially, the field of portable computers was limited to desktop machinery that could be carried from office to home and back, in an automobile. In response to user demands for faster processing, increased storage capacity, higher screen resolution, greater expandability, and devices requiring less power, computer manufacturers developed a myriad of laptop and hand-held portable computers. The laptop computer, a light-weight powerful workstation, has made portable computers popular. Hand-held models, which range from tiny note-taking devices to large calculator formats, are also available.

Computers in the Hospitality Industry ─────────

During the past decade, nothing has enhanced the professionalism nor increased the productivity of the hospitality industry more than the computer. Computers have changed the way hotels and restaurants plan, coordinate, evaluate, and control their operations.

Recent technological developments in the management of computers in the lodging industry have significantly affected both front and back office procedures. Hoteliers are no longer dependent upon an assortment of metal racks, a collection of mechanical equipment, or a set of routine clerical tasks. From the moment potential guests contact a property for reservations to the settlement of their accounts, a computer system is capable of monitoring, charting, and recording all transactions between guests and the hotel. Likewise, computer systems technology has also significantly affected food service and management activities in food and beverage operations. Restaurateurs are no longer dependent upon mechanical cash registers, volumes of sales journals, and routine clerical procedures.

The dependence of the hospitality industry on computer processing is continuing to grow. In fact, many hotels and restaurants employ comprehensive computer-based information systems. These systems are briefly discussed in the following sections.

Hotel Property Management Systems

A computer-based lodging information system is commonly called a **property management system** (PMS). Although the components of a PMS may vary, the term PMS is generally used to describe the set of computer programs that directly relate to front office and back office activities. **Applications software** is the term for computer programs that instruct the hardware of a computer system in what to do, when to do it, and how to do it.

Computerized front office applications consist of a series of software programs (or modules) including reservations, rooms management, and guest accounting functions. A variety of stand-alone applications may also be interfaced with an installed property management system. Popular interfaces include microcomputers, point-of-sale systems, call accounting systems, electronic locking systems, energy management systems, auxiliary guest service devices, and guest-operated devices. Computerized back office applications typically included in back office PMS packages contain modules covering accounting and internal control functions. These hospitality accounting applications are discussed later in this chapter. The following sections briefly describe some of the basic features of PMS front office applications and PMS interfaces.

Front Office Applications

While hotel property management systems differ, many of them offer **front office applications** software in relation to reservations, rooms management, and guest accounting functions.

Reservations Module. A **reservations module** enables a hotel to rapidly process room requests and generate timely and accurate rooms, revenue, and forecasting reports. Reservations received at a central reservations site can be processed, confirmed, and communicated to the destination property before the reservationist finishes talking with the caller on the telephone. When the destination property

Fully automated, stand-alone front desk system. (Courtesy of National Semiconductor DATACHECKER/DTS Corporation)

uses a property management system, the reservations module receives data directly from the central reservation system, and in-house reservations records, files, and revenue forecasts are immediately updated. In addition, the reservations data can be automatically reformatted into preregistration materials and an updated expected arrivals list can be generated.

Rooms Management Module. A **rooms management module** maintains up-to-date information regarding the status of rooms, assists in the assignment of rooms during registration, and helps coordinate many guest ser-vices. Since this module replaces most traditional front office equipment, it often becomes a major determinant in the selection of one PMS over another. This module alerts front desk employees of each room's status just as room and information racks do in non-automated environments. For example, with a room rack, an upside-down card without a folio covering it may signify that the previous night's guest has checked out, but that the room has not yet been cleaned for resale. This status will remain unchanged until housekeeping notifies the front desk that the room is clean and ready for occupancy. In a computerized system, the front desk employee simply enters the room's number at a keyboard and the current status of the room appears immediately on a display screen. Once the room becomes clean and ready for occupancy, housekeeping changes the room's status through a terminal in the housekeeping work area, and the information is immediately communicated to the front desk.

Guest Accounting Module. A **guest accounting module** increases the hotel's control over guest accounts and significantly modifies the night audit routine. Guest accounts are maintained electronically, thereby eliminating the need for folio cards, trays, or posting machinery. The guest accounting module monitors predetermined guest credit limits and provides flexibility through multiple folio formats. When revenue centers are connected to the PMS, remote electronic cash registers or point-of-sale terminals communicate with the front desk, and guest charges are automatically posted to the appropriate folios. At check-out, outstanding account balances are transferred automatically to the city ledger (accounts receivable) for collection. Exhibit 3 shows a sample guest folio used by some automated lodging properties. Exhibit 4 summarizes hotel front office applications.

Property Management System Interfaces

PMS interface applications are stand-alone computer packages that may be linked to a hotel computer system. Although the number and kinds of software packages that may be linked to a hotel system are continuously growing, the most popular interfaces include those discussed in the following sections. Exhibit 5 shows important **PMS interfaces.**

Microcomputer Interfaces. Microcomputer interfaces to larger hotel computer systems have become a popular means of expanding data processing capabilities. Downloading (transferring) data from the hotel systems to a microcomputer enables management to use data contained in the hotel system's software with software applications designed for the microcomputer. For example, the lodging system may maintain all of a hotel's accounting data. When designing next year's budget, management may wish to base projections on actual transactions of the current accounting period. If management is able to download the necessary accounting data from the PMS to the microcomputer, the data can be used by microcomputer software applications that may include word processing, electronic spreadsheets, database management, and communications programs.

Point-of-Sale Systems. A **point-of-sale system**, such as a network of electronic cash registers, is capable of capturing data at point-of-sale (POS) locations and transferring them to the system's guest accounting and financial tracking modules. The ability to communicate such data to both front and back office components can result in numerous benefits derived through comprehensive reporting.

Telephone Call Accounting Systems. Few other interfaces have received more attention than telephone call accounting has. A **telephone call accounting system** (CAS) enables a hotel to take control over local and long-distance telephone services and to apply a markup to switchboard operations. A call accounting system can place and price outgoing calls. When a CAS is interfaced with a front office guest accounting module, telephone charges can immediately be posted to the proper folios. The hotel's telephone department, traditionally a loss leader, can become a potential profit center.

Electronic Locking Systems. Many types of electronic locking systems are available today. Often these systems interface with a front office computer system,

Exhibit 3   Sample Guest Folio Used by Automated Lodging Properties

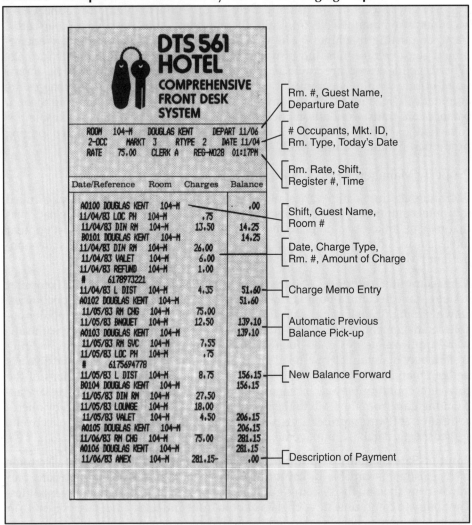

Courtesy of National Semiconductor DATACHECKER/DTS Corporation

thereby enabling management to exercise important key control measures. One kind of **electronic locking system** functions through a computer terminal at the front desk. The terminal selects a code which will permit entry and then produces a card for the guest to use. Once a code is entered and a card produced, all previous codes are canceled, and cards issued to previous guests no longer function.

Energy Management Systems. Interfacing energy management systems with a hotel computer system links guestroom energy controls with the front office rooms

Exhibit 4   PMS Front Office Applications

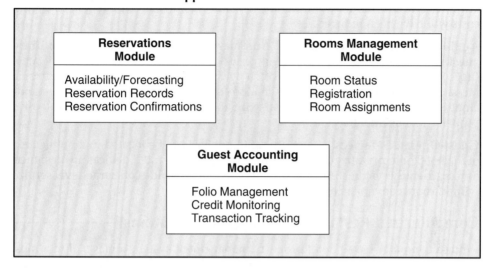

Exhibit 5   Hotel Property Management System Interfaces

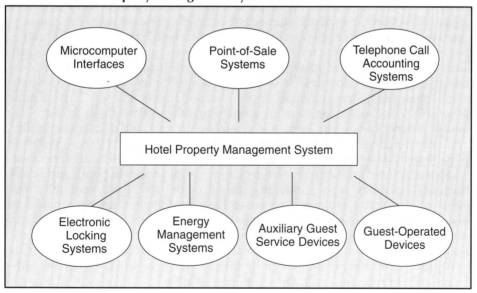

management package. An **energy management system** monitors guestroom temperatures by computer. This may lead to significant reductions in energy consumption and lower energy costs. For example, in the cold winter months, an unoccupied room may be maintained at a temperature of 60°F (15.6°C). When a guest checks in and is assigned a guestroom, the computer can automatically turn up the room's temperature to a more comfortable 70°F (21.1°C). By the time the guest reaches the room, the temperature will be acceptable, and the hotel's energy costs will have been reduced.

Auxiliary Guest Service Devices. Automation has simplified many **auxiliary guest services**, such as the placement of wake-up calls and the delivery of messages to guests. These functions are often performed by devices (such as electronic message-waiting systems and voice mailbox systems) that are marketed as stand-alone systems that can be interfaced with the rooms management module of a property management system.

Guest-Operated Devices. Guest-operated devices can be located in a public area of the hotel or in private guestrooms. In-room guest-operated devices are designed as user-friendly systems. An assortment of devices provide concierge-level service with in-room convenience.

Computerized Restaurant Management Systems

While a computer-based hotel property management system consists of modules, a computer-based **restaurant management system** (RMS) functions through specific hardware components and a wide variety of applications software packages.

Food and beverage service applications vary considerably depending upon the type of operation (quick service, table service, or institutional service), kinds of meals offered (breakfast, lunch, dinner, banquets, etc.), and the degree of autonomy given to restaurant management officials (independent, franchise, or corporate).

For our purposes, the term **service applications** refers to software programs used by restaurant management systems to process data related to front-of-the-house food service activities. Service-oriented applications of a computer-based restaurant management system rely upon electronic cash register (ECR) and point-of-sale (POS) technology to monitor service area transactions through cashier terminals, precheck terminals, remote work station printers, and network controllers.

The term **electronic cash register** refers to an independent (stand-alone) computer system. The cash register frame houses the necessary three components of a computer system: an input/output device, a central processing unit, and storage (memory) capability. A **point-of-sale terminal**, on the other hand, contains its own input/output device and may even possess a small storage (memory) capacity, but does not contain its own central processing unit. In order for POS transactions to be processed, the terminal must be interfaced with (connected to) a central processing unit that is located outside of the terminal's housing. Some food service properties may reduce the cost of automation by interfacing several POS terminals with a large central processing unit. Other operations may find a series of ECRs to be more effective.

ECRs and POS terminals are hardware components. The physical layout and interconnection of hardware components within an automated system is called a **configuration**.

Like all computer hardware components, ECRs and POS terminals require software programs that tell them what to do, how to do it, and when to do it. Service-related applications software programs include prechecking, check tracking, sales

Exhibit 6 Sample Computer-Generated Guest Check

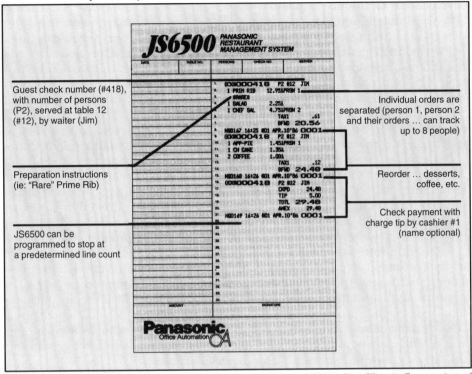

Guest check number (#418), with number of persons (P2), served at table 12 (#12), by waiter (Jim)

Preparation instructions (ie: "Rare" Prime Rib)

JS6500 can be programmed to stop at a predetermined line count

Individual orders are separated (person 1, person 2 and their orders ... can track up to 8 people)

Reorder ... desserts, coffee, etc.

Check payment with charge tip by cashier #1 (name optional)

Source: Panasonic Industrial Company, POS Systems Division of Matsushita Electric Corporation of America.

analysis, and limited attendance and inventory control packages. Exhibit 6 shows a computer-generated guest check. The term **management applications** refers to applications software used by computer-based restaurant management systems to process data related to back-of-the-house food service activities.

Sales and Catering Applications

Hotel sales office staff and food service catering managers spend a great part of each day processing paperwork related to information collected through prospecting, selling, booking, and reporting. Today, at many properties, much of this time-consuming and costly effort is handled with computers.

In a fully automated sales office, every salesperson with a computer terminal has immediate access to guestroom control information. Bookings and cancellations can be quickly processed as they occur—even as the salesperson is on the telephone with the client. This helps ensure that every salesperson has access to exactly the same information, and that "definite" and "tentative" bookings are clearly identified to prevent errors. Also, an automated sales office system can produce reports that provide information on accounts, bookings, market segments, sales staff productivity, average room rates, occupancy, revenue, service history, lost business, and important marketing data. Many of these reports would take several hours to produce manually.

Yield management, sometimes called revenue management, is a set of demand-forecasting techniques used to determine whether prices should be raised or lowered and whether a reservation request should be accepted or rejected in order to maximize revenue. Yield management is based on supply and demand. Prices tend to rise when demand exceeds supply; prices tend to fall when supply exceeds demand. One of the principal computations involved in yield management is **yield**, which is the ratio of actual revenue to potential revenue. Actual revenue is the revenue generated by the number of rooms sold. Potential revenue is the amount of money that the property would receive if all of its rooms were sold at full rack rates.

There are many formulas used to implement yield management strategies. Although the individual computations involving yield management can be performed manually, doing so is very difficult and time-consuming. The most efficient means of handling data and generating yield statistics is through a computer. Sophisticated yield management software can integrate room demand and room price statistics, and project the highest revenue-generating product mix.

Catering software monitors and controls the activities associated with each stage of off-premises catering service. Many of the files created through the use of catering software packages perform functions similar to computer-based restaurant management applications. In addition to containing data on all purchased food and beverage products, catering files include data on such non-food items as labor, serving utensils, production equipment, rental equipment, disposable items, and entertainment options. The more complete this file, the easier it becomes for the caterer to assemble an entire catering service package.

Hospitality Accounting Applications

The number of accounting software modules provided by a back office PMS or RMS may vary widely. A typical back office system contains application software designed to monitor and process accounts receivable and accounts payable transactions, payroll accounting, and financial reporting. Additional back office programs include inventory control and valuation, purchasing, and budgeting. The following sections present an overview of the applications typically included in a PMS back office package.

Accounts Receivable Module. An **accounts receivable module** monitors outstanding balances of guest accounts. An account receivable is a dollar amount representing charged purchases made by a guest who has deferred payment for the products and services rendered by the hotel. Accounts receivable balances can be automatically transferred from front office software applications, or they can be manually posted directly into an accounts receivable program. Once entered into the back office system, account collection begins. Account billings and the aging of accounts receivable can also be monitored by this back office software.

Accounts Payable Module. The **accounts payable module** tracks purchases, creditor positions, and the hotel's banking status. Accounts payable activities normally consist of posting purveyor invoices, determining amounts due, and printing checks for payment. Three major files maintained by an accounts payable module are:

- Vendor master file
- Invoice register file
- Check register file

The vendor master file contains an index of vendor names, addresses, telephone numbers, vendor code numbers, standard discount terms (time and percentage), and space for additional information. An invoice register file is a complete list of outstanding invoices cataloged by vendor, invoice date, invoice number, or invoice due date. This file becomes especially important when management wishes to take advantage of vendor discount rates. The calculation and printing of bank checks for payment to vendors is monitored through the check register file. Check production and distribution is summarized into a payables report and reconciled with bank statements.

Payroll Module. A **payroll accounting module** is an important part of a back office package because of the complexities involved in properly processing time and attendance records, unique employee benefits, pay rates, withholdings, deductions, and required payroll reports. The payroll accounting module must be capable of handling job codes, employee meals, uniform credits, tips, taxes, and other data that affect the net pay of employees. The unique nature of payroll data dictates that special care be taken to maintain an accurate payroll register, to closely control the issuing of payroll checks, and to protect the confidentiality and propriety of payroll data.

Inventory Module. A back office **inventory module** automates several internal control and accounting functions. Internal control is essential to efficient hospitality industry operations. By accessing inventory data maintained by an inventory master file, a back office inventory module is generally able to address three of the most common inventory concerns: inventory status, inventory variance, and inventory valuation. Inventory status refers to an account of how much of each item is in storage; inventory variance refers to differences between a physical count of an item and the balance maintained by the perpetual inventory system; and inventory valuation refers to the value of items in inventory.

Purchasing Module. A back office **purchasing module** maintains a purchase order file and a bid specification file. This module enhances management's control over purchasing, ordering, and receiving practices. Using minimum/maximum inventory level data transferred from the inventory module, the purchasing module generates purchase orders based on an order point established through usage rate and lead-time factors. A purchasing module may also use a zero-based inventory system and generate purchase orders based on projected sales volume.

Financial Reporting Module. The use of a **financial reporting module**, also called a general ledger module, involves the specification of a chart of accounts (a list of

Exhibit 7   Hospitality Accounting Applications

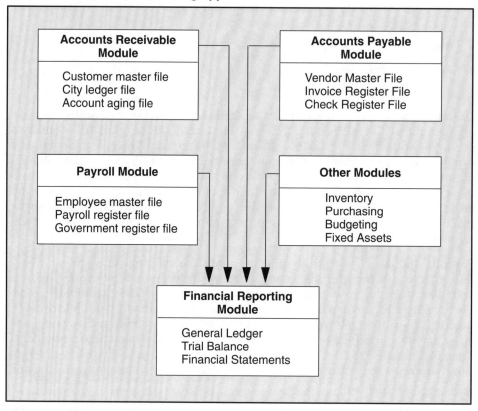

financial statement accounts and their account numbers) and a systematic approach to recording transactions. The design of the general ledger module is often crucial to an effective back office system. The financial reporting module is generally capable of tracking accounts receivable, accounts payable, cash, and adjusting entries. In addition, most financial reporting modules are capable of accessing data from front office and back office modules to prepare financial statements, which include the balance sheet, the statement of income (and supporting departmental schedules), and a variety of reports for use by management. Exhibit 7 summarizes typical hospitality accounting applications.

Summary

Much of this chapter focused on information—one of the most valuable resources of a hospitality business. Information can increase a manager's knowledge of guests, service, labor, finance, and other areas of concern. Information can also reduce the uncertainty that managers may experience when making decisions. And, after decisions have been made, information can provide managers with useful feedback.

Information is the result of data processing that transforms raw facts and isolated figures into timely, accurate, and useful reports. The conversion of data into information is accomplished through a cycle of events identified as input, process, and output. The primary objective of all information systems, including computerized ones, is to transform data into timely, accurate, and useful information. The speed, accuracy, and efficiency required for an effective hospitality information system are often best achieved through electronic data processing. The difference between data processing and electronic data processing lies in the automation of the process and the addition of a memory unit.

A computer is a managerial tool capable of processing large quantities of data much more quickly and accurately than any other data processing method. Three types of computers discussed in this chapter are mainframe computers, minicomputers, and microcomputers (also called personal computers).

The internal memory capacity of computers is often defined in terms of kilobytes. A kilobyte represents approximately one thousand bytes. A byte represents a single character and is made up of a special sequence of bits. A bit is the smallest unit of electronic data. The term bit is short for a *BI*nary digi*T* (which is either zero or one). All characters (letters, numbers, and symbols) are represented by a special sequence of binary digits.

The chapter also presented an overview of the major components of fully automated hotel and restaurant information systems.

Key Terms

Electronic Data Processing

alpha data	information
alphanumeric data	kilobyte
binary code	megabyte
bit	microcomputer
byte	microprocessor
computer	minicomputer
data	numeric data
data processing	silicon chips
data processing cycle	streamlining
electronic data processing	turnaround time
gigabyte	

Hotel Computer Systems

applications software	guest accounting module
auxiliary guest service devices	guest-operated devices
electronic locking system	microcomputer interface
energy management system	point-of-sale system
front office applications	property management system

PMS interfaces   rooms management module
reservations module   telephone call accounting system

Restaurant Computer Systems

configuration   point-of-sale terminal
electronic cash register   restaurant management system
management applications   service applications

Sales and Catering Applications

catering software   yield management
yield

Hospitality Accounting Applications

accounts payable module   inventory module
accounts receivable module   payroll accounting module
financial reporting module   purchasing module

Discussion Questions

1. What are the three phases of the data processing cycle? Describe the functions performed in each phase.

2. How does electronic data processing differ from data processing?

3. What does the term "binary code" mean?

4. What is the difference between a bit and a byte?

5. What are the most common front office components of a property management system?

6. What are some of the computer systems that may interface with a hotel's property management system?

7. What is the difference between an electronic cash register and a point-of-sale terminal?

8. How could yield management software help the sales staff of a hotel maximize revenue?

9. What is the difference between accounts receivable and accounts payable software applications?

10. What are the basic functions performed by a financial reporting module of a hospitality accounting software application?

REVIEW QUIZ

When you feel you have covered all of the material in this chapter, answer these questions. Choose the *best* answer.

Matching

1. Binary code

2. Bit

3. Data

4. Microprocessor

5. Approximately one million bytes

6. Yield

7. Silicon chip

8. Personal computer

   a. The central processing unit of a microcomputer

   b. A counting system based on the digits zero and one

   c. Also called a microcomputer

   d. Based on supply and demand

   e. Facts or figures to be processed into useful information

   f. The smallest unit of electronic data

   g. Kilobyte

   h. Megabyte

   i. Gigabyte

   j. Actual revenue divided by potential revenue

   k. Average daily rate divided by occupancy

   l. Also called a minicomputer

   m. Semi-conductor material containing electronic circuitry

True (T) or False (F)

T   F   9. The result of data processing is information.

T   F   10. Reducing the number of times that data must be handled enhances the accuracy of data processing tasks.

T   F   11. Alphanumeric data can be either numbers or letters, but not both.

T   F   12. A sequence of bits representing a single character is called a bitstream.

Alternate/Multiple Choice

13. A computer-based lodging information system is commonly called:

   a. a property management system.
   b. yield management software.

14. Ranking, sorting, and assembling are examples of:

    a. arithmetic computer functions.
    b. logical computer functions.

15. Which of the following files is not one of the major files maintained by an accounts payable module of a property management system?

    a. invoice register file
    b. vendor master file
    c. guest register file
    d. check register file

Chapter Outline

Input/Output Units
  Keyboards
  Touch-Screen Terminals
  Other Input Devices
  Display Screens
  Printers
  Common I/O Units in the Hospitality
    Industry
The Central Processing Unit
  Read Only Memory (ROM)
  Random Access Memory (RAM)
External Storage Devices
  Magnetic Tapes
  Floppy Disks
  Hard Disks
Anatomy of a Microcomputer
  Microprocessor Characteristics
  CPU Speed
  Bus System
  System Architecture
  Computer Add-Ons
Software
The Operating System
  Operating System Utilities
  Window Environments
  Programming Languages
Summary

Learning Objectives

1. Identify and describe the three hardware components required for a computer system.

2. Identify groups of keys found on a microcomputer keyboard and explain the functions they perform.

3. Describe five types of printers that are used as output devices of computer systems.

4. Explain the difference between read only memory (ROM) and random access memory (RAM).

5. Describe the various external storage devices and explain the advantages of each.

6. Explain the function of an operating system.

7. Distinguish between low-level and high-level programming languages.

2

Essentials of
Computer Systems

THE PHYSICAL EQUIPMENT of a computer system is called **hardware**. Computer hardware is visible, movable, and easy to identify. In order to have a computer system, three hardware components are required: an input/output (I/O) unit, a central processing unit (CPU), and an external storage device.

An input/output unit allows the user to interact with the computer system. For example, the user can input data through a keyboard and receive output on a display screen and/or on paper through a printer.

The central processing unit (CPU) is the control center of the computer system. Inside are the circuits and mechanisms that process and store information and send instructions to the other components of the system. The computer is said to *read* when it takes data in for processing and to *write* when it sends processed data out as information. All input entering the computer system is processed by the CPU before it is sent to the internal memory or to an output device. Similarly, all output (sent to a display screen, printer, or other device) has first been processed by the CPU. There is no direct link between input and output devices. Whenever information moves within the computer system, it passes through the CPU.

An external storage device is a piece of equipment that retains data and/or programs that the CPU can access. Data and programs can be permanently stored on such external devices as magnetic tapes, floppy disks, and hard disks.

This chapter examines various types of each of these components. In addition, the operations of a microcomputer are described as well as common operating systems.

Input/Output Units

Keyboards and touch-screen terminals are common input units. Display monitors and printers are common output units. For most data processing, the computer system needs a keyboard for input and a display screen for output. For a paper record of the processed data, a printer is also needed. Disk drives are also input/output devices; they are capable of sending data in either direction—for input to the central processing unit, or for output to a display screen or printer.

Keyboards

A **keyboard** is the most common input device. However, the number, positioning, and function of the keys on any particular keyboard depend on the type of computer system used and the needs of the individual user. The following discussion focuses on one type of keyboard commonly used as an input device for a microcomputer system. The keys on this keyboard can be grouped in the following sections:

- Function keypad
- Typical typewriter keys
- Cursor control keypad
- Numeric keypad

Function Keypad. The function keypad contains keys (F1 through F12) which perform specific tasks as defined by the particular software application currently running on the computer system. These keys perform different operations when used in conjunction with different software applications. That is, the operation performed by the F3 key in one software application may be entirely different from the operation the F3 key performs in a different software application.

Typical Typewriter Keys. These keys normally function like the keys on a typewriter. Note that there is no typewriter-like carriage return attached to the keyboard. This is because electronic word processing normally performs this function automatically. When keyboard operators wish to force a break in the automatic return (such as at the end of paragraphs), they use the "enter" key (also called the "return" key).

Cursor Control Keypad. This set of keys is used in conjunction with a display screen. The **cursor** is a flashing marker on a display screen which indicates where the next character to be entered will appear. The cursor control keys are marked by arrows. When one of these keys is pressed the cursor moves in the direction of the arrow indicated on the key. Cursor movement is often determined by the particular software application which is run on the computer system. Individual software applications have specifically defined instructions for the cursor control keypad.

Numeric Keypad. When the "Num Lock" key is on, the keys that make up the cursor control keypad are converted to a numeric keypad and perform much like the keys of an adding machine.

Touch-Screen Terminals

Computer manufacturers have developed terminals that enable the user to enter data without having to type a command from a keyboard. One such device is the **touch-screen terminal**. A touch-screen terminal is a cathode ray tube (CRT) with a grid of tiny beams of light over its glass screen. When the screen is touched in a sensitized area, the light beam is broken. This causes a signal to be transmitted to the computer. The touch-screen terminal is especially appealing to those who cannot type well or those interested in simplified input procedures. Since touch-sensitive screens can move large quantities of data easily, they are especially effective as order entry devices in food service operations and are useful for many graphic business applications (such as charts, graphs, and so on).

Other Input Devices

Other input devices include a computer mouse, scanners, and voice recognition systems. A **computer mouse** is a small pointing device designed to fit comfortably under a user's hand. The mouse is connected to the CPU by a long cord. A mouse is used in place of, or in combination with, a computer keyboard. It is capable of choosing commands, moving text and icons, and performing a number of operations. Moving the mouse across a flat surface moves a pointer which is equivalent to a traditional blinking screen cursor. The pointer is a small graphic symbol that shows users where the next entered character will appear. The mouse pointer is usually shaped like an arrow, but may change shape during certain tasks.

A **scanner** is an input device capable of translating a page of text into a machine-readable format. A scanner is used to input text or graphic images into the computer. Scanners convert the images on a page into digitized information that can be recognized by the computer.

Voice recognition systems can respond to a set of instructions spoken by human voice. These systems convert spoken data directly into electronic form suitable for entry into a computer system. Research is being conducted which requires users to possess only a touch-tone telephone, a headset, and a display screen to make full use of a computer system. Experimentation with voice recognition technology is of special interest to the hospitality industry. A hotel reservations program may generate a series of cues on the screen to which the potential guest responds by pushing designated buttons on the telephone and/or by speaking into the mouthpiece of the headset. The computer acknowledges the user's input and may generate an additional series of cues. Although these computer systems today use and understand only a limited vocabulary, the future looks bright.

Display Screens

A **display screen** (also called a monitor or simply a screen) is the most common output unit. The type of display screen depends on the kind of computer system used and the needs of the individual user. Most display screens for microcomputer systems are capable of displaying both text and graphics (e.g., graphs, pie charts, etc.). Many are equipped with controls for adjusting brightness and contrast, and some units can be tilted for optimal viewing position. Display screens may be purchased as monochrome or color units. Those with color capability can produce impressive graphic displays and may be programmed to various foreground and background color combinations while operating many software applications. Types of color monitors include:

- CGA (color graphics adapter); low-end color screen also referred to as RGB (red, green, and blue).

- EGA (enhanced graphics adapter); a step-up from CGA in screen resolution and clarity (uses digital signals).

- VGA (video graphics array); best for desktop publishing and computer-aided design software (uses analog signals).

- LCD (liquid crystal display); blue letters on grayish white background (typically found on a portable computer).

- GP (gas plasma); orange letters on a black screen (normally limited to portable computer monitors)

Printers

Printers are considered output devices and part of the hardware of a computer system. They can be classified in relation to how they actually go about printing processed data. Impact printers, such as dot matrix and daisywheel printers, print character by character and line by line. Non-impact printers include thermal, ink jet, and laser printers.

An **impact printer** depends on the movement of a print head or paper-feeding mechanisms to place data on the page. The simplest printers place characters in a row one after another, then return the carrier to the left margin as the paper is moved up to another line. A **line-printing terminal** (LPT) is an impact printer that prints one line of type at a time.

Some allow for **bidirectional printing** in which the print head goes from left to right only on every other line. On the alternating lines it reverses everything and prints right to left, saving time. Otherwise the time the print head takes to go from the right margin back to the left would be wasted.

All impact printers rely on the durability of their mechanical parts for accurate print positioning, and all are in some degree limited as to the type of data they can print and their ability to move around the page. A **non-impact printer**, on the other hand, achieves accurate print positioning electronically and has the capability of using a greater range of type styles more quickly and efficiently than impact printers.

Printer speed is generally measured in characters per second (cps). Dot matrix printers are capable of 120–250 cps; daisywheel printers 10–60 cps; thermal printers 40–80 cps; and ink jet printers 70–90 cps. Laser printers are so fast that their printer speed is measured in pages per minute (ppm). These printers are capable of 30 ppm. The following sections describe each of these types of printers in some detail.

Dot Matrix Printers. A **dot matrix printer** is inexpensive and, for impact printers, is relatively fast. The text and graphic material which they produce is of fair print quality.

Dot matrix printers form characters by firing a vertical line of pins through an inked ribbon onto the paper. Each time a pin is fired, it strikes the inked ribbon and presses it against the paper to produce a dot. In the case of some dot matrix printers, the dot is about 1/72nd of an inch in diameter. The size varies slightly depending upon the age of the ribbon and the type of paper used. As the print head moves horizontally across the page, pins are fired in different patterns to produce letters, numbers, symbols, or graphics.

For example, to print a capital "T," the print head fires the top pin, moves 1/60th of an inch, fires the top pin again, moves 1/60th of an inch, fires seven pins, moves 1/60th of an inch, fires the top pin, moves another 1/60th of an inch, and fires the top pin once more to finish the letter. All this happens in only 1/100th of a second.

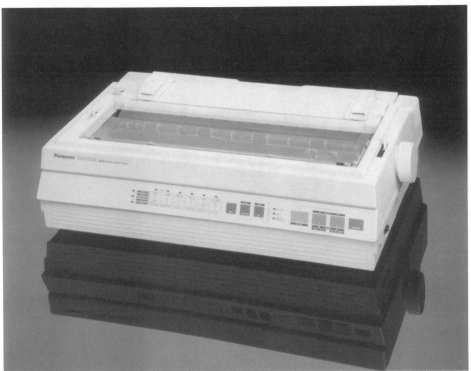

Dot Matrix Printer. (Courtesy of Panasonic Communications & Systems Company, Secaucus, New Jersey)

Daisywheel Printers. A **daisywheel printer** uses solid type (also called preformed characters), not dots, and produces a much higher quality print than dot matrix printers. A daisy wheel is a circular printing head with characters mounted on the ends of spokes radiating from the wheel's center. To print a character, the wheel is rotated at high speed to its proper position and a hammer strikes the spoke pressing the letter on the paper through an inked ribbon.

The similarity between daisywheel printers and wheel-head typewriters should not confuse the reader into believing that there is a direct connection between a keyboard and a daisywheel printer. The printer and the computer to which it is configured do not use or understand letters of the alphabet. Rather, they both function by manipulating binary numbers. When a letter key is pressed at the keyboard, the computer sends a number to its memory. When the computer tells the printer to print that letter, it sends the number to the printer, which must then convert the number to a movement of the print wheel that will activate the correct spoke to produce the desired letter.

Thermal Printers. A **thermal printer**, also referred to as an electrothermal printer, works by burning a protective layer off specially treated paper to reveal ink. Thermal (heat-sensitive) paper has a paper base covered with a layer of ink and a coating of aluminum. The printer forms characters by passing high voltage through printing

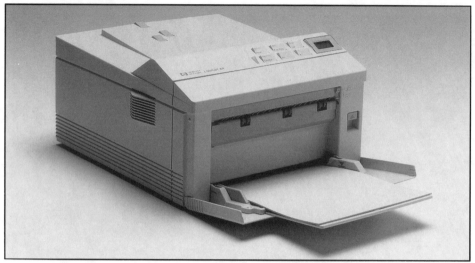

Laser Printer. (Courtesy of Hewlett-Packard Company, Rockville, Maryland)

wires for a fraction of a second. This high voltage burns away the aluminum coating to reveal the ink beneath. Thermal printers are quiet and reliable because they have few moving parts. However, because they require special heat-sensitive paper, their operating costs may be higher than those of other types of printers.

Ink Jet Printers. An **ink jet printer** works by spraying a minute and finely controlled jet of ink onto paper. The printer establishes a high voltage between its paper roller and an ink rod. The ink rod is composed of carbon grains encased in a glass tube. A spark jumps between the paper roller and the ink rod carrying enough carbon from the nozzle to make a dot on the paper. The ink (carbon) is electrically charged as it is sprayed onto the paper. Once charged, the ink can be moved around by electric fields in much the same way an electron beam is used to produce a picture on a television set. Ink jet printer heads have a normal print life of between 150,000 and 200,000 characters. Ink jet printers can be expensive, but they are extremely versatile because they can produce a wide range of characters and high quality graphics.

Laser Printers. A **laser printer** is extremely fast, relatively quiet, and somewhat expensive. Many laser printers are similar in appearance to desktop photocopying machines. While other printers print one character at a time, laser technology enables these devices to print an entire page all at once. Given this speed of output, many laser printers come equipped with collating capabilities. In addition, optional font (print style) cartridges and advanced graphics capabilities are available.

Common I/O Units in the Hospitality Industry

The most common I/O unit used in the hospitality industry is the **CRT unit** ("CRT" is an acronym for cathode ray tube). The CRT unit is composed of a television-like video screen and a keyboard which is similar to a typewriter keyboard. Data entered through the keyboard can be displayed on the screen. The CRT operator can edit and verify the on-screen input before sending it for processing.

A unit that used to be more common in the hospitality industry is the **teletype terminal** (TTY). The TTY is less expensive than the CRT unit but does not include a video display component. Instead, input is entered through a keyboard and printed out on a roll of paper. As the operator enters data into the system, a printed report can be made at the TTY console. The entered data is then communicated to a remote unit for processing. After processing, the information is relayed back to the TTY and printed out on paper.

For example, the housekeeping department of a hotel could use TTYs to communicate up-to-date data regarding room status to the front desk. The TTY would enable the housekeeping department to retain a printed record of the messages which pass between room attendants and front desk personnel.

Other types of I/O equipment common in the hospitality industry include keyboard and operator display units such as electronic cash registers and line-printing terminals. An electronic cash register (ECR) is a computer-based unit which is designed to record cash (and related) transactions and monitor cash balances. A hotel's food and beverage operation may use ECRs to communicate with the front desk. In a computerized hotel system, restaurant charges can be entered into a point-of-sale unit in the restaurant and transmitted to the front office where guest folios are automatically updated with the charges.

One important difference among I/O units is the type of output they produce. A CRT unit displays output on a monitor for the user to examine; this type of output is referred to as **soft copy** because it cannot be handled by the operator or removed from the computer. Printers, however, generate a paper copy of the output called a **hard copy**. Many systems are designed so that they can produce both types of output. For example, a computer at a hotel's front desk might have a CRT unit which the clerk uses to view a soft copy of guest folios at check-in, during the guest's stay, and at check-out. However, when the guest checks out, a hard copy of the folio will be generated from a printer so that the guest can keep a copy. Obviously, output displayed on a screen is much more temporary and its use more constricted than output printed on paper. Generally hospitality managers obtain essential reports in hard copy form, allowing storage outside the computer and providing a base for information backup.

The Central Processing Unit

The **central processing unit** (CPU) is the most important and most expensive hardware component found within a computer system. It is the "brain" of the system and is responsible for controlling all other system components. As shown in Exhibit 1, the CPU is composed of four subunits.

The first subunit is the arithmetic and logical unit (ALU) which performs all the mathematical, sorting, and processing functions.

The second subunit is the control unit, which is responsible for determining which units in the computer system can be accessed by the CPU. If a unit is capable of interacting directly with the CPU, it is said to be on-line; off-line refers to the condition in which there is no established connection between a system unit and

Exhibit 1   Computer Hardware Components

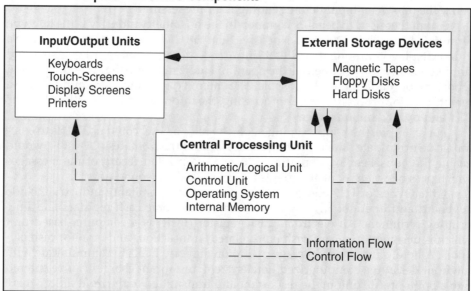

the CPU. It is important to realize that although computer units may be switched on (powered-up), they are not necessarily on-line. For example, when a printer is connected to a CPU and its power switch is turned on, the operator can switch the printer to either on-line or off-line status. The printer will respond to commands from the CPU only when it is on-line.

The third subunit of the CPU houses a portion of the operating system. The **operating system** is responsible for orchestrating the hardware and the software within the computer system. It establishes the system's priorities and directs its resources to accomplish desired tasks. Operating systems are discussed in greater detail elsewhere in this chapter. The final subunit of the CPU is the system's internal memory, which is housed in a set of specialized circuits. One part of internal memory, called **read only memory** (ROM), holds a permanent record of information that the computer needs to use each time it is turned on. Another part of internal memory, called **random access memory** (RAM), holds a temporary version of the programs and/or data which users are processing. These different parts of internal memory are further clarified in the following sections.

Read Only Memory (ROM)

ROM stores a permanent control program entered by the computer manufacturer and may also house the computer's operating system. The control program contains specific sets of commands and instructions which guide the most fundamental routines carried out by the computer system. For example, the control program contains instructions for the conversion of keyboard entries into binary codes for processing by the CPU.

Since ROM is composed of a limited syntax (vocabulary), a computer recognizes only its own pre-programmed commands. If a user tries to enter a different command, the computer will not recognize the input and will respond by reporting that a "SYNTAX ERROR" has occurred. For example, some personal computers start a program's operation if the user types "GO"; others require the user to type "RUN." If the user types the wrong command, the computer responds with a message, such as "UNDEFINED COMMAND," to alert the user to the problem. This is why software designed for one brand of computer may not work on other brands; different ROM contents recognize different commands.

Storing the control program in ROM enables the computer to "read" commands and instructions which program the fundamental operations of the computer system while preventing users from accidentally altering or erasing portions of the control program. Users cannot "write" or save information to the ROM area of the computer's internal memory. In fact, with many systems, users cannot even call up on their display screens any of the programs which are stored in ROM.

The ROM area of the computer's internal memory does not require a constant power supply to retain the commands, instructions, or routines which the manufacturer includes as part of the control program. ROM is described as **non-volatile memory** because programs stored in ROM are not lost when the computer is turned off or otherwise loses electrical power.

Random Access Memory (RAM)

All data which a user enters into the system are temporarily stored in the random access memory (RAM) area of the computer's internal memory. Since data stored in RAM can be accessed and/or altered by the user, RAM is often described as **read/write** memory: the user can both "read" from RAM (retrieve data), and "write" to RAM (store data).

Since all user operations are carried out in RAM, it is important that the amount of RAM supported by a particular computer system be sufficient to meet the user's needs. RAM size is typically designated in terms of the number of bytes which RAM is able to temporarily store. A 256K machine has enough RAM capacity to temporarily store up to 256 kilobytes of data; a 640K machine has enough RAM capacity to temporarily store up to 640 kilobytes of data; and so on. How does storage capacity translate into typed pages?

A single 8 ½ by 11 inch page of double-spaced type contains approximately 2K (2,000 characters). Therefore, a rough conversion of memory capacity to printed pages would be two to one. In other words, 256K converts to approximately 128 pages, 640K to 320 pages; and so on. This relationship holds true even for larger memory formats. Twenty megabytes converts to roughly 10,000 printed pages of text.

Because software application programs vary in the amount of RAM they require, RAM capacity is an important consideration in selecting a computer system. Many users who purchased 256K personal computers just a few years ago have found it necessary to upgrade the RAM capacities of their machines in order to accommodate the more sophisticated software packages available today.

When the computer loses electrical power, or is turned off, all user data stored in RAM is lost. For this reason, RAM is referred to as **volatile memory**. In order to save data stored in RAM for future use, the user must instruct the computer to save it on some type of external storage device.

External Storage Devices

An external storage device is the hardware component of a computer system that retains data and/or programs that can be accessed by the CPU. Data and programs can be permanently saved on a variety of external storage devices.

An important factor in selecting the kind of external storage device for a particular computer system is the kind of access which users wish to have to the stored data. User access to stored data will be addressed in the following sections which discuss some of the more common external storage devices: magnetic tapes (cassette and reel to reel), floppy disks, and hard disks.

Magnetic Tapes

A **magnetic tape** is an external storage device that is made from a polyester base material coated with an oxide compound. It is this compound which gives the tape its durability and electromagnetic properties. Magnetic tapes (cassette and reel to reel) are referred to as a **sequential access medium** because they store data in chronological sequence.

User access to data stored on magnetic tape is similar to the way in which anyone searches for a portion of a recording stored on a cassette tape recorder—the user must wind and rewind the tape until the desired portion of data is found. Because this can be a cumbersome process, magnetic tape is not a feasible storage device for the everyday computer needs of many hospitality operations. However, using magnetic tapes to store some kinds of data may be a great deal less expensive than using disks. Therefore, in some situations, magnetic tapes could serve as an ideal backup system on which to store data which are not required on a regular basis.

Floppy Disks

A **floppy disk** (also called diskette) is a popular external storage device and is frequently used for shipping data and programs from one location to another. It is made of thin, flexible plastic protected by a cardboard jacket. The plastic is coated with a magnetized oxide compound designed to hold electronic information. The size of the floppy disk (eight inch, five and one-quarter inch, or three and one-half inch) depends on the type of computer system used. Exhibit 2 diagrams the basic features of floppy disks.

The surface of a floppy disk is divided into **tracks**, which are invisible concentric rings of magnetic zones. Each track contains a number of **sectors**. The tracks and sectors are numbered, enabling the computer to store information on the disk at specific locations (e.g., sector 7 of track 3, sector 4 of track 23, etc.). The number of tracks and sectors on a floppy disk is largely determined by the computer operating system (DOS, UNIX, OS/2, and others) through a process known as formatting (also called initializing). **Formatting** creates the tracks and sectors on which

Exhibit 2   Diagrams of 5 $^1/_4$- and 3 $^1/_2$-Inch Floppy Disks

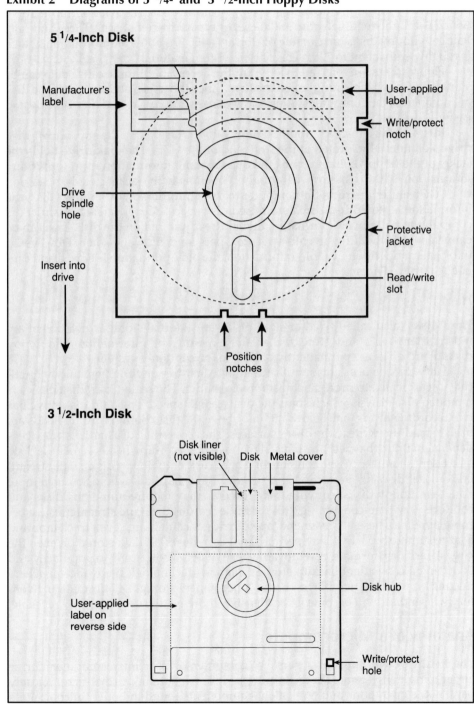

the system is able to read and write information. Once formatted, many five and one-quarter inch floppy disks are capable of storing 360,249 bytes of information, which is roughly equivalent to 180 pages of typewritten material. Three and one-half inch floppy disks are capable of storing 1,456,873 bytes of information, which is roughly equivalent to 728 pages of typewritten material.

Floppy disks are referred to as a **random access medium** because data can be stored in any available location on the disk. Since the tracks and sectors of the disk are numbered, the computer system allows a user to access stored data quickly and easily.

In the case of a microcomputer, a floppy disk is inserted in the appropriate disk drive slot, normally located at the front end of the CPU. The **disk drive** holds the jacket of the floppy still and spins the disk, reading information from (or writing information to) the disk surface through an opening in the jacket called a head slot.

When a user instructs the computer to store information on a floppy disk, the information is stored in an area of unused disk space. A user can also instruct the computer to write over information that is already stored on the disk. This can be convenient for updating inventory records, personnel files, and so on. However, if information is written over old information, the old information is erased and cannot be retrieved again.

Hard Disks

Hard disks (also called fixed or rigid disks) are external storage devices that are much faster to use and store far greater amounts of information than floppy disks. Hard disks are permanently on-line to the computer system.

Hard disk devices are manufactured in a dust-free environment and hermetically (heat) sealed to protect against foreign matter. The sealed hard disk device is mounted on a chassis which spins the disk at high speed. The hard disk drive has two recording heads, one below and one above the disk. Both recording heads are used to read and write to the disk's surfaces. The access time of a hard disk device is dependent upon the mechanism used to move the recording heads across the disk.

Users should copy the contents of a hard disk onto floppy disks, tape streamers, or laser discs for protection and security. Since hard disks hold so much more data than floppy disks, copying their contents may require numerous disks and could be very time-consuming. It is for these reasons that **tape streamers** have become popular. These are magnetic tape cartridges containing seven track tape and a large storage capacity. They permit rapid copying of all data stored on even the largest hard disk formats. A **removable hard disk** is also gaining in popularity and becoming a convenient backup storage method. Technological advancements are making laser discs a feasible medium for permanent storage of information. Eventually, laser discs will become less expensive, more readily available, and reusable.

Anatomy of a Microcomputer

The hardware workings of a personal computer (PC) or microcomputer mirror larger computer systems. The technical descriptions contained in this section closely parallel the operations and equivalent components found in both minicomputers and main frame computers. Exhibit 3 presents a sample illustration of microcomputer components.

Microprocessor Characteristics

The **microprocessor** is the central processing unit of a microcomputer. The number assigned to a microprocessor chip refers to the complexity of its central processing unit (CPU). The microprocessor is the chip that processes instructions and carries out system commands. Central processing units vary in the amount of information they can process. Some microprocessors (numbered 8086 and 8088) process one byte of information at a time. Recall that a byte is eight bits, or the amount of information contained in one character (a letter or numeral). Other microprocessors (numbered 80286 or 286) are designed to process two bytes (16 bits) of information at a time. The more information a computer can process at one time, the faster it operates.

The difference between an 8-bit and 16-bit CPU is akin to the difference between a two-lane and four-lane highway. Surely the four-lane road moves more traffic faster. Also available are 32-bit microprocessors (numbered 80386 or 386). These CPUs are capable of handling 4 bytes of information at a time. Recently developed high speed microprocessors (numbered 80486 or 486) provide even faster information processing. Exhibit 4 relates microprocessor chips with processing characteristics.

CPU Speed

In addition to processing capability of a CPU, speed is also an important factor. The speed of a central processing unit is termed its clock rate or clock speed. Clock speed is measured in **megahertz (MHz)**. One MHz is equivalent to one million cycles per second. A 12 MHz computer, for example, is slower than a 20 MHz computer, even if they have identical microprocessors. Just as CPU processing ability can be compared to the lanes on a highway, so too can the CPU clock speed be related to the highway speed limit. The higher the clock speed, the faster the CPU can process the information.

Bus System

Inside a computer there are channels through which signals travel. A **bus system** is defined as the electronic circuitry over which power, data, and other signals travel. Signals need to get from one location to another, and the system's bus architecture facilitates such movements.

There are three buses within a computer system; together they make up the computer's input/output (I/O) bus system. One transports data (data bus), another directs operations (address bus), and another transmits instructions (control bus). A data bus is the electrical pathway over which data travels between the CPU, disk drives, and peripherals. The address bus is responsible for finding the specific address that contains the requested data, and the control bus transports instruction on what to do with addresses and data. Assume the CPU needs to send two instructions such as "start reading data at address abc" and "stop reading data

Exhibit 3   Sample Microcomputer Illustration

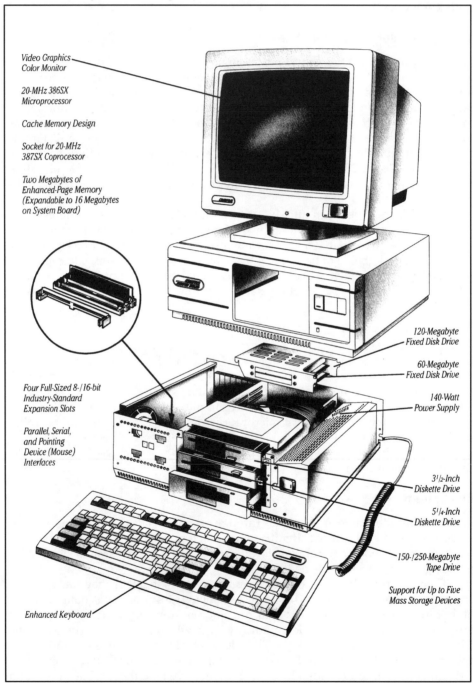

Video Graphics
Color Monitor

20-MHz 386SX
Microprocessor

Cache Memory Design

Socket for 20-MHz
387SX Coprocessor

Two Megabytes of
Enhanced-Page Memory
(Expandable to 16 Megabytes
on System Board)

Four Full-Sized 8-/16-bit
Industry-Standard
Expansion Slots

Parallel, Serial,
and Pointing
Device (Mouse)
Interfaces

Enhanced Keyboard

120-Megabyte
Fixed Disk Drive

60-Megabyte
Fixed Disk Drive

140-Watt
Power Supply

3¹/₂-Inch
Diskette Drive

5¹/₄-Inch
Diskette Drive

150-/250-Megabyte
Tape Drive

Support for Up to Five
Mass Storage Devices

Exhibit 4   Microprocessor Characteristics

Microprocessor	IBM Family	Processing Characteristics
8086 and 8088	XT	8-bit machine
80286 or 286	AT	16-bit machine
80386 or 386	PS/2	32-bit machine

at address xyz." The messages "start reading data" and "stop reading data" will be carried on the control bus. The proper location of data elements would be accessed by the address bus. The requested data would be sent to the CPU through the data bus.

A computer's I/O bus is important since it transports signals among the different input and output devices and the computer's microprocessor. The I/O bus is basically a platform into which peripheral devices (serial ports, parallel ports, or network cards) are inserted. Add-ons to PCs are typically connected to the system's I/O bus.

System Architecture

Advancements in input/output (I/O) architecture are changing the way in which computers process data. The capabilities of the I/O bus should match the number of bits a microprocessor can process at once. For example, a 16-bit bus is a good match for a 286 microprocessor since both move information at the same rate. A bus's clock speed is not the same as a CPU clock speed. Since bus speed is measured in nanoseconds (billionths of a second) and CPU speed is clocked in MHz (millions of cycles per second), I/O bus speed and CPU clock speed typically do not match exactly. Some variance in speeds is tolerable. Similar to differing speeds among motorists on merging highways, major imbalances between I/O bus and CPU speed may lead to traffic jams. Computer traffic jams are termed bottlenecks.

Historically, most computers were built using Industry Standard Architecture (ISA) in which I/O buses have 8-bit or 16-bit widths (referred to as bandwidth). Given the increased capability of microprocessors, ISA is often too slow for CPUs with 386 microprocessors that manage 32 bits of information at a time. Extended Industry Standard Architecture (EISA) and Micro Channel Architecture (MCA) were developed in response to the need for a bus that is compatible with 32-bit microprocessors. A 32-bit bus is designed to more easily handle the workload created by faster, more powerful microprocessors.

Computer Add-Ons

Add-ons are components or devices that are added to a computer system to increase its storage capacity, modify its architecture, or upgrade its performance. An add-on generally requires the insertion of a special circuit board inside the computer unit. Before expanding the capabilities of a computer system, the user must recognize the limitations placed on add-on components by the computer's power supply. The power supply unit provides electrical current to the computer. Power supply is expressed in watts. The more watts, the more internal add-on components a computer will be able to support.

While there are many peripheral devices that may be connected to a computer system and/or microcomputer, the most popular add-on components are expanded memory, extended memory, internal modems, FAX boards, and interface boards.

Expanded Memory. The additional memory capacity that resides outside the computer's basic memory which can be accessed in revolving blocks is referred to as **expanded memory**. Since expanded memory was developed in response to some limited microprocessor capabilities (model 8086 and 8088 microprocessors), it is only available as add-on boards. These boards are inserted into one of the computer's expansion slots. Expanded memory takes advantage of unused reserved memory that the computer believes is in use when, in reality, it is not. For example, the computer system may reserve 128K of space for the system monitor. Should the system monitor require only half of the reserved space, expanded memory can be used to take advantage of this opening. Expanded memory swaps blocks of memory located outside the computer for unused memory located within the computer. The borrowing of this available memory is commonly referred to as bank switching. Some computer operating systems work better with expanded memory than others. Expanded memory is additional memory that enables large programs to use memory beyond conventional limitations (640K limit). Expanded memory is slower than extended memory, but it is compatible with more software. Computers with extended memory can also take advantage of expanded memory, but the opposite is not true.

Extended Memory. The linear memory that reaches beyond a system's basic limits is referred to as **extended memory**. Extended memory often comes built into the system board of some microprocessing units or can be purchased as an add-on (for 286 and 386 machines only). Unlike expanded memory, which swaps unused computer memory within the system's limits, extended memory begins to provide memory outside the system limits. Extended memory is usually required for advanced multitasking (running several applications simultaneously). Older microprocessing machines usually do not possess the ability to take advantage of extended memory. Extended memory operates faster than expanded memory, but doesn't support as much compatible software.

Internal Modem. A modem is a telecommunications device that is used to transmit data over telephone lines from one computer to another. An internal modem is placed inside the computer unit and enables the computer to place and receive data calls. Once a number is dialed and the modem detects a proper answer, data file transfer begins. At the end of the transmission the telephone connection is automatically broken.

FAX Board. FAX is an abbreviation of Facsimile. A **FAX board** allows a computer user to send and/or receive electronic documents. These documents can vary from text copy to pictures, diagrams, and maps. FAX boards prepare data files for transmission and then, using an internal modem, place a telephone call to the destination computer for transmission. Once connected, the FAX board sends the copy.

Interface Boards. Peripheral devices often need more than a cable to communicate with a computer. Some peripherals need both a cable and an interface board. An **interface board** (also referred to as an interface card) is a series of micro chips on a printed circuit board containing an input/output port. The interface board connects to the CPU and allows communications between the CPU and an input/output device. It is the circuitry of the chips and board that allows the peripheral to understand information it receives from the computer. An interface board is placed into an available expansion slot inside the computer. The input/output port (plug point) of the interface board protrudes outside the computer for cable connecting.

Software

The hardware of a computer system does nothing by itself. In order for hardware components to operate, there must be a set of instructions to follow. Instructions that command a computer system to perform useful tasks are called **computer programs**. A set of programs that instructs or controls the operation of the hardware components of a computer system is called **software**. Software programs tell the computer what to do, how to do it, and when to do it.

Many people's first exposure to the power of computers is through applications software such as word processing packages, electronic spreadsheet programs, or database management systems.

Experienced computer users are familiar with **systems software** which must be present for applications software to establish a connection with computer hardware components. The discussion of systems software in this chapter focuses primarily on operating systems, with particular emphasis given to the disk operating systems of microcomputers.

The Operating System

A portion of systems software is called the operating system. Like other types of systems software, the **operating system** controls interactions between hardware components of a computer system and applications software programs. An operating system is necessary for a computer system to be able to carry out instructions generated by applications software programs. The operating system manages routine computer functions while maintaining system priorities. The operating system controls how the computer receives, transfers, and outputs information at the most fundamental levels. The computer cannot function without an operating system. Exhibit 5 illustrates the role of the operating system in mediating applications software and hardware components of a computer system.

A computer system must have a control mechanism if it is to run applications software programs without constant intervention from the user. When a user instructs a computer to save a program or data to an external storage device, something must happen within the computer system so that the entered command successfully initiates the proper sequence of operations for storing the program or data. The management of such routine functions is handled by the computer's operating system.

Exhibit 5   Mediating Role of the Operating System

Hardware Components	O P E R A T I N G S Y S T E M	Applications Software
Input/Output Units Central Processing Units External Storage Devices		Word Processing Electronic Spreadsheets Database Management Communications

In simplest terms, the operating system is the program that controls the execution of other programs. Think of the operating system as the traffic controller of a busy metropolis, directing the flow of traffic by controlling the signals at every street corner. Like the traffic controller, the operating system is at the center of computer activity, directing the flow of data and instructions from applications software programs to the various hardware components of the computer system.

Common types of operating systems in use today include DOS, UNIX, and OS/2. The following sections briefly examine each of these operating systems.

Disk Operating System (DOS). There are a variety of operating systems for different types and brands of computers, and there are different types of operating systems which can run on the same type of computer. Most of the operating systems for microcomputers can be purchased at retail computer outlets. These operating systems are called disk operating systems and contain systems software programs.

Some of these systems software programs operate without user intervention. For example, DOS monitors application programs during their execution, making sure that any operation that is attempted is possible. If the computer system is attempting to print, DOS checks to see that there is a printer on-line with the system. If there is not, DOS signals the user that a problem exists.

Other systems software programs within DOS can be easily commanded by the user to prepare, manipulate, or locate information stored on disks. The user simply inputs the appropriate DOS command, and DOS tells the computer what to do, step by step.

UNIX Operating System. The UNIX operating system is modular and hierarchical in nature. It starts at a single point called the root directory and branches out into different levels of sub-directories, eventually reaching the level of individual program, text, and data files. In UNIX, everything is stored in a file.

UNIX is a powerful multi-user system composed of three levels of programs: the kernel, the shell, and the user environment. The kernel contains the basic operating system. It is the software that is closest to the hardware. The kernel controls access to the resources among users and maintains the file system. The user never interacts directly with the kernel.

The shell is a software program with which the user most commonly interacts. The shell serves as a connection between the user and the kernel, interpreting keyboard input into language the kernel can understand and execute. The shell may also function as a programming language.

The user environment consists of a file system and UNIX utilities or commands. Such commands as copying or removing files, text editing, software development, and the like reside in the user environment section of UNIX.

OS/2 Operating System. A major advantage of OS/2 is its capacity for multitasking. OS/2 is credited with being the first operating system to make working with several applications at once an efficient process.

The OS/2 operating system, originally designed to be a multi-user system, presents the user with a main menu called the program selector. Because it is network-oriented, this approach differs from that of the other operating systems. The program selector is divided into three areas: *start a program, update,* and *switch to a running program.* Selecting START A PROGRAM leads to a second menu containing all available OS/2 programs. UPDATE, as its name implies, offers all the tools necessary to edit the list of OS/2 programs available through the START A PROGRAM option. SWITCH TO A RUNNING PROGRAM allows the user to leave the program selector and to move to an application already in process.

The two terms commonly used to describe OS/2 are multitasking and memory-handling. Multitasking refers to the execution of more than one program simultaneously. Memory-handling is directed at the advantages gained by users of large software applications. Compared to DOS and UNIX, OS/2 requires a lot of internal computer memory. Once installed, the OS/2 operating system overcomes most of the memory limitations associated with running large application software programs under other operating systems. For example, OS/2 provides a DOS window which allows the user to easily switch from OS/2 to DOS and back again.

Operating System Utilities

Regardless of which operating system a user selects, there are several common functions available through operating system commands. Some of the more useful operating system commands include utilities (operations) such as the following:

- Formatting new disks

- Finding out what files are stored on a particular disk

- Copying files from one disk to another, or copying the entire contents of a disk to another disk

- Comparing the contents of files or entire disks to verify that they are identical

- Erasing files

The user's manuals produced by the manufacturers of operating system software give detailed instructions on how to carry out these commands. Users must enter the commands exactly as their manuals instruct. Key substitutions that may work on typewriters (such as typing the numerals 1 and 0 by using the lower case "L" or the upper case "o" letter keys) do not work on computers.

Window Environments

A windowing system provides an easy-to-use interface between an operating system and specific software application packages. Window-based systems use graphics and menus rather than a blank screen with a blinking cursor. Windows show a series of programs, allowing even a novice to move easily from one program to the next.

A window is a rectangular area on a computer screen. Every window has a title bar (window name) and a menu bar (list of application titles). Basically, a windowing system controls a display device and its associated input devices. It takes responsibility for managing the cursor position, ordering the windows on the screen, and coordinating the shared use of input devices (for example, mouse and keyboard). Multiple windows are also useful when working on a number of systems across a network.

Programming Languages

Software applications are sets of computer programs. A computer program is a series of written instructions which guides the computer in carrying out a specific function. The particular language in which a program is written will affect the speed at which the computer responds to instructions, and the ease with which the program can be changed to meet new needs and requirements of users. Programming languages are usually characterized as either low-level languages or high-level languages.

Low-Level Languages. All computers have low-level languages programmed into them because it is at this most basic level that their operations are carried out. **Low-level programming languages** are sometimes referred to as **machine languages** because the computer can understand their instructions directly. Machine languages typically vary from one computer manufacturer to another. Also, machine languages may vary among the different models offered by the same manufacturer.

Initially, all computer programming was done in machine language. These programs were extremely cumbersome because basic instructions had to be written as long strings of binary digits. Programmers had to keep track of hundreds of thousands of zeros and ones; a single misplaced bit (binary digit) could cause the computer to misunderstand an instruction, and the entire program could malfunction. The tedious, laborious nature of programming in machine language also made it difficult to change a program once it had been written.

The difficulties of programming in machine language led to the development of assembly language. An assembly language is very close to machine language, but instead of programming all instructions in strings of binary digits, assembly language eased the programmer's task by making it possible to code some instructions

Exhibit 6   Examples of High-Level Programming Languages

FORTRAN	(FORmula TRANslator) was one of the first high-level languages and was developed for scientific programming.
PASCAL	another scientific programming language, was developed in the mid-1970s and was named after Blaise Pascal, a French mathematician and philosopher. Today, PASCAL is a popular programming language, especially in relation to microcomputers.
COBOL	(COmmon Business Oriented Language) permits programs to be written in a language close to that used by business people. Although this programming language was developed in the late 1950s, many of today's business programs are still written in COBOL.
PL/1	(Programming Language 1) is a general purpose language used for many types of computer processing. It was developed by IBM (International Business Machines Corporation).
C	is a programming language which is relatively easy to learn and use. The name of this programming language is not an acronym. C is considered as powerful as PL/1, yet more efficient.
BASIC	(Beginners' All-purpose Symbolic Instruction Code) was developed at Dartmouth College in the mid-1960s and was intended to introduce students to computer programming—a purpose which it fulfills quite well even today.

in a mnemonic form. But computers do not understand assembly language directly. The mnemonic instructions which make it easier for programmers to write programs must still be converted into machine language. Even so, programmers found it much easier to write a conversion program for their mnemonics than to write an entire program in machine language. Programs written in assembly language run virtually as fast as programs written in machine language.

High-Level Languages. High-level programming languages are made up of familiar words and symbols. They are the most sophisticated programming languages because a relatively simple command instructs the computer to perform complex procedures involving a number of different operations. For example, some computer languages recognize the word SORT and respond to this command by arranging a list of items in a predetermined fashion. High-level languages are easy for a novice programmer to work with because they are similar to the user's own spoken language. Exhibit 6 lists some of the many high-level programming languages in use today.

While high-level languages draw closer to the user's own language, computers can only distinguish between positive and negative electrical charges. A computer cannot understand the commands of a high-level language directly; it must first be

Exhibit 7   Converting Programming Languages into Machine Readable Codes

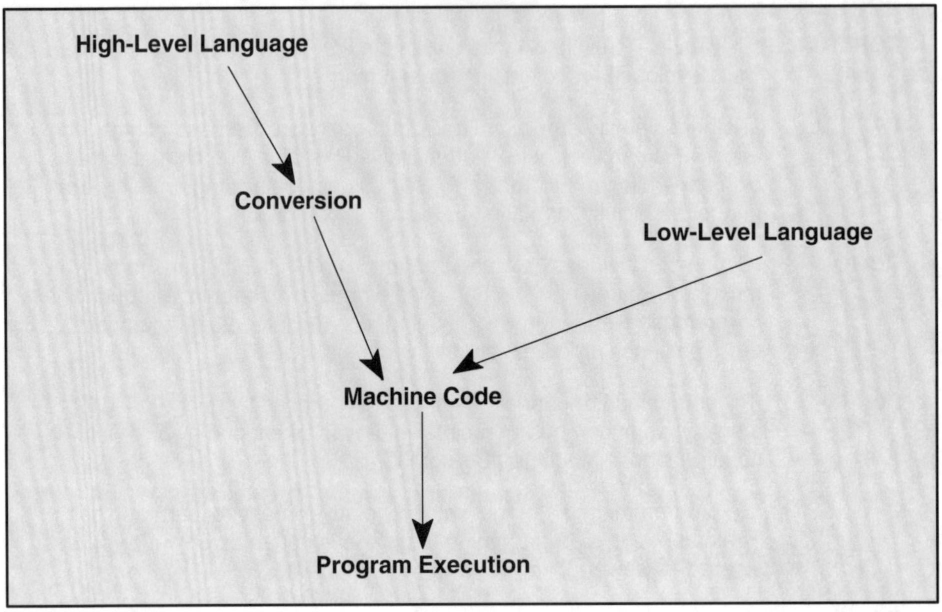

translated into a form of machine language which the computer then executes. Exhibit 7 provides a simple visual representation of the distance separating low-level and high-level programming languages from machine-readable codes which will execute the program functions.

Summary

The physical equipment of a computer system is called hardware. Computer hardware is visible, movable, and easy to identify. In order to have a computer system, three hardware components are required: an input/output (I/O) unit, a central processing unit (CPU), and an external storage device.

Input/output units allow users to interact with the computer system. Input/output units discussed in this chapter include keyboards, touch-screen terminals, display screens, and various kinds of printers. Commonly used input/output units in the hospitality industry are CRT units, teletype terminals, electronic cash registers, and line-printing terminals. There is no direct link between input and output devices. Whenever information moves within the computer system, it passes through the CPU.

The CPU is the control center of the computer system and is the most important and most expensive individual hardware component found within a computer system. It is the "brain" of the system and is responsible for controlling all other system components.

One part of the internal memory of the CPU is known as read only memory (ROM). This memory holds a permanent record of information that the computer needs to use each time it is turned on. Another part of the internal memory of the CPU is called random access memory (RAM). This memory holds a temporary version of the programs and/or data which users are processing. Since data stored in RAM can be accessed and/or altered by the user, RAM is often described as read/write memory: the user can both "read" from RAM (retrieve data), and "write" to RAM (store data). When the computer loses electrical power, or is turned off, all user data stored in RAM is lost.

An external storage device is a piece of equipment that retains data and/or programs that can be accessed by the CPU. Data and programs can be permanently stored on such external devices as magnetic tapes, floppy disks, hard disks, and laser discs.

The operating system is part of systems software and must be present for a computer system to be able to carry out instructions generated by applications software programs. Operating systems for microcomputers discussed in this chapter are DOS, UNIX, and OS/2.

A set of programs that instructs or controls the operation of the hardware components of a computer system is called software. Software programs tell the computer what to do, how to do it, and when to do it. Computer programs can be written in low-level or high-level programming languages. Low-level languages, also referred to as machine languages, can be directly understood by the computer. High-level languages are easier for programmers to use; however, programs written in high-level languages generally do not execute functions as quickly as do programs written in low-level languages.

Key Terms

Input/Output

bidirectional printing	laser printer
CRT unit	line-printing terminal
cursor	mouse
daisywheel printer	non-impact printer
disk drive	scanners
display screen	soft copy
dot matrix printer	teletype terminal
hard copy	thermal printer
impact printer	touch-screen terminal
ink jet printer	voice recognition systems
keyboard	

Computer Systems

bus system	extended memory
central processing unit (CPU)	FAX board
computer program	hardware
expanded memory	high-level programming language

interface board

low-level programming language

machine language

megahertz (MHz)

microprocessor

non-volatile memory

operating system

random access memory (RAM)

read only memory (ROM)

read/write

software

systems software

volatile memory

External Storage

floppy disks

formatting

hard copy

hard disks

magnetic tape

random access medium

removable hard disk

sector

sequential access medium

soft copy

tape streamers

track

Discussion Questions

1. What does the term "hardware" mean? Identify the three hardware components necessary for a computer system, and describe their functions.

2. What are the various types of keys typically found on a microcomputer keyboard?

3. What is the difference between an impact printer and a non-impact printer? Give examples of each type of printer.

4. What is the difference between RAM and ROM?

5. What terms do the following acronyms represent: I/O, CPU, CRT, TTY, LPT, DOS, OS/2, and UNIX?

6. What is meant by the term "computer program"?

7. What are the various functions performed by most operating systems?

8. What is the difference between a sequential access medium and a random access medium?

9. What are some of the typical external storage devices?

10. What is the difference between low-level and high-level computer programming languages?

REVIEW QUIZ

When you feel you have covered all of the material in this chapter, answer these questions. Choose the *best* answer.

Matching

1. The "brain" of a computer system

2. An example of an impact printer

3. Non-volatile memory

4. A random access medium

5. Read/write memory

6. Creating tracks and sectors on a floppy disk

7. Flashing marker on a computer screen

8. Orchestrates the hardware and software within a computer system

a. operating system

b. random access memory (RAM)

c. daisywheel printer

d. cursor

e. volatile memory

f. central processing unit (CPU)

g. laser printer

h. floppy disk

i. read only memory (ROM)

j. magnetic tape

k. formatting

l. display screen

m. bus system

True (T) or False (F)

T   F   9. There is no typewriter-like carriage return attached to a microcomputer system keyboard because electronic word processing usually performs this function automatically.

T   F   10. VGA, LCD, and CGA are types of computer system display screens.

T   F   11. A laser printer works by spraying a minute and finely controlled jet of ink onto the paper.

T   F   12. Magnetic tapes are referred to as a random access medium because data can be stored in any available location on the tape.

Alternate/Multiple Choice

13. A computer system's typical keyboard keys normally function similarly to the keys found on:

    a. a typewriter.
    b. an adding machine.

14. The additional memory capacity that resides outside the computer's basic memory which can be accessed in revolving blocks is called:

    a. extended memory.
    b. expanded memory.

15. The printer that works by burning a protective layer off specially treated paper to reveal ink is called:

a. a thermal printer.
b. an electrothermal printer.
c. an ink jet printer.
d. two of the above.

Chapter Outline

Word Processing Software
    Working with Soft Copy
    On-Screen Editing Techniques
    Formatting Documents
    Special Features
    Desktop Publishing
Electronic Spreadsheet Software
    Spreadsheet Design
    Creating a Spreadsheet
    Updating Data and Recalculations
    Common Spreadsheet Commands
    Graphics Capability
    Special Features
Database Management Software
    Files, Records, and Fields
    Database Structures
    Input Criteria and Output
        Specifications
    Common Database Management
        Commands
    Calculator Feature
Electronic Communications
    Communication Networks
    Telecommunications Hardware
    Electronic Communications Software
    Advanced Features
Summary

Learning Objectives

1. Describe the basic functions of word processing software.

2. Describe "windows" and explain the advantages of using them.

3. Explain what is meant by primary files and secondary files used in a mail merge.

4. Describe the basic functions of electronic spreadsheet software.

5. Define the term "cell" in relation to electronic spreadsheets.

6. Define the term "formula" in relation to electronic spreadsheets.

7. Explain the importance of the recalculation feature of electronic spreadsheet software.

8. Identify the basic function of database management software.

9. Explain how the organization of a database is similar to the organization of an office file cabinet.

10. Identify the differences between hierarchical database structures and relational database structures.

11. Explain how index and sort commands organize records in database files.

12. Describe the basic functions of a modem.

13. Explain what the terms simplex, half-duplex, and full-duplex mean in relation to telecommunications.

Generic Applications Software

In order for a computer system to perform a useful task, there must be a set of programs which instructs the hardware components what to do, how to do it, and when to do it. These programs are called computer software. Applications software programs are designed to perform such tasks as word processing, electronic spreadsheet analysis, and database management.

There are many applications software products on the market. Some of these products are more sophisticated than others, and products often vary in relation to the specific commands which users must master in order to operate the programs. Instead of discussing the details of particular products offered by specific manufacturers, this chapter provides a general explanation of the features found in generic applications software programs. This chapter will provide readers with a basic understanding of what they can expect to accomplish through the use of applications software packages.

In addition, this chapter presents fundamental information regarding hardware and software requirements for electronic communications. This information is intended to be introductory and does not address the details of this highly complex and technical area. However, the discussion will provide readers with a basic understanding of how communication takes place within and between computer systems.

Word Processing Software

Word processing computer software is a valuable office tool that can increase the productivity of personnel engaged in everyday business writing tasks. Before electronic word processing systems were developed, business communications often were first handwritten and then typed on manual or electric typewriters. Revisions to original documents or corrections of typographical errors (typos) often meant hours of lost productivity because entire documents had to be retyped. With electronic word processing, changes can be made and typos can be corrected without re-inputting the entire document.

The first electronic word processing systems were complex and often demanded well-trained and highly skilled operators. This created a division of labor in the production of written communications. Typically, one person wrote a document by hand and gave it to a word processing operator to enter into the system. Then, the operator produced hard copy for the writer to review. The writer revised, edited, and proofread the document and returned it to the operator so that changes could be made. Another hard copy was returned to the writer and the process continued until the document was considered polished and in finished form.

The simplicity of today's word processing computer software has, in many cases, done away with this cumbersome process. Basic word processing techniques can be quickly mastered. This enables writers to input documents themselves and make on-line revisions, editing changes, and proofreading corrections. This process saves both time and money. In addition, it allows the writer to take advantage of the many software features that assist in the writing process, such as the outlining, indexing, and proofreading capabilities of software programs.

Advances in technology, such as **optical character recognition** (OCR) devices, are also increasing the productivity of word processing. OCR devices automate the time-consuming input stage of word processing. These devices are able to scan typed copy produced by ordinary typewriters or electronic printers and convert it into an electronic form which can be entered into the word processing system.

Word processing computer software and electronic printers have also dramatically increased the quality of written business communications. The layout and design of letters, memos, reports, and typical business forms can reflect the powerful capabilities of sophisticated word processing software packages. The options available through these software packages often eliminate the need for hospitality businesses to contract the services of local printers. Direct mail advertising, menu printing, and personalized form letters are examples of the kind of work that some businesses are now producing in-house. This capability not only saves time and money, it also increases management's control over projects that have important deadlines which must be met.

The following sections describe some basic electronic word processing techniques. These packages vary widely not only in relation to specific features, but also in terms of the particular keystrokes which carry out basic functions. Instead of describing the details of a specific product offered by a single software manufacturer, the following sections provide an overview of what can be done by almost any of today's sophisticated word processing computer software products.

Working with Soft Copy

A word processing document appearing on the computer's display screen can be thought of as a very long sheet of paper. Just as you cannot see all of a sheet of paper when it is rolled onto a typewriter's carriage, so only a certain number of lines of a word processing document can be seen at a time on the computer's screen. The user accesses portions of the document by pressing the keys on the cursor control keypad.

The cursor is a flashing marker on a display screen that indicates where the next character to be entered will appear. The cursor control keys on the computer keyboard are marked by arrows. When one of these keys is pressed, the cursor moves in the direction of the arrow indicated on the key. The cursor control keys move the cursor through the document one character space at a time. However, special keys and key combinations permit a user to **scroll** through a document a full page at a time. As the user presses the appropriate keys, the document appears on the screen in a rolling manner, similar to the way in which a very long sheet of paper would roll through a typewriter's carriage. As lines successively disappear at the top of the screen, new lines appear at the bottom.

To accommodate the needs of users who typically work with long documents, special commands exist which can move the cursor immediately to any desired page in a document. Also, some word processing packages reserve space on the display screen to identify the current position of the cursor within the document appearing on the screen. This information lets the user know the exact cursor position in terms of page number, line number, and position along a line.

The ability of a word processing package to match soft copy (what is seen on the display screen) with hard copy (the printed version of the word processed document) is often described as a "what you see is what you get" (WYSIWYG) software feature. For many types of word processing tasks, it is helpful to have the document appear on the display screen exactly as it will appear in printed form. Not all word processing software packages provide this feature. In some cases, the commands entered by a user to perform certain editing tasks will appear as part of the soft copy on the display screen but not as part of the hard copy produced when the document is printed.

On-Screen Editing Techniques

Electronic word processing enables users to easily edit documents and to immediately observe the results of their editing work. As the user enters basic editing commands (such as insert, delete, copy, move, search, replace), the changes are immediately reflected in the textual material appearing on the display screen.

Since these functions are carried out in the CPU's temporary memory (RAM), all of the textual material will be lost if the computer is turned off or if it loses power. In order to save the current version of textual material, the user must transfer it to an external storage device, such as a disk. Word processing systems contain specific instructions for saving processed material. Once saved on an external storage device, the textual material can be retrieved at any time for reprinting, updating, editing, or any further processing.

Inserting and deleting large blocks of text are important parts of word processing and are two of the functions that make word processing such a valuable tool. When new material is inserted within the document, words are automatically moved to allow space for the new characters. Also, when material is deleted from a document, the spacing is adjusted to fill any gaps created by the deleted material. Whole pages can be inserted (or deleted), and the spacing within the document will be adjusted to accommodate the changes. All this rearranging is accomplished within seconds by simply pressing keys that initiate the commands.

Relatively simple commands enable a user to cut a portion of a document, save it in a temporary file, and insert it later in the same document or in an altogether different document. This electronic "cut and paste" technique avoids the laborious retyping involved in non-computerized office tasks. There are also commands that permit a user to copy a portion of a document (or even the entire document), save it in a temporary file, and later insert it within another document. A variation of this technique will be discussed shortly in relation to the use of boilerplate files.

Many word processing software packages permit a user to view more than one document at a time on the computer's display screen. Special keystroke commands split the screen into any desired number of sections. These sections of the screen are called **windows**. Each window can contain textual material from a separate document. Space limitations on the user's screen determine the number of windows the user can effectively work with at any given time. However, just two or three windows can permit a user to efficiently perform a variety of editing tasks. For example, textual material from one document on the screen can be copied, moved, and inserted into a second document which appears on the same screen. Having both documents on the screen at the same time enables the user to verify the success of the transfer immediately.

Sophisticated word processing software enables a user to search through an entire document and quickly find a word, phrase, or even an entire sentence. A few simple keystrokes automatically move the cursor through the document, stopping only at each occurrence of the sought-after word or phrase. When the search function is coupled with a replace function, the user can replace a word or phrase with another word or phrase. This can be an enormous time-saver when editing documents. Changes which would once have entailed retyping the entire document can be made within seconds.

Formatting Documents

In the context of word processing, the term "formatting" refers to techniques for preparing a document's printed appearance. These techniques include setting line spacing, page lengths, margins, tabs, and indents; boldfacing, underlining, or centering important words or phrases; and transforming single-column documents into two, three, or more columns. Each of these document formatting techniques can be implemented with just a few keystrokes.

Word processing software programs generally preset some document formatting controls. These preset controls are called **default settings**. For example, when the user begins to input characters, the margins of the document are usually already set to conform to the requirements of typical typing tasks. Users can change these default settings at any time—for the entire document or for any portion within the document. For example, wide documents can be produced by simply changing the setting for the right margin. However, if the right margin setting makes the line length longer than the number of characters per line which the display screen can show at any one time, it will not be possible for the user to see the whole width of the document. The cursor will be able to span across the line of the document, but the entire width will not appear on the display screen at one time. Default settings typically control margins, tabs, indents, page lengths, and other basic characteristics of a document's visual appearance.

Document formatting techniques which are not preset by the software manufacturer include underlining, boldfacing, and centering. **Underlining** and **boldfacing** are formatting techniques which are used to emphasize words, phrases, titles, or formulas by making them stand out from the rest of the text. The user controls these formatting techniques by initiating start/stop commands at the keyboard. For example, if the underlining command is turned on and the user forgets to turn it off, the rest of the textual material input by the user will be automatically underlined. **Similarly, if the command for boldfacing is turned on and the user forgets**

to turn it off, the rest of the textual material input by the user will be automatically boldfaced.

The command for centering textual material between margins functions in a similar manner. Generally, the user must issue one command which turns the centering function on and another command which turns the function off.

Other document formatting techniques include controlling line justification, creating document headers/footers, and automatically numbering the pages of a document.

When a line of textual material is right justified, the spacing between words is varied so that each line of the document aligns with the right margin setting. When working with multiple columns of text (which necessitate short line lengths), right justification may create unacceptable gaps of blank space between the words on a line. In these cases, the user may either turn off the right justification function, or run an automatic hyphenation routine which will break words and even out the spacing between words in the columns of textual material.

Header/footers are generally used with long documents. A header is information placed at the top of a page above the regular textual material of the document. A footer is information placed at the bottom of the page below the regular textual material of the document. Sophisticated software packages normally permit the user to control the placement of headers and/or footers. These options include placing them flush left, flush right, or centered between the margins of the textual material.

Automatic page numbering is an extremely useful function in the processing of long documents. Word processing packages generally enable the user to control the placement of page numbers in much the same way that the user controls the placement of headers and footers.

Special Features

Sophisticated word processing packages enable the user to do more than create, edit, and format documents. They also may provide math features for calculating figures or creating limited types of spreadsheets. Some of the more useful features related to processing textual material include running an automatic spell check, creating boilerplate files and style sheets, and personalizing form letters.

Automatic Spell Check. Many word processing software packages include **automatic spell check** programs that can help users proofread documents by automatically checking for spelling errors. The words in the document are electronically compared to entries in the spell checker's dictionary. When a word appears in the document that does not appear in the program's dictionary, it is generally highlighted on the display screen so it can be corrected by the operator. Automatic spell checks can be used to look up one word at a time, all of the words on a given page, or all of the words in a particular document. Normally, spell checkers do not automatically replace misspelled words with correctly spelled words. Users are typically given several options, such as skipping over the identified word, correcting the misspelled word, and others.

Skipping over a word highlighted by the spell checker is an important option. The spell checker's dictionary may be limited in size and therefore may not contain all words commonly used by hospitality operations. Also, when proper nouns (such as people's names) are not words which appear in the spell checker's dictionary, the program highlights them, alerting the user to verify that they are correct. Hospitality businesses deal with a great many proper nouns such as the names of guests, employees, suppliers, sales contacts, and so on.

An advanced feature of some sophisticated word processing packages enables users to add words to the spell checker's dictionary or even create their own special-purpose dictionaries. Also, some packages enable the user to activate an on-screen thesaurus or to look up the spelling of a difficult word by merely typing a phonetic version (sound pattern) of the word. For example, a user could ask for the correct spelling of "muzium" and the dictionary could respond with "museum."

None of these options takes the place of careful proofreading, but they can be useful time-savers when deadlines for important projects are approaching.

Boilerplate Files and Style Sheets. Some types of written business communications use standard phrases and/or paragraphs over and over again in a number of different contexts. When such standard textual material is stored on floppy disks, the files on the disks are often referred to as **boilerplate files.** The standard content stored in boilerplate files can be retrieved and automatically inserted into appropriate documents as needed. This eliminates retyping and ensures consistency of content.

A **style sheet** is a predesigned form, also called a format, for typical documents processed by a particular business. While boilerplate files store *contents*, style sheets store *formats*. Some word processing packages provide style sheets which format typical business documents such as memos or letters. The style sheet feature can be used to format business letters so that the proper spacing is allotted to accommodate output onto letterhead stationery.

Personalizing Form Letters. Advanced word processing software programs enable users to personalize form letters quickly and accurately through a process which is sometimes referred to as **mail merge.** Mail merge involves the use of two files—a primary file and a secondary file. The primary file contains the standard textual material that the user wishes to distribute. The secondary file contains variable textual material, such as a mailing list consisting of individual names and addresses.

When creating the primary file, the user instructs the computer that special information from a secondary file will be required at various points within the document. When the document is printed, the primary and secondary files *merge* to produce a distribution copy with proper names and addresses inserted. Exhibit 1 illustrates the process involved in personalizing form letters by merging primary and secondary files.

Some printers will not be able to carry out all of the special word processing options offered by a sophisticated word processing package. Other printers may be able to carry out many of these options, but only at the expense of additional printer hardware (such as print wheels or font cartridges) which is typically purchased

Exhibit 1   Personalizing Form Letters

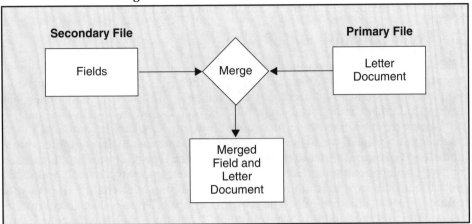

separately from the basic printer components. The user's manual provided by the software manufacturer generally identifies the types and models of printers which can support application features. The degree to which a particular printer supports the special printing features of a word processing package is an important consideration when selecting printers.

Desktop Publishing

Desktop publishing can be defined as the writing, assembling, and design of printed materials using a personal computer. In the hospitality industry, desktop systems are sometimes used to develop printed menus, company newsletters, business forms, promotional literature, advertising copy, training manuals, and the like.

Computer hardware and software requirements for desktop publishing systems are relatively straightforward. Hardware components include a microcomputer system, external storage devices, and a quality printer (usually a laser printer). Desktop publishing software consists of a page layout program capable of integrating text with graphics. Several sophisticated word processing software packages are capable of importing graphics designed within other applications software programs. However, these programs are neither as efficient nor as effective as software programs designed specifically for desktop publishing.

Templates assist those desktop publishing users who are not experienced graphic designers. Templates are used to produce recurring features and formats of documents. A template is basically a group of rules that describe what a document will look like in terms of margins, columns, lines, boxes, and so on. For example, a lunch menu format that is used each day regardless of changes in items or prices could be designed as a template. Each time that management wanted to produce a new lunch menu, the lunch template would provide consistent design information to the desktop system. This eliminates the need for the user to create a new menu design from scratch. The template serves as a style sheet, providing set-up information and simplifying the production of a document.

Electronic Spreadsheet Software

With a computerized accounting system, figures are entered only once into the accounting records. These entered amounts can then be accessed by programs which prepare mathematically correct journals, ledgers, and financial statements. This feature and others are made possible by electronic spreadsheet software.

An electronic spreadsheet program allows a user to input a model of the accountant's traditional worksheet in the temporary memory of the computer system and view it as output generated on a display screen. The electronic model is essentially a blank page of a worksheet which is divided into rows (usually numbered from top to bottom) and columns (usually lettered from left to right). The rows and columns intersect to form **cells**. The coordinates of a cell (the particular column letter and row number) identify what is typically called the address of a cell.

Cells can hold different types of data: alpha data, such as labels for the columns and rows; numeric data, such as dollar amounts; and **formulas**, which instruct the computer to carry out specific calculations, such as adding all numbers in a certain range of cells. The cells in which formulas are entered will display the results of the calculations. If any of the amounts entered in the range of cells change, a formula is able to immediately recalculate the amounts and place the new total in the same designated cell.

Electronic spreadsheet software is not limited to bookkeeping functions; it is capable of performing many different kinds of tasks which may be extremely useful to managers in the hospitality industry. The recalculation feature of electronic spreadsheet programs offers managers opportunities to explore "what if" possibilities. For example, an electronic spreadsheet could be created to indicate the effects that different room occupancy levels may have on a hotel's food and beverage operation, telephone revenue, gift shop sales, and other revenue-producing centers. Information which could take hours to calculate manually takes only seconds when calculated electronically.

The speed with which electronic spreadsheet software can generate information is an important factor that increases a manager's ability to make decisions. A manager is less likely to request certain kinds of information or reports when he or she knows that valuable personnel will be tied up for hours. With electronic spreadsheet software, a manager has all kinds of information and reports at his or her fingertips—and in a matter of seconds.

Most electronic spreadsheet software packages have graphics capability. That is, the programs are able to generate graphs (bar charts, line graphs, pie charts, etc.) from data entered in worksheets. This can be a valuable management tool for communicating information. However, in order for users to view the graphic designs that they create, their display screens must have graphics capability. This is an important consideration when selecting computer hardware. Printers may have limited graphics capability as well. Just because a particular bar chart appears as soft copy on a display screen does not mean that the printer can produce hard copy of the chart. When selecting hardware components for a computer system, users must make sure that the components fully support the capabilities of the software applications that they plan to run on the system.

Since an electronic spreadsheet program creates a worksheet in the temporary memory (RAM) of the computer system, if a user turns off the computer or exits from the program without saving the worksheet, all the work that went into creating the worksheet will be lost. If a worksheet is to become a permanent record, it must be saved on some type of external storage device such as a disk. Once a worksheet has been properly stored, it can be retrieved at any time and brought into the computer's temporary memory for updating and additional processing. Many programs permit users to save material to external storage devices while they are still in the process of creating their worksheets. Once material is stored to a disk, additional backup is recommended to protect a disk from being damaged, lost, or simply worn out. Therefore, it is extremely important to make at least one extra copy of every disk that is used.

Spreadsheet Design

Along the horizontal border at the top of an electronic spreadsheet are letters of the alphabet which are used to identify individual columns within the spreadsheet. Since spreadsheet software packages normally provide many more columns than there are letters in the alphabet, the alphabet is repeated in a number of different series (such as, from AA through AZ, then from BA through BZ, and so on) until all the columns are identified. Some electronic spreadsheets have 256 columns or more. Along the vertical border on the left side of the spreadsheet are numbers which are used to identify the rows within the spreadsheet. Some electronic spreadsheets have more than 2,000 rows. The rows and columns intersect to form cells. The coordinates of a cell (the particular column letter and row number) identify what is typically called the **cell address**. Exhibit 2 illustrates the format of an electronic spreadsheet. The addresses of several cells are identified within the exhibit for illustrative purposes only. Before the user inputs data, the cells of an electronic spreadsheet are empty.

In order to operate sophisticated spreadsheet programs, the user's computer system must have a large memory capacity. If the random access memory (RAM) of the user's computer system is unable to handle the software programs, the computer will either fail to load the programs or, at some point, completely stop functioning.

Display screens typically provide space for an 8-column by 20-row spreadsheet. Therefore, only a small portion of the spreadsheet (160 cells) can appear on the screen at a time. However, the cursor control keypad enables the user to move through the spreadsheet cell by cell, or scroll up or down through the spreadsheet full screens at a time. Other cursor key combinations allow the user immediate access to any cell within the spreadsheet. A simple "go to" command followed by a cell address immediately places the cursor within the desired cell.

Some electronic spreadsheet software packages refer to the flashing cursor as a **pointer**. The cell that contains the pointer at any particular time is called the **current cell**. Data entries are always made to the current cell. The user defines the content of each cell and thus creates a unique spreadsheet which will perform the desired task.

Exhibit 2   Electronic Spreadsheet Format

	A	B	C	D	E	F	G	H
1	A1	B1	C1	D1	E1	F1	G1	H1
2	A2	B2						
3	A3		C3					
4	A4			D4				
5	A5				E5			
6	A6					F6		
7	A7						G7	
8	A8							H8

Creating a Spreadsheet

Spreadsheet cells can hold different types of data: alpha data, such as labels to identify the contents of columns and rows; numeric data, such as dollar amounts; and formulas, which instruct the computer to carry out specific calculations, such as adding all the numbers in a certain range of cells. A **cell range** is a group of adjacent cells.

When textual information is entered into a cell, it is referred to as a **label**. Labels are used as column heads and row titles to organize and identify **numeric values** which are eventually entered into cells from the keyboard's numeric keypad. Spreadsheet software programs are normally able to immediately distinguish data input as labels from data input as numeric values. However, when entering formulas, the user must enter a special character or command before entering the formula. This alerts the program that the entry is a formula and not a label or numeric value.

Exhibit 3 illustrates a spreadsheet designed to calculate occupancy percentages for a large hotel. The spreadsheet contains labels in cells B1, C1, D1, E1, F1, G1, A2, A3, and A5. Note that the cell width of column A was altered to accommodate descriptive labels. Cells B2, C2, D2, E2, F2, G2, B3, C3, D3, E3, F3, and G3 all contain numeric values necessary for calculating occupancy percentages.

The results of stored formulas appear in cells B5, C5, D5, E5, F5, and G5. Note that the formulas themselves do not appear within cells. Cells that contain formulas only display the results of calculations produced by the formulas. Since occupancy percentage is calculated by dividing rooms sold by rooms available for sale, the formula used to generate the result in cell B5 was +B2/B3. This formula references the cell addresses (B2 and B3) whose numeric values are needed in order to calculate the occupancy percentage for Day 1.

Exhibit 3 Spreadsheet Calculation of Occupancy Percentages

	A	B	C	D	E	F	G
1		Day 1	Day 2	Day 3	Day 4	Day 5	Day 6
2	Rooms Sold	2950	3000	2750	3090	2850	2925
3	Rooms Available	3100	3100	3100	3100	3100	3100
4							
5	Occupancy % =	.9516	.9677	.8871	.9968	.9194	.9435
6							

Note that the addition symbol (+) is part of the formula input. This symbol is used to alert the spreadsheet program that the input involves a formula and not a label or numeric value. The symbol is not a command to add; it is a **formula prefix** defined by the manufacturer of the software package. Formula prefixes may vary from manufacturer to manufacturer and are defined by the user manuals which accompany the particular spreadsheet programs. The slash symbol (/) within the formula indicates the mathematical operation (division) which is to be carried out. Similarly, the values in cells C5, D5, E5, F5, and G5 were generated from the formulas + C2/C3, + D2/D3, + E2/E3, + F2/F3, and + G2/G3, respectively.

Updating Data and Recalculations

Since entered formulas become part of the spreadsheet, amounts within a cell or range of cells can be changed and the formulas will immediately recalculate a new total. This **recalculation** feature of electronic spreadsheet software enables users to update spreadsheet data and obtain the results almost instantly. It also offers managers opportunities to explore *what if* possibilities. For example, hotel managers could analyze costs and revenues under different circumstances and arrive at the best room rate to charge guests in order to maximize profits.

The ability of users to input formulas prevents electronic spreadsheets from simply being glorified word processing programs capable of generating specialized reports. A person might think that the spreadsheet illustrated in Exhibit 3 was generated by a word processing program. There is nothing in the exhibit to contradict this belief, because, when formulas are entered into cells, the cells display only the values which result from the calculations carried out by formulas. However, many word processing software packages do not have electronic spreadsheet capability. And those which do are much more limited in scope than software designed specifically for spreadsheet functions. Also, few word processing systems carry the graphics capabilities of advanced electronic spreadsheet software.

Common Spreadsheet Commands

Specific commands enable the user to expand the pointer to cover a range of cells and then issue other commands which will affect the entire range of cells. While the specific names of commands vary among software programs, simple keystrokes are able to initiate the following actions:

- Retrieve a spreadsheet from a disk.

- Insert a number of rows or columns.

- Delete a number of rows or columns.

- Copy a cell or a range of cells.

- Move a cell or a range of cells.

- Erase all data entered into the spreadsheet.

- Save a spreadsheet to a disk.

- Print a spreadsheet.

- Create a graph from spreadsheet data.

Creating a spreadsheet involves a great deal more than merely entering data. The user must master many formatting techniques which affect the spreadsheet's printed appearance. Often, column widths must be enlarged to support lengthy labels, entered data must be consistently aligned within cells, and so on.

Preformatted electronic spreadsheet programs are available. These preformatted spreadsheets, called **templates**, enable the user to simply enter data into predefined data cells. The columns and rows are identified by labels, and formulas are already entered into cells which display the results of calculations. The user enters numeric values in the appropriate cells and the template program does virtually everything else. Templates save time and may also enable the user to acquire powerful, proven technology at a fraction of its development cost.

Graphics Capability

Once a spreadsheet has been created and the data and formulas have been entered correctly, the spreadsheet can be saved on an external storage device (such as a floppy disk) for future use or it can be printed immediately as a hard copy report. Spreadsheet data can also be used to generate graphic materials which reflect information contained in the spreadsheet.

Even well-designed spreadsheets may not convey the real importance of the information they contain. With a properly equipped computer system, spreadsheet data can be displayed in the form of bar, line, or pie graphs. Although graphic displays do not usually provide a great deal of detail, managers can more easily track recent performance trends by displaying the results of operations in line graphs. Pie charts can be used to identify the proportions of individual departmental expenses; and bar charts can be used to show the amounts of total revenue generated by departments over several months.

Spreadsheet graphics. (Courtesy of International Business Machines Corporation)

What if simulation projections can also be displayed visually. Any graph created from spreadsheet data will be instantly updated each time spreadsheet data are changed. When a single piece of data is changed to explore *what if* possibilities, a new graphic output can emphatically depict the impact of the changed data on the total net result. This enables managers to use graphics as a valuable simulation tool.

Special Features

Advanced electronic spreadsheet programs enable the user to take advantage of such sophisticated features as on-line assistance, linking spreadsheets, multiple windowing, macro commands, and integrating spreadsheets with other software applications.

On-Line Assistance. While creating a spreadsheet, a user may often need information which explains how to initiate a certain command. Some electronic spreadsheet packages provide users with on-line assistance. A few simple keystrokes enable the user to leave the current spreadsheet and call up needed information onto the display screen. After receiving the information, a few more keystrokes return the user to exactly the same working position within the spreadsheet.

Some spreadsheet packages provide a menu, also referred to as a control panel, which generally appears directly above the spreadsheet. The menu alerts the user to helpful information, such as the address of the current cell and cell contents. One line of the menu may show spreadsheet data, character by character, as it is input at the keyboard. Other messages may appear in the menu which inform the user of available commands and the status of the spreadsheet.

Linking Spreadsheets. Large and intricate spreadsheets are difficult to construct and may be cumbersome to operate. Users find that it is much easier to develop and refine a series of smaller, separate spreadsheets. Advanced spreadsheet software programs enable users to work with smaller spreadsheets and yet achieve the same results as they would with a single intricate spreadsheet. These programs operate by **linking spreadsheets** in such a way that they share data and can interact to perform functions which none of them could perform individually.

Multiple Windowing. While the ability to link spreadsheets enables a user to work with smaller spreadsheets, each of these spreadsheets will probably not be small enough to allow a user to view all of the columns and rows at one time on the display screen. Advanced spreadsheet programs provide **multiple windowing** capability enabling a user to split the display screen (either vertically, horizontally, or both) and view separate areas of a spreadsheet simultaneously. This function allows a user to enter data in one portion of the spreadsheet and immediately observe its effects on other areas.

Macro Commands. Sophisticated spreadsheet software packages also enable a user to create programs which minimize keystrokes. These **macro commands** allow for greater speed of data entry, consolidation, and reporting. For example, a macro command could be programmed to print several versions of a projected budget with each version incorporating several different values for specified expense areas.

Integrating Spreadsheets. The ability to integrate electronic spreadsheets with other software applications (such as word processing systems, database management programs, and electronic cash register systems) is becoming increasingly important to users in the hospitality industry. Integrated software applications enable users to access important data and enhance the appearance of printed reports.

Database Management Software

Database management software is a term for programs which allow users to catalog and store information about their businesses for future use. A **database** is a collection of related facts and figures designed to serve a specific purpose.

Although the term database is relatively new, the function which a database performs is not. People have been routinely using dozens of databases for centuries. For example, a personal checkbook is a database; it collects facts and figures which are designed to monitor personal finances. Other common databases include an address book, a telephone book, and a dictionary.

The design and organization of these everyday databases are essential to users. The data within an address book, telephone book, and dictionary are sorted alphabetically so that users can quickly access the particular data they need. The checks in a personal checkbook are numbered sequentially. If an individual keeps to this numbered sequence when issuing checks, the returned cancelled checks can

Exhibit 4   Database Files, Records, and Fields

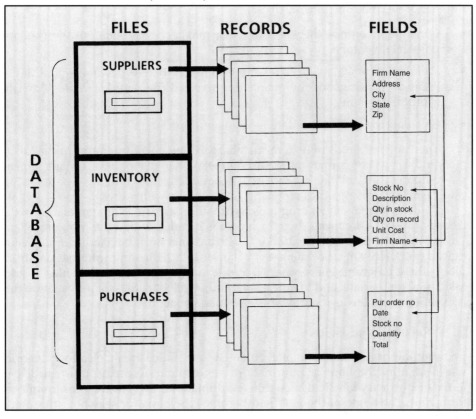

be stored in the same numbered sequence, enabling the person to easily retrieve any particular check with minimal effort.

Think of a database management system as a filing cabinet. The way information is organized within a filing cabinet will depend on the kind of information which is stored and the particular needs of the user. File cabinets have separate file drawers. Each file drawer contains separate file folders. The folders within each drawer contain similar records of related information. Each record within a folder contains specific facts and/or figures.

Exhibit 4 diagrams the similarity between a typical office file cabinet and a database management system. In the language of database management software, the file cabinet is called the database, the drawers of the cabinet are called **database files**, the folders within the drawers are called **database records**, and the detailed facts and/or figures in the records are called **database fields**.

For example, an inventory database might be set up for inventory control. Assume that this database is made up of a single file. The file would contain one record for each inventory item, and each record would contain a number of fields, such as the item's name, number, cost, quantity on hand, re-order point, and so on.

Different users of the computer system can access this database to perform any number of desired functions, such as:

- Generate inventory checklists to assist managers and supervisors in taking physical inventory.

- Perform variance analyses on the differences between actual quantities of items on hand versus the quantities projected (perpetual inventory) by the computer system.

- Calculate the total value of items in inventory.

There are hundreds of uses for database management programs in the hospitality industry. These programs are used in relation to personnel file management, payroll processing, marketing research, general ledger accounting, tax reporting, direct mail advertising, sales reporting, and countless other areas.

Database management programs control the structure and organization of databases as well as the means by which data is handled within a computer system. These programs limit the number of times that data must be handled and ensure that all users accessing the database are working with the same information. In addition, these programs enable users to create, access, and merge data files; to add, select, and delete data; and to index, sort, and search data files for information that is eventually printed as reports for use by management.

Files, Records, and Fields

In a computerized database management system, fields are labeled by categories which identify the kind of information they contain. Records are identified in terms of a primary key field, also called a primary key, which contains unique information. The name of the key field becomes the basis for searching through a data file for a particular record.

Consider the organization of a master payroll file. The file would contain a record for each employee. Each record would be made up of fields identified by labels such as employee number, employee name, address, pay rate, withholdings, deductions, and so on. One of these fields would serve as the primary key field which could be used to search the data file for a particular record. Since the primary key field must contain unique information, the employee number field would function best as the key field of the master payroll file. Different employees may, by chance, have the same name, but when a company assigns employee numbers on a sequential basis, it guarantees that a particular number in the sequence identifies one particular employee named John Smith, who lives at a particular address, and so on.

The database of a hospitality business may be organized into many data files (such as personnel files, financial data files, guest history files, etc.). These files may contain dozens of records and scores of fields containing thousands of pieces of data. Database management software programs structure the relationships among files, records, and fields in a way that ensures rapid access to information. However, not all database management software programs structure a database in the same manner.

Exhibit 5   Hierarchical Database Structure

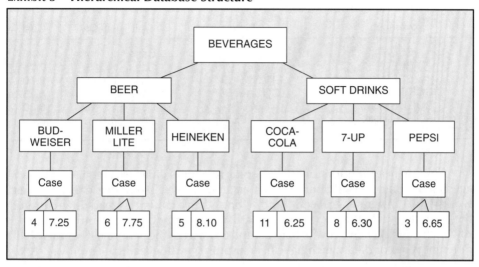

Database Structures

Database management programs structure a database by organizing data files, records, and fields in ways that facilitate searching for data, updating data, and generating accurate, timely, and useful reports for management. Database software programs manage databases through either hierarchical structures or relational structures.

A **hierarchical database structure** arranges data files, records, and fields into formations which resemble the structure of the roots of a tree. As the trunk of a tree leads into major roots which in turn branch off into entire networks of roots, so a hierarchically structured database begins with a data file (the trunk) which opens onto a number of master records (the major roots) which in turn lead to intricate root-like networks of other subordinate records. Exhibit 5 illustrates the structure of a hierarchical database.

In order to access data contained in subordinate records, the database management system must first access the data file, then the parent root, then a key field of the subordinate record network.

Database management software programs that arrange data in hierarchical structures are able to carry out precise data searches and generate comprehensive statistical analyses. However, they are dependent upon rigid parameters which define the nature of fields and records. It may be difficult and time-consuming to incorporate new data definitions into a hierarchically structured database.

Relational database structures have become the most popular type of database management system because of the simplicity of data arrangement, the ease of data manipulation, and the flexibility of data handling. The data files of a relational database management program are formatted as rectangular tables of rows and columns and are similar in appearance to electronic spreadsheets.

Exhibit 6   Relational Database Structure

Beverages	Brand	Unit	Qty.	Cost
BEER	BUDWEISER	Case	4	7.25
BEER	MILLER LITE	Case	6	7.75
BEER	HEINEKEN	Case	5	8.10
SOFT DRINK	COCA-COLA	Case	11	6.25
SOFT DRINK	7-UP	Case	8	6.30
SOFT DRINK	PEPSI	Case	3	6.65

Column headings identify fields (some relational database management packages refer to fields as attributes) such as an employee's number, name, address, work history, pay rate, skill code, and so on. When a column is read down through the rows it reveals the same type of data about many different employees. Each row is a record. When a row is read completely across the columns it reveals all the different types of data which have been input regarding a single employee. A key field attribute (such as, in our previous example, employee number) is used to identify the record. Exhibit 6 illustrates how the same data presented in Exhibit 5 would appear in a relational database structure. Exhibit 7 uses personnel data to illustrate the difference between hierarchical and relational database structures.

Input Criteria and Output Specifications

Database applications require users to define an input area for data entry, a criteria area to direct queries, and an output area to direct results. Although database software programs usually provide predetermined specifications (also referred to as default settings), users are encouraged to define specifications for these areas that best meet their particular needs.

Input area specifications define data entry procedures. Screen templates can be designed to guide users with data input responsibilities. For example, the display screen at the front desk of a hotel may guide front desk employees in entering specific data regarding guests during check-in. The use of a screen template would ensure that important data is collected and properly entered into the computer system.

Criteria area specifications define query procedures. A query is usually a request for a few pieces of data which does not necessitate a lengthy report, such as information regarding a guest's credit limit. Most database management programs support a query language which enables users to make requests through the keyboard. Criteria area specifications define the necessary sequence of keystrokes. For example, inputting a query may necessitate the following keystrokes:

- Entering a command

- Defining the scope of the command

- Specifying command conditions

Database management commands are usually entered by keying a simple word (such as DISPLAY, SUM, COUNT, LOCATE, LIST, and so on). Defining the

Exhibit 7   Personnel Data

Hierarchical Database Structure

Name: Dagan, Toby
Emp. Number: 48824

Emp. No. 48824	Emp. No. 48824	Emp. No. 48824
Personal Data	Work History	Salary History
29 Market Street	Start: 4/29/87	Start: 3.50
(413) 247–0962	End:	Current: 3.85

Rational Database Structure

Fields

	Name	Address	City, State	Emp. No.
R E C O R D S	Dagan, Toby	29 Market St.	E. Natick, MA	48824
	Michael, Greg	11 Arnold Pl.	N. Hampton, MA	48895
	Steven, Liz	87 E. 204 St.	S. Queens, MA	48864
	Vaugh, Betty	42 Summer St.	Carrick, MA	48827

---

scope of the command identifies which areas of the database will be affected by the command. Specifying command conditions stipulates the circumstances under which the command will operate. For example, given a particular database management program, entering the following sequence of keystrokes:
DISPLAY NAME, ADDRESS, CITY, STATE FOR SOCSEC = '277-42-9991' would lead the system to carry out the command (DISPLAY) for the field names listed (NAME, ADDRESS, CITY, STATE) when a specified condition is met (the existence of a social security number of 277-42-9991). The system will respond by displaying the person's name, address, city, and state only if there actually is an employee in the database with the specified social security number.

Output area specifications control the generation and formatting of reports. Since data stored in a database is independent of its application, database management programs are able to separate related information and generate a variety of report formats.

Common Database Management Commands

Once a database has been designed and the data input, records within database files can be accessed by a number of different users, and various types of information can be obtained through database management commands. Database management software programs provide a number of commands which enable users to organize records within database files and to search for information which may be contained in a number of different files. A few of the more common commands are briefly described in the following sections.

Organizing Records in Database Files. Two of the most frequently used commands which organize records in database files are the index and sort commands. The **index command** does not rearrange the records of a database file. Instead, it provides a limited working file which identifies records containing certain data, somwhat as the index of a textbook identifies page numbers containing a certain type of information. When a database file is retrieved and the **sort command** issued, a new database file is created which is equal in size and content of the original (source) file. However, the sort command changes the order of the records in the source file according to a field category designated by the user.

Assume that a large hospitality corporation is considering increasing the life insurance benefits of employees who have been continuously employed by the company for ten years. A user retrieves the personnel database file and the records containing employee numbers, employee names, addresses, length of employment, etc., and discovers that the records are arranged by employee number. Through the database management program, the user issues a command to sort the file and reorder the records by length of employment. The sorted file can then be printed as a report revealing the employees affected by the new insurance benefit, or the sorted file can become the basis for further processing.

It is important to note that an indexed file generally maintains a direct connection with the source file from which it was created. Therefore, the indexed file will immediately reflect any changes which are made to the source file, and vice versa. This is not the case with sorted files. A sorted file is generally independent of the source file from which it was created. Therefore, any changes made to the source file, such as updating the records, will have to be transferred to the previously sorted file. If extensive updating of database records occurs regularly, new sorted files must be created.

Searching Records. The **find command** or the **locate command** is used to search for specific records in database files. The find command normally functions more quickly than the locate command. However, it generally works only with files that have been indexed in terms of the specific field category for which the user is searching. The locate command functions by matching file entries with the character string for which the user is searching. Searches issued by the locate command tend to be less efficient and more time-consuming than searches issued by the find command, especially when large database files are involved.

Multiple Searches. The real strength of a database management software package lies in its ability to perform **multiple searches** across a broad spectrum of field categories. For example, consider the advantages of a multiple search routine for processing room requests from walk-ins. Assume that a guest arrives at the front desk of a large hotel and requests an upper floor suite with two double beds. The front desk employee conducts a multiple search through the rooms availability database file. The first search indexes the database file in terms of a **primary key**

field, which is the broadest field category involved in the search. In our example the primary key would be the type of room—a suite. Subsequent searches focus on **secondary keys,** which order and limit the primary key field. In our example, the number of beds in a room and floor location would be the secondary keys which order the primary key field of suites. Using the multiple search feature of a database management program, the front desk employee would have the necessary information for the guest within seconds.

Multiple search routines can be extremely useful when users work with large and complex databases. Consider how a multiple search routine can be used by a large food and beverage operation to find a substitute server who is available on Tuesday evenings between 4 and 7 P.M. Initially, a personnel database file would be searched for all persons qualified as a food server. Subsequent search passes through the file would result in a selective deletion of names whose work availability schedules fail to coincide with the day and time criteria.

Calculator Feature

Advanced database management software packages have built-in calculators which are capable of carrying out basic arithmetical and statistical operations. Standard mathematical conventions are adhered to, with multiplication and division taking precedence over addition and subtraction. The **calculator feature** can be extremely useful because it can be accessed at any point in a database application.

Since the results of calculations can be stored and later referenced, the calculator dimension extends the usefulness of the software into wide areas of application. For example, a specific command files the results of calculations under a named memory variable. A hotel's average room rate, which is calculated by dividing rooms revenue by the number of rooms sold, can be computed and filed under a unique name, such as "avgrate." Later, when the data is needed, it can be easily retrieved.

Database management programs allow the user to store both numeric and alpha data as memory variables. This feature enhances the recall capabilities of the software programs without necessitating the creation of separate database files which would have to be indexed, sorted, or searched.

Electronic Communications

Electronic communications is an extremely complex and technical area. Specific hardware and software requirements must be met before communication can take place within a computer system or between one computer system and another. This section first addresses electronic communications in relation to the hardware components necessary for transforming individual work stations into a local area network and the hardware components required for telecommunications. Next, fundamental conditions for electronic communications to take place are addressed in terms of the parameters which must be set through the aid of communications software programs. The section closes with a discussion of special features which enable users to take advantage of advanced techniques of telecommunications.

Communication Networks

Work stations within an office or a business can be cabled together. The cabling serves as a hardware interface linking individual work stations into a **local area network**. The network enables user groups to communicate with one another and share data, programs, and the use of output devices (such as printers). The presence of cables is just one of the necessary conditions for successful communications to take place within a local area network. Other necessary conditions are technical and complex; however, their basic features can be explained by making an analogy to the conditions which are necessary for a stereo system to function correctly.

Just as a stereo system needs wires to connect speakers to an amplifier, so the communications system of a computer network needs cables to connect its various hardware components. Like the speaker wires which must be inserted into the jacks (plugs) of the stereo amplifier, the cables of the computer network must be inserted into the correct **ports**, or connectors, on each hardware component which is to be linked to the network. And, finally, just as the amplifier relays signals to the speakers of the stereo system, so each hardware component in the computer network must have a **communications controller** responsible for sending (or receiving) data to (or from) its connector and the cable.

However, correctly linking the speaker wires, jacks, and amplifier does not guarantee that the stereo system will function correctly. A stereo system manufactured for use in the United States is configured to accept electricity in the form of an alternating current of 120 volts. This type of stereo system will not operate (in fact, it may be totally ruined) if it is taken to England, plugged into a wall socket, and receives electricity of double the designated voltage (240 volts). Similarly, in relation to computer networks, the type of cables, the specific ports to which the cables attach, and the nature of work that the communications controller performs all depend on the form in which data is transferred. Data transfers can be made in either parallel or serial form.

Parallel transmission uses multiple channels to transmit several bits of data simultaneously. In this type of data transfer, the bits that encode a character travel as a single pulse along a set of wires within the communications cable. Timed pulses that coordinate the flow of data are sent on other wires within the same cable. In order for a computer network to support parallel data transfer, special parallel communications cables must connect to the parallel ports of the hardware components, and the communications controllers must be configured to interpret the timed pulses that coordinate the flow of data.

Serial transmission uses a single channel to transmit data bit by bit. In this type of data transfer, the data bits travel as a sequence of pulses over a single wire. Eight bits encode a single character. Data flow is coordinated by start and stop bits which are transformed into pulses which precede and follow each character. In order for a computer network to support serial data transfer, special serial communications cables must connect to the serial ports of the hardware components and the communications controllers must be configured to interpret the start/stop bits that coordinate the flow of data.

The manner in which data is transferred determines to a great extent the compatibility of hardware components within any computer system. Some hardware components are not capable of supporting both types of data transfer. For example, printers are generally configured for only one type of data transfer. Before selecting the hardware components of any type of computer system, managers must be sure that all components are capable of supporting the same method of transferring data.

Most microcomputers use parallel data transfer for internal operations and for moving data short distances—such as through the cables of a local area network. Serial data transfer is used for moving data long distances, and for transmissions where a limited number of wires is available to carry the data, as is the case with telephone wires. The next section describes the hardware components necessary for telecommunications and briefly addresses the complex area of communications software.

Telecommunications Hardware

Since all telecommunications involve transferring data along a limited number of wires, all transmissions are serial. In order to convert the parallel pulses which computers generally use for internal operations into serial pulses for telecommunications, the following hardware components are necessary:

- An asynchronous communications adapter

- A modem device

- A special cable connecting the communications adapter and the modem

The asynchronous communications adapter is a circuit board which can be inserted within an expansion slot inside the CPU. A **modem** translates the electronic pulses of the computer into the type of signals that can be carried along telephone wires. The adapter card and the modem are connected by a **cable** containing multiple wires. Although the serial transmission sends pulses in sequence through a single wire, other wires are used to provide two-way links and to coordinate the dialogue between modem and computer.

Detailed explanations of the asynchronous adapter card and the intricate wiring of the special connecting cable are beyond the scope of this chapter. Although explanations of modems can become just as technical, some understanding of their basic features is essential in the realm of telecommunications.

Exhibit 8 diagrams how modems function in the telecommunications process. Digital microcomputers communicate through distinct digital signals (zeros and ones). The telephone system, on the other hand, processes communications which are transmitted and received in the form of continuous analog signals (tones). To enable communication along telephone wires between two digital computers, a modulator must convert the digital signals transmitted by the first computer into analog signals. The data can then be carried along the telephone wires. At the other end of the communication line, a demodulator must reconvert the analog signals into digital signals which can be received by the second computer. A modem performs both the modulator and demodulator functions. The word *MODEM* is a contraction of *MOdulate/DEModulate*.

Exhibit 8   The Function of a Modem

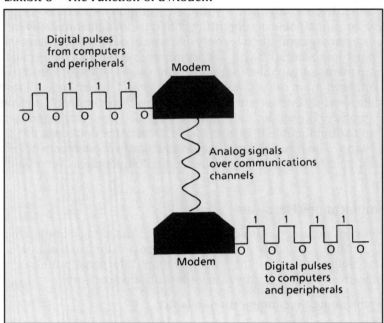

External modems connect with telephone lines by using one of two kinds of hardware devices, acoustic couplers or direct connection devices. These devices are illustrated in Exhibit 9. An acoustic coupler is designed so that the telephone handset (used for voice communication) may be placed into special cups on the modem. The modulator is placed next to the mouthpiece and the demodulator is placed next to the earpiece. Digital signals which are transmitted through the modem are converted by the modulator into audible tones, and the audible tones received by the modem are converted into digital signals for the computer to process. Direct connection devices perform the same modulation/demodulation function, but they are connected directly to the telephone jack by a wire that bypasses the telephone handset.

Compatibility between modems is determined by manufacturing design and by operating characteristics (also referred to as communication parameters) which are defined by communications software programs.

Electronic Communications Software

The appropriate hardware components do not ensure that successful communications will take place between two computer systems. Communications software programs are necessary to instruct the hardware components in what to do, how to do it, and when to do it.

Exhibit 9   Types of External Modems

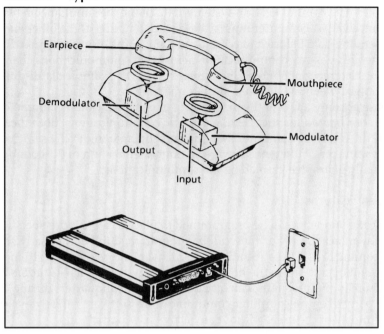

There are many communications software packages available. Most of these programs are user-friendly; that is, they prompt the user to respond with information regarding the **communications parameters** under which the transmitting computer and the receiving computer will operate. Communications parameters which must be set include, but are not limited to, baud rate (the speed at which the computers will transfer data) and how data will flow through the communication channel.

Baud rate is the rate of modulation or the number of times the carrier signal is modulated per second. Baud is a measure of the speed by which data is transferred, approximately the number of data bits sent in one second. The higher the baud rate, the faster the transfer. Most microcomputers can communicate at a baud rate of 2,400 data bits per second (bps). However, communication is possible only when the modem used by the transmitting computer system is set at the same rate as the modem used by the receiving computer system. If the baud rates are set differently, either no communication will take place or unintelligible data will be transferred.

Communications parameter settings which determine how data will flow through the communication channel are termed simplex, duplex, or half-duplex. A **simplex connection** carries data in only one direction. Television and radio use simplex communication. A **half-duplex connection** permits an alternating two-way communication over a single channel. A CB radio is an example of half-duplex communication, because only one person is permitted to communicate at a time. In half-duplex data communication systems, data cannot be simultaneously transmitted and received. A computer must wait for the computer at the other end of a line to stop sending data before it may transmit data. A **full-duplex connection** allows simultaneous two-way communication across two communications channels, one going in each direction. A telephone conversation is an example of full-duplex communication between two persons at the same time.

These are only a few of the many types of communications parameters which must be coordinated for successful electronic communications. Both the transmitting and the receiving computer systems must operate under the same communications parameters. Different software settings at either end of the communication line virtually guarantee garbled or lost communications.

Advanced Features

Sophisticated modems can be programmed to place a call to a pre-specified phone number at an exact time, or they can be programmed to be in a ready state to receive incoming calls. These **autodial/auto-answer** features can be extremely useful to multi-unit operations in the hospitality industry. Data, such as orders and sales reports from individual units, can be transferred to headquarters during off hours. The company's central computer communications software can retrieve the information from all of the units without any active user participation.

Telecommunications capability also enables users to take advantage of electronic mail systems. The use of an **electronic mailbox** involves reserving an addressable storage location on a rental company's disk. The sender then telephones the rental company (instead of the receiver) and transmits the document to the pre-specified mailbox. Information may even be passed to a computerless receiver by having the documents sent to a designated **remote print site** for immediate hard copy dissemination.

Other advantages of a telecommunications system include the use of information service companies. These companies, also called information utilities, provide, for a fee, access to data that are stored and regularly updated at a central location. Such data include news and stock market information, indexes of published information, and services such as automated shopping, travel reservations, and message systems for contacting other users.

Telecommunications technology within a multi-unit operation also provides, on a company-wide basis, the same advantages as the local area networks which may operate at each company unit. Remote users are able to share data, programs, and output devices (such as printers). This enables unit microcomputers located at different sites to share the power and data storage capability of a minicomputer or mainframe computer at company headquarters.

Summary

The generic applications software addressed in this chapter are word processing, electronic spreadsheet, database management, and communications programs.

Exhibit 10   Features of Word Processing Software

Basic Features

Document creation	Underlining
Retention	Boldfacing
Updating/editing	Centering
Scrolling	Text movement
Cursor control	Line/page formatting
Screen windowing	Headers/footers

Advanced Features

Optical character recognition
Calculator functions
Automatic spelling check
Boilerplate files
Style sheets
Mail merge
Integrated software capability

Sophisticated word processing extends beyond simply writing, editing, storing, and printing textual material. Many word processing systems are also able to carry out mathematical functions, proofread with spell checkers, create useful business forms, and "personalize" mailings by merging names and textual material. Exhibit 10 summarizes basic and advanced features provided by many word processing packages.

An electronic spreadsheet program allows a user to input a model of an accountant's traditional worksheet in the temporary memory of the computer system and view it as soft copy generated on a display screen. The electronic model is essentially a blank page of a worksheet which is divided into rows and columns that intersect to form the addresses of cells. Cells can hold different types of data: alpha data, such as labels for the columns and rows; numeric data, such as dollar amounts; and formulas, which instruct the computer to carry out specific calculations, such as adding all the numbers in a certain range of cells. Exhibit 11 summarizes basic and advanced features provided by many electronic spreadsheet packages.

Database management software is a term for programs which allow users to store information about their businesses for future use. A database is a collection of related facts and figures designed to serve a specific purpose. The structure of the database provides a means of organizing related facts and figures and arranging them in ways that facilitate searching for data, updating data, and generating accurate, timely, and useful reports for management. Exhibit 12 summarizes basic and advanced features provided by many database management packages.

Specific hardware and software requirements must be met before communication can take place within a computer system or between one computer system and another.

Exhibit 11   Features of Electronic Spreadsheet Software

Basic Features

Spreadsheet creation   Screen windowing
Retention   Cell definition
Updating/editing   Automatic recalculation
Scrolling   Spreadsheet templates
Cursor control   Graphics capability

Advanced Features

On-line assistance
Linked spreadsheets
Multiple windowing
Macro commands
Integrated software capability

Exhibit 12   Features of Database Management Software

Basic Features

Database creation   Relational structure
Retention   Input area
Updating/editing   Criteria area
Files   Output area
Records   Index command
Fields   Sort command
Hierarchical structure

Advanced Features

Calculator feature
Multiple searches

Key Terms

Word Processing Software

automatic spell check   header/footer
boilerplate file   mail merge
boldfacing   optical character recognition
default setting   scroll

style sheet
underlining

windows

Electronic Spreadsheet Software

cell address
cell range
cells
current cell
formula prefix
formulas
integrating spreadsheets
label

linking spreadsheets
macro commands
multiple windowing
numeric values
pointer
recalculation
templates

Database Management Software

calculator feature
criteria area specifications
database
find command
hierarchical database structure
index command
input area specifications
locate command
multiple searches

database fields
database files
database records
output area specifications
primary key field
relational database structure
secondary keys
sort command

Electronic Communications

autodial/auto-answer
baud rate
cable
communications controller
communications parameters
compatibility
electronic mailbox
full-duplex connection

half-duplex connection
local area network
modem
parallel transmission
port
remote print site
serial transmission
simplex connection

Discussion Questions

1. How can word processing computer software increase the productivity of personnel engaged in everyday business writing tasks?

2. How does the cursor control keypad provide a user with access to portions of a word processing document?

3. What does the phrase "what you see is what you get" mean? Explain why this feature of some word processing software packages would be useful to hospitality operations.

4. What is meant by the term "default setting"? Explain how default settings may be useful for performing various writing tasks in hospitality operations.

5. In what ways can electronic spreadsheet software be useful to the managers of hospitality operations? Identify functions these programs can perform and explain the "recalculation" feature common to many spreadsheet programs.

6. What does the term "database" mean? Explain how database management programs can be useful to managers of hospitality operations.

7. What are "files," "records," and "fields"? Explain how they are organized within hierarchical and relational database structures.

8. How do primary and secondary keys function in relation to multiple searches across a broad spectrum of field categories within a large database?

9. How does parallel transmission differ from serial transmission?

10. What function is performed by a modem in computer-based telecommunications?

REVIEW QUIZ

When you feel you have covered all of the material in this chapter, answer these questions. Choose the *best* answer.

Matching

1. A particular column letter and row number

2. Preformatted electronic spreadsheets

3. Uses a single channel to transmit data

4. In spreadsheets, user-created programs that minimize keystrokes

5. Define query procedures

6. Preset document formatting controls

7. Information placed at top of page above regular text

8. Flashing cursor

   a. scroll

   b. default settings

   c. windows

   d. header

   e. cell address

   f. pointer

   g. cell range

   h. *what if* possibilities

   i. templates

   j. macro commands

   k. criteria area specifications

   l. serial transmission

   m. baud rate

True (T) or False (F)

T   F   9. Word processing software enables writers to input documents themselves and make on-line edits and corrections.

T   F   10. The process of mail merge enables users to personalize form letters more quickly and accurately.

T   F   11. The function that a database performs is a new concept.

T   F   12. Television and radio use simplex communication.

Alternate/Multiple Choice

13. Which of the following common word processing software formatting controls are *not* considered default settings?

   a. margins, tabs, and page lengths
   b. centering, boldfacing, and underlining

14. Most electronic spreadsheet packages _____ graphics capability.

   a. have
   b. do not have

15. Word processing software style sheets store:

   a. contents.
   b. formats.
   c. cells.
   d. edits.

Part II

Computer-Based Hotel Property Management Systems

Chapter Outline

Central Reservation Systems
    Affiliate and Non-Affiliate Systems
    Central Reservation System Functions
    Additional Central Reservation
      Services
    Intersell Agencies
    Global Reservation Systems
Property-Level Reservation Module
    Reservation Inquiry
    Determination of Availability
    Creation of the Reservation Record
    Confirmation of the Reservation
    Maintenance of the Reservation Record
    Generation of Reports
New Developments
Summary

Learning Objectives

1. Explain the similarities and differences between affiliate and non-affiliate reservation systems.

2. Outline the functions provided by a central reservation office.

3. Describe the services provided by a central reservation office.

4. Explain how an intersell agency functions.

5. Describe global reservation systems.

6. Identify the typical activities associated with the use of a property-level reservation module.

7. Describe reservation inquiry procedures.

8. Describe the confirmation letters produced by property-level reservation modules.

9. Explain how a property can use data maintained by reservation records.

10. Describe the kinds of reports produced by property-level reservation systems.

11. Outline recent developments in computerized hotel reservations.

4

Computer-Based Reservation Systems

WHILE MANY INDUSTRIES computerized during the 1960s, the hotel industry did not actively pursue the possibilities of automation until the early 1970s. This relatively late start in computerization enabled the hotel industry to benefit from advances in computer technology. When other industries were struggling to upgrade their existing computer systems, hoteliers received greater value for dollars spent on newer computer hardware components and easier-to-operate software packages. This is especially true in regard to the first generation of computerized reservation systems. However, these reservation systems became outdated as technological advances linked reservations directly to comprehensive property management systems. Today, these second generation systems are beginning to mature and are often pushed to their maximum processing capabilities. The design of a third generation of reservation systems has already begun. These systems will more effectively link hotel reservations to systems developed for airlines, car rental agencies, travel agencies, and other travel-related businesses.

The proper handling of reservation information is critical to the success of hotel companies and individual properties. Reservations can be made for individuals, groups, tours, or conventions. Each request for accommodations creates a need for an accurate response in relation to the room types and rates available at a given point in time.

This chapter examines computer-based reservations management systems involving central reservation systems, intersell agencies, and property-level reservation modules.

Central Reservation Systems

Since the early 1970s, the hospitality industry has witnessed many independent central reservation systems enter and leave the marketplace. The problems encountered by these systems are not related to difficulties in generating demand for their services. Rather, they are related to servicing demand at an acceptable level of profitability. Expensive computer equipment (hardware components and communication devices), high overhead, and extensive operating costs have made it difficult for many independent central reservation systems to succeed. The staff required to process individual reservation requests and maintain diverse reservation records for a multitude of hotel properties can lead to dwindling revenues and soaring operating costs.

Increased on-line interaction between hotel properties and a **central reservation office** (CRO) decentralizes the reservation function but centralizes marketing and sales efforts in relation to the reservations process. This results in greater control of reservations handling at the property level and increased sales efforts at the CRO on behalf of the participating properties.

Affiliate and Non-Affiliate Systems

There are two types of **central reservation systems**: affiliate and non-affiliate systems. An **affiliate reservation system** refers to a hotel chain's central reservation system (CRS) in which all participating properties are contractually related. Each property is represented in the computer system database and is required to provide room availability and inventory data to the central reservation office on a timely basis. Chain hotels link their operations in order to streamline reservations processing and reduce total system costs. Typically, a central reservation office of an affiliate system performs the following functions:

- Deals directly with the public

- Advertises a central telephone number

- Provides participating properties with necessary communications equipment

- Communicates room availability and inventory data to global and non-affiliate reservation systems based on information supplied by individual properties

- Performs data entry services for remotely located or non-automated properties

- Delivers reservations and related information to properties quickly and cost-effectively

- Maintains statistical information on the volume of calls, talk time, conversion rates, denial rates, and other statistics

- Performs administrative functions for corporate-sponsored guest recognition programs

- Maintains a property profile of demographic information, policies, and other information

- Bills properties for handling reservations

Some affiliate systems enter into agreements with non-chain properties, allowing them to join the system as overrun facilities. An **overrun facility** refers to a property selected to receive reservation requests after chain properties have exhausted room availabilities in a geographic region.

A **non-affiliate reservation system** refers to a subscription system linking independent properties. A hotel subscribes to the system's services and takes responsibility for updating the system with accurate room availability data. Non-affiliate systems generally provide the same services as affiliate systems, thus enabling independent hotel operators to gain benefits otherwise available only to chain operators. However, many non-affiliate systems process reservations solely on the basis of the availability of room types. With this method, room types are classified as either "open" or "closed." Most affiliate systems process reservations on the basis of a declining inventory of both room types and room rates. This method helps participating properties to maximize revenue potential and occupancy.

Central Reservation System Functions

Central reservation services are provided by the central reservation office (CRO). The CRO receives room rate and availability information from participating properties. Non-automated properties send this information in the form of hard copy and the CRO manually enters the information into the electronic data base. Information from automated properties is typically sent over communication lines and enters the data base directly. With this system, the responsibility and control of central reservation information lies with managers at the property level. The key to successful central reservation management is that the property and the central system must have access to the same room and rate availability information. When this is the case, reservationists at the CRO can directly confirm room rates and availability at the time of reservation.

The timely delivery of reservation confirmations from a CRS to individual properties is vital. Many chain systems provide multiple delivery alternatives to ensure that properties receive all new reservations, modifications, or cancellations. For example, some central reservation systems relay processed transactions to member properties through on-line interfaces and telephone call-out techniques. Although on-line interfacing between central reservation offices and property-level computers is fast and effective, some networks place telephone calls to properties to ensure successful completion of the reservation process.

The goals of a central reservation system are to improve guest service while enhancing profitability and operating efficiency. A CRO accomplishes these goals by:

- Providing access to special room rates and promotional packages

- Instantly confirming reservations

- Communicating with major airline, travel, and car rental agencies

- Building extensive guest files

Basic services provided by most central reservation systems include automatic room availability updating and corporate-wide marketing.

Automatic Room Availability Updating. As a room is sold, whether through the CRO, the individual property, or a remote intersell agency, the inventory of rooms available for sale is automatically updated at both the property and the CRO. Having current room availability information for each participating property provides a central reservation system with the ability to automatically close out room types without obtaining direct property approval. The advantage of an effective CRO is that reservationists can directly confirm room rates and availability at the time reservations are made.

To appreciate this capability, consider that only a few years ago system-wide updating may have taken hours or days. In the past, the CRO was provided room availability data from participating properties at regularly scheduled intervals. This meant that when a property booked its own reservations, there would be no immediate record sent to the CRO; updating waited until the next scheduled reporting period. As the CRO booked reservations for a property, messages were sent to the property and printed on dedicated reservation printing devices. The property was often required to enter these printed transactions into its in-house reservation system so that accurate room availability data could be recalculated. In turn, this recalculated data was sent back to the CRO as an update on room availability.

Corporate-Wide Marketing. A CRO can function as a powerful marketing resource. The CRO information system contains important marketing data on individual guests and may provide individual properties with profiles of groups booked. New central reservation systems technology allows hotels to vary room rates for each room type on a daily basis. Varying conditions of supply and demand enable the room rates to slide within the ranges prescribed by each individual property.

Guest history data can be extremely helpful in processing reservations. This data also serves as the basis for determining demographic and geographic patterns of guests staying at participating hotel properties. Repeat guests may qualify for special frequent traveler programs offered by a hotel chain or individual property. By accessing guest history data, central reservation systems are usually able to direct and support these frequent traveler programs. For example, data maintained in relation to guests in a frequent traveler program generally includes:

- Guest identification number.

- Level of membership in the program.

- Home and business address and telephone numbers.

- Full name and preferred salutation.

- Type of guestroom preferred.

- Amenities, such as newspaper preference.

For each guest's stay, the system tracks the guest's arrival and departure dates, number of room nights by room type, and a revenue breakdown by rooms, food and beverage, and other categories.

Additional Central Reservation Services

In addition to maintaining up-to-date information about room availability and rates, a comprehensive hotel central reservation system typically maintains such data as:

- Room types

- Room rates

- Room decor

- Room location

- Promotional packages

- Travel agent discounts

- Alternative booking locations
- Guest recognition programs
- Special amenities

In addition to processing reservations, a CRO may perform a variety of other services. A reservation system may serve as an administrative network for inter-property communications. The reservation system may also be used to transfer accounting data from individual properties for processing at company headquarters. In addition, the system may operate as a destination information center by serving as a communications channel for local weather, news, and reports on special hotel features. Central reservation systems can report:

- Travel or airline agent performance statistics.
- Effectiveness of special promotional packages.
- Sales forecasting information.

Newer systems enable the participating hotels to build in specific rules and procedures for each of the hotel's promotional packages or products. Some central reservation systems expand their basic services to include such functions as:

- Yield management.
- Centralized commission reporting.
- Deposit/refund accounting.

Yield management, also called revenue management, is a set of demand forecasting techniques which are used to develop pricing strategies that will maximize rooms revenue for a lodging property. Centralized commission reporting details the amounts payable to agencies booking business with a hotel through the central reservation system. Hotel companies that require advance deposits to ensure reservations may find the central reservation system helpful in maintaining accounting records. Records can be kept of deposits made with reservation requests and of amounts refunded to individuals or groups who cancel reservations within the allotted time specified by management.

Intersell Agencies

Competition for hotel reservation commissions is intense since other segments of the travel industry also operate reservation systems. Airline carriers, travel agencies, car rental companies, and chain hotels offer stiff competition to independent central reservation systems entering the reservations marketplace.

The term **intersell agency** refers to a reservation network that handles more than one product line. Intersell agencies typically handle reservations for airline flights, car rentals, and hotel rooms. The spirit of an intersell promotion is captured by the expression "one call does it all." Although intersell agencies typically channel their reservation requests directly to individual hotels, some may also communicate with central reservation systems.

Exhibit 1   Interrelationships Among Reservation Systems

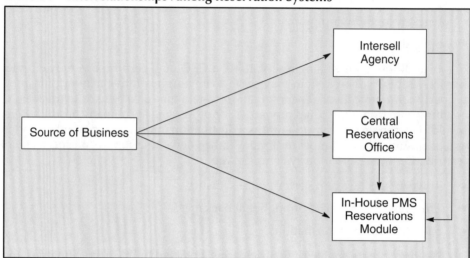

It is important to note that an intersell arrangement does not exclude a hotel property from participating in a central reservation system or from processing reservations directly with an in-house front office reservations module. Exhibit 1 illustrates the interrelationships which may exist among various reservation systems.

Although there are a variety of options for interconnecting various intersell agencies with a CRO and individual properties, the goal of integrating operations is to minimize suspense time. Suspense time refers to the elapsed time from system inquiry to response. Minimal suspense time results when, instead of communicating with participating CROs and individual properties, intersell agencies are able to automatically share reservation system databases. Sharing databases provides intersell reservation agents with a simplified method for booking a guest's complete travel requirements, and also provides participating hotels with a way to simultaneously update the CRO. Intersell systems enhance product distribution while providing a basis for cost-effective CRO operations. The CRO simply increases its exposure while reducing its operating expenses.

Global Reservation Systems

Global reservation systems are often formed as joint ventures linking a number of diverse businesses. By directly linking the reservation systems of hotel, airline, car rental, and travel agency companies on a world-wide basis, global reservation systems provide access to travel and tourism inventories around the world. A global reservation system can represent a significant portion of reservations business for many airport and resort properties.

Although all global reservation systems perform similar functions, each maintains unique internal system formats in relation to room rate, room type, and availability information. A key to the success of global reservation systems is the **smart**

switch. This switch translates reservations transactions into as many unique formats as required, allowing users to share data from different reservation systems without having to deal with complex formats, files, and operating systems. The smart switch can access reservation system files and convert the data into easy-to-use formats and files.

Hotels and central reservation systems participating in a global reservation system are likely to be competitors. Therefore, global reservation systems must provide a security system that protects the proprietary nature of room and rate availability data. Security is usually maintained through passwords. Users of the system are issued passwords that restrict access to proprietary data. Although passwords may need to be changed frequently, they offer effective measures of security.

Property-Level Reservation Module

Property-level reservation systems are specifically designed to meet the particular needs of the lodging industry. These systems have streamlined hotel operations with respect to guest, staff, and management needs. The specific needs and requirements of individual properties determine whether application software is purchased and operated separately or as a part of an overall property management system (PMS).

A reservations module of a computer-based property management system enables a reservationist to respond quickly and accurately to callers requesting future accommodations. The module significantly reduces paperwork, physical filing, and other clerical procedures. This provides the reservationist with more time for giving personal attention to callers and for marketing the various services the hotel offers. Stored information can be accessed quickly, and many of the procedures for processing requests, updating information, and generating confirmations are simplified.

The reservationist's initial inquiry procedures create a **reservation record** that initiates the hotel guest cycle. Reservation records identify guests and their needs before their arrival at the property and enable the hotel to personalize guest service and appropriately schedule needed personnel. In addition, reservation modules can generate a number of important reports for management's use. The following sections describe typical activities associated with the use of a reservation module. These activities include:

- Reservation inquiry
- Determination of availability
- Creation of the reservation record
- Confirmation of the reservation
- Maintenance of the reservation record
- Generation of reports

Reservation Inquiry

A reservation request can be received in person, over the telephone, in the mail, or through an interface with an external reservation system. Regardless of its origin, the reservation request is formulated into a **reservation inquiry** by the reservationist. This inquiry typically collects the following data:

- Date of arrival
- Type and number of rooms requested
- Number of room nights
- Room rate code (standard, special, package, etc.)
- Number of persons in party

The reservationist enters the data through a computer terminal according to rigidly defined inquiry procedures. Simultaneous processing involves a **real time capability**. This means that the reservationist receives the necessary feedback from the system in order to respond to a caller's requests during the telephone call. The real time capability of many reservation modules is designed to provide quick responses (less than five seconds) and, therefore, enables the reservationist to edit, alter, or amend the inquiry while the caller is still available for comment. Once the inquiry is matched with rooms availability data, the PMS assigns and blocks a room, thus removing it from the availability file.

Determination of Availability

Once entered, the reservation inquiry is compared to rooms availability data according to a predetermined system algorithm. The algorithm is a computer-based formula designed to sell rooms in a specified pattern (by zone, floor, block, etc.). Processing a reservation request may result in one of several system-generated responses which appear on the reservationist's display screen:

- Acceptance or rejection of the reservation request
- Suggestions of alternative room types or rates
- Suggestions of alternative hotel properties

Creation of the Reservation Record

Once the reservation request has been processed and the room blocked, the system requires that the reservationist complete the reservation record by collecting and entering necessary data, such as:

- Guest's personal data (name, address, and telephone number)
- Time of arrival
- Reservation classification (advance, confirmed, guaranteed)
- Confirmation number
- Caller data (agency or secretary)
- Special requirements (handicapper, crib, no smoking, etc.)

Non-automated procedures generally require that this information be recorded early in the reservation process. However, computerized reservation systems do not

Exhibit 2   Sample Reservation Confirmation Letter

```
              T H E   K E L L O G G   C E N T E R
    MICHIGAN STATE UNIVERSITY, E. LANSING, MICHIGAN 48824   (517) 332-6571
  O Name      Arrival Date   Arrival Time   Departure Date   No Guest   No. Rooms   Preferred Accommodations
             05/23                          05/24            1          1                    TWIN BEDS

  Remarks    THANK YOU FOR YOUR PATRONAGE.   ALL SPECIAL REQUESTS ARE SUBJECT TO
  AVAILABILITY.



         LORIN BUCKNER                            We will not knowingly rent a guest room on which we already have an advance
         777 RED CEDAR RD                         deposit or guaranteed payment reservation from a customer. If, for any reason be-
                                                  yond our control, a room should not be available for a customer who has either an
         PLYMOUTH, MICHIGAN 48995                 ADVANCE DEPOSIT RESERVATION, CREDIT CARD GUARANTEED RESERVA-
                                                  TION, or COMPANY GUARANTEED RESERVATION, we shall arrange for accom-
                                                  modations at another hotel or motel, pay for such room, provide complimentary
                                                  transportation to that property (and back to this property if for more than one
                                                  night), and honor the payment of one long distance phone call to notify business
                                                  or family contact of these arrangements
                                                  If your plans change, please notify us. Thank you


         CONFIRMATION        05/17
                                   CHECK IN TIME AFTER 1 P.M.
```

Courtesy of Kellogg Center, Michigan State University, East Lansing, Michigan

clutter the initial inquiry routine with the collection of this secondary type of data. This often proves to be more efficient to callers and property personnel. For example, if all data were collected and the system denied the reservation request, the reservationist and the caller would have spent a lot of time exchanging information which turned out to be of little use.

Confirmation of the Reservation

Property management systems can automatically generate letters of confirmation on the day a reservation request is received. Information can be retrieved from the reservation record and printed on a specially designed hotel form. Exhibit 2 illustrates one type of confirmation letter. While there are probably as many formats and styles of confirmation letters as there are automated hotels, acknowledgments within confirmation letters generally include:

- Guest's name and address
- Date and time of arrival
- Type, number, and rates of rooms
- Number of nights
- Number of persons in party
- Reservation classification (advance, confirmed, guaranteed)
- Special services requested by the guest
- Confirmation number
- Request for deposit or prepayment
- Update of original reservation (reconfirmation, modification, or cancellation)
- Cancellation policy

Reservation confirmations may be printed at any time. However, they are normally printed as part of the stream of output produced during the time of system update. A **system update** performs many of the same functions as those performed by the night audit routine in non-automated properties. System updates are run daily to allow for report production, system file reorganization, and system maintenance, and to provide an end-of-day time frame.

Maintenance of the Reservation Record

Reservation records are stored in an electronic file and commonly segmented by date of arrival (year, month, day), group name, and guest name. File organization and the method of file retrieval are critical to an effective reservations module because callers frequently update, alter, cancel, or reconfirm their reservations. For example, should a caller request a cancellation, the reservationist must be able to quickly access the correct reservation record, verify its contents, and process the cancellation.

Data from reservation records may be used to generate preregistration forms. Exhibit 3 shows one type of preregistration form created from reservations data. Reservation records can also serve as preregistration folios for pre-sale guest cycle transactions. Prepayments, advance deposits, and cash payouts are examples of transactions that can be posted to the reservation record and later transferred to the guest's in-house folio.

In addition, the reservation module has the ability to interface with other front office functions. Reservation record data can be:

- Printed onto preregistration cards to facilitate faster check-in procedures.

- Used as the basis for printing in-house guest folios and guest information lists (alphabetical listings or sequential room number listings).

- Transferred to commission agent files for later processing.

- Formatted for eventual inclusion in a guest history file.

Generation of Reports

Similar to many computer applications, the number and type of reports available through a reservation module are functions of the user's needs, software capability, and database contents. An in-house reservation module is designed to maximize room sales by accurately monitoring room availabilities and providing a detailed forecast of rooms revenue. A computer-generated **rooms availability report** lists, by room type, the number of rooms available each day (net remaining rooms in each category). Exhibit 4 shows one type of rooms availability report. A **revenue forecast report** projects future revenue by multiplying predicted occupancies by current house rates. Exhibit 5 depicts one type of revenue forecast report. The reservation module, which replaces non-automated reservations processing, can also automatically compile and generate:

- Reservation transaction records.

- Expected arrival and departure lists.

Exhibit 3   Sample Reservation Preregistration Form

NAME BUCKNER, LORIN	ROOM
FIRM	TYPE TB
ADD 777 RED CEDAR RD	# PTY 1
CITY PLYMOUTH, MICHIGAN 48995	DEP 05/24
RATE 47.00	ARR 05/23
TELE	CLERK 19

MY ACCOUNT WILL BE SETTLED BY:

☐ AMEX
☐ VISA/M. CHG   ☐
☐ CASH   ☐
☐ CB   ☐ OTHER

SPECIFY

IF ABOVE INFORMATION IS NOT CORRECT,
PLEASE SPECIFY IN AREA BELOW.

PLEASE PRINT

(LAST)   (FIRST)   (INITIAL)

NAME _____   ☐ HOME
STREET _____   ☐ BUSINESS
CITY _____ STATE _____ ZIP ___
COMPANY _____ .
SIGNATURE

SS CODES: RESV#: 38923

BC4423000015692435

NAME DONOVAN, JOHN	ROOM 727
FIRM ATLAS INC.	TYPE LD
ADD 1299 MICHIGAN BLVD.	# PTY 2
CITY FLINT, MICHIGAN 48458	DEP 05/24
RATE 75.00	ARR 05/23
TELE 313-686-0099	CLERK 19

MY ACCOUNT WILL BE SETTLED BY

☐ AMEX
☐ VISA/M. CHG   ☐
☐ CASH   ☐
☐ CB   ☐ OTHER

SPECIFY

IF ABOVE INFORMATION IS NOT CORRECT,
PLEASE SPECIFY IN AREA BELOW.

PLEASE PRINT

(LAST)   (FIRST)   (INITIAL)

NAME _____   ☐ HOME
STREET _____   ☐ BUSINESS
CITY _____ STATE _____ ZIP ___
COMPANY _____
SIGNATURE

SS CODES: UF SS   RESV#: 38921

NGUAR

** MSU IS AN AFFIRMATIVE ACTION/EQUAL OPPORTUNITY INSTITUTION**
```
    BUCKNER, LORIN            05/23
                             47.00
    777 RED CEDAR RD          05/24
    PLYMOUTH, MICHIGAN 48995  #G  1

        BC4423000015692435
```

** MSU IS AN AFFIRMATIVE ACTION/EQUAL OPPORTUNITY INSTITUTION**
```
727  DONOVAN, JOHN            05/23
     ATLAS INC.              75.00
     1299 MICHIGAN BLVD.      05/24
     FLINT, MICHIGAN 48458    #G  2

          UF SS

                            NGUAR
```

```
ROOM:          RATE:   47.00
NAME: BUCKNER, LORIN
DEPARTING: 05/24
SS CODES:
QNAME:
```

```
ROOM:  727    RATE:   75.00
NAME: DONOVAN, JOHN
DEPARTING: 05/24
SS CODES: UF SS
QNAME:
```

Courtesy of Kellogg Center, Michigan State University, East Lansing, Michigan

- Commission agent reports.
- Turnaway statistics.

A **reservation transaction record** provides a daily summary of reservation records that were created, modified, or canceled. Exhibit 6 illustrates one kind of reservation transaction record. Reservation modules may also generate supplemental

Exhibit 4   Sample Rooms Availability Report

```
AVAILABLE ROOMS — KELLOGG CENTER
05/18          11:24
AR—PAGE    1  _ = BLOCKED,    * = EXPECTED DEPARTURE,    # = NOT READY
```

CC— 201 *#	TB— 206 #	DD— 209	ED— 222	LT— 227	TB— 232
TB— 233	ED— 301	TB— 302	TB— 303	TB— 304	TB— 305
TB— 306	TB— 307 #	LD— 309	TB— 312	ED— 316	ET— 323
LD— 327	SD— 328 #	TB— 330	TB— 331 #	TB— 332	TB— 333
ED— 401 *#	TB— 402	TB— 403 #	TB— 405	TB— 406	TB— 407 *#
LT— 409	TB— 413	TB— 414	TB— 515 *#	DB— 416 *#	ED— 417
BT— 420 #	ED— 422	LD— 427	SD— 428	TB— 429 #	TB— 430 #
TB— 431 #	TB— 432 #	ED— 501 #	TB— 502 #	TB— 506 #	SD— 508 #
LD— 509 #	TB— 512	DB— 516	ED— 517	BD— 519	BT— 520
ED— 522	LD— 527	SD— 528 #	TB— 529 #	TB— 532	TB— 533
ET— 601	TB— 603	TB— 606	TB— 607	SD— 608 #	LT— 609
TB— 612	TB— 613 *#	TB— 615	ED— 617 #	BD— 619	ED— 622
LD— 627	SD— 628	TB— 629	TB— 630	TB— 631	TB— 632 #
TB— 633	TB— 702	TB— 703	TB— 704	TB— 705	TB— 706 #
SD— 708 _#	LT— 709	TB— 712	TB— 713	TB— 714	TB— 715
DB— 716 #	ED— 717 #	BD— 719 #	BT— 720 #	ED— 722 #	LD— 727 # ,
SD— 728 #	TB— 729	TB— 730	TB— 731	TB— 732	TB— 733

Courtesy of Kellogg Center, Michigan State University, East Lansing, Michigan

summaries of specialized activities, such as cancellation reports, blocked room reports, and no-show reports. Exhibit 7 depicts one type of no-show report. **Expected arrival and departure lists** are daily reports showing the number of guests expected to arrive and depart, the number of stay-overs (the difference between arrivals and departures), and the names of guests associated with each transaction. **Commission agent reports** delineate reservation transactions and commissions payable, by agent. Agents, having contractual agreements with a hotel, may earn commissions for the business they book at the property. A **turnaway report**, also called a refusal report, tracks the number of room nights refused because rooms were not available for sale. This report is especially helpful to hotels with expansion plans.

New Developments

Reservations was the first functional area of hotels to be computerized and, therefore, has received a great deal of vendor research and development. Additionally, the airline industry has spent millions of dollars developing its own reservation

Exhibit 5   Sample Revenue Forecast Report

```
FORECAST REPORT — KELLOGG CENTER
05/18      10:05
FR-PAGE  1  RUN  1
NO MODIFICATIONS
```

DATE	ARRIVALS DEF	TEN	DEPART EF	TEN	STAYOVERS DEF	TEN	RMS RES	SOLD ALL	UN-SOLD RES	ALL	# GUESTS DEF	TEN	#GPS AR	DP	EXPCTD REVENUE
05/18	52	0	6	3	46	-3	98	95	49	52	118	-5	4	1	
MON	52		9		43		67%	65%			113		9		
															4,516.50
05/19	32	0	55	0	43	-3	75	72	72	75	90	-5	1	6	
TUE	32		55		40		51%	49%			85		4		
															3,412.00
05/20	58	0	48	0	27	-3	85	82	62	65	99	-5	5	2	
WED	58		48		24		58%	56%			94		7		
															4,216.34
05/21	17	1	57	0	28	-3	45	43	102	104	63	-3	2	2	
THU	18		57		25		31%	29%			60		7		
															1,946.00
05/22	16	0	31	1	14	-3	30	27	118	121	44	-5	3	7	
FRI	16		32		11		20%	18%			39		3		
															1,380.00
05/29	31	10	11	0	47	22	78	110	70	38	114	54	1	0	
FRI	41		11		69		53%	74%			168		7		
															5,234.00

```
AVG ROOM RATE:       47.40

MONTHLY TOTALS                               719     1053                        26
           429                               40%                      961
                                                                                      34,081.84

GRAND TOTALS                                 719     1053                        26
           429                               40%                      961
                                                                                      34,081.84
```

Courtesy of Kellogg Center, Michigan State University, East Lansing, Michigan

techniques, many of which have been adapted to the needs of hotels. Two of the more interesting recent developments in the reservations area are self-reservation systems and voice output systems.

Individuals with microcomputers are presently able to place their own reservations on airline flights. Soon, consumers may use this same tech-nology to book their own hotel reservations. Interactive **self-reservation systems** allow users with telecommunications equipment to retrieve computer-stored reservation packages and view them on their television screens or display monitors. These reservation programs typically require users to respond to a series of questions. Users may enter their responses through a specially designed keypad (or touch-tone phone) and thereby create their own bookings.

Currently under development are interactive multi-media presentations for microcomputers that travel agents use. Companies are developing digitized maps and property photographs as well as full-motion property tours that can be displayed on a screen and viewed by travel agency clients as they make travel decisions.

Exhibit 6   Sample Reservation Transaction Record

```
RESERVATION TRANSACTION REPORT
===================================================================
```

RESV#	GROUP	UNIT	PC	REF.	EMP	FOOD/PRI $	DATE	TIME	CC	RESV#
1999	0	403	1	12356487	3	1500	0327	1216		1999
1999	0	403	1	12345678	3	0	0327	1216		1999
2000	1996	106	1		3	−1000	1211	1646		2000
2000	0	504	1	12345678	3	0	0327	1217		2000
2000	1996	106	12		3	1000	0614	1055		2000
2005	1996	511	1		3	−1000	1211	1646		2005
2005	1996	511	12		3	1000	0614	1055		2005
2008	1996	215	1		3	−21150	1211	1647		2008
2008	1996	215	7	215, 1	0	450	0608	0907		2008
2008	1996	215	7	215, 1	0	450	0609	1049		2008
2008	1996	215	11	215, 1	0	9500	0608	0907		2008
2008	1996	215	11	215, 1	0	375	0609	1049		2008
2008	1996	215	11	215, 1	0	375	0608	0907		2008
2008	1996	215	11	215, 1	0	9500	0609	1049		2008
2008	1996	215	12		3	500	0614	1055		2008
2076	0	506	1	TA999988	3	−50000	0703	1449		2076
2076	0	506	1		3	−52040	1211	1645	DC	2076

Source: Lodgistix, Wichita, Kansas.

Exhibit 7   Sample No-Show Report

ACCT	ROOM	TYPE	S	GUEST NAME	FIRM/TA NAME		PLAN	ARR DATE	DEPRT	RESERVED	IATA#
1984	1003	SUTE	3	HUTCHINGSON, MR. AND ADDRESS 1 LINE XXXXX	CAMELBACK TRAVELS CITY FIELD XXXXX	ST 25478	03–27	03/30 DC 65465468716165487	03/26	88885555
1985	1003	SUTE	S	LEXINGTON, PHILLIP C ADDRESS 1 LINE XXXXX	CAMELBACK TRAVELS CITY FIELD XXXXX	ST 25478	03/27	04/01 DC 65465468716165487	03/26	88885555
1986	2002	DDBL	3	LIVINGSTON, JONATHAN ADDRESS 1 LINE SSSSS	MUSSELSHELL VALLEY CITY FIELD DDDDD	ST 21547	03/27	03/31 AX 32165414651654365	03/26	77776666
1987	2002	DDBL	S	LIVINGSTON, ROBERT ADDRESS 1 LINE SSSSS	MUSSELSHELL VALLEY CITY FIELD DDDDD	ST 21547	03/27	03/31 AX 32165414651654365	03/26	77776666
1989	110	QUEN	3	JENKINS, ROBERT ADDRESS LINE 1	FIRM LINE CITY FIELD	ST 565466	03/27	03/27 DC 64321646432164643	03/27	
1994	501	KING	6	JORGENSON, MICHAEL ADDRESS 1 LINE TEST	FIRM LINE TESTDDDDDD CITY FIELD	ST 321311	03/27	03/27 CA	03/27	
2012	101	KING	C	WEST, MR. KERRY 1938 N. WOODLAND	LODGISTIX INC. WICHITA	KS 58201	03/27	03/30 AX 21257464326454246	03/27	

Source: Lodgistix, Wichita, Kansas.

Experimentation with **verbal recognition/synthesis** technology (talking computers) is promising and may significantly affect hotel reservation modules in the near future. Research is presently being conducted which requires users to possess a touch-tone telephone, a headset, and a display screen. The reservations program generates a series of cues on the screen to which the potential customer responds by pushing designated buttons on the telephone or speaking into the mouthpiece of the headset. The computer acknowledges the user's input and may generate an additional series of cues. Although these computer programs presently use and understand only a limited vocabulary, the future looks bright for this application.

Summary

A central reservation office (CRO) is responsible for maintaining a rooms availability inventory for each property participating in the system. Transactions are handled instantaneously through on-line connections between property-level and CRO computer systems.

The advantage of an effective CRO is that reservationists have the ability to directly confirm room rates and availability at the time of reservation. On-line central reservation systems are single-inventory based so that they need only maintain a single depleting inventory of rooms. This concept produces one image of room inventory network-wide.

A global reservation system links a variety of travel and tourism companies, improving communications and increasing market exposure. The smart switching component of the global reservation system enables rapid and easy access to data. Because many of the participating companies are likely to be competitors, global reservation systems restrict access through computer security procedures, such as issuing passwords.

A reservation module enables a hotel to rapidly process room requests and generate timely and accurate rooms, revenue, and forecasting reports. Reservation records are stored in an electronic file segmented by date of arrival (year, month, day), group name, and guest name. File organization and the method of file retrieval are critical to an effective reservations module because guests frequently update, alter, cancel, or reconfirm their reservations. Reservation records can also serve as preregistration folios for pre-sale guest cycle transactions.

Key Terms

affiliate reservation system
central reservation office
central reservation system
commission agent report
expected arrivals list
expected departures list
global reservation system
intersell agency
non-affiliate reservation system
overrun facility
real time capability

reservation inquiry
reservation record
reservation transaction record
revenue forecast report
rooms availability report
self-reservation system
smart switch
system update
turnaway report
verbal recognition/synthesis

Discussion Questions

1. How do affiliate reservation systems differ from non-affiliate reservation systems?

2. What services are provided by a central reservation office?

3. How does a central reservation system use overrun facilities?

4. What does the term "intersell agency" mean?

5. Why is data security a concern of global reservation systems?

6. What are the typical activities associated with the use of a property-level reservations module?

7. What data are collected through reservation inquiry procedures?

8. What data are generally included in confirmation letters produced by property-level reservation modules?

9. How can a property use data maintained by reservation records?

10. What kinds of reports can be produced by property-level reservation systems?

REVIEW QUIZ

When you feel you have covered all of the material in this chapter, answer these questions. Choose the *best* answer.

Matching

1. Initiates the hotel guest cycle

2. Verbal recognition/synthesis technology

3. A CRS in which all participating properties are contractually related

4. "One call does it all"

5. Projects future revenue by multiplying predicted occupancies by current house rates

6. Can access reservation system files and convert the data into easy-to-use formats and files

7. Tracks the number of room nights refused because rooms were not available for sale

8. Performs many of the same functions as non-automated night audit

a. overrun facility

b. smart switch

c. revenue forecast report

d. reservation inquiry

e. turnaway report

f. intersell agency

g. affiliate reservation system

h. real time capability

i. system update

j. rooms availability report

k. non-affiliate reservation system

l. talking computers

m. reservation record

True (T) or False (F)

T   F   9. A non-affiliate reservation network refers to a subscription system linking independent properties.

T   F   10. Computer-based property management systems may automatically generate letters of confirmation on the day a reservation request is received.

T   F   11. A reservation module may be capable of printing reservation data onto preregistration cards in order to facilitate faster check-in procedures.

T   F   12. Rooms management was the first functional area of hotels to be computerized.

Multiple Choice

13. In a fully computerized property management system, which of the following initiates the hotel guest cycle?

    a. a room status report
    b. creation of a reservation record
    c. assignment of room and rate
    d. creation of a customer master file

14. Which of the following is *not* associated with the use of a reservation module of a hotel property management system?

    a. determination of room availability
    b. creation of a reservation record
    c. generation of a rooms status report
    d. confirmation of a reservation

15. A daily summary of reservation records that are created, modified, or canceled is called:

    a. an expected arrival and departure list.
    b. a rooms availability report.
    c. a turnaway statistics report.
    d. a reservation transaction record.

Chapter Outline

Rooms Management Module
    Room Status
    Room and Rate Assignment
    In-House Guest Information Functions
    Housekeeping Functions
    Generation of Reports
Guest Accounting Module
    Types of Accounts
    Posting Entries to Accounts
    Night Audit Routine
    Account Settlement
    Generation of Reports
Summary

Learning Objectives

1. Explain what functions a rooms management module performs.

2. Explain the importance of keeping track of room status and eliminating room status discrepancy.

3. Describe how a rooms management module performs room and rate assignments.

4. Discuss how a rooms management module provides a review of guest data.

5. Describe how a rooms management module can be used to schedule housekeeping employees and measure room attendant productivity.

6. Describe some of the reports that a rooms management module can generate.

7. Discuss the primary functions a guest accounting module performs.

8. Briefly describe the five types of folios that a guest accounting module might produce.

9. Explain why identification codes and reference codes are important to on-line posting procedures.

10. Explain the advantages a system update routine has over a non-automated night audit routine.

11. Describe how accounts are settled in an automated property.

12. Discuss the reports a guest accounting module can produce.

5

Rooms Management and Guest Accounting Applications

A COMPUTER-BASED HOTEL MANAGEMENT SYSTEM carries out a number of front office and back office functions while supporting a variety of applications software which may relate to front office and back office activities. While not all property management systems (PMS) operate identically, a rooms management applications module is typically an essential component of front office software.

A rooms management module maintains up-to-date information on the status of rooms, assists in the assignment of rooms during registration, and helps coordinate many guest services. A guest accounting module processes and monitors financial transactions that occur between guests and the hotel. When remote electronic cash registers, situated at various revenue centers throughout the hotel, are interfaced with a guest accounting module, guest charges are communicated to the front desk and automatically posted to the appropriate electronic guest folios.

Rooms Management Module

The rooms management module is an important information and communications branch within a front office property management system. It is primarily designed to strengthen the communication links between the front office and the housekeeping department. Most rooms management modules perform the following functions:

- Identify current room status.

- Assist in assigning rooms to guests at check-in.

- Provide in-house guest information.

- Organize housekeeping activities.

- Provide auxiliary services.

- Generate useful reports for management.

A rooms management module alerts front desk employees of the status of each room, just as room racks do in non-automated operations. A front desk employee simply enters the room's number at a keyboard, and the current status of the room appears immediately on the terminal's display screen. Once a room becomes clean

Exhibit 1   Sample Rooms Status Report

```
ROOM STATUS REPORT — KELLOGG CENTER
05/19     18:56
RU–PAGE  1                                              FLOOR(S) 2, 3, 4, 5, 6, 7
     201  OOO    202  O/D    203  CO     204  V/C    205  V/C    206  O/C
     207  V/C    208  V/C    209  V/C    215  O/C    216  V/C    217  V/C
     219  OOO    220  V/C    222  O/D    223  OOO    224  OOO    225  OOO
     227  V/C    230  OOO    231  V/C    232  V/C    233  O/C    301  V/C
     302  O/D    303  O/D    304  O/D    305  O/D    306  O/D    307  O/C
     308  O/C    309  O/D    311  O/C    312  O/D    313  O/C    314  V/C
     316  V/D    317  O/D    319  OOO    320  V/C    322  V/C    323  V/C
     325  OOO    327  V/C    328  V/C    329  O/D    330  O/D    331  O/D
     332  O/D    333  O/D    401  V/C    402  V/C    403  V/C    404  V/C
```

```
     715  V/C    716  V/C    717  V/C    719  V/C    720  V/C    722  V/C

     77  V/C   2  V/D   18  OOO   54  OCC   5  CO
```

Courtesy of Kellogg Center, Michigan State University, East Lansing, Michigan

and ready for occupancy, housekeeping staff change the room's status through a terminal in their work area, and the information is immediately communicated to terminals at the front desk. Rooms status reports may also be printed at any time for use by management. Exhibit 1 illustrates one type of **rooms status report**.

Rooms management modules are also capable of automatic room and rate assignments at the time of check-in. In addition, their ability to display guest data on terminals at the front desk, switchboard, and concierge station eliminates the need for traditional front office equipment, such as room racks and information racks. These modules also enable management to efficiently schedule needed housekeeping staff and to review detailed housekeeping room attendant productivity reports. In addition, automated wake-up systems and message-waiting systems can be interfaced with the rooms management module to provide greater control over these auxiliary guest services. Exhibit 2 summarizes functions performed by a rooms management module.

Room Status

Before assigning rooms to guests, front desk employees must have access to current, accurate information on the status of rooms in the property. The current status of a room can be affected by information about future availability (determined through reservations data) and information about current availability (determined through housekeeping data).

Information about future availability is important because it may affect the length of stay of in-house guests. Access to rooms availability data which extends

Exhibit 2   Functions of a Rooms Management Module

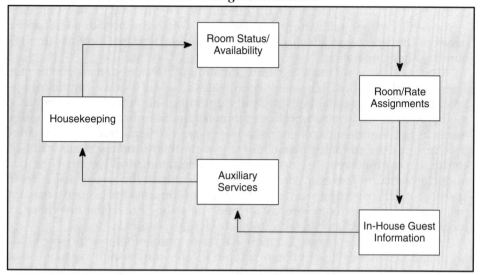

several days into the future gives front desk employees reliable **room status** information and enhances their ability to satisfy the needs of guests while maximizing occupancy. Consider the following example.

Mr. Gregory checks in on Thursday for a one-night stay. However, during the course of his work on Friday, he finds it necessary to stay over through the weekend. The front desk employee may be inclined to approve this extension based on the fact that Friday night's business is light. Later, upon checking reservations data, the employee learns that although the hotel has a low occupancy forecasted for Friday evening, all rooms are reserved on Saturday night. This obviously poses a problem that needs to be resolved according to hotel policy, but it is better for the problem to surface Friday than on Saturday night when the house is full.

Housekeeping's description of the current status of a room is crucial to the immediate, short-run selling position of that room. Common housekeeping descriptions of a room's status include:

- On-makeup

- On-change

- Out-of-order

- Clean

- Ready for inspection

Information about current availability is absolutely essential in order for front desk employees to properly assign rooms to guests at the time of check-in. Nonautomated front office systems often experience problems because of a breakdown in communication between housekeeping staff and front desk employees. Computerized front office systems, on the other hand, ensure timely communications by converting data input by front desk employees, housekeepers, or guest services personnel into messages which are available at several terminal locations throughout the lodging operation.

The hotel property management system routes data through the rooms management module and, thereby, helps coordinate the sale of rooms. Computer-based hotel technology is capable of instantly updating the housekeeping status of rooms, enabling front desk employees to make quick and accurate room assignments to guests at the time of check-in. For example, when a housekeeping attendant informs the property management system that a room's status has been changed from on-makeup to clean, a notice may be automatically printed at a room inspector's station. This notice informs the inspector that the room is ready for inspection. After inspecting the room, the inspector informs the property management system that the room is ready for sale. A message conveying this change in room status is immediately relayed to the front desk terminals.

Room status discrepancy is a term that refers to situations in which the housekeeping department's description of a room's status differs from the room status information that guides front desk employees in assigning rooms to guests. These discrepancies can seriously affect a property's ability to satisfy guests and maximize rooms revenue. Non-automated properties experience room status discrepancies not only because of time delays in communicating room status information from the housekeeping department to the front desk, but also because of the cumbersome nature of comparing housekeeping and front desk room status information. Consider the following scenario.

Mr. Gregory checks out of a non-automated hotel and the desk clerk forgets to change his room's status in the room rack. When housekeeping attendants clean the room, they may notice that Mr. Gregory's luggage and belongings have been removed (since the room has been vacated). However, if the housekeeping report does not indicate that Mr. Gregory may be a check-out and not a stay-over, the actual status of the room may go undetected. As long as the room status discrepancy exists, the hotel will not sell Mr. Gregory's vacated room because the room rack at the front desk erroneously indicates that the room continues to be occupied. Unfortunately, this situation, termed a **sleeper,** arises all too often in non-automated hotels. Why is it called a sleeper? Since the guest's card remains undisturbed in the room rack, it is described as being asleep. It remains so until corrected (awakened).

A computer-based property management system operates without a room rack. Instead, the rooms management module generates a **rooms discrepancy report** which signals to management the specific rooms whose status must be investigated to avoid sleepers. The report notes any variances between front desk and housekeeping room status updates. This is an important dimension of the rooms management module.

Room and Rate Assignment

Rooms management modules may be programmed to assist front desk employees in assigning rooms and rates to guests at the time of check-in. Modules may make automatic assignments or require front desk personnel to input data to initiate room assignments.

Automatic room and rate assignments are made according to parameters specified by hotel management officials. Rooms may be selected according to predetermined floor zones (similar to the way in which guests are seated in a dining room) or according to an index of room usage and depreciation. The computer system may track room histories (frequency of sales) and rank rooms according to usage data. The system uses this information to assign rooms on a basis which evenly distributes occupancy loads across the full inventory of rooms.

Interactive room and rate assignments are popular programs in the lodging industry. These programs give front desk personnel direction in decision-making situations while increasing their control over actual room assignments. For example, in a property with 800 rooms, a front desk employee can narrow the search routine by clarifying the guest's needs through a series of room and rate category queries. In addition, the front desk employee may use the rooms management module to display an abbreviated list of available rooms selected by type and rate. This abbreviated list enables the front desk employee to quickly suggest a room to a guest waiting to check in. This ensures a faster check-in process than would a random search through the entire rooms availability database.

To accommodate guest preferences and to ensure smooth check-in procedures, rooms management modules typically feature an override function that front desk employees can use to bypass the room or rate assignments automatically generated by the system. An override function is often a useful feature. For example, most automatic room and rate assignment programs will assign guests only to rooms whose status is clean and available for occupancy. However, many times it may be necessary to assign a particular guest to a room whose status is on-makeup or on-change. For example, a guest may arrive for check-in and have to leave immediately to attend an afternoon meeting. An override function permits the front desk employee to carry out check-in procedures while informing the guest that the room won't be available for occupancy until some time later in the day.

In-House Guest Information Functions

The rooms management module is also designed to provide a limited review of guest data. Guest data can be displayed on terminal screens, enabling a guest services coordinator, switchboard operator, or front desk employee to quickly identify the name, room number, and telephone extension of a particular guest. This function of the rooms management module also contributes to the elimination of such traditional information sources as information racks, room racks, and telephone lists. Terminals may also be located at room service order stations, garage outlets, and other high guest-contact areas to enhance employees' recognition of guests, thereby personalizing the services provided.

Guest data may also be transferred from a rooms management module to a point-of-sale area to expedite the verification and authorization of charge purchases guests make. When an electronic cash register system in a dining area is interfaced with the hotel's property management system, guest data can be reviewed before charges are accepted. This capability allows cashiers to verify that a particular room is occupied and that the correct guest name is on the room record. Access to this data minimizes the likelihood of charges being accepted for the wrong guest folios, for guests who have vacated their rooms, or for guests who have been denied charge privileges.

Housekeeping Functions

Important housekeeping functions performed by the rooms management module include:

- Forecasting the number of rooms to be cleaned
- Scheduling room attendants
- Assigning workloads
- Measuring productivity

A rooms management module forecasts the number of rooms which will require cleaning by processing current house counts and expected number of arrivals. After determining the number of rooms which will require cleaning, most modules can print out schedules for individual room attendants and assign a specific number of rooms to each attendant on the basis of property-defined standards.

Upon first entering a room to be cleaned, a room attendant may use the room's telephone interface to the PMS to enter his or her identification code number, room number (not always necessary), and the code identifying the room's current status. The computer system automatically logs the time of the call. When a room is clean and ready for inspection, the room attendant again uses the room's telephone interface to notify the inspector's station, and the computer system once again logs the time of the call. The log of times in and out by room attendants enables the rooms management module to determine productivity rates. Productivity rates are determined by calculating the average length of time an attendant spends in a room and the number of rooms attended to during a shift. Productivity reports keep management apprised of potential inefficiencies while also tracking the location of housekeeping personnel throughout a shift.

Generation of Reports

The number and types of reports which can be generated by a rooms management module are functions of the user's needs, software capacity, and the contents of the rooms management file database. A large number of reports are possible because the rooms management module overlaps several key areas, such as the rooms department, housekeeping department, and auxiliary services. Most rooms management modules are designed to generate reports that focus primarily on room availability, room status, and room forecasting. These reports are designed to assist management in scheduling staff and distributing work loads.

A **rooms allotment report** summarizes rooms committed (booked or blocked), by future date. One type of **expected arrival/departure report** is shown in Exhibit 3. A **registration progress report** provides the rooms department with a summary of current house information. The report may list present check-ins, number of occupied rooms, names of guests with reservations who have not yet registered, and the

Exhibit 3   Sample Expected Arrival/Departure Report

ARRIVALS, STAYOVERS, DEPARTURES FOR KELLOGG CENTER
DA–PAGE 001
05/13   8:40

DATE	ARRIVE	STAYON	DEPART	GUESTS	SOLD	UNSOLD	REVENUE
05/13	27	112	23	143	139	7	6,435.00
05/14	27	117	22	151	144	2	6,593.00
05/15	20	126	18	162	146	0	6,806.00
05/16	72	21	125	143	93	53	4,907.00
05/17	35	16	77	62	51	95	2,460.00
05/18	43	41	10	100	84	62	3,995.00
05/19	27	33	51	72	60	86	2,837.00
05/20	53	21	39	86	74	72	3,874.34
05/21	14	26	48	49	40	106	2,002.00

Courtesy of Kellogg Center, Michigan State University, East Lansing, Michigan

Exhibit 4   Sample Registration Progress Report

HOUSE COUNT DISPLAY   COMPLEX   1
03/28   15:20:02

VACANT/READY ROOMS	144	ROOMS RESERVED	23
OCCUPIED ROOMS	4	BLOCKS RESERVED	23
VACANT ROOMS ON CHANGE	0	DAY RNTL RESVD	0
MAINT 0		ROOMS STAYING OVER	6
CLEAN 0		ROOMS DEPARTING	0
DIRTY 0		DAY RNTL DEPT	0
ROOMS DUE ON MAINTENANCE	0		
DISCREPANT ROOMS	2	CURRENT ROOMS TO SELL	121
		CURRENT OCCUPANCY PERCENT	4
—GUEST STATISTICS—		PROJECTED ROOMS TO SELL	121
GUEST ACCTS TO CHECK-IN	0	PROJECTED ROOMS OCCUPIED	29
GUEST ACCTS TO CHECK-OUT	0	PROJECTED OCCUPANCY PERCENT	19
GUESTS TO ARRIVE 0			
GUESTS ARRIVED 0		—ROOMS RESERVED—	
GUESTS TO DEPART 0		C 0 6 0	
GUESTS DEPARTED 0		1 0 7 0	
CURRENT # OF GUESTS	4	2 0 8 0	
		3 0 9 0	
WALK-INS 0 EARLY DEPT 0		4 0 B 23	
		5 0 ALL 23	

Source: Lodgistix, Wichita, Kansas.

number of rooms available for sale. A registration progress report may also profile room status, rooms revenue, and average room rate. Exhibit 4 shows one type of registration progress report. A **rooms activity forecast** provides information on anticipated arrivals, departures, stay-overs, and vacancies. This report assists managers in staffing front desk and housekeeping areas. An **actual departures report** lists the names of guests who have checked out, their room numbers, billing addresses, and folio numbers.

A **housekeeper assignment report** is used to assign floor and room numbers to room attendants and to list room status. This report may also provide space for special messages from the housekeeping department. System-generated **house-keeper productivity reports** provide a relative productivity index for each house-keeper by listing the number of rooms cleaned and the amount of time taken to clean each room.

At the end of each month, quarter, and year, rooms management modules are capable of generating **rooms productivity report**s which rank room types by percentage of occupancy and/or by percentage of total rooms revenue. Rooms management modules may also produce a **rooms history report** depicting the revenue history and use of each room by room type. This report is especially useful to those properties using an automatic room assignment function.

Guest Accounting Module

The most critical component of a hotel front office system is the guest accounting module. The creation of electronic folios enables remote point-of-sale terminals to post charges directly to guest and non-guest accounts. The guest accounting module gives management considerable control over financial aspects of the hotel guest cycle. This front office module is primarily responsible for on-line charge postings, automatic file updating (auditing) and maintenance, and folio display/printing upon demand. In addition, guest accounting modules may provide electronic controls over such areas as folio handling, account balances, cashier reconciliation, food and beverage guest check control, account auditing, and accounts receivable. Exhibit 5 diagrams the sequence of activities involved in the process of guest accounting. The following sections discuss guest accounting modules in relation to:

- Various types of guest accounts (also referred to as folios)
- Common procedures for posting charges to folios, updating accounts, and managing account settlement
- Typical reports generated for use by management

Types of Accounts

A computer-based property management system ensures that preregistration folios are prepared for guests arriving with reservations. Preregistration folios are typically produced by the PMS reservations module when a reservation record is created. When guests arrive without reservations, front desk employees enter the necessary data into the guest accounting module at check-in. Data elements needed to create a folio are referred to as **header information**. Common header elements include:

- Guest name
- Address

Exhibit 5   Guest Accounting Activities

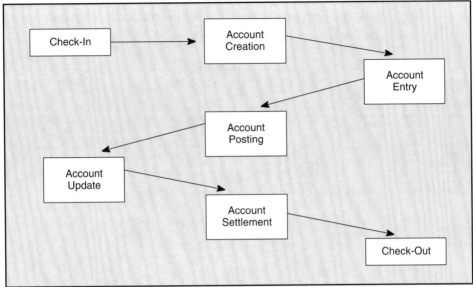

- Room number
- Folio number

If self check-in terminals are available at the property, guests may enter the necessary data themselves by responding to system-generated cues. Header information collected by these terminals is used for folio creation.

While not all hotel guest accounting modules offer the same folio formats, common types of folios include:

- Individual folios
- Master folios
- Non-guest folios
- Employee folios
- Control folios

Individual folios are assigned to in-house guests for the purpose of charting their financial transactions with the hotel. Exhibit 6 presents a sample guest folio. **Master folios** generally apply to more than one guest or room and contain a record of transactions which are not posted to individual folios. Master folios are commonly created to provide the kind of billing service required by most groups and conventions. For example, consider the needs of the International Gymnastics Conference. While attendees at this conference are responsible for their own food and beverage expenses, the sponsoring organization pays all room charges. As participants dine at various food and beverage outlets in the hotel, their deferred payments are posted to their individual folios. Each night's room charges, however, are

Exhibit 6   Sample Guest Folio

```
          The Kellogg Center              |           The Kellogg Center
          Michigan State University       |           Michigan State University
        East Lansing, Michigan 48824      |         East Lansing, Michigan 48824
               517-332-6571               |                517-332-6571


   DOE, JOHN              ROOM   307      |    DOE, JOHN              ROOM   307

   1000 ARROW DR.                         |    1000 ARROW DR.
   OXFORD, OH   45056                     |    OXFORD, OH   45056

                      page    01          |                       page    01
   arrive 05/16       folio   CH-(A)      |    arrive 05/16        folio   CH-(A)
   depart 05/18       acct#   122032      |    depart 05/18        acct#   122032
   guests   1         sdate   05/16       |    guests   1          sdate   05/16
   qname   JOHNSO     edate   05/18       |    qname   JOHNSO      edate   05/18
   s-code  YG         clk#    17          |    s-code  YG          clk#    17
   settle MC5298003010027534             |    settle MC5298003010027534


   travel agent/caller                    |    travel agent/caller
   name                                   |    name
   firm                                   |    firm
   street                                 |    street
   city                                   |    city
```

DATE	REFERENCE NO.	DESCRIPTION	CHARGES/CR
1987			
MAY16	1014271817	STATE ROOM	4.85
MAY16	1014271817	TAX S. R.	.19
MAY16	1014271817	F & B TIP	1.50
MAY16	5111651332	L. D. CALL	4.20
MAY16	0010001700	TELE-SVCS	.50
MAY16	0110122800	ROOM CHG	42.00
MAY16	0110122800	ROOM TAX	1.68
MAY17	1014286332	STATE ROOM	2.60
MAY17	1014286332	TAX S. R.	.10
MAY17	1014286332	F & B TIP	1.00
MAY17	0010001700	TELE-SVCS	.50
MAY17	0110122800	ROOM CHG	42.00
MAY17	0110122800	ROOM TAX	1.68
MAY18	0010000917	VISA/M. CHG	102.80−
		TOTAL-DUE	.00

DATE	REFERENCE NO.	DESCRIPTION	CHARGES/CR
1987			
MAY16	1014271817	STATE ROOM	4.85
MAY16	1014271817	TAX S. R.	.19
MAY16	1014271817	F & B TIP	1.50
MAY16	5111651332	L. D. CALL	4.20
MAY16	0010001700	TELE-SVCS	.50
MAY16	0110122800	ROOM CHG	42.00
MAY16	0110122800	ROOM TAX	1.68
MAY17	1014286332	STATE ROOM	2.60
MAY17	1014286332	TAX S. R.	.10
MAY17	1014286332	F & B TIP	1.00
MAY17	0010001700	TELE-SVCS	.50
MAY17	0110122800	ROOM CHG	42.00
MAY17	0110122800	ROOM TAX	1.68
MAY18	0010000917	VISA/M. CHG	102.80−
		TOTAL-DUE	.00

```
   I hereby declare to be personally      |    I hereby declare to be personally
   liable for payment of this bill.       |    liable for payment of this bill.
                                          |
                                          |    SIGNATURE:.........................
```

Courtesy of Kellogg Center, Michigan State University, East Lansing, Michigan

posted to the group's master folio. At check-out, each guest receives a folio documenting only the charges for which he or she is responsible. The conference administrator is responsible for settling the master folio containing the room charges.

Non-guest folios are created for individuals who have in-house charge privileges but are not registered as guests in the hotel. These individuals may include health club members, corporate clients, special club members, political leaders, or local celebrities. Non-guest account numbers are assigned at the time that the accounts are created and may be printed (or imprinted) on specially prepared account cards. When purchases are charged to non-guest accounts, cashiers may request to see the account card as a verification that a valid posting status exists.

Procedures for posting transactions to non-guest folios are similar to those required for on-line posting of transactions to guest folios. Instead of inputting a room number, the cashier, front desk employee, or auditor inputs the designated account number. The use of a unique billing number alerts the guest accounting module to the type of account being processed. For example, a six-digit account number may signal a non-guest account, while a four-digit number may signal an in-house guest account. The major difference between accounting for non-guest and in-house guest transactions is in the area of account settlement. Guest folios are settled at check-out; terms for settlement of non-guest accounts are usually defined at the time these accounts are created. The term "settlement" refers to bringing an active folio to a zero balance by posting cash received, or by transferring the folio balance to the city ledger or credit card company account.

When properties offer charge privileges to employees, transactions may be processed in a manner similar to non-guest accounts. **Employee folios** can be used to track employee purchases, compute discounts, monitor expense account activity, and separate authorized business charges from personal expenditures.

The efficiency of a guest accounting module in carrying out continuous posting and auditing procedures often depends upon the existence of control folios. **Control folios** may be constructed for each revenue center and used to track all transactions posted to other folios (individual, master, non-guest, or employee). Control folios provide a basis for double entry accounting and for cross-checking the balances of all electronic folios. For example, as an in-house guest charges a purchase at the hotel's restaurant, the amount is posted (debited) to the appropriate individual folio, and the same amount is simultaneously posted (credited) as a deferred payment to the control folio of the food and beverage outlet. Control folios serve as powerful internal control documents and greatly simplify ongoing auditing functions.

Posting Entries to Accounts

Account entries can be made from terminals at the front desk or from remote POS terminals that interface with the PMS guest accounting module. Account entries can also be made internally, that is, from within the guest accounting module itself. For example, during the system update routine, room charges and taxes may automatically be posted to all active guest folios. Although guest accounting modules vary in the specifics of their operation, most modules rely on specific data entry requirements in order to ensure that amounts are properly posted to the appropriate folios. Data entry requirements may consist of the following sequence:

- Room number (or account number)

- Identification code

- Reference code

- Charge total

After a room number (or account number) is entered, a guest accounting module may require that an identification code be entered as well. This is generally done by inputting the first few letters of the guest's last name. An **identification code** enables the guest accounting module to process a charge to the correct folio when two separate accounts exist under the same room number. In these situations, simply inputting a room number does not guarantee that the correct folio is retrieved and held ready to accept a charge. Therefore, a guest identification code is part of the required data entry sequence.

Before a charge can be posted to a folio, the guest accounting module may also require that a **reference code** be entered. This is typically done by inputting the serial number of a departmental source document. Departmental **source documents** are usually serially numbered for internal control purposes. This numbering system helps the guest accounting module conduct investigative searches and analyze account entries made by individual employees through POS terminals within the property.

The final data entry requirement is that the amount of the charge be input. However, before accepting a charge and posting it to a folio, the guest accounting module initiates a **credit monitoring routine**. This routine compares the current folio balance with a predetermined credit limit (also called a **house limit**) which is determined by management. Although most guest accounting modules allow managers to specify a single house limit, some provide for further options based on guest history information, such as whether the guest is a repeat customer or a known business associate. Other options may include setting a house limit on the basis of the type of reservation or the credit authorization limits established by individual credit card companies.

Regardless of how the credit limit is set, an attempt to post a charge to an account initiates a credit monitoring routine, thus ensuring that the outstanding balances during a guest's stay do not exceed the account's credit limit. When hotel policy dictates that a line of credit is not to be extended to a guest, a folio can be set at a no-post status. The guest accounting module will not permit charges to be posted to a folio with a no-post status.

When in-house guests make charge purchases throughout their stay at the hotel, they are typically asked to present their room key as verification that a valid posting status exists for their individual folios. Some types of electronic locking systems, which may be interfaced with a PMS guest accounting module, depend upon the insertion of plastic electronic keycards (containing strips of encoded magnetic data) to authorize the posting of charges from remote POS terminals. If a guest presents a keycard for an unoccupied room, an account with a no-post status, or a guest account which already has been closed (settled), the system will not permit the cashier to post the charge. Entering the guest's identification code (the first few letters of the purchaser's last name) may provide further evidence that the person making the charge is not a currently authorized guest at the hotel.

Night Audit Routine

In a non-automated property, the night auditor must post all room rates, taxes, and any departmental charges not posted earlier in the day. The night auditor also balances all guest, non-guest, and departmental accounts. In an automated property, the system update routine takes responsibility for completing these tasks. The ongoing nature of the property management system design has led to a simplification of the audit and enables hotels to perform auditing tasks much more rapidly than is possible in non-automated environments.

A system update performs many of the same functions as those performed by the night audit routine in non-automated properties. System updates are run daily to allow for report production, system file reorganization, and system maintenance, and to provide an end-of-day time frame.

The update routine normally requires the user (auditor, system manager, or another designated employee) to respond to brief system instructions and then monitor the computer's execution of a predetermined set of software applications. Employees no longer have to perform tedious auditing tasks during the slow early morning hours; an equivalent routine may be initiated at any time during the day.

As part of the system update, the guest accounting module automatically posts charges for room rates and taxes to folios for every occupied guestroom. In addition, the module automatically balances departmental accounts by cashier shift, and generates the equivalent of a traditional trial balance. Although postings from remote POS terminals are processed electronically (and in some instances automatically), managers can attach a voucher printer to each POS terminal. This creates a tangible cross-reference document. Guest accounting modules can also automatically transfer entries between two folios and perform multiple guest splits for any accounting transaction. **Multiple guest splits** involve charges that are to be divided among a group of guests. For example, the cost of a cocktail reception may be shared by several in-house guests.

A computer-based audit trail consists of cross-references from source document serial numbers, workshifts, cashiers, POS terminals, and departmental (control folio) accounts. Guest accounting modules generally use enough reference codes to enable cashiers to identify the origin (location) of entries and to verify amounts posted to folios with minimal cross-checking against charge vouchers or source documents. Well-documented folios reduce the chance of error when charges are posted to accounts. Reducing posting errors may also minimize guest discrepancies at check-out. **Guest discrepancies** refer to charges disputed by guests.

Account Settlement

The ability to print clear, itemized guest statements (with reference code detail) may significantly reduce guest disputes about folio charges. For example, assume that at check-out time Ms. Nessy has found what she believes to be a discrepancy in regard to a long-distance telephone charge appearing on her folio. The hotel cashier uses the reference code number on the folio to locate the proper telephone call record. The cashier then verifies the source (room number) from which the call was placed and the telephone number which was called. This procedure enables the hotel to quickly, objectively, and efficiently resolve disputes regarding amounts posted to guest folios.

System update routines can be programmed to generate pre-printed folios (usually by 7:00 A.M.) for guests expected to check out that day. Pre-printing folios significantly speeds up the check-out process and minimizes guest discrepancies. When additional charges are posted to folios which have already been pre-printed, the pre-printed folios are simply discarded and updated folios, with the correct account balances, are printed at the time of check-out.

On-line, instantaneous posting of all charges leads to a major victory in the hotel's battle against late charges and charges made under false pretenses. **Late charges** are charged purchases made by guests which are posted to folios after guests have settled their accounts. Electronic folios are closed at the time of settlement. Accounts that are accidentally closed can easily be re-opened. Check-out, however, triggers a communication to housekeeping and internally sets the account to a no-post status. Because the guest accounting module can be interfaced with other front office modules, better communications among staff members are possible and more comprehensive reports are available for use by management.

Generation of Reports

Guest accounting modules are capable of producing a myriad of formatted statements and reports summarizing financial transactions which occur between guests and the hotel, activities within revenue centers, and audit findings. The analytical capacity of this module has simplified traditional hotel auditing procedures while providing increased control over guest accounting procedures. The ability to print guest and non-guest folios at any time during the guest cycle provides management with important accounting information on a timely basis. Room statistics and revenue reports, detailing occupancy loads and revenue generated by room night, give managers such essential information as occupancy percentages, average rate (per room and per guest), and departmental revenue summaries.

Ledger summary reports present guest, non-guest, and credit card activity by beginning balance, cumulative charges, and credits. **Revenue center reports** show cash, charge, and paid-out totals by department and serve as a macro-analysis of departmental transactions. **Guest check control reports** compare guest checks used in revenue outlets, such as in food and beverage outlets, with source documents to identify discrepancies. Transfers to non-guest (city) ledgers from guest accounts are automatically logged onto a **transfer report** along with the printing of an initial dunning letter. A **dunning letter** is a request for payment of an outstanding balance (account receivable) owed by a guest or non-guest to the hotel.

Some system vendors provide an optional output format that enables the transfer of guest accounting data onto microfilm or microfiche. This increases the system's capacity to store information on minimal active file space.

Summary

A rooms management module maintains up-to-date information on the status of rooms, assists in room assignment during registration, and helps coordinate many guest services. Since this module replaces most traditional front office equipment, it often becomes a major factor when selecting a complete front office applications package.

A guest accounting module increases management's control over guest accounts and significantly alters the night audit routine. Guest accounts are maintained electronically, thereby eliminating the need for folio cards, trays, and mechanical posting equipment. The guest accounting module monitors predetermined guest credit limits and is capable of creating several types of folio formats. When revenue centers are interfaced with the PMS, remote electronic cash registers communicate with the front desk and guest charges are automatically posted to the appropriate folios. At check-out, outstanding appropriate account balances are transferred automatically to the city ledger (accounts receivable) for collection.

Key Terms

Rooms Management Module

actual departures report	room status
automatic room and rate assignment	room status discrepancy
	rooms activity forecast
expected arrival/departure report	rooms allotment report
	rooms discrepancy report
housekeeper assignment report	rooms history report
housekeeper productivity report	rooms productivity report
interactive room and rate assignment	rooms status report
	sleeper
registration progress report	

Guest Accounting Module

control folio	late charges
credit monitoring routine	ledger summary report
dunning letter	master folio
employee folio	multiple guest splits
guest check control report	non-guest folio
guest discrepancies	reference code
header information	revenue center report
house limit	source document
identification code	transfer report
individual folio	

Discussion Questions

1. What primary functions does a rooms management module perform?

2. How does a rooms management module help reduce room status discrepancies?

3. How does a rooms management module automatically perform room and rate assignments? Explain how an override option may be useful to management.

4. How can a rooms management module be used to schedule housekeeping staff and measure the productivity of room attendants?

5. What are some of the reports that a rooms management module can generate?

6. What are the primary functions a guest accounting module performs?

7. What five types of folios might a guest accounting module use? Give brief descriptions of each.

8. Why are identification codes and reference codes important to on-line posting procedures?

9. What are some of the advantages of the system update routine performed by a guest accounting module?

10. How are account settlement procedures influenced by a guest accounting system?

REVIEW QUIZ

When you feel you have covered all of the material in this chapter, answer these questions. Choose the *best* answer.

Matching

1. Provides information on anticipated arrivals, departures, stay-overs, and vacancies

2. Assigned to in-house guests for charting their financial transactions with the hotel

3. Ranks room type by percentage of occupancy and/or by percentage of total rooms revenue

4. Charges divided among a group of guests

5. A predetermined credit limit established by the hotel for a guest

6. Generally, the first few letters of the guest's last name

7. A vacant guestroom believed to be occupied

8. Guest-charged purchases posted to folios after guests have settled their accounts

a. identification code

b. late charges

c. multiple guest split

d. control folio

e. transfer report

f. sleeper

g. rooms activity forecast

h. house limit

i. header information

j. individual folio

k. guest discrepancies

l. rooms productivity report

m. reference code

True (T) or False (F)

T   F   9. A computer-based property management system instantly updates the housekeeping status of rooms, thereby enabling front desk employees to make quick and accurate room assignments at the time of check-in.

T   F   10. Rooms management modules typically feature an override function that front desk employees can use to bypass the room and/or rate assignments automatically generated by the system.

T   F   11. A rooms allotment report provides the rooms department with a summary of current house information.

T   F   12. Master folios are created for individuals who have in-house charge privileges but are not registered as guests in the hotel.

Alternate/Multiple Choice

13. In an automated property, the system update performs many of the same functions as those performed by:

 a. a night audit routine in a non-automated property.
 b. the credit monitoring routine.

14. Which one of the following front office modules is primarily designed to strengthen the communication links between the front office and housekeeping departments?

 a. reservations module
 b. guest accounting module
 c. general management module
 d. rooms management module

15. Which one of the following front office property management modules forecasts the number of rooms that will require cleaning by processing current house counts and expected number of arrivals?

 a. reservations module
 b. rooms management module
 c. guest accounting module
 d. general management module

Chapter Outline

Point-of-Sale Systems
    POS Postings and Account Entries
    Management Concerns
Call Accounting Systems
    HOBIC System Interface
    Features of Call Accounting Systems
    CAS/PMS Advantages and
        Management Concerns
Electronic Locking Systems
    Hard-Wired Systems
    Micro-Fitted Systems
    ELS Features
    ELS Reports
Energy Management Systems
Auxiliary Guest Services
Guest-Operated Devices
    Self Check-In/Check-Out Systems
    In-Room Movie Systems
    In-Room Beverage Service Systems
    Guest Information Services
Summary

Learning Objectives

1. Distinguish a point-of-sale terminal from an electronic cash register.

2. Identify typical POS data entry requirements for charges to appropriate guest folios.

3. List management concerns regarding interfacing of a POS system and in integrated PMS system.

4. Explain the basic operation of the HOBIC system.

5. Identify and describe the basic features of an active call accounting system.

6. Distinguish between hard-wired and micro-fitted electronic locking systems.

7. Describe three features commonly included in the design of energy management systems.

8. Identify and describe automated guest-operated devices.

6

Property Management System Interfaces

A FULLY INTEGRATED hotel computer system provides management with an effective means with which to monitor and control many front office and back office activities. Other areas of a lodging operation may also benefit from automation. Rather than function as part of a property management system design, some automated systems may perform more effectively as independent, stand-alone devices which can be interfaced with the property management system. Interfacing permits the property management system to access data and information processed by stand-alone systems, without affecting the primary structure of the property management system.

This chapter presents a detailed discussion of property management system interfaces. Important interfaces for hotel operations include:

- Point-of-sale systems

- Call accounting systems

- Electronic locking systems

- Energy management systems

- Auxiliary guest services

- Guest-operated devices

Some hotels have gone beyond installing basic property management systems by offering a variety of automated guest-operated devices. These devices are described in the final sections of this chapter. As the world's traveling public becomes more familiar with and skilled in using computers, there will be additional growth in this area of lodging services.

Point-of-Sale Systems

A point-of-sale (POS) system is made up of a number of POS terminals that interface with a remote central processing unit. A **point-of-sale terminal** contains its own input/output component and may even possess a small storage (memory) capacity, but usually does not contain its own central processing unit. In order for POS transactions to be processed, the terminal must be interfaced with a CPU located outside the terminal's housing. Generally, the POS system's processing unit is a stand-alone device, but connection to an electronic cash register (ECR) is also possible. An **electronic cash register** is normally defined as an independent, stand-alone computer system. The ECR frame houses all the necessary components of a computer system: an input/output device, a central processing unit, and storage (memory) capacity.

Newer POS system designs place a microprocessor at each terminal location. These microprocessors are networked to form a complete POS system which functions without a large, remote CPU. These systems are referred to as **micro-based POS systems**.

When the main processor of a POS system interfaces with a property management system (PMS), data can be directly transferred from the POS system to various front office and back office PMS modules for further processing. This interface accomplishes the basic objectives of electronic data processing. The amount of time required to post charge sales to guest folios is significantly reduced, and the number of times that pieces of data must be handled is minimized. Relaying data collected by POS terminals to the property management system also tends to significantly reduce the number of posting errors and minimizes the possibility of late charges.

The number and location of POS terminals throughout a property is a function of a variety of factors, such as:

- Size and type of operation

- Physical design limitations

- Communication requirements

- Security considerations

For example, a large resort hotel may place POS terminals at every revenue collection area, including:

- Restaurants

- Bar and lounge areas

- Room service stations

- Gift shops

- Pool areas

- Pro shops

POS Postings and Account Entries

Account entries can be made from terminals at the front desk or from remote POS terminals that interface with the property management system guest accounting module. Account entries can also be made internally, that is, from within the guest accounting module itself. For example, during the system update routine, room charges and taxes may automatically be posted to all active guest folios. Although guest accounting modules vary in the specifics of their operation, most modules rely on specific data entry requirements in order to ensure that amounts are properly posted to the appropriate folios. Data entry requirements may consist of the following sequence:

- Room number (or account number)

- Identification code

- Reference code

- Charge total

After a room number (or account number) is entered, a guest accounting module may require that an identification code be entered as well. This is generally accomplished by inputting the first few letters of the guest's last name. An identification code enables the guest accounting module to process a charge to the correct folio when two separate accounts exist under the same room number. In these situations, simply inputting a room number does not guarantee that the correct folio is retrieved and held ready to accept a charge. Therefore, a guest identification code is part of the required data entry sequence.

Before a charge can be posted to a folio, the guest accounting module may also require that a reference code be entered. This is typically accomplished by inputting the serial number of a departmental source document. Departmental source documents are usually serially numbered for internal control purposes. This numbering system helps the guest accounting modules conduct investigative searches and analyze account entries made by individual employees through POS terminals within the property.

The final data entry requirement is that the amount of the charge be input. However, before accepting a charge and posting it to a folio, the guest accounting module initiates a credit monitoring routine. This routine compares the current folio balance with a predetermined credit limit (also called a house limit) which is set by management officials, thus ensuring that the outstanding balances during a guest's stay do not exceed the account's credit limit. Although most guest accounting modules allow management officials to specify a single house limit, some provide for further options based on guest history information, such as whether the guest is a repeat customer or a known business associate. Other options may include setting a house limit on the basis of the type of reservation or the credit authorization limits established by individual credit card companies. When hotel policy dictates that a line of credit is not to be extended to a guest, a folio can be set at a no-post status. The guest accounting module will not permit charges to be posted to a folio with a no-post status.

When in-house guests make charge purchases throughout their stay at the hotel, they are typically asked to present their room key as verification that a valid posting status exists for their individual folios. Some types of electronic locking systems, which may be interfaced with a property management system guest accounting module, depend upon the insertion of plastic electronic keycards (containing strips of encoded magnetic data) to authorize the posting of charges from remote POS terminals. If a guest presents a keycard for an unoccupied room, or an account with a no-post status, or a guest account which has already been closed (settled), the system will not permit the cashier to post the charge. Entering the guest's identification code (the first few letters of his or her last name) may provide further evidence that the person making the charge is not a currently authorized guest at the hotel.

Management Concerns

Although a POS/PMS interface offers lodging properties significant advantages, there are also important concerns to address. Problems which may arise include:

- Data transferred from the POS system may not meet the specific needs of the property management system.

- POS system data may be lost during the property management system update routine.

- General limitations of interface technology may interfere with effective system operations.

The amount and type of data communicated from a POS system to a property management system varies in relation to the particular type of POS system and property management system design employed by a property. Problems may arise when the type of data needed by front office or back office property management system modules cannot be collected by or transferred from the POS system. For example, a POS system may not be able to:

- Break out amounts for food and for beverage from the total amount of a guest check.

- Transfer data relating to special hotel meal plans and promotions.

- Track taxes and tips.

Management officials may also have to address questions such as these:

- Will individual transactions or consolidated transactions be transmitted?

- Will data be transmitted as it is collected or at a later time?

- How much data will be stored in property management system files and how much will be retained in POS system memory?

- How and when will settlement affect stored transaction data?

- What audit procedures will be followed to ensure proper posting and monitoring of transactions?

A hotel's property management system must undergo a system update routine (an automated version of the traditional night audit functions). This generally occurs sometime during the evening hours. While the system is being updated, the POS interface may be inoperable. The interruption of data flow along the interface channel may lead to lost transactions or bottlenecks at either the POS or PMS end. Care should be taken to schedule the property management system update when food and beverage outlets and other revenue-producing centers are closed, or during their slack business hours. When this cannot be done, non-automated procedures may have to be implemented at revenue outlets for the duration of the property management system update routine.

Before interfacing a POS system to a PMS, management may have to resolve problems related to interface technology. For example, a POS system may be dependent upon a unique set of applications software unrelated to the needs of the hotel's property management system. Should this be the case, the primary applications software of the POS system may need to be enhanced before the system is interfaced with the property management system.

Call Accounting Systems

Since 1981, it has been legal for lodging properties to resell telephone service to guests. This resale capability has enabled the hotel's telephone department, traditionally a loss leader, to become a potential profit center. A call accounting system (CAS) enhances management's control of expenses relating to local and long-distance telephone services.

A CAS may operate as a stand-alone system or it may be interfaced with a hotel's property management system. Generally, a CAS is able to handle direct-distance dialing, distribute calls through a least-cost routing network, and price outgoing calls. When a CAS is interfaced to a property management system front office guest accounting module, telephone charges can be posted immediately to the proper guest folio.

Call accounting systems conserve valuable space and often reduce maintenance and labor costs associated with traditional telephone systems. CAS hardware takes up much less space and requires less maintenance than the bulky switchboard equipment it replaces. Labor costs decrease since a telephone operator is not involved in CAS call placement and distribution functions. Similarly, the automatic pricing of calls eliminates the need for manually calculating and posting charges.

Calls which are direct-distance-dialed are channeled through the CAS; outgoing calls requiring operator assistance are channeled through a HOBIC interface. **HOBIC** is an acronym for Hotel Billing Information Center. A CAS may include such features as:

- Automatic identification of outward dialing (AIOD)
- Automatic route selection (ARS)
- Least-cost routing (LCR)
- Call rating program
- HOBIC system interface

Exhibit 1 diagrams a CAS designed to monitor administrative (non-guest) and guest telephone traffic. Since all telephone extensions are interconnected through the hotel's switchboard, the switchboard serves as a primary control device for the entire call accounting system. The switchboard may contain an optional station message detail record (SMDR) which takes responsibility for charting and monitoring telephone traffic.

The following sections examine CAS features. The HOBIC interface is addressed first because many properties continue to process telephone traffic through this system.

Exhibit 1   Overview of a Call Accounting System

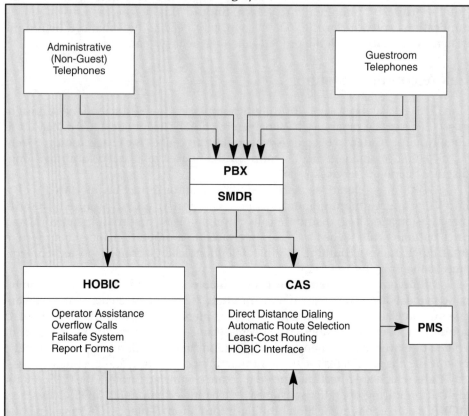

HOBIC System Interface

Before 1981, lodging properties used the HOBIC system to provide telephone service to guests. This system is still in use today and often serves as a backup system for properties which have installed call accounting systems.

The HOBIC system is a service supplied by a telephone company that records time and charges on each long-distance call made by guests. Guest calls are placed on special telephone lines called HOBIC lines. When a guest places a call over these lines, the telephone company operator intervenes and asks the guest for his or her room number. Upon receiving the room number, the operator allows the call to go through. After completion of the call, the hotel receives the "time and charges" either from an operator calling the property or through a telephone company transmission received at a front desk teletype machine.

Before January 1983, hotels received a commission from the telephone company for collecting charges from guests. The commission was a 15 percent discount on the property's telephone bill. However, due to the cost of installing and operating telephone system equipment and problems associated with the HOBIC system, hotel telephone departments were barely able to break even financially. HOBIC operators had no way of verifying the room number given by a guest, and time delays (between when a guest completed a call and when the property received the time and charges) often resulted in uncollectible late charges.

Despite its drawbacks, the HOBIC system is often interfaced with a CAS to perform the following functions:

- Supervise all operator-assisted calls.

- Process overflow telephone service from the CAS.

- Serve as a fail-safe telephone service.

For example, if a direct-dial call is placed and all available CAS lines are busy, the HOBIC lines are automatically engaged to complete the call. When the HOBIC system is used to process overflow calls, the calls are usually sent to the CAS for final pricing, recording, and reporting. Also, if (for whatever reason) the CAS is inoperable, the HOBIC system serves as a fail-safe mechanism by processing calls in the same manner as for properties without call accounting systems. This ensures continuous telephone service for guests.

Features of Call Accounting Systems

Exhibit 2 presents a simplified flowchart of the operation of a call accounting system. Functions which may be performed by a CAS include:

- Call placement
- Call distribution
- Call routing
- Call rating
- Call record

Call accounting systems have significantly simplified the sequence involved in call placement. Guests can direct-distance dial, eliminating operator intervention. With the HOBIC system, an operator intercepts outgoing calls to identify the guest's room number. The **automatic identification of outward dialing** (AIOD) feature of a CAS immediately identifies the extension from which a call is placed.

As an outgoing call is placed, the CAS's call distribution equipment is engaged. How and where a specific call is routed is essential in determining its cost. With a **passive call accounting system**, there are no options available to the call distribution network. Selection of a route is based on convenience rather than on minimizing expense. An **active call accounting system**, on the other hand, employs an automatic route selection (ARS) switch with a least-cost routing (LCR) device. The **automatic route selection** (ARS) feature has become an essential CAS component and is usually capable of connecting with a variety of common carriers. A **common carrier** is any recognized entity that transmits messages or other communication for general use at accepted rates. The **least-cost routing** (LCR) device directs calls over the least-cost available line, regardless of carrier. When the least-cost line is busy, the

Exhibit 2   Simplified Flowchart of a CAS Operation

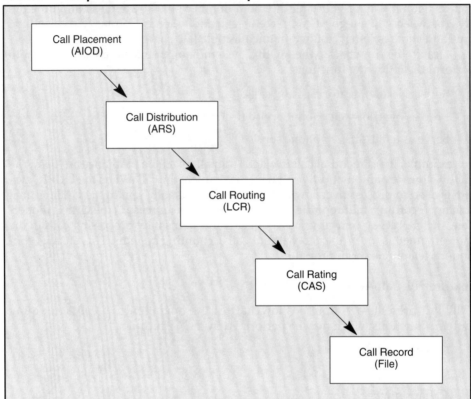

LCR prompts the system to seek out the next least expensive line. This search procedure is performed at high speed and with remarkable precision.

The manner by which a call is rated will vary in relation to vendors, equipment packages, and electronic switches. A **station message detail record** (SMDR) may be employed to chart and monitor telephone traffic. The data collected by the SMDR is used to rate calls. Some systems base calls on a ringback mechanism; others incorporate a timeout feature. With a **ringback mechanism**, the guest is charged only for calls which are answered. With a **timeout feature**, callers begin paying for calls after a predetermined amount of placement time. After a call is rated, it is entered into a call record file.

The **call record file** monitors details regarding calls processed by the CAS. This file may include:

- Date

- Guestroom extension number

- Telephone number dialed

- Time call was placed

- Duration of call

- Cost of call

- Tax and markup charges

While most call rating systems calculate the price and tax of a call and automatically post the necessary data to appropriate call record files, other systems price and tax calls but may require data to be manually posted to call record files. A **call record** is hard copy documentation containing essential transactional support data for individually placed telephone calls. Call records are typically referenced on a guest folio and provide a means for resolving guest discrepancies relating to telephone charges.

Call records are automatically logged in a traffic transaction file. The **traffic transaction file** maintains data necessary for generating reports for management. Typically, records are organized by time of call placement (chronological file) or room extension number (sorted file). The extent of report detail is a function of management needs. A **daily telephone revenue report**, also referred to as a daily profit report, sorts traffic transaction data by type of call and records the cost, price, and gross profit earned on each call processed by the CAS. Exhibit 3 groups an assortment of reports which may be generated by a CAS.

CAS/PMS Advantages and Management Concerns

A CAS/PMS interface offers lodging properties a number of significant advantages, such as:

- Enhanced guest services and guest satisfaction

- Improved communications networking

- Improved call pricing methods

- Minimized telephone traffic expenses

- Automatic charge posting to guest folios

- Automatic call detail records

- Detailed daily reports of telephone transactions

Since the CAS reduces operator intervention, the hotel telephone department can save both time and labor. Eliminating telephone meter readings and reducing guest telephone charge discrepancies also contribute to faster check-out times and more efficient front desk operation.

Contingency backup procedures should be a major management concern in relation to a call accounting system and its interface with a property management system. The CAS/PMS interface is itself backed up by the HOBIC call system. Various CAS reports provide information backup through hard copies of processed transactions. Energy backup for the CAS, however, may require access to an uninterruptible power supply.

Exhibit 3   Assorted CAS Reports

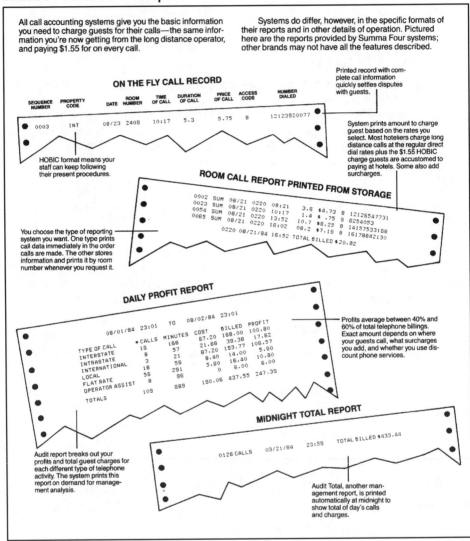

All call accounting systems give you the basic information you need to charge guests for their calls—the same information you're now getting from the long distance operator, and paying $1.55 for on every call.

Systems do differ, however, in the specific formats of their reports and in other details of operation. Pictured here are the reports provided by Summa Four systems; other brands may not have all the features described.

ON THE FLY CALL RECORD

Printed record with complete call information quickly settles disputes with guests.

System prints amount to charge guest based on the rates you select. Most hoteliers charge long distance calls at the regular direct dial rates plus the $1.55 HOBIC charge guests are accustomed to paying at hotels. Some also add surcharges.

HOBIC format means your staff can keep following their present procedures.

ROOM CALL REPORT PRINTED FROM STORAGE

You choose the type of reporting system you want. One type prints call data immediately in the order calls are made. The other stores information and prints it by room number whenever you request it.

DAILY PROFIT REPORT

Profits average between 40% and 60% of total telephone billings. Exact amount depends on where your guests call, what surcharges you add, and whether you use discount phone services.

Audit report breaks out your profits and total guest charges for each different type of telephone activity. The system prints this report on demand for management analysis.

MIDNIGHT TOTAL REPORT

Audit Total, another management report, is printed automatically at midnight to show total of day's calls and charges.

Another important concern is the storage capacity of the CAS. Before purchasing and installing a CAS, management must be sure that telephone traffic throughout the hotel has been properly evaluated so that the proposed CAS will have adequate storage capacity for processing and storing telephone data. Management may also wish to ensure that the proposed system is able to distinguish administrative (non-guest) calls from guest calls. Other important concerns focus on system maintenance, service, and vendor support. In many cases, management officials may need to initiate new telephone maintenance programs.

Electronic Locking Systems

An electronic locking system (ELS) replaces traditional brass keys and mechanical locks with sophisticated computer-based guestroom access devices. Installing electronic locks on existing guestroom doors may be a minor job or it could involve a major reconstruction effort. Some systems require only the drilling of a small hole for wires to pass from the outside to the inside portion of the lock. In many cases, existing deadbolt and latch hardware are retained as part of the new lock. Other systems may require all-new hardware or even new doors.

Currently, there are a variety of electronic locking systems available to lodging properties. Most of them are either hard-wired or micro-fitted locking systems. The following sections describe these systems in some detail.

Hard-Wired Systems

Hard-wired electronic locking systems operate through a centralized master code console interfaced to every controlled guestroom door. The console may be a slotted switchboard centrally located at the front desk. With this type of **hard-wired system**, a front desk employee follows a check-in procedure by inserting a previously encoded keycard into the proper room location slot on the console. The console immediately transmits the keycard's code to the remote guestroom door lock. By the time the guest leaves the front desk, the keycard which he or she has been issued is the only workable guestroom access key. Keycards issued to previous guests who occupied the same room become invalid.

Since every controlled door must be cabled to the master console, hard-wired systems present both a challenge (expensive design) and an opportunity (improved security). Before such a system is installed, management should identify emergency energy backup sources. Hard-wired locking systems use AC (house current) as their primary energy source, with DC (battery pack) serving as emergency backup. Management must also determine when keycards are to be created (initially encoded) and how they are to be maintained.

Micro-Fitted Systems

Micro-fitted electronic locking systems operate as individually configured stand-alone units, thus avoiding the complex dedicated circuitry required by hard-wired locking systems. Each door has its own microprocessor which contains a unique, predetermined sequence of codes. A master console at the front desk contains a record of all code sequences for each door. With a **micro-fitted locking system**, the front desk employee completes guest check-in by encoding a keycard with the next code in the predetermined sequence of codes for an assigned room

With hard-wired systems, codes are directly communicated from the master code console to the controlled doors. Micro-fitted systems do not possess this kind of communications capability. The front desk console and the microprocessors of controlled doors are essentially separate units. What connects them is the predetermined sequence of codes. This means not only that the front desk console must be programmed with the same predetermined sequence of codes that is contained within each microprocessor, but also that the console and each microprocessor must agree on which code in the sequence is currently valid.

For example, assume that at check-in a family requests two rooms with a connecting door. The parents plan to stay in one of the rooms while their children stay in the other. Upon reaching the rooms, the family enters the first room and finds the connecting door to the other room already open. The next morning, the family checks out of both rooms, having never used the second room's keycard. The locking mechanism in the second room's door will not advance to the next code in the predetermined sequence because the keycard was never used. The master console at the front desk, however, will automatically advance to the next code in the sequence when another guest checks into that room because it assumes that the last issued keycard has been used. Should this happen, the new guest (receiving the next keycard) will find that the keycard he or she has been issued fails to activate the lock. A front desk employee must then use a specially designed keycard to reprogram the room door's microprocessor so that the current code synchronizes with the front desk control console.

An important energy feature of micro-fitted electronic locking systems is that the microchips in each door are powered by battery packs and therefore do not require wiring to an external energy source. Some systems employ penlight size batteries, some D-size cells, and others even larger battery units.

ELS Features

Electronic locking systems may produce various levels of master keys. Most systems are sophisticated enough to provide several distinct levels of security. One level may be established for housekeeping personnel, another for hotel security officers, and yet another for property management officials.

Some ELS designs provide a "do not disturb" option for guests. This option typically employs an indicator which displays a notice when the guest wants privacy. The notice is often given by a flashing red light located within the locking mechanism. This indicator may be triggered when a room attendant inserts a keycard into the locking mechanism. No longer must the housekeeping staff test the door's chain to realize that the guest is still in the room!

A safety feature built into some electronic locking systems prevents the door from opening while the keycard remains in the lock. This prevents a guest from entering a guestroom while forgetting to take the keycard from the lock. One system permits entry without keycard removal; however, it tracks the length of time the keycard is in the door. If the keycard remains in the locking mechanism beyond a predetermined time interval, the system destroys the keycard by scrambling its code. The reason for scrambling a keycard's code relates to guestroom security. A keycard that remains in a lock may be taken by someone other than the room's occupant. To avoid problems, hotel staff must inform guests that failure to promptly remove the keycard will cause it to become invalid.

Electronic locking systems may become an essential hotel feature as self-service terminals which enable unassisted guest check-in and check-out appear throughout the lodging industry. There is an even newer form of electronic locking system that does not require guests to possess keys or cards at all. With this system, guests set the locking mechanism by programming their own four-digit code number. This system has not had time to significantly affect the marketplace. Guest acceptance may be an overwhelming factor in determining the future success of this system.

Some electronic locking system vendors provide additional technology that enables guests to use their personal credit cards for room entry. At the time of check-in, the guest's credit card is moved ("swiped") through a magnetic strip reader. The reader captures and encodes the information contained on the card's magnetic strip and sends it as the access code for the appropriate guestroom door. When the guest arrives at the assigned room, the credit card operates as the room key.

ELS Reports

One of the most significant advantages of an electronic locking system is that management can find out which keycards opened which doors, by date and time. Communicating this ELS capability to hotel staff and guests may help reduce the number of guestroom incidents.

An ELS typically maintains an audit trail of all activities involving the use of system-issued keycards. Some systems print reports detailing activities in chronological sequence. A system that records events as they occur generally does so because of limited memory, not because the resulting printouts are intrinsically more useful or effective. Other systems record and store activity data which can be formatted to provide printed reports on demand. The creation of reports, as well as other system functions, should be controlled by operator identification and password security codes.

Energy Management Systems

Heating, lighting, ventilating, and air-conditioning equipment are essential to a hotel's existence. The greater the efficiency of this equipment, the better the hotel serves the needs of guests. Energy management systems may conserve energy, contain energy costs, and tighten operational controls over guestroom and public area environments. An important feature of these systems is their ability to minimize the building's energy needs while not significantly affecting the hotel's comfort conditions.

An energy management system may eventually become a standard feature of the rooms management module. However, these systems are currently marketed as stand-alone systems and, therefore, must be interfaced to the rooms management module to provide maximum efficiency.

An energy management system (EMS) is a computer-based control system designed to automatically manage the operation of mechanical equipment in a property. The programming of this system enables management to determine when equipment is to be turned on or off or otherwise regulated. For example, if the meeting rooms of a property will be used from 10:00 A.M. to 2:00 P.M., the computer can be programmed to automatically conserve energy during the hours the rooms will not be in use, while ensuring that by 10:00 A.M. the rooms reach a satisfactory comfort level for guests. This programming technique can usually be applied to equipment affecting various spaces throughout the property.

Although actual operating features of energy management systems vary, common energy control designs include:

- Demand control

- Duty cycling

- Room occupancy sensors

Demand control maintains usage levels below a given limit by shedding energy loads in an orderly fashion. Equipment units assigned to demand control programs are those that can be turned off for varying periods without adversely affecting environmental comfort conditions. Unfortunately, hotels and motels do not have very many equipment units that can be shed without adversely affecting the overall operation of the property and the comfort of its guests.

Duty cycling turns off equipment sequentially for a period of time each hour. Heating, ventilating, and air conditioning systems may be duty-cycled to reduce energy consumption while maintaining space comfort conditions. However, duty cycling is not normally applied to large horsepower motors which cannot be stopped and started on a frequent basis without overheating.

Room occupancy sensors use either infrared light or ultrasonic waves to register the physical occupancy of a room. Whenever a guest enters a monitored space, sensors turn on whatever devices are under their control, such as lights, air conditioning equipment, heating equipment, and so on. When a guest leaves a monitored room, sensors react and, after a short delay, turn off the lights and/or automatically reset the temperature.

An EMS/PMS interface offers a number of opportunities for energy control. For example, assume that, on a particular night, a 50 percent occupancy is forecasted for a 300-room property. Minimizing the hotel's energy consumption on this night becomes a factor in determining which rooms to sell. One approach would be to assign guests only to the lower floors of the property and significantly reduce the energy demands of rooms on the upper floors. By interfacing an energy management system to a front office rooms management module, it is possible to automatically control room assignments and achieve desired energy cost savings. In many cases, energy cost savings are tracked by an in-house microcomputer through specially created electronic spreadsheets.

Comfort conditions in guestrooms, meeting and function rooms, public spaces, administrative offices, and other EMS-monitored areas can be controlled through a system console. Energy management systems typically provide rapid access to heat, ventilating, and air conditioning (HVAC) levels at remote locations and display these readings on the console screen.

No matter how sophisticated an energy management system may be, energy controls are virtually worthless if they are operating an energy system that is poorly designed or inadequately maintained.

Auxiliary Guest Services

Automation has simplified many auxiliary guest services, such as the placement of wake-up calls and the delivery of messages to guests. These functions are often performed by devices marketed as stand-alone systems which can be interfaced to the rooms management module of a property management system.

Perhaps the main reason for interfacing auxiliary guest services to a property management system lies in the comprehensive coordination and tracking of guest-related functions. While automated wake-up call devices are often best operated as stand-alone units, it may be beneficial to interface a guest messaging system to the PMS. The ability to notify guests about messages waiting for them depends on access to the PMS mechanism that links with guestroom telephones and televisions.

An automated wake-up system permits front desk employees to input a guest's room number and requested wake-up time. At the specified time, the system automatically rings the room and calls back at predetermined intervals until the guest answers the phone. If there is no response on the third or fourth try, the system stops calling and makes note of the guest's failure to answer. If the guest answers the call, the system completes a prerecorded morning greeting and then disconnects. Some sophisticated wake-up devices require that the guest actually speak into the phone to confirm that he or she is awake. A notation of the answered call is often stored for the day within the system.

Electronic message-waiting systems are designed to let a guest know that a message is waiting at the front desk. Traditional message-waiting devices are capable of flashing a light on a telephone or television in the guest's room. Electronic systems are now available which actually display messages on the television screen in the guest's room. Other systems employ an automatic telephone calling pattern similar to that used in automated wake-up systems. The system's ability to keep calling until the guest answers is more economical and efficient than employing the time, patience, and persistence of a switchboard operator.

Recently, hotels have begun experimenting with voice mailboxes. These are devices that record telephone messages for guests. A caller who wishes to leave a message for a guest simply does so over the phone, and the message is recorded for the guest to access later. To retrieve a message, the guest typically dials a special telephone number, connects with the voice mailbox, and listens to the message delivered in the caller's own voice. By interfacing the voice mailbox service with the PMS, the recording of the message trips the message-waiting mechanism in the guestroom, leaving the switchboard staff free to perform more productive tasks.

Guest-Operated Devices

Guest-operated devices can be located in a public area of the hotel or in private guestrooms. In-room guest-operated devices are designed to be user-friendly. An assortment of devices provide concierge-level service with in-room convenience. Guest-operated devices discussed in the following sections include:

- Self check-in/check-out systems
- In-room movie systems
- In-room beverage service systems
- Information service systems

Exhibit 4   Self Check-In/Check-Out Device

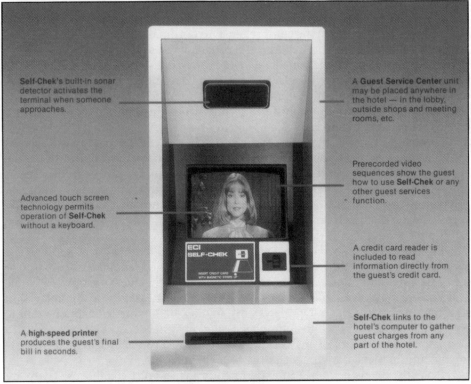

Self-Chek's built-in sonar detector activates the terminal when someone approaches.

A **Guest Service Center** unit may be placed anywhere in the hotel — in the lobby, outside shops and meeting rooms, etc.

Prerecorded video sequences show the guest how to use **Self-Chek** or any other guest services function.

Advanced touch screen technology permits operation of **Self-Chek** without a keyboard.

A credit card reader is included to read information directly from the guest's credit card.

A **high-speed printer** produces the guest's final bill in seconds.

Self-Chek links to the hotel's computer to gather guest charges from any part of the hotel.

Source: ECI, EECO Computer Inc., Santa Ana, California.

Self Check-In/Check-Out Systems

Self check-in/check-out terminals are typically located in the lobbies of fully automated hotels. These terminals vary in design. Some resemble automatic bank teller machines, while others are unique in design and may possess both video and audio capability. Exhibit 4 shows one type of self check-in/check-out device.

In order to use one of these terminals, a guest typically must arrive at the hotel with an advance reservation and must possess a valid credit card. The guest initiates the self-registration process by inserting the credit card into the terminal. The terminal then prompts the guest to use a keypad and enter necessary information. After collecting registration data, the terminal screen may display room types and rates. Since most terminals are interfaced to a property management system rooms management module, automatic room and rate assignment is possible. Once a room and rate have been determined, the terminal automatically dispenses an electronic keycard or tells the guest how to obtain a room key.

Lobby terminals are also capable of handling self check-out procedures. Typically, the guest uses the credit card used at check-in to access the appropriate folio and review its contents. After the guest completes the designated check-out

CAPDATA Night Express. (Courtesy of CAPDATA, Inc., Scottsdale, Arizona)

procedures, the system automatically posts the account balance to the credit card for billing and dispenses an itemized statement for the guest.

Self check-in/check-out systems are also available for small properties. These systems allow the busy owner/manager of a small property to capitalize on technological advances that, in the past, have been available primarily to large properties. One system is capable of registering guests, assigning rooms, handling credit card or cash transactions, providing a room key or keycard, and printing a receipt for the guest.

One type of system has a secured face plate that mounts on an interior or exterior wall. For the convenience of guests, step-by-step instructions are printed on the face plate. The only way to access the machine's contents (such as cash) is from the rear of the machine, which generally opens into the manager's office or another secure area. As a security precaution, the system does not disburse cash. If a late-arriving guest uses the system and a credit is due from a cash overpayment, the guest is instructed to receive the change at the front desk in the morning. When a guest pays by credit card, credit authorization is secured by telecommunications capability. If the guest's use of credit card is declined, special instructions can be displayed asking the guest to use another card or to pay by cash.

Recent technological advances offer guests the opportunity for both in-room folio review and **in-room check-out**. These systems may use in-room computer terminals, the property's television cable station, or guestroom telephones to access and display guest folio data on the guestroom television screen. When in-room computers are interfaced with a property management system guest accounting module, they are able to access folio data and provide guests with a means to approve and settle their accounts. Guestroom telephones, interfaced with the property management system, can also be used to access and display folio data on the television screen. Newer in-room folio review technology uses a guestroom telephone interface with the property management system to provide computer-synthesized voice responses. This system provides guests with folio totals (or details) and directs a self check-out procedure. Folio copies are typically available for guests to pick up at the front desk.

Regardless of which kind of guest-operated device is used, self check-in/check-out terminals and in-room computer interfaces can significantly reduce the time it takes to process guest registrations, check-ins, and check-outs. In addition, some automated terminals have enhanced video capability enabling the property to introduce guests to the facilities and amenities available. Automated check-in and check-out devices can free front office employees to spend more time with those guests who require personal attention.

In-Room Movie Systems

In-room movie systems can be interfaced with a hotel's property management system or they can function as independent, stand-alone systems. Exhibit 5 illustrates the components of one type of in-room movie system.

When interfaced with the property management system, in-room movie systems provide guestroom entertainment through a dedicated television pay channel. The interface includes a timing device. After the channel has been tuned in for a predetermined amount of time (usually several minutes), the device triggers an automatic charge posting to the appropriate guest folio.

Guest-disputed charges have haunted in-room movie systems since their inception. A guest may inadvertently turn on the television set for background entertainment, only to discover at check-out that the set was tuned to a pay channel. Incorporating a pay television preview channel can significantly reduce the number of disputed charges. The preview channel permits a guest to view a small segment of each available program. In order to view an actual program, the guest must then physically switch the television from normal viewing to a pay movie channel.

Stand-alone in-room movie systems generally require the guest to dial an in-house service and request that the pay channel be turned on. The operator who turns on the program is also responsible for posting the charge to the proper guest

Exhibit 5   Sample In-Room Movie System Hardware

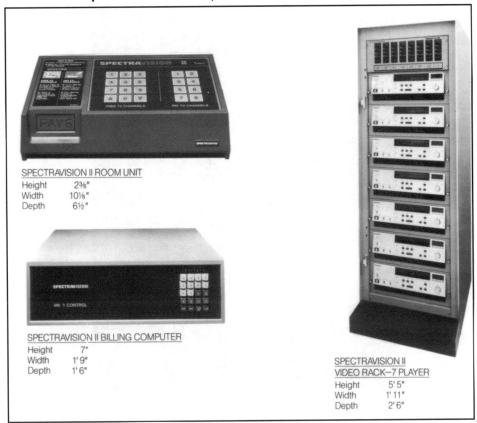

SPECTRAVISION II ROOM UNIT
Height   2⅜"
Width   10⅛"
Depth   6½"

SPECTRAVISION II BILLING COMPUTER
Height   7"
Width   1' 9"
Depth   1' 6"

SPECTRAVISION II
VIDEO RACK—7 PLAYER
Height   5' 5"
Width   1' 11"
Depth   2' 6"

Source: Spectradyne Inc., Richardson, Texas.

folio. Although the telephone call approach is not fully automated, it does provide a sound basis for minimizing guest-disputed charges.

In-Room Beverage Service Systems

In-room beverage service systems are capable of monitoring sales transactions and determining inventory replenishment quantities. Two popular in-room beverage service systems are non-automated honor bars and microprocessor-based vending machines.

Non-automated honor bars typically involve stocks of items which are held in both dry and cold storage areas within a guestroom. Changes in the bar's beginning inventory level are noted either by housekeeping room attendants during their normal rounds or by designated room service employees. In either case, the employee typically uses a touch-tone telephone in the guestroom to connect with the dedicated bar computer. Once connection has been made, the employee enters the product code numbers of items which have been consumed. The bar system's

In-room folio review. (Courtesy of Spectradyne Inc., Richardson, Texas)

CPU relays guestroom information and charges for consumed items to the property management system for proper folio posting and issues a stock replacement report.

Although non-automated honor bar systems are extremely convenient for guests, they may pose several problems for the hotel. For example, since the bar is always open, consumption is almost impossible to regulate. This service problem could result in frequent late charges. Another potential problem is the high labor costs associated with taking the necessary physical inventory of each in-room bar.

Microprocessor-based vending machines contain beverage items in see-through closed compartments. The compartment doors may be equipped with fiber optic sensors that record the removal of stored products. Once triggered, the sensors relay the transaction to a built-in microprocessor for recording. Individual room microprocessors are typically cabled to a large CPU, which stores recorded transactions. This CPU converts transactions into accounting entries, and relays them to the property management system guest accounting module for folio posting. The bar system's CPU also maintains perpetual inventory replenishment data, which directs the restocking of vending units.

Microprocessor-based vending systems avoid some of the problems associated with honor bars. For example, hotel managers may use a remote central console to lock in-room vending units. Some systems enable guests to lock their in-room bar units with their guestroom keys. In addition, property management system interfacing minimizes late charges. Also, since microprocessor-based vending systems maintain a perpetual inventory record, labor costs associated with manual inventory tracking are reduced.

Guest Information Services

Just as shopping malls have installed information terminals, so too have many hotels. Automated **guest information services** include devices in public hotel areas that allow guests to inquire about in-house events and local activities. When a line-printing terminal (LPT) is connected with a lobby information terminal, guests may receive individually prepared hard copy lists of events. Transient guests, conference attendees, and casual observers alike can access information about the hotel, its outlets, and surrounding attractions.

Guest information systems, also called in-room electronic services, are an important guest amenity revolutionizing the guestroom. These systems connect to cable broadcast systems, wire news services, transportation schedules, and restaurant and room service menus, and may also access external computer systems. When in-room computers are able to link with external computer information services, guests may access:

- Airline schedules

- Local restaurant guides

- Entertainment guides

- Stock market reports

- News and sports updates

- Shopping catalogs

- Video games

If every guestroom terminal were directly interfaced with a property management system, a great deal of system processing would be needed to respond to all of the activity coming from in-room terminals. To avoid overloading the property management system, in-room computers are typically connected to a remote CPU which is interfaced with the CPU of the property management system. Since only one connection must be made to the property management system, this configuration simplifies the guest information services interface. Exhibit 6 presents a simplified diagram of an interface configuration for in-room computers.

In addition to the property management system interface, in-room guest information terminals may also be connected to the hotel's cable television band. This connection enables the property to keep convention attendees informed about

Exhibit 6   Interface Configuration for In-Room Guest Information Systems

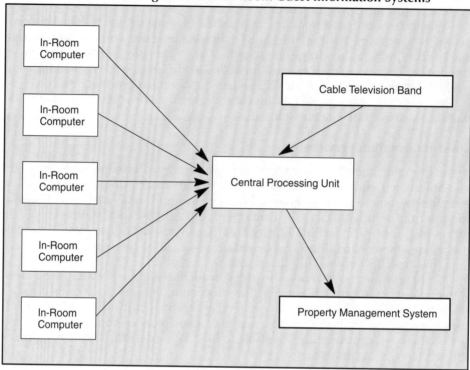

events and functions, to provide tourists with information about local attractions, and to inform business travelers about support services provided by the property.

Summary

This chapter examined independent, stand-alone computerized systems which may interface with a property management system. These PMS interfaces are:

- Point-of-sale systems
- Call accounting systems
- Electronic locking systems
- Energy management systems
- Auxiliary guest services
- Guest-operated devices

A point-of-sale (POS) system is made up of a number of point-of-sale terminals that typically interface with a remote central processing unit. The processing unit interface is usually a stand-alone CPU or a host electronic cash register. When the remote CPU or the host electronic cash register is interfaced with a property management system, data can be transferred from the POS system to various front office and back office property management system modules for further processing.

A call accounting system (CAS) increases the control of hotel management over expenses relating to local and long-distance telephone services. Generally, a call accounting system is able to handle direct-distance dialing, distribute calls through a least-cost routing network, and price outgoing calls. When a call accounting system is interfaced with a property management system front office guest accounting module, telephone charges can be posted immediately to the proper guest folio.

This chapter examined two types of electronic locking systems—hard-wired systems and micro-fitted systems. Hard-wired systems employ a key code console or master control board which determines a door's lock combination and relays that code to the door. Some systems are sophisticated enough to operate as a two-way communication relay. Micro-fitted systems rely upon a predetermined sequence of code numbers residing in each individual door lock. All codes and code sequences are stored in a central console at the front desk. The insertion of a keycard into a microprocessor lock advances the stored sequence to the next number and makes all previous codes invalid. Transaction data collected and stored by electronic locking systems form the basis of security reports for use by management.

A computerized energy management system (EMS) is designed to automatically manage the operation of some types of equipment responsible for maintaining comfort levels throughout a hotel property. The programming of these systems enables management to determine when equipment is to be turned on or off or otherwise regulated.

Guest auxiliary services include the automation of wake-up calls, electronic message systems, and the use of voice mail boxes. The recent introduction of advanced technology to auxiliary services has enhanced the hotel's productivity, especially with regard to guest support services.

This chapter also examined guest-operated devices such as self check-in/check-out technology, in-room movie systems, in-room beverage service systems, and guest information services.

Key Terms

Point-of-Sale Systems

electronic cash register

micro-based POS system

point-of-sale terminal

Call Accounting Systems

active call accounting system

automatic identification of
  outward dialing

automatic route selection

call record

call record file

common carrier

daily telephone revenue report

HOBIC system

least-cost routing

passive call accounting system

ringback mechanism

station message detail record
timeout feature

traffic transaction file

Energy Management Systems

demand control
duty cycling

room occupancy sensors

Electronic Locking Systems

hard-wired system

micro-fitted system

Guest-Operated Devices

guest information services
in-room beverage service system
in-room check-out
in-room movie system

microprocessor-based vending
   machine
non-automated honor bar
self check-in/check-out terminals

Discussion Questions

1. How do micro-based POS systems differ from other POS systems?

2. What are typical POS data entry requirements for posting charges to appropriate guest folios?

3. What are some concerns that management should address in relation to interfacing a POS system to an integrated PMS system?

4. What are the advantages of a call accounting system when compared with the HOBIC system?

5. What data are maintained by a CAS call record file? Explain how this data may be useful to management.

6. What are the major differences between hard-wired and micro-fitted electronic locking systems? Identify advantages and disadvantages of each system.

7. What are three energy control strategies which may be used by an energy management system?

8. How can lodging properties benefit from automated self check-in/check-out systems?

9. What are two in-room beverage service systems? Explain the advantages and disadvantages of each.

10. What external information services may guests be able to access from in-room computer terminals?

REVIEW QUIZ

When you feel you have covered all of the material in this chapter, answer these questions. Choose the *best* answer.

Matching

1. POS terminal

2. Automatic identification of outward dialing

3. HOBIC system

4. Passive call accounting system

5. Common carrier

6. Traffic transaction file

7. Hard-wired electronic locking system

8. Duty cycling

a. Contains call records

b. Uses centralized master code console

c. Does not use least-cost routing

d. Also called micro-fitted locking system

e. Interfaces with remote CPU

f. Also called electronic cash register

g. Uses least-cost routing

h. Also called demand control

i. Energy management system feature

j. Non-automated honor bars

k. Telephone company service

l. Identifies extension placing a call

m. Transmits messages for general use at accepted rates

True (T) or False (F)

T   F   9. POS systems that place microprocessors at each terminal location are called micro-based POS systems.

T   F   10. Call accounting systems often reduce the labor costs associated with traditional telephone systems.

T   F   11. A least-cost routing device directs telephone calls over the least-cost available line, regardless of carrier.

T   F   12. When a ringback mechanism is used in a call accounting system, callers begin paying for calls after a predetermined amount of time.

Alternate/Multiple Choice

13. Which of the following maintains energy usage levels below a given limit by shedding loads in an orderly fashion?

    a. demand control
    b. duty cycling

14.   Which in-room beverage system is more likely to result in late charges?

   a. microprocessor-based vending machines
   b. non-automated honor bars

15.   Which of the following enables a guest to retrieve a message and hear it delivered in the caller's own voice?

   a. electronic message-waiting system
   b. ringback dial system
   c. voice mailbox
   d. in-room computer system

Part III

Computer-Based Food and Beverage Management Systems

Chapter Outline

ECR/POS Hardware Components
    Keyboards
    Display Screens
    Printers
    Printer Controllers
Computer-Based Guest Checks
ECR/POS Software
    Menu Item File
    Labor Master File
    Inventory File
    Consolidated Reports
Automation Advances
    Touch-Screen Technology
    Bar Code Terminals
    Wireless Terminals
    Magnetic Strip Readers
Automated Beverage Control Systems
    Order-Entry Devices
    Delivery Networks
    Dispensing Units
Summary

Learning Objectives

1. Identify the different functions performed by precheck terminals and registers as part of an ECR/POS system.

2. Identify and explain the function of the different types of keys found on the keyboard of an ECR/POS system terminal.

3. Describe the kinds of printing devices that may be part of an ECR/POS system.

4. Describe major files maintained by ECR/POS software.

5. Explain the value of touch-screen, bar code, and wireless terminals for food and beverage operations.

6. Identify the functions performed by magnetic strip readers, power platforms, and debit cards.

7. Describe two types of automated beverage systems. Identify and describe the three hardware components required for a computer system.

8. Identify the basic features of a sophisticated automated beverage control system.

7

Food and Beverage Applications—Service

W<small>HILE COMPUTER-BASED</small> hotel property management systems tend to consist of modules, computer-based restaurant management systems function through specific hardware components and a wide variety of applications software packages. This chapter focuses on service-oriented applications of a computer-based restaurant management system. These applications rely upon electronic cash register (ECR) and point-of-sale (POS) technology to monitor service area transactions through precheck terminals, remote work station printers and displays, printer controllers, and registers.

This chapter begins by identifying the necessary hardware components of a restaurant-wide ECR/POS system. Input/output devices such as keyboards, display screens, printers, and printer controllers are discussed in great detail. In addition, computer-based guest checks are examined in relation to enhancing management's control of operations.

Like other computer hardware components, ECRs and POS terminals require software programs to instruct them in what to do, how to do it, and when to do it. ECR/POS software not only directs internal system operations, it also maintains files and produces reports for management's use. The chapter examines the types of data stored in major ECR/POS files and the kind of information contained in some of the more significant reports that can be generated.

The chapter also examines recent automation advances for food and beverage service operations. Sophisticated input devices are described as well as the use of ECR/POS power platforms. The chapter closes with a section on automated beverage control systems. The discussion focuses on order-entry devices, delivery networks, and dispensing units.

ECR/POS Hardware Components

Although some food service operators and computer system vendors may use the terms "register" and "terminal" interchangeably, the terms actually refer to different equipment functions. In this chapter, the term **register** refers to an ECR/POS device which is connected to a cash drawer. All other ECR/POS devices are called terminals.

Since ECR/POS devices are generally sold as modular units, everything but the basic terminal is considered optional equipment. The cash drawer is no exception. Management may connect up to four cash drawers to a single register. Multiple cash drawers may enhance management's cash control system when several cashiers work at the same register during the same shift. Each cashier can be assigned a separate cash drawer so that, at the end of the shift, cash drawer receipts are individually reconciled.

A terminal without a cash drawer is commonly called a **precheck terminal**. Precheck terminals are used to enter orders, not to settle accounts. For example, a server can use a precheck terminal located in a dining room service station to relay orders to the appropriate kitchen and bar production areas, but cannot use the terminal to settle guest checks.

An ECR/POS device with a cash drawer can normally support both prechecking and cashiering functions. For example, an employee at a cashier stand in a hotel restaurant may serve as the cashier for the food service outlet and as an order-taker for room service. When answering room service calls, the employee uses the register as a precheck terminal. The register relays the room service orders to the appropriate kitchen and bar production areas. Before delivering the room service order, a room service employee stops at the cashier station and picks up the printed guest check from the cashier. After delivering the order, the room service employee presents the settled guest check to the cashier, who then uses the register to close the guest check within the system.

ECR/POS system hardware components consist of keyboards, display screens, various printers, and a printer controller. The following sections discuss these hardware components. Keyboards are examined in relation to keyboard design, types of keys, and keyboard overlays. The section on display screens addresses important concerns, such as the size and function of operator and customer displays. Features of guest check printers, receipt printers, remote work station printers, and journal printers are discussed next. The final section focuses on the function of a printer controller.

Keyboards

The two primary types of keyboard surfaces are micro-motion and reed style. The micro-motion keyboard design has a flat, wet-proof surface, while the reed keyboard design contains wet-proof keys raised above the surface of the keyboard. More important than the physical design of the keyboard's surface is the number of hard and soft keys the keyboard provides. **Hard keys** are dedicated to specific functions programmed by the manufacturer. **Soft keys** can be programmed by users to meet the specific needs of their restaurant operations.

Both keyboard designs can usually support interchangeable menu boards. A **menu board** overlays the keyboard surface and identifies the function performed by each key during a specific meal period. Menu boards can be developed to meet the specific needs of individual properties. Exhibit 1 shows a sample menu board for a dinner period. Menu boards for both micro-motion and reed style keyboard designs identify a number of different types of keys. Key types may include:

- Preset keys
- Price look-up (PLU) keys
- Function keys

Exhibit 1   Sample Menu Board

CARAFE WHITE WINE	CARAFE RED WINE	BOURBON	VODKA	DECAF COFFEE	COFFEE	SALAD	BAKED POTATO	HASH BROWNS	FRENCH FRIES	SOUR CREAM	TIME IN
CARAFE ROSE WINE	SCOTCH	SODA	WATER	BLOODY MARY	TEA	WITH	WITH-OUT	BREAD	STEWED TOMATO	VEGETAB	TIME OUT
RARE	GIN	TONIC	COLA	SCREW-DRIVER	MILK	HOUSE DRESS	FRENCH DRESS	VINEGAR & OIL	EXTRA BUTTER	MUSHRM SAUCE	ACCOUNT #
MEDIUM	WELL	SAUTEED MUSHRMS	SHRIMP COCKTAIL	FRENCH ONION SOUP	CRAB MEAT COCKTAIL	OYSTERS ON 1/2 SHELL	ITALIAN DRESS	BLEU CHEESE DRESS	COUPON 1	COUPON 2	COUPON 3
PRIME RIB	T-BONE	SHRIMP	LOBSTER	CIGARS	CASH BAR	CLEAR	ERROR CORRECT	CANCEL TRANS	CHECK TRANSFER	PAID OUT	TIPS PAID OUT
CHATEAU-BRIAND	FILET	CLAMS	TROUT	CANDY	SERVER #	TRAN CODE	SCREEN	NO SALE	CASHIER #	EMPL DISC	MGR DISC
TOP SIRLOIN 16 OZ	TOP SIRLOIN 12 OZ	SEA BASS	SCALLOPS	SNACKS	VOID ITEM	7	8	9	QUANTITY	ADD CHECK	CREDIT CARD 2
PORTER-HOUSE	CHOPPED SIRLOIN	OYSTERS	ALASKAN KING CRAB	# PERSONS ADD ON	REVERSE RECEIPT	4	5	6	VOID TRANS	CHARGE TIPS	CREDIT CARD 1
STEAK & CHICKEN	SURF & TURF	RED SNAPPER	SEA FOOD PLATTER	DINING ROOM SERVICE	PRICE LOOK UP	1	2	3	NEW CHECK	CASH BAR TOTAL	CHARGE
LEG OF LAMB	ROAST DUCK	PORK CHOPS	CHICKEN LIVERS	LOUNGE SERVICE	MODE SWITCH	0		MENU 1	PREVIOUS BALANCE	CHECK TOTAL	CASH TEND

Source: Validec, Inc., San Carlos, California.

- Settlement keys
- Modifier keys
- Numeric keypad

Servers enter orders by using preset keys and price look-up (PLU) keys. Modifier keys may be used in combination with preset and PLU keys to detail preparation instructions (such as rare, medium, well-done) for food production areas. Modifier keys may also be used to alter prices according to portion sizes (such as small, medium, and large). A numeric keypad facilitates various data-entry operations and enables cashiers to ring items by price when prices for items are not identified by preset keys or PLU numbers. Function keys and settlement keys are used to correct and complete transactions. Touch-screen ECR/POS devices and magnetic strip readers may soon replace traditional keyboard entry procedures. These automation advances are described in detail later in the chapter.

Generally, restaurant managers determine the positioning of most keys on a keyboard overlay. By positioning keys for similar items and functions together and arranging groups logically, managers can improve system performance and enhance operational controls. The following sections briefly discuss the types of keys commonly found on ECR/POS system keyboards.

Menu Board Overlay. (Courtesy of National Cash Register Corporation)

Preset Keys. These keys are programmed to maintain the price, descriptor, department, tax, and inventory status for a limited number of menu items. Automatic menu pricing speeds guest service, eliminates pricing errors, and permits greater menu flexibility. The term **descriptor** refers to the abbreviated description of a menu item, such as "SHRMPCKT" for shrimp cocktail or "PRIME" for prime rib. Although systems vary in the number of descriptor characters which they can accommodate, most support descriptors 8 to 10 characters long.

Each **preset key** is normally associated with a department code and a printer routing code. A **department code** refers to the menu category to which the preset item belongs—appetizer, entrée, dessert, and so on. A printer routing code is used to direct preparation instructions to the proper production area. For example, the porterhouse steak on the keyboard in Exhibit 1 has a department code associated with entrée items. The porterhouse steak also has a printer routing code designating it as an item prepared at the hot food station of the kitchen. Other items on the same keyboard (salad, wine, etc.) are assigned different department and printer routing codes.

Once a preset key is pressed, a description of the item and its price are retrieved from memory and appear on the operator's display screen. This data may also be relayed (along with preparation instructions) to the appropriate production station and may be printed on a guest check. In addition, the sales represented by this transaction are retained for revenue reporting and for tracking inventory levels. Sales data of individual items are important for guest check totalling as well as for production of management reports.

Price Look-Up Keys. Since terminals have a limited number of preset keys, **price look-up (PLU) keys** are used to supplement transaction entries. PLU keys operate

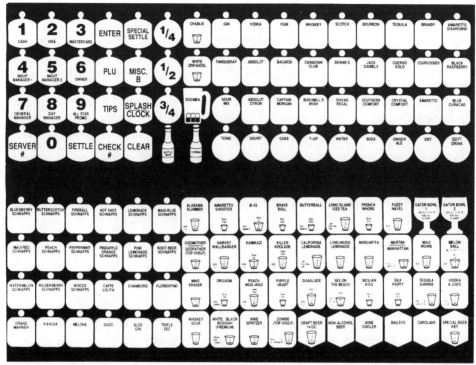

Keyboard for an Automatic Dispensing System. (Courtesy of American Business Computers)

like preset keys, except that they require the user to identify a menu item by its reference code number (up to five digits) rather than by its name or descriptor. A server entering an order for prime rib on a preset keyboard would merely press the item's designated key. In the absence of a prime rib preset key, the server would enter the item's code number (e.g., 7807) and then press the PLU key. PLU keys perform the same functions as preset keys. Preset keys and PLU keys enable the system to maintain a file for most menu items in terms of price, descriptor, tax, department, and inventory status.

Function Keys. While preset and PLU keys are used for order-entry purposes, **function keys** assist the user in processing transactions. Sample function keys include: clear, discount, void, and no-sale. Function keys are important for error correction (clear and void), legitimate price alteration (discount), and proper cash handling (no-sale). For example, a restaurant may attempt to increase weekly lunch sales by issuing coupons to nearby local businesses. When a coupon is used at the time of settlement, the cashier typically enters the value of the coupon and then presses the "discount" key. The value of the coupon is credited to the guest check and the remainder of the bill is settled through standard settlement procedures. The success of the promotion can be tracked if the system can print itemized discounts and daily discount totals.

Settlement Keys. These keys are used to record the methods with which accounts are settled: by cash, credit card, house account, charge transfer, or other payment method. **Settlement keys** enhance revenue accounting controls because they classify transactions at the time of settlement. Although restaurants may use any one of a number of revenue accounting methods, most operations use either server banking or cashier banking. Server banking places the responsibility for guest check settlement on the server. Cashier banking involves a non-server handling account settlement. In either case, tracking the identification of the banker and the transaction settlement method facilitates a fast and accurate sales reconciliation.

Modifier Keys. These keys allow servers to relay preparation instructions (such as rare, medium, or well-done) to remote work station printers or video display screens located in food production departments. Typically, a server enters the item ordered and then presses the appropriate preparation modifier. **Modifier keys** may also be used to legitimately alter menu item prices. For example, modifier keys may be useful to a restaurant that sells house wine by the carafe and half-carafe. Instead of tying up two preset keys (one for carafe, the other for half-carafe), a single preset key can be designated for house wine by the carafe and a modifier key can be programmed as a half-portion modifier. When a half-carafe is sold, the server simply presses both the carafe preset key and half-portion modifier key to register a half-carafe sale. The system maintains total wine revenue by adding the dollar amount for the half-carafe sale only. In addition, the system adjusts inventory records accordingly.

Numeric Keypad. This set of keys can be used to ring up menu items by price, access PLU data by menu item code number, access open guest check accounts by serial number, and perform other data entry operations. For example, if the register is used to record and store payroll data, employee identification numbers can be entered as employees begin and end their workshifts. In addition, menu item code numbers may be entered through the numeric keypad to access various files in order to make adjustments approved by management. The numeric keypad is also used to enter report codes that initiate the production of management reports.

Display Screens

In addition to a keyboard, a register terminal typically contains an operator display screen and may support a customer display unit as well. An **operator display screen** is generally a standard system component that enables the operator to view and edit transaction entries. The unit allows a user to monitor transactions in progress and also may serve as a prompt for various system procedures. The length and number of lines displayed is often an important consideration when selecting ECR/POS devices. Line lengths generally range from 7 to 80 characters, and the number of lines available varies from 1 to 24. An operator display screen is typically encased in the primary housing of the ECR/POS device. This is not always true for customer display units.

The design of **customer display units** include those that rest atop, inside, or alongside the ECR/POS device. Although customer display units are more restricted in size and scope than operator display screens, they permit a guest to observe the operator's entries. In many table service restaurants, settlement activities often take place outside the view of guests; therefore, a customer display unit may not be warranted. In those restaurants where guests can view settlement transactions, serious consideration should be given to the use of a customer display screen.

Customer display units also permit management to spot-check cashier activities. For example, an employee operating a register without a customer display unit might ring up a $5 transaction as 50 cents. Later, to balance the register's cash, the employee might take the $4.50 for personal use. This kind of theft is riskier when the terminal contains a customer display unit because a manager might observe the bogus 50-cent entry and take appropriate corrective action. Customer display screens are often more important for this purpose than for the assurance they offer guests.

Printers

Register printers are sometimes described as either on-board or remote printing devices. On-board printing devices are normally located within six feet of the terminal that they serve. These devices include guest check printers and receipt printers. Remote printing devices include work station printers and journal printers that are located more than six feet from the terminal that they support. These printing devices require separate cabling.

Guest Check Printers. These on-board printing devices are sometimes called slip printers. The **guest check printers** of most ECR/POS systems are capable of:

- Immediate check printing
- Delayed check printing
- Retained check printing

Immediate check printing refers to the ability of the system to print items as they are input at a terminal; delayed check printing prints items at the end of a complete order entry; and retained check printing prints the guest check at any time following order entry and before settlement. Sophisticated guest check printers may be equipped with an automatic form number reader (AFNR) and possess automatic slip feed (ASF) capabilities.

An **automatic form number reader** facilitates order-entry procedures. Instead of a server manually inputting a guest check's serial number to access the account, a bar code imprinted on the guest check presents the check's serial number in a machine-readable format. A server simply slips the guest check into the terminal's AFNR unit, and the AFNR provides rapid access to the guest check account.

An **automatic slip feed** capability prevents overprinting items and amounts on guest checks. ECR/POS systems without ASF capability require that a server insert a guest check into the printer's slot and manually align the printer's ribbon with the next blank printing line on the guest check. This can be an awkward procedure for servers to follow during busy meal periods. If the alignment is not correct, the guest check appears disorganized and messy with items and amounts printed over one another or with large gaps between lines. A system with ASF capability retains the number of the last line printed for each open guest check. The server simply aligns the top edge of a guest check with the top edge of the printer's slot, and the terminal automatically moves the check to the next available printing line and prints the order-entry data. Since guest checks are placed within the printer's slot the same way every time, servers may spend less time manipulating machinery and more time meeting their guests' needs. In addition, guests receive neatly printed, easy-to-read checks for settlement.

Exhibit 2 presents an itemized guest check produced by a guest check printer with an automatic form number reader and automatic slip feed capability. The bar code is printed in the upper right-hand corner of the guest check. The printed order follows a sequence of departments rather than the sequence in which the server actually wrote the order or entered the order at a precheck terminal.

Receipt Printers. These on-board printing devices produce hard copy on narrow register tape. Although the usefulness of a **receipt printer** is somewhat limited, these devices may help control the production of menu items that are not prepared at departments receiving orders through remote display or printing devices. For example, when servers prepare desserts and the pantry area is not equipped with a remote communication device, desserts could be served without ever being entered into the system. When this happens, it is also possible that desserts could be served without amounts ever being posted to guest checks. This situation can be avoided with a receipt printer. Servers preparing desserts can be required to deliver a receipt tape to the dessert pantry area as proof that the items are properly posted to guest checks for eventual settlement. This procedure ensures that every menu item served is printed somewhere in the system, enhancing management's internal control.

Work Station Printers. These remote printers are usually placed at kitchen preparation areas and service bars. As orders are entered at precheck terminals, they are sent to a designated remote **work station printer** to initiate production. Exhibit 3 shows printouts produced by remote work station printers. The printouts correspond to items printed on the sample guest check illustrated in Exhibit 2. This communications system enables servers to spend more time meeting their guests' needs while significantly reducing traffic in kitchen and bar areas.

If the need for hard copy output in production areas is not critical to an operation's internal control system, video display units (also called **kitchen monitors**) may be viable alternatives to work station printers. Since these units display several orders on a single screen, kitchen employees do not have to handle numerous pieces of paper. An accompanying cursor control keypad enables kitchen employees to easily review previously submitted orders by scrolling full screens at a time.

Journal Printers. These remote printers produce a continuous detailed record of all transactions entered anywhere in the system. **Journal printers** are usually located in secure areas away from service and production areas. Hard copy is produced on narrow register tape (usually 20 columns wide) and provides management with a thorough system audit. In addition to providing an audit trail, journal printers also print a variety of management reports. Management routinely reviews journal printouts to verify that the system is being used properly.

Exhibit 2   Sample Guest Check

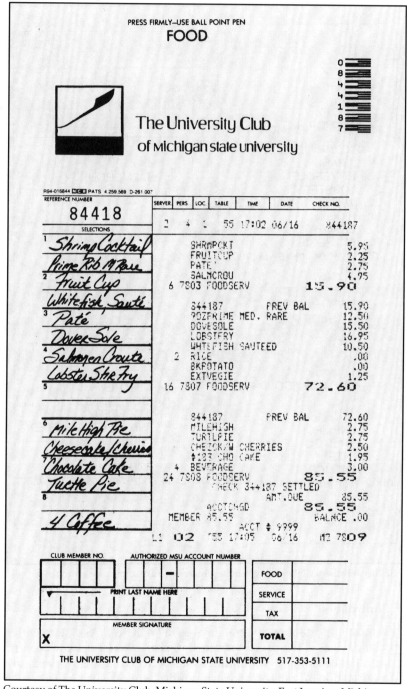

Courtesy of The University Club, Michigan State University, East Lansing, Michigan

Exhibit 3   Sample Work Station Printouts

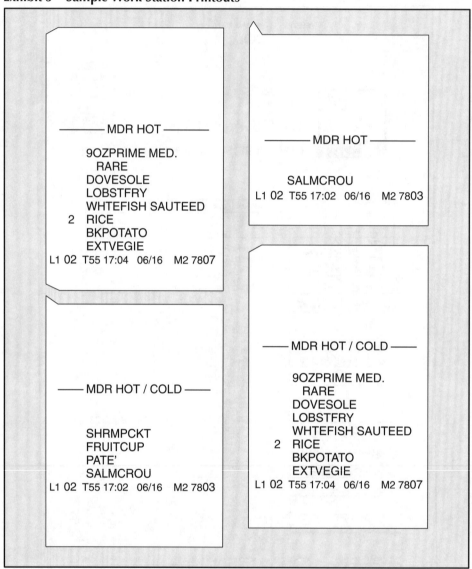

———— MDR HOT ————

  9OZPRIME MED.
    RARE
  DOVESOLE
  LOBSTFRY
  WHTEFISH SAUTEED
2 RICE
  BKPOTATO
  EXTVEGIE
L1 02 T55 17:04 06/16   M2 7807

———— MDR HOT ————

  SALMCROU
L1 02 T55 17:02   06/16   M2 7803

———— MDR HOT / COLD ————

  SHRMPCKT
  FRUITCUP
  PATE'
  SALMCROU
L1 02 T55 17:02 06/16   M2 7803

———— MDR HOT / COLD ————

  9OZPRIME MED.
    RARE
  DOVESOLE
  LOBSTFRY
  WHTEFISH SAUTEED
2 RICE
  BKPOTATO
  EXTVEGIE
L1 02 T55 17:04 06/16   M2 7807

Courtesy of The University Club, Michigan State University, East Lansing, Michigan

Printer Controllers

One of the most important peripheral devices in an ECR/POS system with remote work station devices is the **printer controller**, also called a network controller. A printer controller coordinates communications between cashier or precheck terminals and work station printers or kitchen monitors, while ensuring that servers need only enter their orders once. Exhibit 4 diagrams the function of a printer controller.

Kitchen Monitor and Cursor Control Keypad.

Exhibit 4   The Function of a Printer Controller

Cashier Terminal		Hot Food Printer or Display
Precheck Terminal		
Precheck Terminal	Printer Controller	
Precheck Terminal		Cold Food Printer or Display
Cashier Terminal		

When several precheck terminals send data to the same work station printer or kitchen monitor simultaneously, the printer controller processes data from one of the terminals immediately and temporarily stores (buffers) other communications until the printer becomes available. As the remote printer or kitchen monitor outputs data sent from one terminal, the printer controller sends the next set of data, and so on, until all orders are printed. Since remote work station units are typically very fast, the time delay between order entry and printout is minimal— even for those orders temporarily held by the printer controller.

Without a printer controller, a remote work station unit would be able to receive and print only one set of data at a time. When the remote printer is receiving data from one terminal, servers entering orders at other precheck terminals would receive a response like a telephone busy signal. Orders would have to be re-input, since the original orders were not received or stored anywhere in the ECR/POS system.

Computer-Based Guest Checks

Many automated systems use pre-printed, serially numbered guest checks like those used in manual guest check systems. Before entering an order, the server "opens" the guest check within the system by inputting his or her identification number and the guest check's serial number. Once the system has recognized the server and opened the guest check, orders are entered and relayed to remote printers at production areas. The same items (with their selling prices) are printed on the server's guest check.

Once a guest check has been opened, it becomes part of the system's **open check file**. For each opened guest check, this file may contain the following data:

- Terminal number where the guest check was opened
- Guest check serial number
- Server identification number
- Time guest check was opened
- Menu items ordered
- Prices of menu items ordered
- Applicable tax
- Total amount due

A server adds orders to the guest check at the precheck terminal by first inputting the guest check's serial number and then entering the additional items.

There are many variations of this automated prechecking system. As described earlier in this chapter, some systems use guest checks with bar codes corresponding to the pre-printed serial numbers. This eliminates the need for servers to input the guest check's serial number when opening a guest check or when adding items to guest checks already in use. When the guest check is placed in the guest check printer, the system reads the bar code and immediately accesses the appropriate file.

Newer systems eliminate the traditional guest check altogether. These systems maintain only an electronic file for each open guest check. A narrow, receipt-like guest check can be printed at any time during service, but is usually not printed until after the meal when the server presents it to the guest for settlement. Since no paper forms are used, the table number often is the tracking identifier for the order. With some systems, seat numbers are used for tracking multiple checks per table. When presenting these checks to guests for settlement, the receipt-like guest checks can be inserted in high-quality paper, vinyl, or leather presentation jackets.

Some systems are experimenting with a receipt-like guest check that also serves as a credit card voucher. This could reduce the time it takes servers to settle guest checks. Instead of presenting the guest check, collecting the guest's credit card, printing a credit card voucher, transferring information from the guest check to the voucher, and then presenting the voucher to the guest to sign, servers are able to present the guest check and the credit card voucher simultaneously.

Electronic cash registers and point-of-sale technology simplify guest check control functions and eliminate the need for many time-consuming manual audit procedures. Automated prechecking functions eliminate mistakes servers make in pricing items on guest checks or in calculating totals. When items must be voided, a supervisor (with a special identification number) accesses the system and deletes the items. Generally, automated systems produce a report which lists all guest checks with voided or returned items, the servers responsible, and the supervisors who voided the items. It is important for automated systems to distinguish voided from returned items because returned items should be included in inventory usage reports while voided items should not. If an item is voided after it has been prepared, the item would be classified as "returned."

At any point, managers and supervisors can access the system and monitor the status of any guest check. This check-tracking capability can help identify potential walkouts, reduce server fraud, and tighten guest check and sales income control.

The status of a guest check changes from open to closed when payment is received from the guest and it is recorded in the system. Most automated systems produce an **outstanding checks report** that lists all guest checks (by server) that have not been settled. These reports may list the guest check number, server identification number, time at which the guest check was opened, number of guests, table number, and guest check total. This makes it easier for managers to determine responsibility for unsettled guest checks. Exhibit 5 presents a sample server check-out report. Note that the report lists time in, time out, hours worked, number of guests served, tables attended, net sales, and tip information.

ECR/POS Software

The hardware of any computer system does nothing by itself. There must be a set of software programs directing the system in what to do, how to do it, and when to do it. ECR/POS software programs not only direct internal system operations, they also maintain files and produce reports for management. Files which may be stored and maintained by sophisticated ECR/POS systems include:

Exhibit 5   Sample Server Check-Out Report

MRS
DEMONSTRATION

Server: **ANNA**

Date: **11/20**

In Time	Out Time	Total
12:36	15:23	02:47
15:25	15:26	00:01

Total Hours Worked: **02:48**

	Persons	Tables	Net	Tips
Lunch:	19	6	290.55	39.71
Dinner:	0	0	0.00	0.00
Total:	19	6	290.55	39.71

Tips on Credit Cards:	39.71
Credit Card Surcharge:	1.99
Net Total Tips:	37.72
Balance Due:	**37.72**

Source: Genlor Systems, Inc., Northport, New York.

- Menu item file
- Labor master file
- Inventory file

Data maintained by these files (and others) can be accessed by ECR/POS terminals and formatted reports can be printed out on narrow register tape. The following sections briefly examine the types of data stored by major ECR/POS files and the kind of information contained in some of the more significant reports that can be produced.

Menu Item File

A **menu item file** usually contains data for all menu items sold in the restaurant. Records within this file may contain the following data:

- Identification number
- Descriptor

- Price
- Tax
- Applicable modifier keys
- Amount totals for inventory reporting
- Printer routing code

This file is generally used to monitor menu keyboard operations. Management can control information about current menu items for various meal periods. Reports can be produced for each meal period identifying menu item descriptor, price, and applicable tax table. When menu items, prices, or tax tables need to be changed, the menu item file is accessed and appropriate changes are entered according to procedures indicated in the user's manual provided by the system's vendor.

Labor Master File

The **labor master file** contains one record for each employee and typically maintains the following data:

- Employee name
- Employee number
- Social security number
- Authorized job codes and corresponding hourly wage rates

This file may also contain data required to produce labor reports for management. Each record in the labor master file may accumulate:

- Hours worked
- Total hourly wages
- Declared wages
- Tips
- Credits for employee meals
- Number of guests served (if appropriate)
- Gross sales

Many ECR/POS systems are unable to compute net pay figures because of restricted processing ability and limited internal memory capacity. Data accumulated by the labor master file can be accessed to produce a number of reports, such as a labor master report and daily, weekly, and period labor reports.

A **labor master report** contains general data maintained by the labor master file. This report is commonly used to verify an employee's hourly rate(s), job code(s), or social security number.

A **daily labor report** typically lists the names, employee numbers, hours worked, wages earned, and wages declared for each employee on a given workday. A **weekly labor report** contains similar information and may be used to determine which employees are approaching overtime pay rates. A **period labor report**

Exhibit 6   Sample Daily Labor Report

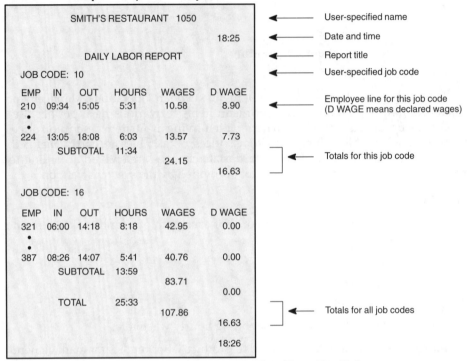

Source: International Business Machines Corporation, White Plains, New York.

generally lists hour and wage information for each employee who worked during the period specified by management. Exhibit 6 illustrates a sample daily labor report.

Data stored in the labor master file may also be used to produce daily, weekly, and period employee meals reports which show amounts for meals provided to employees. Also, a weekly and period employee tips report may be printed showing the total tips reported by each employee.

Inventory File

The **inventory file** maintained by an ECR/POS system may not meet all the needs of some restaurant properties. Many registers are incapable of tracking the same item as it passes through the control points of receiving, storing/issuing, and production. Inventory data must be specific to each of these control points because purchase units (e.g., case, drum, etc.) commonly differ from storeroom inventory units (e.g., #10 can, gallon, etc.), which, in turn, differ from standard recipe units (e.g., ounce, cup, etc.). Many systems are not able to support the number of conversion tables necessary to track menu items through ingredient purchase, storage, and use (standard recipe).

Since restaurant operators do not purchase their inventory ingredients on a pre-portioned basis, they very often encounter significant problems when trying to

Exhibit 7   Sample Sales and Payment Summary Report

SALES			LUNCH	DINNER	BRUNCH	TOTAL
1 NUMBER OF CUSTOMERS			110	89	.	199
2 TAXABLE FOOD TOTAL			2455.50	2093.00	.	4558.50
3 TAXABLE BEVERAGES TOTAL			1371.00	1382.75	.	2753.75
TOTAL FOOD & BEVERAGE (before tax)			3826.50	3475.75	.	7302.25
SALES TAX			315.69	286.75	.	602.44
4 NONTAXABLE FOOD TOTAL			.	.	.	.
5 NONTAXABLE BEVERAGE TOTAL			.	.	.	.
TOTAL			4142.19	3762.50	.	7904.69
% OF SALES			52.40	47.60	.	

PAYMENTS	#CKS	TAXABLE	NONTAX.	TAX	TIPS	GROSS	CARD FEE	NET
6 CASH	3	482.50	.	39.81	.	522.31	.	482.50
7 CHECK	3	318.25	.	26.26	.	344.51	.	318.25
8 HOUSE CH.	3	1017.00	.	83.90	57.00	1157.90	.	1017.00
9 AMEX	40	5484.50	.	452.47	298.50	6235.47	222.64	5261.86
10 DC	0	.	.	.	.	.	.	.
11 VISA/MC	0	.	.	.	.	.	.	.
CARD SUBTOT	40	5484.50	.	452.47	298.50	6235.47	222.64	5261.86
TOTAL	49	7302.25		602.44	355.50	8260.49	222.64	7079.61

Source: Integrated Restaurant Software, Fort Lee, New Jersey.

implement a register-based inventory control system. In addition, the initial creation of an ingredient file and the subsequent file updates (daily, weekly, monthly, etc.) can be an overwhelming task for some food service operations. For example, a restaurant typically carries an average of 400 menu items and an inventory of 1,500 ingredients and monitors at least 18 high-cost inventory items on a perpetual basis. ECR/POS systems may not be able to support the files necessary for effective register-based inventory control.

Consolidated Reports

ECR/POS systems may access data contained in several files to produce consolidated reports for use by management. Such reports typically include daily revenue reports, sales analysis reports, summary **activity reports**, and productivity reports.

A **sales and payment summary report** provides managers with a complete statement of daily or monthly sales (by shift or broken down by food and beverage categories). The report also summarizes settlement methods. Exhibit 7 illustrates a sample sales and payment summary report.

A **sales by time of day report** enables management to measure the sales performance of individual menu items by department or product category within certain time intervals. Time intervals may vary in relation to the type of food service operation. Quick service restaurants may desire **sales analysis reports** segmented by 15 minute intervals, table service restaurants by the hour, and institutional food service operations by meal period. This report allows management to track individual item

Exhibit 8   Sample Sales by Time of Day Report

Date	8–30										
Time	5:31 A.M.			SALES BY TIME OF DAY							
			CURRENT				TO DATE				
	Stn	Sales	Trans	Cvrs	Avg $/Trns	Avg $/Cvr	Sales	Trans	Cvrs	Avg $/Trns	Avg $/Cvr
08:01– 09:00	01–	141.85	9	25	15.76	5.67	141.85	9	25	15.76	5.67
	02–	372.75	13	43	28.67	8.67	372.75	13	43	28.67	8.67
	–	514.60	22	68	23.39	7.57	514.60	22	68	23.39	7.57
09:01 – 10:00	01–	12.30	2	5	6.15	2.46	12.30	2	5	6.15	2.46
	–	12.30	2	5	6.15	2.46	242.40	18	36	13.47	6.73
10:01 – 11:00	01–	183.85	10	34	18.39	5.41	183.85	10	34	18.39	5.41
	02–	464.90	13	74	35.76	6.28	1,173.80	50	196	23.48	5.99
	–	648.75	23	108	28.21	6.01	1,357.65	60	230	22.63	5.90
11:01 – 12:00	01–	22.75	1	2	22.75	11.38	22.75	1	2	22.75	11.38
	02–	24.55	2	4	12.28	6.14	178.40	12	35	14.87	5.10
	–	47.30	3	6	15.77	7.88	201.15	13	37	15.47	5.44
12:01 – 13:00	01–	54.20	3	6	18.07	9.03	54.20	3	6	18.07	9.03
	02–	45.20	4	8	11.30	5.65	45.20	4	8	11.30	5.65
	–	99.40	7	14	14.20	7.10	99.40	7	14	14.20	7.10
13:01 – 14:00	01–	31.15	2	8	15.58	3.89	31.15	2	8	15.58	3.89
	02–	38.90	2	4	19.45	9.73	38.90	2	4	19.45	9.73
	–	70.05	4	12	17.51	5.84	70.05	4	12	17.51	5.84
Total	–	1,392.40	61	213	22.83	6.54	2,485.25	124	397	20.04	6.26

Source: American Business Computers, Akron, Ohio.

sales, analyze product acceptance, and monitor advertising and sales promotional efforts. A sample sales by time of day report is shown in Exhibit 8.

Exhibit 9 presents a sample **daily transactions report** that provides an in-depth analysis of sales transactions by individual server. **Productivity reports** typically detail sales activity for all assigned server sales records. Daily productivity reports may be generated for each server and cashier in terms of guest count, total sales, and average sales. In addition, a weekly productivity report may be generated, showing average sales per guest for each server.

Automation Advances

The importance of practical, easy-to-use, fast, and reliable input devices has prompted the development of touch-screen terminals, bar code terminals, and

Exhibit 9 Sample Daily Transactions Report

Date	8–30												
Time	5:31 A.M.				DAILY TRANSACTIONS								

Guest Check	Tabl/ Covrs	Employee	ID	Time In	Time Out	Elapsed Time	Food	Bar	Wine	Guest Total	Tax	Tip	Settlement Method	Settlement Amount
11378	2–2	Jones	4	8:23	9:00	0:37	13.75	0.00	3.50	17.25	0.87	2.00	CASH	20.12
11379	2–1	Jones	4	8:25	9:00	0:35	2.35	0.00	0.00	2.35	0.12	0.00	COMP 1 0004	2.47
11380	3–3	Jones	4	8:32	9:01	0:29	13.15	0.00	5.50	18.65	0.93	0.00	CASH COMP 2 0033	9.58 10.00
11381	4–4	Jones	4	8:34	9:16	0:42	9.05	0.00	0.00	9.05	0.47	0.00	MC	9.52
11382	3–2	Jones	4	8:40	9:18	0:38	6.20	0.00	5.50	11.70	0.60	0.00	Cancelled	
11383	3–2	Jones	4	8:41	9:19	0:38	4.35	0.00	0.00	4.35	0.22	0.00	COMP 1 0004	4.57
11384	4–4	Jones	4	8:43	10:16	1:33	33.80	11.00	0.00	44.80	2.25	0.00	AMEXPRESS	47.05
11385	4–2	Jones	4	8:46	10:17	1:31	0.00	9.75	0.00	9.75	0.49	0.00	VISA	10.24
11386	4–5	Jones	4	8:51	10:17	1:26	0.00	18.50	0.00	18.50	0.91	0.00	MC	19.41
11387	8–2	Jones	4	8:54	10:18	1:24	14.65	2.50	0.00	17.15	0.85	0.00	COMP 1 0004	18.00
11388	4–3	Jones	4	9:23	10:17	0:54	4.70	3.00	0.00	7.70	0.39	1.00	CASH	9.09
11389	2–2	Jones	4	9:34	10:16	0:42	4.60	0.00	0.00	4.60	0.24	0.00	CASH	4.84
11398	3–2	Jones	4	12:09	12:10	0:01	11.35	0.00	0.00	11.35	0.57	0.00	CASH	11.92
11399	3–2	Jones	4	12:20	12:21	0:01	10.25	2.00	0.00	12.25	0.61	0.00	CASH	12.86
21615	3–2	Jones	4	11:39	11:41	0:02	13.15	0.00	0.00	13.15	0.65	0.00	CASH	13.80
21616	1–2	Jones	4	11:40	11:41	0:01	7.90	0.00	3.50	11.40	0.58	0.00	CASH	11.98
	Total cancelled			11.70										
	**** Totals						143.05	46.75	12.50	202.30	10.15	3.00		215.45

Source: American Business Computers, Akron, Ohio.

wireless server terminals. Advances in automation have also simplified settlement procedures with magnetic strip readers that reduce the time it takes to obtain credit card authorizations. The following sections discuss each of these advances in detail.

Touch-Screen Technology

There is perhaps no area of ECR/POS hardware that has received more research and development than touch-screen technology. Touch-screen terminals are replacing the traditional keyboard as order-entry devices for many POS systems. Touch-screen terminals have been developed for fast food operations that allow customers to place their orders without interacting with counter employees.

A **touch-screen terminal** contains a unique adaptation of a cathode ray tube (CRT) screen and a special microprocessor to control it. The self-contained microprocessor displays data on areas of the screen that are sensitive to touch. Touching one of the sensitized areas produces an electronic charge which is translated into digital signals telling what area was touched for transmission to the microprocessor. This signal also instructs the microprocessor to display the next screen.

Terminal design varies from vendor to vendor. Flat touch-screen terminals are available that require significantly less space than the traditional POS terminals that they replace. Flat screens measure only three and one-half inches thick and can be mounted from walls, ceilings, counters, or shelving units. The design offers restaurants flexibility in determining where to locate the terminals.

Touch-Screens and POS Systems. Touch-sensitive screens simplify data entry and may be used in place of traditional CRT screens and POS keyboards. The previous discussion of POS system keyboards pointed out that price look-up keys (PLUs) must often be used to enter orders because many systems maintain a limited number of preset keys. Using PLUs generally requires additional order-entry procedures related to product code numbers assigned to menu items. In some cases, servers memorize these codes, or management tapes a list of the code numbers at keyboard terminals. Most touch-screen terminals eliminate the need for PLUs altogether, decreasing the time necessary to enter orders into the system.

Touch-screen terminals are also interactive. That is, the system provides on-screen prompts guiding servers through order-entry or settlement procedures. For example, after a server enters an order for a menu item that needs preparation instructions (such as a New York strip steak), the screen shifts to display the appropriate modifiers (rare, medium rare, medium, medium well done, well done). This eliminates the possibility of servers sending incomplete orders to production areas. The interactive nature of these systems decreases the time it takes to train new employees.

Touch-screen terminals may also be equipped with magnetic strip reader devices that allow servers and managers to use bar-coded company identification cards to sign in and out of the system. One type of system ensures that immediately after employees sign into the system, a message screen is displayed. This message screen enables management to deliver different messages to different categories of employees, or to individual employees as well. For example, employees with job codes corresponding to food servers might receive messages about daily specials and prices. Or an individual employee might receive a message from a supervisor about work schedule changes. Since employees must touch the message screen to complete sign-in procedures, management is assured that employees have received their messages.

Touch-Screens and Customer Order-Entry Systems. Some fast food operations are installing counter-top recessed touch-screen terminals that customers can use to place their orders without interacting with counter employees. This new self-service option helps to reduce labor costs and speed up service. Some systems have color graphic components that induce customers to use the terminals. For example, icons (graphic images) can be used: caricature drawings representing chicken, fish, french fries, burgers, etc; and company logos representing specific soft drink choices. Condiments can also be creatively displayed—with a lasso indicating ranch salad dressing, the Eiffel Tower indicating french salad dressing, and so on.

One system enables customers to place orders by following six simple steps. The customer activates the terminal by pressing a start feature on the screen. The screen then shifts to a display asking the customer to indicate whether the order will be take-out or whether the customer will dine on premises. Next, the screen shifts to display menu options. To order, the customer simply touches the desired item on the screen. As items are touched, a "video receipt" appears on the right side of the screen that keeps a running total during the ordering process. When the order is complete, the customer touches a "finished" box on the screen. At this point, a suggestive selling display appears asking the customer if he or she would

Exhibit 10 Sample Bar-Coded Menu

COLD APPETIZERS	HOT APPETIZERS	PASTA	PASTA SIDES	MODIFIERS
ANTIPASTO MISTO	1/2 HOT ANTIPASTO	ANGEL HAIR PRIMAVERA	ANGEL HAIR PRIMAVERA	*DISCOUNT AMOUNT
ANTIPASTO CASALINGO	ARTICHOKE CASINO	BAKED ZITI	BAKED ZITI	*WITH
CLAM COCKTAIL	CALAMARI FRITTI	CANNELLONI	CANNELLONI	*NO
CRAB MEAT COCKTAIL	CLAMS OREGANATE	FETT FILETTO DI POM	FETT FILETTO DI POM	*EASY ON
INSALATA MARINA	HOT ANTIPASTO	FETT ROMANISSIMO	FETT ROMANISSIMO	*EXTRA
H.C SHRIMP & LOBSTER	MOZZ IN CARROZZA	FETTUCINE ALFREDO	FETTUCINE ALFREDO	*ON SIDE
MOZZ, PROSC, & TOM	SNAILS BOURGUIGNONE	GNOCCHI	GNOCCHI	*INSTEAD OF
OYSTER COCKTAIL	SNAILS FRA DIAVOLO	LASAGNA	LASAGNA	*BAKED
PEPPERS & ANCHOVIES	SPIEDINI ALLA ROM	LINGUINE - GAR & OIL	LINGUINE - GAR & OIL	*STEAMED
PROSCIUTTO & MELON	STUFFED MUSHROOMS	LINGUINE - RED CLAM	LINGUINE - RED CLAM	*BOILED
SCUNGILLI SALAD	ZUPPA DI CLAMS	LINGUINE - WH CLAM	LINGUINE - WH CLAM	*HOT
SHRIMP & LOBSTER	ZUPPA DI MUSSELS	MANICOTTI	MANICOTTI	*COLD
SHRIMP COCKTAIL	*TODAY'S APPETIZER	RAVIOLI	RAVIOLI	*SPICY
SUN D.TOM.MOZZ.& B.P	**SALADS**	SPAGH.BOLOGNESE	SPAGH.BOLOGNESE	*NOT SPICY
*TODAY'S APPETIZER	*NO	SPAGH.MARINARA	SPAGH.MARINARA	*BLACK & BLUE
CHICKEN	*EXTRA	SPAGH.PESTO	SPAGH.PESTO	*PINK
CHICKEN CACCIATORE	*DRESSING	SPAGH.PUTANESCA	SPAGH.PUTANESCA	*VERY RARE
CHICKEN CHAMPAGNE	*ON SIDE	SPAGH.TOMATO SAUCE	SPAGH.TOMATO SAUCE	*RARE
CHICKEN FRANCESE	ROQUEFORT	ZITI ARRABIATI	ZITI ARRABIATI	*MED RARE
CHICKEN OREGANATA	ARUGULA & ORANGE	ALFREDO	ALFREDO	*MEDIUM
CHICKEN PARMIGIANA	BROCCOLI SALAD	ARRABIATI	ARRABIATI	*MED WELL
CHICKEN PARM W/SPAG	CAESAR SALAD	BOLOGNESE	BOLOGNESE	*WELL
CHICKEN PICCATA	ENDIVE SALAD	FILLETTO DI POMODORO	FILLETTO DI POMODORO	*VERY WELL
CHICKEN PORTAFOGLIO	HEARTS OF PALM	GARLIC & OIL	GARLIC & OIL	*DRY
CHICKEN SCARPARIELLO	HOUSE SALAD	MARINARA	MARINARA	*SOFT
CHICKEN ZINGARA	SPINACH SALAD	PESTO	PESTO	*ANCHOVIES
ROASTED BABY CHICKEN	TOMATOES & ONION	PRIMAVERA	PRIMAVERA	*ARTICHOKES
BEEF	**VEAL**	PUTANESCA	PUTANESCA	*BALSAMIC VINEGAR
FILET MIGNON	VEAL CHAMPAGNE	RED CLAM SAUCE	RED CLAM SAUCE	*BASIL
MEDALIONS OF BEEF	VEAL CHOP MILANESE	ROMANISSIMO	ROMANISSIMO	*BEL PAESE
NEW YORK SIRLOIN	VEAL FRANCESE	TOMATO SAUCE	TOMATO SAUCE	*BREAD CRUMBS
STEAK ARRABBIATA	VEAL MARSALA	WHITE CLAM SAUCE	WHITE CLAM SAUCE	*BUTTER
STEAK PIZZAIOLA	VEAL PARMIGIANA	*TODAY'S PASTA	*TODAY'S PASTA	*CHEESE
FISH	VEAL PARM W/SPAG	*ANGEL HAIR	*ANGEL HAIR	
BROILED FILET SOLE	VEAL PICCATA	*FARFALLE	*FARFALLE	
CALAMARI MARINARA	VEAL PIZZAIOLA	*FETTUCINE	*FETTUCINE	
FILET OF SOLE	VEAL ROLLATINI	*GNOCCHI	*GNOCCHI	
FILET SOLE MEUNIER	VEAL SALTIMBOCCA	*LINGUINE	*LINGUINE	Copyright January 1989
FRIED CALAMARI	VEAL VALDAOSTANA	*PENNE	*PENNE	Standard Commercial Systems
LOBSTER TAILS ROM		*RIGATONI	*RIGATONI	Ridgewood, NJ 07450
				201-447-5350 * 212-505-9416

Source: Standard Commercial Systems, Ridgewood, New Jersey.

like soft drinks or desserts (if not ordered). The final screen displays the total amount due.

Bar Code Terminals

Bar code terminals also simplify data entry and may be used in place of traditional keyboards or touch-screen terminals. With this system, servers use hand-held, pen-like bar code readers to enter orders at service station terminals from a laminated bar-coded menu. Exhibit 10 presents a sample bar coded menu.

Orders can be entered quickly at bar code terminals because no keystrokes are involved. Also, servers do not have to keep switching from one screen to another as with touch-screen terminals. In addition, server training time can be reduced because all orders are entered from one bar-coded menu.

Wireless Terminals

Wireless order-entry terminals are revolutionizing ECR/POS technology. When these terminals are small enough to hold in one's hand, they are called **hand-held terminals** (HHTs). When they are as large as the size of a normal terminal keyboard, they are called portable server terminals. These devices perform most of the functions of a precheck terminal. Wireless technology can be a major advantage for

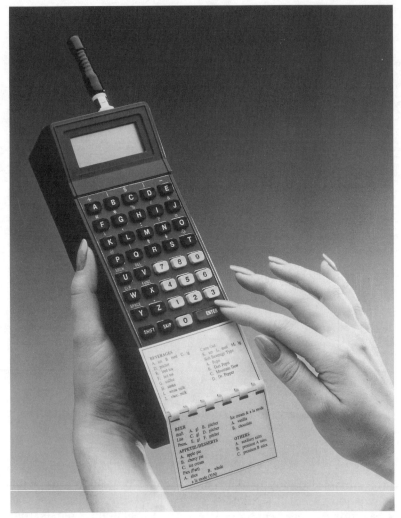

Hand-Held Server Terminal. (Courtesy of Norand Corporation, Cedar Rapids, Iowa)

large establishments with drive-through facilities, long distances between service stations, outdoor dining areas, or very busy lounges where it is difficult to reach a precheck terminal. In any establishment, service may be quicker because servers do not have to wait to use a precheck terminal during peak business periods and orders can be entered at tableside.

Two-way communications not only allow a server to include special instructions, such as "no salt" or "medium rare" as part of an order, but also can immediately alert a server if an item is out of stock. Typically, when an order is ready for pick-up, the server receives a signal on the hand-held unit. In some cases, appetizers and drinks may be ready just seconds after a server has finished entering the orders and left the table.

Since all items must be entered through the server's hand-held unit, the frequent problem of coffee or desserts inadvertently left off guest checks can be eliminated. Some units enable managers to monitor service through their own hand-held devices.

Exhibit 11 diagrams one type of hardware configuration for hand-held server terminals. The hand-held units have low-frequency FM radio transmitters and receivers. As orders are entered at the guest's table, analog signals are sent to **antenna units** located within the dining area. These antenna units relay the analog signals to a **radio base station** where a modem converts the analog signals into digital signals which are cabled to the restaurant computer system processing unit. From the restaurant computer processing unit, signals are relayed to remote work station printers or kitchen monitors.

Up to four antenna units may be connected to one radio base station. Before installation, a site survey should be conducted to determine the optimum locations for each antenna unit. The amount and location of metal structures in a restaurant are important installation concerns. Generally, each antenna unit requires separate cabling to the radio base station.

A charged battery pack powers each hand-held server terminal. Fully charged, these battery packs may last for eight hours. It is recommended that two fully charged battery packs be available for each hand-held unit.

Magnetic Strip Readers

A **magnetic strip reader** is an optional input device that connects to a register. Magnetic strip readers do not replace keyboards, touch-screen devices, or bar code terminals. Instead, they extend their capabilities. Magnetic strip readers are capable of collecting data stored on a magnetized film strip typically located on the back of a credit card or house account card. As explained earlier, terminals equipped with magnetic strip readers can be used by employees with plastic, bar-coded identification cards to sign into the system. Also, managers can use specially encoded cards to access ongoing transactions and other operational data.

With magnetic strip readers, credit card and house account transactions can be handled directly within an ECR/POS system. The connection of a magnetic strip reader to a cashier terminal allows rapid data entry and efficient settlement processing.

Power Platforms. Processing credit card transactions is simplified when a **power platform** is used to consolidate electronic communications between a hospitality establishment and a credit card authorization center. An ECR/POS power platform connects all ECR/POS terminals to a single processor for transaction settlement. This eliminates the need for individual telephone lines at each ECR/POS cashier terminal. Power platforms can capture credit card authorizations in three seconds or less. This swift data retrieval helps reduce the time, cost, and risk associated with credit card transactions.

Exhibit 11 Hardware Configuration for Hand-Held Server Terminals

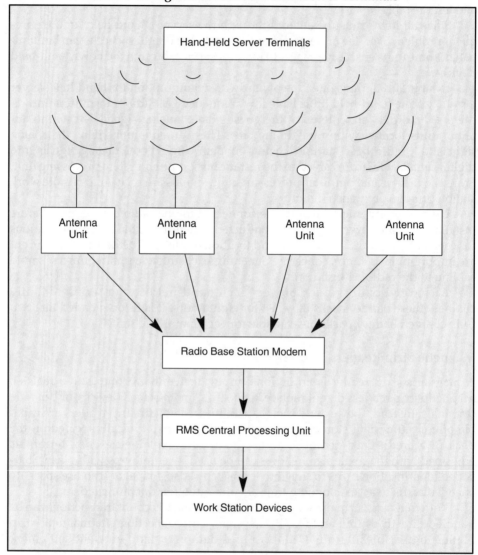

Smart Cards. Smart cards are made of plastic and are about the same size as credit cards. Microchips embedded in smart cards store information that can be accessed by a specially designed card reader. Smart cards can store information in several files that are accessed for different functions. For example, a smart card could store a person's vital health statistics, dietary restrictions, credit card number, and bank balance. The security of information stored in smart cards is controlled because a personal identification number (PIN) must be used to access files.

Since smart cards contain the necessary information for authorizing credit purchases, a specially designed card reader secures credit authorizations quickly. There is no waiting for telephone lines to clear as with the use of magnetic strip readers and power platforms.

Debit Cards. Debit cards differ from credit cards in that the cardholder must deposit money in order to give the card value. The cardholder deposits money in advance of purchases through a debit card center or an electronic debit posting machine. As purchases are made, the balance on the debit card falls. For example, a cardholder who has deposited $300 to a debit card account has a value of $300 encoded on the magnetic strip section of the plastic debit card. As the cardholder makes purchases, the value of the debit card decreases accordingly. To settle the transaction, the establishment bills the debit service center identified through information recorded in the magnetic strip section of the user's card.

One variation of a debit card system is the use of automatic teller machine (ATM) cards to settle guest checks. Restaurants that accept ATM card payment have specially designed equipment at cashier stations. After the amount of payment is entered into an electronic cash register, a display on the back of the register asks the guest to swipe the ATM card through a card reader. The guest then enters his or her personal identification number (PIN) on a numeric key pad that is out of the cashier's sight. Usually within eight seconds, cash is transferred from the guest's checking account to the restaurant's bank account.

Automated Beverage Control Systems

Automated beverage systems reduce many of the time-consuming management tasks associated with controlling beverage operations. While automated beverage systems vary, most systems can dispense drinks according to the operation's standard drink recipes and count the number of drinks poured.

Automated beverage systems can be programmed to dispense both alcoholic and non-alcoholic drinks with different portion sizes. They can also generate expected sales information based on different pricing periods as defined by management. With many systems the station at which drinks are prepared can be connected to a guest check printer that records every sale as drinks are dispensed. As a control technique, some systems require that a guest check be inserted into the printer before a drink can be dispensed. Most equipment can, and should, be connected to the bar cash register to automatically record all sales generated through automated equipment.

With one type of automated beverage system, liquor is stored at the bar. Price-coded pourers (special nozzles) are inserted into each bottle. These pourers cannot dispense liquor without a special activator ring. The bartender slips the neck of a liquor bottle (with the price-coded pourer already inserted) into the ring and prepares the drink with a conventional hand-pouring motion. A cord connects the activator ring to a master control panel which records the number of drinks poured at each price level. The master control panel may be connected to a point-of-sale system which records the sale. Some master control panels are equipped with printers and

Exhibit 12   Keyboard-Operated Automated Beverage System

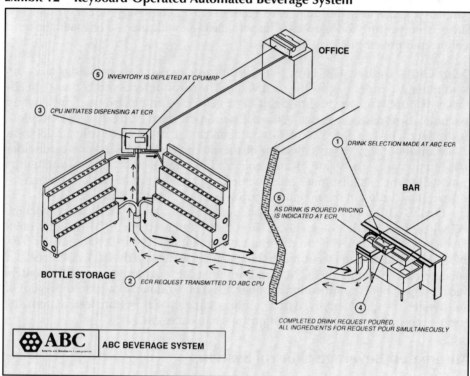

Source: American Business Computers, Akron, Ohio.

can produce sales reports for each station. Reports indicate the number of drinks poured at different price levels and the total expected income from each station.

With another type of automated beverage system, liquor is stored in racks in a locked storage room. The bartender prepares a drink by pushing the appropriate key on a keyboard. The liquor and necessary mixes travel to a dispensing device at the bar through separate plastic tubing. The system pours the drink when the bartender holds the glass (with ice) under the dispensing device. The drink is then garnished and served to the guest. Exhibit 12 diagrams the layout of one type of keyboard-operated automated beverage control system.

Keyboard-operated automated beverage control systems may employ different types of sensing devices which increase operational controls and maintain data integrity within the system. Three common sensing devices are glass sensors, guest check sensors, and empty bottle sensors. A **glass sensor** is an electronic mechanism located in a bar dispensing unit that will not permit liquid to flow from the dispensing unit unless there is a glass in place to catch the liquid below the dispensing head. **Guest check sensors** prevent the system from fulfilling beverage orders unless they are first recorded on a guest check. When a server places a beverage order whose ingredients are close to becoming out-of-stock, an **empty bottle sensor** relays a signal to the order-entry device.

Automated beverage control systems can enhance production and service capabilities while improving accounting and operational controls. Sophisticated systems are able to record data input through order-entry devices, transport beverage ingredients through a controlled delivery network, dispense ingredients for ordered items, and track important service and sales data that can be used to produce various reports for management. The following sections examine the basic components of an automated beverage control system: order-entry devices, delivery networks, and dispensing units.

Order-Entry Devices

In an automated beverage control system, the primary function of an order-entry device is to initiate activities involved with recording, producing, and pricing beverage items requested by guests. There are two basic order-entry devices: a group of preset buttons located on a dispensing unit, and keyboard units that function as precheck terminals.

A group of preset buttons on a dispensing unit is the most popular order-entry device. These devices may result in lower system costs because the dispensing unit serves as both an order taker and a delivery unit. However, since dispensing units may only support up to sixteen preset buttons, the number of beverage items under the control of the automated beverage system is limited.

Keyboard units function like precheck terminals; beverage dispensing is performed by a separate piece of hardware. Since they support a full range of keys (including preset keys, price look-up keys, and modifier keys), keyboard units place a large number of beverage items under the control of the automated system. Keyboard units are most effective when equipped with a guest check printer with automatic form number reader (AFNR) and automatic slip feed (ASF) capabilities.

Delivery Networks

An automated beverage control system relies on a **delivery network** to transport beverage item ingredients from storage areas to dispensing units. Exhibit 13 diagrams one kind of delivery network. The delivery network must be a closed system capable of regulating temperature and pressure conditions at various locations and stages of delivery. To maintain proper temperature conditions, the delivery network typically employs a cooling sub-system which controls such mechanisms as cold plates, cold boxes, and cold storage rooms.

Most systems are able to deliver beverage ingredients by controlling pressure sources such as gravity, compressed air, carbon dioxide, and nitrous oxide. Gravity and compressed air are used for delivering liquor, nitrogen or nitrous oxide for wine, compressed air for beer, compressed air for perishables, and a carbon dioxide regulator for post-mixes. A post-mix soft drink dispenser places syrup and carbonated water together at the dispenser instead of storing, transporting, and distributing the soft drink as a finished product.

The particular pressure source selected to transport a specific ingredient is a function of its effect on the taste and wholesomeness of the finished beverage item. For example, if carbon dioxide were attached to a wine dispenser, the wine would be carbonated and spoiled. Similarly, if compressed air were hooked up to a post-mix

Exhibit 13   Delivery Network of an Automated Beverage Control System

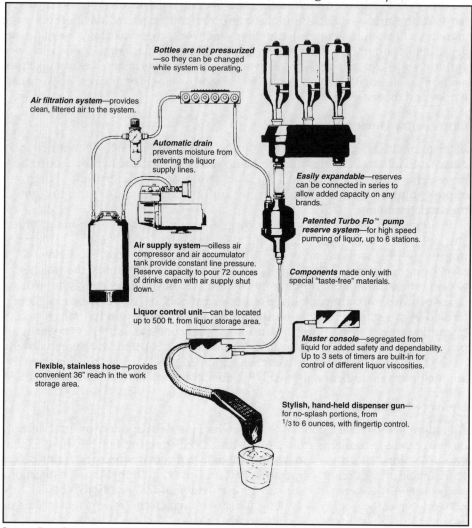

Bottles are not pressurized
—so they can be changed
while system is operating.

Air filtration system—provides
clean, filtered air to the system.

Automatic drain
prevents moisture from
entering the liquor
supply lines.

Easily expandable—reserves
can be connected in series to
allow added capacity on any
brands.

*Patented Turbo Flo™ pump
reserve system*—for high speed
pumping of liquor, up to 6 stations.

Air supply system—oilless air
compressor and air accumulator
tank provide constant line pressure.
Reserve capacity to pour 72 ounces
of drinks even with air supply shut
down.

Components made only with
special "taste-free" materials.

Liquor control unit—can be located
up to 500 ft. from liquor storage area.

Master console—segregated from
liquid for added safety and dependability.
Up to 3 sets of timers are built-in for
control of different liquor viscosities.

Flexible, stainless hose—provides
convenient 36" reach in the work
storage area.

Stylish, hand-held dispenser gun—
for no-splash portions, from
1/3 to 6 ounces, with fingertip control.

Source: Berg Company, A Division of DEC International, Inc., Madison, Wisconsin.

soft drink dispenser, the finished beverage item would not have any carbonation. Pressure sources not only affect the quality of finished beverage items, but may also affect the timing, flow of mixture, portion size, and desired foaming.

Almost any brand of liquor and accompanying liquor ingredient can be stored, transported, and dispensed by an automated beverage control system. Portion sizes of liquor can be controlled with remarkable accuracy. Typically, systems can be calibrated to maintain portion sizes ranging from one-half ounce to three and one-half ounces.

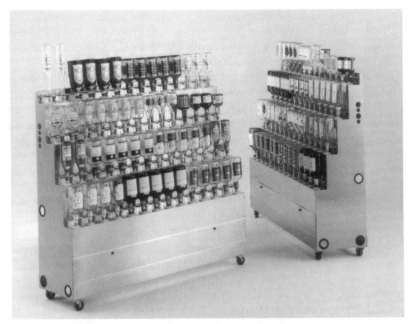

An Automated Beverage Control and Storage System. (Courtesy of American Business Computers, Akron, Ohio)

Dispensing Units

Once beverage item ingredients are removed from storage and transported by the delivery network to production areas, they are ready to be dispensed. Automated beverage control systems may be configured with a variety of dispensing units. Common dispensing units include:

- Touch-bar faucet
- Hose and gun
- Console faucet
- Mini-tower pedestal
- Bundled tower

A touch-bar faucet can be located under the bar, behind the bar, on top of an ice machine, or on a pedestal stand. These devices may not have the versatility, flexibility, or expandability of other dispensing units. Typically, touch-bar faucets are dedicated to only a single beverage type and are preset for one portion size output per push on the bar lever. A double shot of bourbon, therefore, may require the bartender to push twice on the bar lever.

The hose and gun device is a popular dispensing unit. Control buttons on the handle of the gun can be connected to liquors, carbonated beverages, water, and wine tanks. These dispensers can be installed anywhere along the bar and are frequently included as standard equipment on portable bars and at service bar locations. Pressing a control button produces a pre-measured flow of the desired beverage. The number of beverage items under the control of a hose and gun dispensing unit is limited to the number of control buttons the device supports. Some newer units offer the bartender up to 16 buttons.

Console faucet dispensing units are similar to touch-bar faucet devices in that they can be located in almost any part of the bar area. In addition, these units may be located up to 300 feet from beverage storage areas. Unlike touch-bar faucet devices, console faucet units can dispense various beverages in a number of portion sizes. Using buttons located above the faucet unit, a bartender can trigger up to four different portion sizes from the same faucet head. An optional feature of this kind of dispensing device is a double hose faucet unit which provides the capability to transport large quantities of liquids in short amounts of time.

The mini-tower pedestal dispensing unit combines the button selection technique of hose and gun devices with the portion size capabilities of console faucet units. In addition, the mini-tower concept offers increased control of bar operations. In order for a beverage to be dispensed, the mini-tower unit requires that a button be pressed and a glass sensing device requires that a glass be placed directly under the dispensing head. This automated dispensing unit has been popular for dispensing beverage items which need no additional ingredients before service, such as wine, beer, and call brand liquors. A mini-tower unit can also be located on a wall, ice machine, or pedestal base in the bar area.

The most sophisticated and flexible dispensing unit is the bundled tower unit, also referred to as a tube tower unit. The bundled tower unit is designed to dispense a variety of beverage items. Beverage orders must be entered on a separate piece of hardware, not on the tower unit. Bundled tower units may support in excess of 110 beverage products and contain a glass-sensing element. Each liquor has its own line to the tower unit, and a variety of pressurized systems can be used to enhance delivery from storage areas. While other units sequentially dispense beverage item ingredients, the bundled tower unit simultaneously dispenses all ingredients required for a specific beverage item; bar servers merely garnish the finished product. This dispensing unit can be located up to 300 feet from beverage storage areas.

Summary

This chapter focused on service-oriented applications of a computer-based restaurant management system. Important hardware components of an ECR/POS system were examined. These components included cashier terminals and precheck terminals, keyboards, display screens, printers, kitchen monitors, and printer controllers.

Keyboards were discussed in relation to design, menu boards, and types of keys. The chapter identified two types of ECR/POS terminal displays: operator display screens and customer display units. On-board printers were distinguished from remote printers, and several kinds of ECR/POS printing devices were described. These devices included guest check printers, receipt printers, work station printers, and journal printers. Kitchen monitors were also discussed as alternative remote work station devices.

This chapter also examined ECR/POS software and identified data contained by records within a menu item file, open check file, labor master file, and inventory files. Data maintained by these files and others can be accessed by ECR/POS terminals, and formatted reports can be printed on narrow register tape. Several important management reports were also described.

The chapter discussed advanced input devices, such as touch-screen terminals, bar code terminals, and wireless server terminals. In addition, magnetic strip reader devices were discussed in relation to rapid data entry and settlement processing.

The chapter closed by examining features of automated beverage control systems such as order-entry devices, delivery networks, and dispensing units.

Key Terms

ECR/POS System Hardware

automatic form number reader (AFNR)

automatic slip feed (ASF)

customer display unit

department code

descriptor

function keys

guest check printer

hard keys

journal printer

kitchen monitor

menu board

modifier keys

operator display screen

precheck terminal

preset key

price look-up (PLU) key

printer controller

receipt printer

register

settlement keys

soft keys

work station printer

ECR/POS System Software

activity report

daily labor report

daily transactions report

inventory file

labor master file

labor master report

menu item file

open check file

outstanding checks report

period labor report

productivity reports

sales analysis report

sales and payment summary report

sales by time of day report

weekly labor report

Automation Advances

antenna units

bar code terminal

debit card

hand-held terminal

magnetic strip reader

power platform

radio base station

smart card

touch-screen terminal

Automated Beverage Control Systems

delivery network   glass sensor
empty bottle sensor   guest check sensor

Discussion Questions ────────────────────────────

1. What are the necessary hardware components of an ECR/POS system? Describe the varieties of each component.

2. How do preset keys differ from PLU keys?

3. What functions do modifier and numeric keys perform?

4. How can a customer display unit on an ECR/POS register enhance management's internal control system?

5. What are two important features available for guest check printers?

6. How are guest checks opened and closed within an ECR/POS system?

7. What types of data are kept by the major files maintained by ECR/POS systems?

8. Why would managers prefer touch-screen, bar code, or wireless terminals to conventional keyboard order-entry devices?

9. What kinds of sensor devices do some types of automated beverage systems have?

10. What are the basic components of an automated beverage control system?

REVIEW QUIZ

When you feel you have covered all of the material in this chapter, answer these questions. Choose the *best* answer.

Matching

1. Overlays the surface of a keyboard and identifies the function performed by each key

2. Simplifies processing credit card transactions

3. Keys on an ECR/POS terminal that are dedicated to specific functions programmed by the manufacturer

4. The holder of this card must deposit money before using it to make purchases

5. An automated beverage control device that can be used when liquor is stored at the bar

6. ECR/POS software that records the amount of tips earned

7. An ECR/POS device used to enter orders, not to settle accounts

8. Keys on an ECR/POS terminal that can be programmed by users to meet specific needs

a. smart card

b. soft keys

c. menu board

d. open check file

e. labor master file

f. menu item file

g. power platform

h. touch-screen terminal

i. price-coded pourer

j. sales by time of day report

k. precheck terminal

l. hard keys

m. debit card

True (T) or False (F)

T F 9. Once activated, price look-up keys perform the same function as preset keys.

T F 10. Receipt printers are remote printing devices that produce a continuous detailed record of all transactions entered anywhere in the ECR/POS system.

T F 11. Empty bottle sensors of an automated beverage dispensing unit will not permit liquid to flow unless there is a glass positioned to catch the liquid from the dispensing head.

T F 12. In an automated beverage control system, compressed air is often used a a pressure source to transport post-mixes.

Alternate/Multiple Choice

13. A printer equipped with an automatic form number reader and an automatic slip feed capability would be:

    a. a work station printer.
    b. a guest check printer.

14. Which of the following ECR/POS terminal keys are used for such functions as clear, discount, void, and no-sale?

    a. preset keys
    b. price look-up keys
    c. modifier keys
    d. function keys

15. Which of the following files is accessed to close a guest check at the time of settlement?

    a. menu item file
    b. open guest check file
    c. labor master file
    d. inventory file

Chapter Outline

Recipe Management
    Ingredient File
    Standard Recipe File
    Menu Item File
Sales Analysis
Menu Management
    Data Input
    Menu Engineering Analysis
    Menu Item Evaluation
    Menu Item Classification
    Four-Box Analysis
    Menu Summary Sheet
    Menu Engineering Graph
Integrated Food Service Software
    Generic Software
    Precosting/Postcosting Applications
Management Reports from Automated
   Beverage Systems
Summary

Learning Objectives

1. Identify data maintained by an ingredient file of a recipe management application.

2. Explain the function of conversion tables within an ingredient file of a recipe management application.

3. Identify data maintained by a standard recipe file of a recipe management application.

4. Explain what is meant by chaining recipes.

5. Describe the contents of a daily sales report produced by a sales analysis application.

6. Explain the function of a menu engineering application.

7. Describe the advantages of integrated software capability in relation to precosting and postcosting functions.

8. Describe the reports that can be produced by sophisticated automated beverage control systems.

8

Food and Beverage Management Applications

RESTAURANT MANAGERS are constantly challenged to find new ways to increase sales while controlling and reducing costs. A major stumbling block for many managers is the lack of detailed, timely information about restaurant operations. Managers need timely information to measure current effectiveness and plan business strategies. The cost of collecting detailed information manually is often prohibitive. But, a computer-based restaurant management system can provide needed information while improving operations and enhancing management's control.

Food and beverage management applications process data related to back-of-the-house food service activities. This chapter examines common management applications such as:

- Recipe management

- Sales analysis

- Menu management

This chapter also discusses the importance of integrated food service software for precosting and postcosting software applications. In addition, reports generated by sophisticated automated beverage control systems are described in detail.

Recipe Management

The recipe management application maintains three of the most important files of an automated restaurant management system:

- Ingredient file

- Recipe file

- Menu item file

Most other food service applications have to access data contained within these files in order to effectively carry out their processing functions.

Ingredient File

An **ingredient file** contains important data on each purchased ingredient. Data may include:

Exhibit 1   Sample Ingredient Cost List

```
01 - CHICKEN DELICIOUS, INC.              INGREDIENT COST LIST                    SA1222
001 - CHICKEN DELICIOUS #1                                                        10.35.19

   EXPENSE      INGRED.   INGREDIENT      PURCHASE    PURCHASE   RECIPE    RECIPE    RECIPE
   CATAGORY     NUMBER    DESCRIPTION     UNIT        COST       YIELD     UNIT      COST

     01           1       Chicken         Case         51.00     32.00     Head      1.5937
     02           41      Shortening      50 lb        19.12     50.00     1b         .3824
     03           42      Milk & Egg Dip  24 lb/cs     28.51     24.00     1b        1.1879
     03           43      Fine Salt       80 lb         7.98     80.00     1b         .0097
     03           44      Seasoning       24 lb/10     61.38     24.00     Pkts      2.5575
     03           45      Flour           25 lb         3.89      1.00     Bag       3.8900
     04           2       Roll            80/cs         6.76    180.00     Each       .0375
     05           3       Potato Mix      6 #10 Cans   31.88     34.80     1b         .9160
     06           49      Cabbage         50 lb        11.75     50.00     1b         .2350
     06           50      Onions          1b            1.70     50.00     1b         .0340
     06           52      Mayonnaise      4 Gal.       17.81     40.00     Gal.       .4452
     06           53      Salad Oil       4 Gal.       16.43     32.00     Pint       .5134
     06           54      Vinegar         4 Gal.       11.92     32.00     Pint       .3725
     06           55      Sugar           25 lb         8.98     25.00     1b         .3592
     06           56      Salt            80 lb         4.90     80.00     1b         .0612
     07           6       Gravy Mix       24 lb/cs     16.07     24.00     1b         .6695
     07           65      Pepper          1 1b          4.41      1.00     1b        4.4100
     07           66      Margarine Qtrs  30 lb        11.22     30.00     1b         .3740
     09           12      Bucket          100 cs       20.72    100.00     Each       .2072
     09           15      Dinner Box      250 cs       13.32    250.00     Each       .0532
     09           16      Snack Box       300 cs       12.54    300.00     Each       .0418
     09           17      Plastic Forks   6000 cs      37.47   6000.00     Each       .0062
     09           19      Napkins         6000 cs      31.68   6000.00     Each       .0052
     09           28      3.5 oz cup      2000 cs      29.10   2000.00     Each       .0145
     09           29      3.5 oz lid      2000 cs      14.20   2000.00     Each       .0071
     09           69      Labels          1000 cs       2.71   1000.00     Each       .0027
     10           75      Milk            1/2 Pint       .19      1.00     Each       .1900
     15           21      Chicken Livers  Case         72.00     72.00     1/2 lb    1.0000
     15           22      Breading        25 lb        25.00    650.00     1 Cup      .0384
```

Source: Tridata, Inc., Atlanta, Georgia.

- Ingredient code number
- Ingredient description
- Purchase unit
- Purchase unit cost
- Issue unit
- Issue unit cost
- Recipe unit
- Recipe unit cost

Exhibit 1 shows a sample ingredient cost list produced from some of the data maintained by an ingredient file. This report shows the current cost of each ingredient, the unit of measure by which each ingredient is purchased, the number of recipe portions by unit, and the recipe cost of each portion. The report is useful for verifying the accuracy of entered data, detailing unit expenditures at current costs, and monitoring relationships among various product units (such as purchase, issue, and recipe units of the same ingredient).

Some ingredient files may specify more than one recipe unit. For example, the recipe unit for bread used for french toast is the slice; however, the recipe unit for bread used for stuffing is the ounce. In addition, most restaurant operations enter non-food items into an ingredient file to ensure that the ingredient file contains a complete list of all purchased products. This list becomes especially important if purchase orders are eventually generated for complete ingredient inventory.

Additional data contained by the ingredient file may provide the basis for effective inventory control. **Conversion tables** can be maintained by which to track ingredients (by unit and by cost) as they pass through purchasing/receiving, storing/issuing, and production/service control points. In order to efficiently maintain a perpetual inventory record, a food service system must be able to automatically convert purchase units into issue units and recipe units (also called usable units).

Assume that an ingredient is purchased, issued, and used in different units. When a shipment of the ingredient arrives, it should be easy to update the inventory record by simply entering the purchase unit received. The computer should then automatically convert this entry into issue units. Without this conversion capability, it would be necessary to manually calculate the number of units which will be stored, and increase the inventory record accordingly. Similarly, at the end of a meal period the system should update the inventory record by entering the standard recipe units which were used to prepare menu items. If the restaurant management system cannot convert issue units into recipe units, these calculations might also have to be performed manually and the inventory record decreased.

The system should also track the costs associated with these various ingredient units. Assume that bottle ketchup is purchased by the case (24 12-ounce bottles), issued from the storeroom to the kitchen by the bottle, and used in recipes by the ounce. Given information regarding the purchase unit's net weight and cost, the computer extends costs for issue and recipe unit(s). If the purchase unit's net weight is 18 pounds and its purchase price is $20.40, the system computes issue unit cost at $0.85 and recipe unit cost at slightly more than $0.07. To arrive at these costs through manual calculations an employee would first compute the price per ounce of the purchase unit. This is done by first converting 18 pounds to 288 ounces and then dividing $20.40 by 288 ounces to arrive at the recipe unit cost of $0.07 per ounce. Multiplying $0.07 by 12 ounces yields the issue unit cost of $0.85. Performing these calculations manually for every ingredient purchased can be a tedious, error-prone, time-consuming process. A food service management applications package can perform these calculations in fractions of a second. Care must be taken to ensure that the ingredient file contains the necessary data, conversions definitions, and algorithms.

Standard Recipe File

A standard recipe file must contain recipes for all menu items. Important data maintained by the standard recipe file may include:

- Recipe code number
- Recipe name
- Number of portions

Exhibit 2   Sample Recipe File Printout

Item Name: New York Steak Dinner			Code: 4			Category: Dnnr = 2	
No. Ingredient	Code	Price/Oz.	Meas.	Lrg. Units	Sml. Units	Extension
0 New York Strip	2	$0.2484	1	0.0 Pnds	8.0 Ozs.	$1.9872
1 Russet Potatoes	1	$0.0125	1	0.0 Pnds	9.0 Ozs.	$0.1125
2 Butter Chips	10	$0.1375	1	0.0 Pnds	2.0 Ozs.	$0.2750
3 Salad Batch	2R	$0.0247	1	0.0 Pnds	6.0 Ozs.	$0.1482
4	0	$0.0000	1	0.0 Pnds	0.0 Ozs.	$0.0000
5	0	$0.0000	1	0.0 Pnds	0.0 Ozs.	$0.0000
6	0	$0.0000	1	0.0 Pnds	0.0 Ozs.	$0.0000
7	0	$0.0000	1	0.0 Pnds	0.0 Ozs.	$0.0000
8	0	$0.0000	1	0.0 Pnds	0.0 Ozs.	$0.0000
9	0	$0.0000	1	0.0 Pnds	0.0 Ozs.	$0.0000

Selling Price: $8.95   Yield: 100%   Total Food Extension: $2.5228
Total Ozs. 25.0   Cost/Oz.: $0.1189   +   Misc. Food Cost: $0.0000
Base Recipe Code: 3 Dinner Set Up   + Cost of Base Recipe: $0.4500
Food Cst % = $2.9728 × 100/ $8.95   =33.2%   =   Total Food Cost: $2.9728
                         High Warning Flag Set At: 35%   Labor or Non-Food: $0.0000
Profit = Selling Price − Total Cost = $5.98   =   Total Cost: $2.9728

* ENTER <1> TO MODIFY FILE, <2> TO EXIT *

Source: Advanced Analytical Computer Systems, Tarzana, California.

- Portion size

- Recipe unit

- Recipe unit cost

- Menu selling price

- Food cost percentage

Exhibit 2 presents a sample printout of some of the data contained in a recipe file. Up to ten ingredients can be listed for this specific application. A feature of this recipe record is the "high warning flag," which signals when the current food cost exceeds a level designated by management. Recipe records are integral to purchase order systems, because stored recipes can indicate needed quantities before production and provide an index of perpetual inventory replenishment following production.

Some data in the standard recipe file overlap data within the ingredient file. This simplifies the creation and maintenance of recipe records, because data should not have to be re-entered. Recipe management applications can access specific elements of data contained in ingredient and recipe files and format different management reports. Exhibit 3 shows a summary recipe cost list. This report can be useful in the menu planning process.

Some recipe management applications provide space for preparation instructions (also called as assembly instructions) that are typically found on standard recipe cards. Although this information is not accessed by other food service

Exhibit 3   Sample Summary Recipe Cost List

```
01  – CHICKEN DELICIOUS, INC.        RECIPE COST LISTING              A1322   PAGE 1
001 – CHICKEN DELICIOUS #1                                            10.25.58 10/01
```

	RECIPE NUMBER	DESCRIPTION	NUMBER OF UNITS	UNIT OF MEASURE	COST PER ITEM	TOTAL COST
RECIPE	10	Chicken Batch	18.0000	Piece		
INGREDIENTS:						
	1	Chicken	2.0000	Head	1.5937	3.1874
	41	Shortening	.4800	lb	.3824	.1836
	42	Milk & Egg Dip	.0500	lb	1.1879	.0594
	43	Fine Salt	.0694	lb	.0997	.0069
	44	Seasoning	.0694	Pkts	2.5575	.1775
	45	Flour	.0694	Bag	3.8900	.2700
**** TOTAL COST		$3.8862				

- -

	RECIPE NUMBER	DESCRIPTION	NUMBER OF UNITS	UNIT OF MEASURE	COST PER ITEM	TOTAL COST
RECIPE	43	Liver and Onions	4.000	1/2 lb		
INGREDIENTS:						
	50	Onions	.0250	lb	.0340	.0009
	44	Seasoning	.0694	Pkts	2.5575	.1775
	45	Flour	.0750	Bag	3.8900	.2918
	41	Shortening	.0500	lb	.3824	.0191
	43	Fine Salt	.0250	lb	.0997	.0025
	22	Breading	.0500	1 Cup	.0384	.0019
	21	Chicken Livers	1.0000	1/2 lb	1.0000	1.0000
***** TOTAL COST		$ 1.4940				

- -

	RECIPE NUMBER	DESCRIPTION	NUMBER OF UNITS	UNIT OF MEASURE	COST PER ITEM	TOTAL COST
RECIPE	44	Liver and Onion Pack	1.0000	Each		
SUBRECIPES:						
	43	Liver and Onions	1.0000	1/2 lb	.3735	.3735
	30	Mashed Potatoes	.1363	lbs	.2140	.0292
	60	Gravy	.0688	lbs	.0579	.0040
INGREDIENTS:						
	69	Labels	1.0000	Each	.0027	.0027
	2	Roll	2.0000	Each	.0375	.0750
	16	Snack Box	1.0000	Each	.0418	.0418
	19	Napkin	1.0000	Each	.0052	.0052
	17	Plastic Forks	1.0000	Each	.0062	.0062

```
***** TOTAL COST    $ .5376    PRICE    $2.55    % FP COST: 21.08    PROFIT: $2.0124
```

- -

Source: Tridata, Inc., Atlanta, Georgia.

management applications, it allows management to print recipes for production personnel. This can be a useful feature when batch sizes (number of portions yielded by a particular standard recipe) need to be expanded or contracted to accommodate forecasted needs. For example, if a standard recipe is designed to yield 100 portions (batch size) but 530 portions are needed, it may be possible (depending on the item) to instruct the system to proportionately adjust the corresponding ingredient quantities. When batch size can be modified, unique recipes can be printed which include preparation information, providing a complete plan for recipe production.

Few restaurants purchase all menu item ingredients in ready-to-use or pre-portioned form. Some ingredients are made on the premises. This means that the ingredients within a standard recipe record may be either inventory items or references to other recipe files. Recipes included as ingredients within a standard recipe record are called **sub-recipes.** Including sub-recipes as ingredients for a particular standard recipe is called **chaining recipes.** Chaining recipes enables the restaurant management system to maintain a record for a particular menu item that requires an unusually large number of ingredients. When ingredient costs change, computerized recipe management applications must be capable of updating not only the costs of standard recipes, but also the cost of sub-recipes used as ingredients. If not, new cost data would have to be separately entered into each sub-recipe record. This can be a time-consuming and error-prone process. Note that the sample recipe data shown in Exhibit 2 contains an ingredient called "salad batch." This reference illustrates the use of a sub-recipe as an ingredient in another recipe.

Menu Item File

A **menu item file** contains data for all meal periods and menu items sold. Important data maintained by this file may include:

- Identification number

- Descriptor

- Recipe code number

- Selling price

- Ingredient quantities for inventory reporting

- Sales totals

This file also stores historical information on the actual number of items sold. Generally, after a meal period, the actual number of menu items served is manually entered into the menu item file, or automatically transferred from an ECR/POS system through an interface to the restaurant management system. This data can be accessed by management or by sophisticated forecasting programs to project sales, determine the number of ingredient quantities to purchase, and schedule needed personnel. In addition, computer-based sales analysis applications access data in the menu item file to produce sales analysis reports for management. When menu items, prices, or tax tables need to be changed, the menu item file is accessed and appropriate changes are entered according to procedures indicated in the user's manual provided by the system's vendor.

Sales Analysis

Sophisticated ECR/POS systems can store or maintain files that contain important data regarding daily restaurant operations. When an ECR/POS system is interfaced to a fully integrated restaurant management system, data maintained by ECR/POS system files can be accessed by computer-based management applications. Such an interface enables a sales analysis application to merge data from ECR/POS files with data from files maintained by a recipe management application. The sales analysis application can then process this combined data into numerous reports to help management direct daily operations in such specific areas as:

- Menu planning
- Sales forecasting
- Menu item pricing
- Ingredient purchasing
- Inventory control
- Labor scheduling
- Payroll accounting

The consolidated reports produced by an ECR/POS system might be supplemented by information which the ECR/POS system may be unable to provide. Management reports can be printed on paper larger than the narrow tape used by registers and journal printers.

Exhibit 4 shows four sales analysis reports that may be produced by a restaurant management system sales analysis application. A **daily sales report** summarizes all sales revenue activity for a day. Revenue is itemized by the following categories:

- Net sales
- Tax
- Number of guest checks
- Number of covers
- Dollars per check
- Dollars per cover
- Sales category
- Day-part totals

In addition, affected general ledger accounts are listed, and associated food costs and sales percentage statistics are noted. A **weekly sales spreadsheet** provides a weekly summary of all information reported by daily sales reports.

A **sales category analysis report** shows relationships between amounts sold by sales category and day-parts defined by management. This report enables management to see at a glance which menu items sell and when they sell. A **marketing category report** compiles weekly totals summarizing the revenue earned by food and beverage departments (or categories).

Menu Management

While most automated food service management applications sort and index data into timely, factual reports for management, menu management applications help management answer such questions as:

Exhibit 4 Assorted Sales Analysis Reports

```
08-29-                    DAILY SALES REPORT - FC 1001
                              01-ABC RESTAURANT
-------------------------------------------------------------
NET SALES          $  1270.10
EXCLUSIVE TAX      $    50.80
INCLUSIVE TAX      $     0.00
NO. OF CHECKS          112    DOLLARS PER CHECK $  11.79
NO. OF COVERS          190    DOLLARS PER COVER $   6.95
-------------------------------------------------------------
SALES CATEGORY     SALES $     FC%      % SALES    DEBIT   CREDIT

FOOD           $   944.45    34.22%    74.36%     200220  310010
LIQUOR         $   180.00    21.00%    14.17%     200220  310020
BEER           $   123.75    19.62%     9.74%     200220  310040
WINE           $    21.90    41.10%     1.72%\    200220  310050

               $  1270.10    31.04%

DAY PART TOTALS

BREAKFAST      $     0.00
LUNCH          $   310.70
DINNER         $   959.40
LATE NIGHT     $     0.00
```

```
08-29-                  01 - ABC RESTAURANT WEEKLY SALES SPREADSHEET                              PAGE 1

                    Fri.      Sat.      Sun.      Mon.      Tue.      Wed.      Thu.
                   07/04/    07/05/    07/06/    07/07/    07/08/    07/09/    07/10/    TOTALS

NO. OF CHECKS....      110       136       105        78        85       123        92       729
NO. OF COVERS....      269       340       248       210       274       248       198      1787
CASH.............  3045.10   5336.55   4311.55   2995.50   3247.15   3977.65   2444.55  25358.05
TTL. CHARGES.....   713.14   1403.05   1428.57   1318.71   1493.08    959.14    366.14   7681.83
TTL. COMPS.......    87.36     76.41      0.00    115.44     78.06     26.16     55.53    438.97
PROMOS..........      0.00      0.00     50.41      0.00      0.00    210.56      0.00    260.97
PETTY CASH.......    10.50      0.00     12.45     20.12     10.15      0.00      0.00     53.22
OVER/SHORT.......     2.36      0.00      .27     12.88      4.21     10.89      5.65     37.26
TAX.............    192.28    340.82    287.00    215.51    240.91    248.14    143.31   1667.97
FOOD COST %......    34.06     35.13     37.81     37.67     31.06     34.73     34.38     35.09
NET.............   3845.60   6816.01   5790.53   4429.65   4818.29   5173.51   2866.22  33739.83
CATEG. SALES.....  3653.32   6475.19   5503.53   4214.14   4577.38   4925.37   2722.91  32071.85
CATEG. COGS......  1244.38   2274.83   2080.89   1587.50   4214.15   4577.38   2722.91  32071.86
                                                           1421.59   1710.34    936.00  11255.55
AM. EXPRESS......   475.66    693.22    596.32    369.52    465.32    521.01    158.32   3279.37
MASTER CARD......   128.41    475.32    412.53    789.32    864.23    369.22     73.41   3114.44
VISA............     23.66      0.00    231.55    100.25    107.21      0.00     56.32    518.99
DINERS..........     85.41     89.25     86.32      0.00      0.00      0.00     65.84    326.82
CARTE BLANC......     0.00    145.26     75.76      0.00      0.00     45.26     10.25    276.23
DISCOVER........      0.00      0.00     26.39      0.00     23.65     23.65      0.00     50.94
HOUSE...........      0.00      0.00      0.00      0.00     56.32      0.00      0.00    115.94
COMPANY.........      0.00      0.00      0.00     59.62      0.00      0.00      0.00      0.00
  *** COMPS
PROBLEM FULL....     21.04     28.66      0.00     16.32     52.21     10.21     10.21    138.65
PROBLEM PART....     66.32     47.75      0.00      0.00      0.00      0.00     43.32    243.94
VIP
STA
WAS
STA               08-29-                     01 - ABC RESTAURANT
PRO                                        SALES CATEGORY ANALYSIS
OUT
  ***        -------------------------------------------------------------
FOO
LIQU         FRI. 07/04/    FOOD    LIQUOR   BEER   WINE  NOT USED  NOT USED  NOT USED  NOT USED  NOT USED  NOT USED  TOTALS    %
BEE
WIN          BREAKFAST     951.35    0.00    0.00   0.00    0.00      0.00      0.00      0.00      0.00      0.00    951.35  26.0
NOT          LUNCH         942.61   66.00   59.58 146.67    0.00      0.00      0.00      0.00      0.00      0.00   1214.86  33.3
NOT          DINNER        942.61   66.00   59.58 146.67    0.00      0.00      0.00      0.00      0.00      0.00   1214.86  33.3
NOT          LATE NIGHT      0.00   66.00   59.58 146.67    0.00      0.00      0.00      0.00      0.00      0.00    272.25   7.4

             TOTALS       2836.57  198.00  178.75 440.00    0.00      0.00      0.00      0.00      0.00      0.00   3653.32
             %              77.64    5.42    4.89  12.04    0.00      0.00      0.00      0.00      0.00      0.00    100.00

             END OF COMPANY
```

```
08-29-               01 - ABC RESTAURANT WEEKLY SALES SPREADSHEET
                            MARKETING CATEGORY REPORT
-------------------------------------------------------------
FRI. 07/04/            DAY TOTAL:      3653.32

1) DOMESTIC B   101.75   5) LIQUOR      198.00   9) POULTRY DI  695.32  13) DESSERTS     0.00  17) CANDY          0.00
2) IMPORTED B    77.00   6) BEEF LUNCH  265.33  10) SEAFOOD LU  210.02  14) BEVERAGES  201.42  18) TOBACCO IT     0.00
3) DOMESTIC W   220.00   7) BEEF DINNE  456.88  11) SEAFOOD DI  266.39  15) APPETIZERS   0.00  19) NOT USED       0.00
4) IMPORTED W   220.00   8) POULTRY LU  741.21  12) MEAL SALAD    0.00  16) TOYS         0.00  20) NOT USED       0.00

END OF COMPANY
```

Source: Datachecker Systems Inc., a subsidiary of National Semiconductor Corporation, Santa Clara, California.

- What is the most profitable price to assign to a menu item?
- At what price level and sales mix does a food service operation maximize its profits?
- Which current menu items require repricing, retention, replacement, or repositioning on the menu?
- How should daily specials and new items be priced?

- How can the success of a menu change be evaluated?

Menu engineering is a menu management application used for evaluating decisions regarding current and future menu pricing, design, and contents. This application requires that management focus on the number of dollars a menu contributes to profit and not simply monitor cost percentages.

Menu engineering begins with an interactive analysis of menu mix (MM) and contribution margin (CM) data. Competing menu items are categorized as either high or low. A menu item is high when its MM is greater than or equal to 70 percent of its equal menu share, low when its MM is less than 70 percent of its equal menu share. The item's individual CM is similarly compared with the menu's average CM and categorized as either high or low. This analysis produces the following classifications:

- Menu items high in both MM and CM are stars (winners).

- Menu items high in MM but low in CM are plowhorses (marginal).

- Menu items low in MM but high in CM are puzzles (potential).

- Menu items low in MM and low in CM are dogs (losers).

The application goes a step further and identifies practical approaches by which to re-engineer the next menu. For example, simple strategies include:

- Retain stars

- Reprice plowhorses

- Reposition puzzles

- Remove dogs

The following sections examine the menu engineering application in greater detail.

Data Input

Data for analysis can be entered into the program's database manually, automatically (from an integrated restaurant management applications package), or electronically (via an external ECR/POS system interface). A stand-alone version of menu engineering requires that the user input each menu item's product cost, selling price, and sales history. This minimal input is sufficient to generate a complete menu engineering analysis. Food service operators who use computer-based recipe management applications to provide accurate product cost data can program a menu engineering application to read this data from a file, rather than rely upon user input. Other data already collected by an ECR/POS system, such as selling price and number of items sold, can be electronically transmitted to the menu engineering application for processing. An establishment using both integrated food service management applications and ECR/POS system interface capabilities will experience a minimal amount of data preparation and handling. Once the data requirements are fulfilled with pre-service, post-service, or simulated information, program execution can begin.

Exhibit 5   Menu Item Evaluation

Date:			Menu: MENUTEXT	
Menu Item Name	Menu Revenue	Menu Cost	Menu CM	No. Sold
Fried Shrimp	$ 1,669.50	$ 1,018.50	$ 651.00	210
Fried Chicken	2,079.00	928.20	1,150.80	420
Chopped Sirloin	405.00	175.50	229.50	90
Prime Rib	4,770.00	2,970.00	1,800.00	600
King Prime Rib	597.00	339.00	258.00	60
NY Strip Steak	3,060.00	1,620.00	1,440.00	360
Top Sirloin	4,054.50	2,193.00	1,861.50	510
Red Snapper	1,668.00	948.00	720.00	240
Lobster Tail	1,425.00	742.50	682.50	150
Tenderloin Tips	2,322.00	1,440.00	882.00	360
Totals	$22,050.00	$12,374.70	$9,675.30	3,000

Menu Engineering Analysis

Following data input and selection of the analysis option, the menu engineering application begins its work. As the analysis progresses, a menu item's contribution margin and sales activity will be categorized as relatively high or low. Procedures performed here are identical to those described for the manual analysis. Eventually each item will be further classified for both its marketing and pricing success. These classifications, resulting from a series of internal mathematical and logical procedures, will help identify proper decision strategies. The menu engineering output is composed of five reports:

- Menu item evaluation
- Menu item classification
- Four-box analysis
- Menu summary sheet
- Menu engineering graph

Menu Item Evaluation

Exhibit 5 shows the initial report in the menu engineering analysis—the menu item evaluation. This report lists menu items and, for a specified period of time, indicates the revenue generated by each, the food cost incurred in generating the revenue, the contribution margin of each item, and the number of items sold. The primary purpose of this report is to increase the user's awareness of the importance of each menu item's contribution to the menu's overall performance.

Menu Item Classification

Exhibit 6 illustrates a menu item classification report. This report lists each menu item and indicates for each item:

Exhibit 6   Menu Item Classification

Date:						Menu: MENUTEXT
Menu Item Name	Selling Price	Item Cost	Item CM	No. Sold	Menu Mix %	Item Class
Fried Shrimp	$7.95	$4.85	$3.10	210	7.0%	PLOWHORSE
Fried Chicken	$4.95	$2.21	$2.74	420	14.0%	PLOWHORSE
Chopped Sirloin	$4.50	$1.95	$2.55	90	3.0%	<< DOG >>
Prime Rib	$7.95	$4.95	$3.00	600	20.0%	PLOWHORSE
King Prime Rib	$9.95	$5.65	$4.30	60	2.0%	?PUZZLE?
NY Strip Steak	$8.50	$4.50	$4.00	360	12.0%	* STAR *
Top Sirloin	$7.95	$4.30	$3.65	510	17.0%	* STAR *
Red Snapper	$6.95	$3.95	$3.00	240	8.0%	PLOWHORSE
Lobster Tail	$9.50	$4.95	$4.55	150	5.0%	?PUZZLE?
Tenderloin Tips	$6.45	$4.00	$2.45	360	12.0%	PLOWHORSE
Totals				3,000	100%	

- Selling price
- Cost
- Contribution margin
- Number sold
- Menu mix percentage
- Classification

The menu mix percentage is determined by dividing the number of the item sold by the total number of menu items sold during the period. The menu engineering application analyzes the data and classifies each menu item according to the following table:

MM Rank	CM Rank	Classification
High	High	Star
High	Low	Plowhorse
Low	High	Puzzle
Low	Low	Dog

These classifications are not unique to menu engineering analysis.

Four-Box Analysis

Exhibit 7 depicts a four-box analysis that indexes the menu classifications developed in the menu item classification report. Since menu engineering leads to a series of decision strategies specific to each menu classification, the four-box analysis provides the user with insight relative to the number of items found in each category. For example, Exhibit 7 displays a menu composed of items classified as five plowhorses, two stars, two puzzles, and one dog. Five items are classified as

Exhibit 7   Four-Box Analysis

Date:	Menu: MENUTEXT

PLOWHORSE	* STAR *
Fried Shrimp Fried Chicken Prime Rib Red Snapper Tenderloin Tips	NY Strip Steak Top Sirloin
<< DOG >>	?PUZZLE?
Chopped Sirloin	King Prime Rib Lobster Tail

Exhibit 8   Menu Summary Sheet

Menu: MENUTEXT
Date:

	Total	Average	Low	Median	High
Price	$22,050.00	$7.35	$4.50	$7.23	$9.95
Food Cost	$12,374.70	$4.12	$1.95	$3.80	$5.65
Contribution Margin	$ 9,675.30	$3.23	$2.45	$3.50	$4.55
Demand Factor	3,000	300	60	330	600
Food Cost Percentage	56.1%		43.3%	52.8%	62.3%
Number of Items	10				

plowhorses. Is that too many? This type of evaluation process begins with the four-box matrix and continues through the menu summary sheet and the menu engineering graph.

Menu Summary Sheet

Exhibit 8 shows a menu engineering summary sheet. This report is perhaps the most informative report produced by the menu engineering application. Important information is presented in capsule form, providing a concise statement of operations.

The row labeled "price" shows total menu revenues, average item selling price, lowest item selling price, median item selling price, and highest item selling price. Similarly, the food cost row contains total menu costs, average item food cost, lowest cost item, median cost, and highest cost item.

The contribution margin row indicates total menu contribution margin, average item contribution margin, lowest item contribution margin, median item contribution margin, and highest item contribution margin.

The demand factor row details the total number of items sold during the period, the average number of a menu item sold, the lowest number of a menu item actually sold, the median number of menu items sold, and the highest number of a menu item actually sold.

The report also lists the menu's overall food cost percentage for the period covered by the report and indicates the lowest food cost percentage of an item on the menu, the median food cost percentage of menu items, and the highest food cost percentage of an item on the menu.

While much of the information in this report can be gathered by other menu management applications, the menu engineering application provides data on a single report for management. The lowest and highest selling prices on the menu, often called price points, can help managers assess the degree to which they are satisfying their target markets.

Menu Engineering Graph

Exhibit 9 is a menu engineering graph, and Exhibit 10 contains the legend for the numbers appearing on the graph. The menu engineering graph is a useful means by which to evaluate decision strategies. Since it indicates each competing menu item's position relative to all others, the menu engineering graph is the most powerful report a menu engineering application produces. The vertical axis of the graph corresponds to menu mix, and the horizontal axis corresponds to contribution margin. Each item is then graphed according to its CM and MM coordinates. It is especially important to note that not all items in the same classification have the same characteristics. This technique points out that a different strategy may be appropriate for items even though they are similarly segmented. Prime rib, for example, has a profile that is very different from fried shrimp's profile. A food service operator may be more willing to raise the price of prime rib (even if it means selling less) than the price of fried shrimp. Menu engineering strategies are concerned with trade-offs based upon elasticities of price and demand.

Menu engineering is an objective way to develop strategies for menu improvement. It also supports the objective of menu planning, which is to increase contribution margin—not simply decrease food cost percentage.

Integrated Food Service Software

Perhaps the most common mistake in choosing a food service computer system is deciding on computer hardware before considering software. Computer hardware is typically purchased on the basis of brand, advertising, price, accessories, and the like. Only after the purchase is made does the search for software begin.

Identifying software aimed at an operation's needs can be time-consuming and frustrating, but learning that the software selected is incompatible with already-purchased hardware can be devastating. The best way to avoid this disaster is to remember that finding hardware to support software packages is much easier than making do with inadequate software.

Generic Software

Standard word processing, electronic spreadsheet, and database management programs are powerful and versatile management tools, but they can also become

Exhibit 9   Menu Engineering Graph

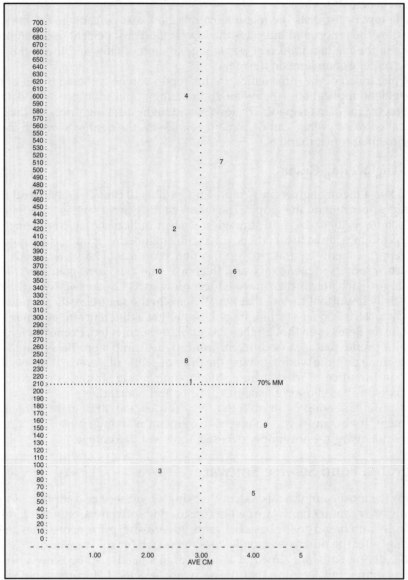

an endless source of frustration. Consider the operator who selects a spreadsheet program to generate budgets, food costs, and daily reports. Each application requires that separate data be entered into specific cells located in distinct worksheet files. If the operator also wants to monitor inventory, the work it takes to support the computer applications may outweigh the other savings of time and

Exhibit 10   Graph Legend

Menu Item Number	Menu Item Name
1	Fried Shrimp
2	Fried Chicken
3	Chopped Sirloin
4	Prime Rib
5	King Prime Rib
6	NY Strip Steak
7	Top Sirloin
8	Red Snapper
9	Lobster Tail
10	Tenderloin Tips

money. A food service operator who uses a word processing program for correspondence, an electronic spreadsheet program for financial analysis, and a database management program for inventory control may find that automation is more trouble than it is worth.

The limitations of free-standing, non-integrated, generic software become apparent when management tries to share or exchange data between programs. Non-integrated applications software seldom achieves the chief objectives of data processing. These objectives are:

- To minimize the time it takes to process input (data) into output (information).

- To minimize the handling and rehandling of data (streamlining).

Integrated food service software applications enable data to pass directly from one application to another. Data is entered only once. The following section illustrates the differences between integrated and non-integrated food service applications while describing precosting and postcosting applications.

Precosting/Postcosting Applications

Precosting is a special type of forecasting which compares forecasted guest counts with standard menu item recipe costs to yield an index of expense before an actual meal period. Precosting software applications can project costs on a portion, batch, or meal period basis. This projected cost of sales figure enables management to review and adjust operations before an actual service period begins. If precosting finds projected costs to be outside an acceptable range, management may consider raising prices, decreasing portion sizes, altering accompaniments, or substituting menu items.

Precosting predictions are based on three types of data: an accurate cost of every ingredient item purchased by the restaurant; a set of standard recipes containing a precise list of ingredients and their quantities along with a description of production procedures for particular batch and portion sizes; and a menu plan specifying each item on the menu and the projected number of portions to be consumed during a

Exhibit 11   Files Accessed by Precosting Applications

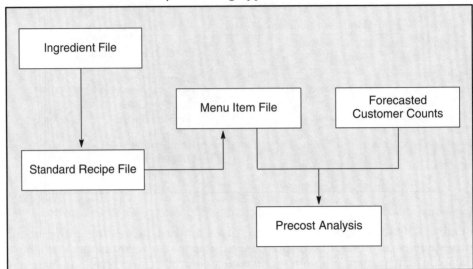

meal period. A commercial restaurant with a fixed menu and standard recipes would need to focus most of its attention on maintaining cost data and developing sound sales mix forecasts.

Although most non-automated restaurants have access to the data needed for precosting calculations, few actually perform the analysis because it can be time-consuming. It can be almost as time-consuming for restaurants with non-integrated software packages. In a non-integrated food service software design, the necessary data—ingredient costs, recipe formulations, and menu plans—most likely would reside in separate software programs. Applying each ingredient data element against its recipe and menu plan would require intervention by the user, intermediate calculations, and re-entry of data, all of which can be both time-consuming and error-prone. To achieve accurate and timely precosting, the best approach is to use integrated software. Integrated file structures free restaurateurs to concentrate on designing menu plans without getting mired in repetitive clerical procedures. Exhibit 11 outlines the files accessed by a precosting management application.

Postcosting multiplies the number of menu items sold by standard recipe costs to determine a potential food cost amount. When actual recipe costs are known, these figures are multiplied by the number of menu items sold to produce an actual cost figure. Exhibit 12 outlines the files accessed by a postcosting management application.

Management Reports from Automated Beverage Systems ———

Electronic bar registers record and store data which can be accessed to produce valuable reports for management. Data may include:

Exhibit 12   Files Accessed by Postcosting Applications

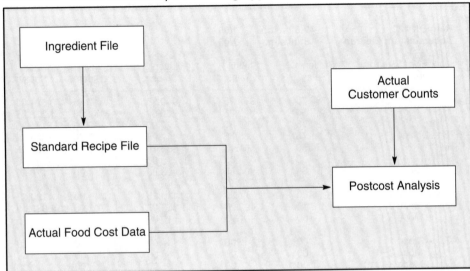

- Beverage item
- Individual brands
- Portion sizes
- Prices
- Sales
- Tax
- Tips
- Bar check numbers
- Server identification codes
- Service location(s)

Bar registers are usually programmed to access specific types of data and print reports on narrow register tape. Reports produced by an automated beverage system are similar to those produced by typical ECR/POS systems. These reports may include sales mix reports, inventory usage reports, missing check reports, server productivity reports, and others. Journal printers typically provide a print format larger than that used by an ECR/POS system and may be programmed to produce detailed accounting and financial reports.

For each shift and each station during a shift, sophisticated automated systems can produce separate reports indicating:

- Sales by major beverage category
- Sales by time of day

Exhibit 13   Sales by Major Beverage Category Report

Ring Off #22 Accumulators Cleared	— 2:52 a.m. — 8:00 a.m.	1/06 1/05		
Sales by Major Category	Station 1 Sales	Station 2 Sales	Station 3 Sales	Station 4 Sales	Total Sales
Liquor	1,185.75	977.25	1,040.25	417.75	3,621.00
Beer	469.50	372.25	236.50	144.00	1,222.25
Wine	29.75	45.00	77.00	19.50	171.25
Soft Drinks	1.75	20.75	17.25	8.75	48.50
Misc A	34.50	61.15	88.70	117.90	302.25
Btl Wine	.00	.00	.00	.00	.00
Lookups	57.85	94.55	23.80	.00	176.20
Price Mode 1	3.00	77.00	110.25	.00	190.25
Mode 2	1,776.10	1,492.20	1,363.25	707.90	5,339.45
Mode 3	.00	1.75	10.00	.00	11.75
Tax—Mode 1	.00	.00	.00	.00	.00
Mode 2	.00	.00	.00	.00	.00
Mode 3	.00	.00	.00	.00	.00
Tips	1.50	.00	11.10	.00	12.60
Gross Sales	1,780.60	1,570.95	1,494.60	707.90	5,554.05
Net Sales	1,779.10	1,570.95	1,483.50	707.90	5,541.45
Accumulated Sales	919,058.24	43,281.83	50,696.30	30,780.18	
Transactions	16	190	24	93	323

Source: American Business Computers, Akron, Ohio.

- Sales by server
- Settlement methods
- Outstanding guest checks
- Sales mix by beverage product

Exhibits 13 through 19 show a series of reports generated by a sophisticated automated beverage control system. The reports cover a single shift and integrate data from four separate stations.

Exhibit 13 reports the expected beverage **sales by major beverage category** for the four separate stations, as well as total sales figures combining the four stations. Exhibit 14 shows a **sales by beverage server report.** Note that the total sales figure at the bottom of this report ($5,524.05) is $30 less than the total standard beverage income listed on Exhibit 13 as $5,554.05 (total gross sales). An **outstanding guest checks report** (Exhibit 15) resolves this discrepancy. When bartenders close their stations, the system generates a **settlement methods report** (Exhibit 16)

Exhibit 14   Sales by Beverage Server Report

Ring Off #22	—2:52 a.m.	1/06								
Accumulators Cleared	—8:00 a.m.	1/05								

Server	Reported Tips	Total Sales	Cash	Visa	Dine	(All Sales Include Tax and Tips) Amex	Prom	Comp	Disc	Dire
1	6.10	1252.05	1160.45	.00	.00	91.60	.00	.00	.00	.00
4	.00	197.45	197.45	.00	.00	.00	.00	.00	.00	.00
5	.00	223.40	223.40	.00	.00	.00	.00	.00	.00	.00
6	.00	493.50	493.50	.00	.00	.00	.00	.00	.00	.00
12	1.50	785.65	553.70	.00	179.70	52.25	.00	.00	.00	.00
15	.00	644.75	644.75	.00	.00	.00	.00	.00	.00	.00
16	.00	5.00	5.00	.00	.00	.00	.00	.00	.00	.00
17	.00	288.90	288.90	.00	.00	.00	.00	.00	.00	.00
27	.00	111.75	111.75	.00	.00	.00	.00	.00	.00	.00
35	.00	21.00	21.00	.00	.00	.00	.00	.00	.00	.00
37	.00	28.25	28.25	.00	.00	.00	.00	.00	.00	.00
39	.00	36.50	36.50	.00	.00	.00	.00	.00	.00	.00
40	.00	276.20	276.20	.00	.00	.00	.00	.00	.00	.00
41	.00	18.00	18.00	.00	.00	.00	.00	.00	.00	.00
43	.00	244.25	233.50	10.75	.00	.00	.00	.00	.00	.00
44	.00	5.95	5.95	.00	.00	.00	.00	.00	.00	.00
45	.00	85.95	85.95	.00	.00	.00	.00	.00	.00	.00
47	5.00	30.50	25.50	.00	.00	5.00	.00	.00	.00	.00
56	.00	166.25	166.25	.00	.00	.00	.00	.00	.00	.00
58	.00	84.25	84.25	.00	.00	.00	.00	.00	.00	.00
60	.00	7.75	7.75	.00	.00	.00	.00	.00	.00	.00
65	.00	13.00	13.00	.00	.00	.00	.00	.00	.00	.00
66	.00	235.50	235.50	.00	.00	.00	.00	.00	.00	.00
67	.00	2.50	2.50	.00	.00	.00	.00	.00	.00	.00
68	.00	21.00	21.00	.00	.00	.00	.00	.00	.00	.00
71	.00	24.25	.00	.00	.00	24.25	.00	.00	.00	.00
78	.00	208.25	208.25	.00	.00	.00	.00	.00	.00	.00
80	.00	10.50	10.50	.00	.00	.00	.00	.00	.00	.00
93	.00	1.75	1.75	.00	.00	.00	.00	.00	.00	.00
Totals	12.60	5524.05	5160.50	10.75	179.70	173.10	.00	.00	.00	.00

Source: American Business Computers, Akron, Ohio.

Exhibit 15   Outstanding Guest Checks Report

Ring Off #22	— 2:52 a.m.	1/06
Accumulators Cleared	— 8:00 a.m.	1/05

Outstanding Guest Checks	Server	Check Total
#4567	05	30.00
Total		30.00

Source: American Business Computers, Akron, Ohio.

Exhibit 16   Settlement Methods Report

Ring Off #22   —2:52 a.m.   1/06
Accumulators Cleared—8:00 a.m.   1/05

Settlement Methods	STATION 1 SALES	STATION 2 SALES	STATION 3 SALES	STATION 4 SALES	TOTAL SALES
Cash	1548.65	1560.20	1368.00	683.65	5160.50
Visa/MC	.00	10.75	.00	.00	10.75
Diners	179.70	.00	.00	.00	179.70
Amex	52.25	.00	96.60	24.25	173.10
Promo	.00	.00	.00	.00	.00
Company	.00	.00	.00	.00	.00
Discovery	.00	.00	.00	.00	.00
Direct Bill	.00	.00	.00	.00	.00
Total Settlements	1780.60	1570.95	1464.60	707.90	5524.05

Source: American Business Computers, Akron, Ohio.

Exhibit 17   Net Sales by Time of Day Report

Ring Off #22   — 2:52 a.m.   1/06
Accumulators Cleared   — 8:00 a.m.   1/05

Net Sales by Time of Day	Station 1 Sales	Station 2 Sales	Station 3 Sales	Station 4 Sales	Total Sales
6 – 7 A.M.	.00	.00	.00	.00	.00
7 – 8	.00	.00	.00	.00	.00
8 – 9	.00	.00	.00	.00	.00
9 – 10	.00	.00	.00	.00	.00
10 – 11	.00	.00	.00	.00	.00
11 – 12	.00	.00	.00	.00	.00
12 – 1 P.M.	.00	.00	.00	.00	.00
1 – 2	.00	.00	.00	.00	.00
2 – 3	.00	.00	.00	.00	.00
3 – 4	.00	.00	.00	.00	.00
4 – 5	.00	3.25	16.50	.00	19.75
5 – 6	.00	14.00	32.25	.00	46.25
6 – 7	.00	43.00	68.25	.00	111.25
7 – 8	40.70	58.00	112.50	6.25	217.45
8 – 9	123.75	77.40	170.85	55.40	427.40
9 – 10	297.75	272.50	217.00	180.15	957.40
10 – 11	343.50	361.65	282.90	221.50	1,209.55
11 – 12	346.00	250.40	218.75	194.85	1,010.00
12 – 1 A.M.	276.90	276.05	208.50	49.75	811.20
1 – 2	233.00	183.45	126.00	.00	542.45
2 – 3	117.50	31.25	30.00	.00	178.75
3 – 4	.00	.00	.00	.00	.00
4 – 5	.00	.00	.00	.00	.00
5 – 6 A.M.	.00	.00	.00	.00	.00
Total Net Sales	1,779.10	1,570.95	1,483.50	707.90	5,541.45

Source: American Business Computers, Akron, Ohio.

which indicates the amounts due in the form of credit card vouchers, house account charges, and cash. Note that the total of the settlement report (the amount of sales income that the bartenders will be held accountable for) does not include the $30 from the outstanding guest check.

Exhibit 17 shows a **net sales by time of day report.** This report is useful for forecasting sales and for scheduling servers and bartenders according to expected demand. Exhibit 18 shows the **sales mix by major product report** for the shift. Managers use these reports to monitor product sales trends and to adjust par inventory levels when necessary. The **product usage report** shown in Exhibit 19 enables managers to minimize inventory control problems.

Automated beverage systems can greatly enhance management's control of beverage operations. At the least, the system provides accurate information about the number of drinks and/or ounces sold. At best, such a system will not allow a drink to be served without its being entered as a sale within the system.

However, automated equipment cannot solve the problem of assessing standard income from beverage sales completely because:

- Some beverage products will not be on the system. For example, bottled beer and some mixed cocktails such as frozen daiquiris are not generally metered by automated equipment.

- Dishonest personnel can almost always find a way to work outside or around the system.

- Should the equipment break down, manual income control systems are still necessary.

Perhaps the best approach for controlling sales income with an automated beverage system is to make sure that it complements the income collection system used in the food and beverage operation.

Summary

Computer-based restaurant management applications process data related to back-of-the-house food service activities. Common management applications examined in this chapter included:

- Recipe management
- Sales analysis
- Menu management

Three important files maintained by the recipe management application were examined. These files were the ingredient file, the recipe file, and the menu item file. The chapter stressed that most other food service management applications must be able to access data in these files to carry out their processing functions.

The chapter pointed out that a restaurant management system sales analysis accesses data from various sources and produces a number of reports that help management direct daily operations. Four sales analysis reports discussed were a

Exhibit 18 Sales Mix by Major Product Report

Ring Off #22	—2:52 a.m.	1/06
Accumulators Cleared	—8:00 a.m.	1/05

Sales Mix By Major Product	STATION 1 SALES	STATION 2 SALES	STATION 3 SALES	STATION 4 SALES	TOTAL SALES
Scotch	30.00/ 12	46.00/ 22	45.00/ 18	15.00/ 6	136.00/ 58
Chivas	.00	.00	12.50/ 6	.00	12.50/ 6
Cutty	.00	.00	4.50/ 2	.00	4.50/ 2
Dewar's	46.75/ 17	30.00/ 12	36.50/ 14	46.75/ 17	160.00/ 60
J&B	11.00/ 4	8.25/ 3	32.00/ 12	.00	51.25/ 19
JW Black	8.25/ 3	13.75/ 5	2.75/ 1	2.75/ 1	27.50/ 10
Bourbon	47.50/ 19	15.50/ 7	21.50/ 9	5.00/ 2	89.50/ 37
Granddad	.00	5.25/ 3	.00	.00	5.25/ 3
WildTurk	5.50/ 2	8.25/ 3	.00	.00	13.75/ 5
JDaniels	74.25/ 27	90.75/ 33	65.25/ 27	35.75/ 13	266.00/100
Seag 7	52.50/ 21	15.00/ 6	13.00/ 6	30.00/ 12	110.50/ 45
MakrMark	5.50/ 2	18.25/ 7	2.75/ 1	11.00/ 4	37.50/ 14
Seag VO	22.00/ 8	40.00/ 16	45.75/ 17	27.50/ 10	135.25/ 51
Cr Royal	13.75/ 5	19.25/ 7	2.75/ 1	.00	35.75/ 13
C Club	8.25/ 3	82.00/ 32	35.75/ 13	8.25/ 3	134.25/ 51
Tanquray	60.50/ 22	46.75/ 17	51.00/ 20	22.00/ 8	180.25/ 67
Beefeatr	2.75/ 1	2.75/ 1	8.25/ 3	.00	13.75/ 5
Gin	25.00/ 10	10.00/ 4	7.50/ 3	2.50/ 1	45.00/ 18
Bombay	11.00/ 4	.00	.00	.00	11.00/ 4
Absolut	16.50/ 6	38.50/ 14	16.50/ 6	2.75/ 1	74.25/ 27
Vodka	145.00/ 58	130.00/ 52	205.50/ 85	45.00/ 18	525.50/213
Stoli	46.75/ 17	40.25/ 15	76.00/ 28	19.25/ 7	182.25/ 67
Smirnoff	24.75/ 9	13.75/ 5	.00	.00	38.50/ 14
Rum	30.00/ 12	5.00/ 2	28.00/ 12	5.00/ 2	68.00/ 28
Bacardi	.00	.00	.00	11.00/ 4	11.00/ 4
Trip Sec	.00	2.50/ 1	.00	.00	2.50/ 1
Peach	75.00/ 30	27.50/ 11	5.00/ 2	17.50/ 7	125.00/ 50
Sloe Gin	.00	2.50/ 1	.00	.00	2.50/ 1
Dom Beer	428.25/191	321.00/145	218.25/ 99	119.25/ 53	1086.75/488
Imp Beer	41.25/ 15	51.25/ 19	18.25/ 7	24.75/ 9	135.50/ 50
Tequilla	5.00/ 2	.00	12.50/ 5	2.50/ 1	20.00/ 8
Cuervo G	2.75/ 1	24.75/ 9	5.50/ 2	.00	33.00/ 12
Gr Marn	.00	6.50/ 2	19.50/ 6	6.50/ 2	32.50/ 10
Brandy	12.50/ 5	.00	.00	.00	12.50/ 5
Menthe L	17.50/ 7	.00	7.50/ 3	.00	25.00/ 10
Menthe G	.00	.00	2.50/ 1	.00	2.50/ 1
Cacao Dk	2.50/ 1	.00	.00	.00	2.50/ 1
Drambuie	19.50/ 6	.00	6.50/ 2	.00	26.00/ 8
Di Saron	6.50/ 2	.00	3.25/ 1	.00	9.75/ 3
Amorita	19.50/ 6	.00	7.50/ 3	.00	27.25/ 9
Frngelco	.00	.00	3.25/ 1	.00	3.25/ 1
Chrdonay	.00	3.00/ 1	.00	3.00/ 1	6.00/ 2
Kamora	32.50/ 10	.00	4.50/ 2	.00	37.00/ 12
Midori	3.25/ 1	.00	.00	.00	3.25/ 1
Chablis	5.25/ 3	15.75/ 9	21.75/ 13	8.75/ 5	51.50/ 30
Sambuca	.00	26.00/ 8	45.50/ 14	.00	71.50/ 22
TiaMaria	.00	.00	7.75/ 3	.00	7.75/ 3
Zinfndel	21.00/ 7	21.00/ 7	36.00/ 12	6.00/ 2	84.00/ 28
Soda	.00	.00	1.75/ 5	.00	1.75/ 9
LemLime	1.75/ 2	.00	1.75/ 2	.00	3.50/ 4
SeagCool	12.25/ 7	.00	.00	1.75/ 1	14.00/ 8
Cola	.00	1.75/ 3	10.25/ 10	1.75/ 2	13.75/ 15
Tonic	.00	.00	1.75/ 2	.00	1.75/ 2
Diet	.00	5.00/ 3	1.75/ 1	7.00/ 6	13.75/ 10
Martini	10.25/ 3	13.75/ 4	21.25/ 7	78.75/ 23	124.00/ 37
Manhattn	3.25/ 1	3.25/ 1	40.25/ 13	.00	46.75/ 15
Mai-Tai	11.00/ 3	.00	.00	.00	11.00/ 3
Wh Sour	5.75/ 2	28.75/ 10	15.50/ 5	.00	50.00/ 17
TCollins	5.00/ 2	7.50/ 3	10.00/ 4	.00	22.50/ 9
Daiquiri	.00	.00	1.50/ 1	3.00/ 1	4.50/ 2
Bl Russn	13.00/ 4	2.25/ 1	2.25/ 1	.00	17.50/ 6
Rusty Nl	.00	.00	6.50/ 2	.00	6.50/ 2
Stinger	19.50/ 6	.00	.00	.00	19.50/ 6
Kamikaze	85.00/ 34	85.00/ 34	27.50/ 11	.00	197.50/ 79
Spritzer	1.75/ 1	3.50/ 2	17.50/ 10	1.75/ 1	24.50/ 14
Ice Tea	26.00/ 8	32.50/ 10	26.00/ 8	6.75/ 3	91.25/ 29
Lemonade	.00	6.50/ 2	.00	3.25/ 1	9.75/ 3
W Cooler	1.75/ 1	1.75/ 1	1.75/ 1	.00	5.25/ 3
Margrita	12.50/ 5	2.50/ 1	.00	.00	15.00/ 6
PeachDaq	.00	3.50/ 1	.00	.00	3.50/ 1
B-52	52.00/ 16	6.50/ 2	3.25/ 1	.00	61.75/ 19
V Hammer	.00	.00	.00	7.00/ 2	7.00/ 2
LaBoomer	.00	.00	3.50/ 1	.00	3.50/ 1
Spec Ctl	58.50/ 18	9.75/ 3	35.75/ 11	.00	104.00/ 32
Totals	1686.75	1415.25	1371.00	590.00	5063.00

continued

Sales Mix By Produce Lookup	STATION 1 SALES	STATION 2 SALES	STATION 3 SALES	STATION 4 SALES	TOTAL SALES
Moet Chandon	38.00/ 1	38.00/ 1	.00	.00	76.00/ 2
Cajun	.00	.00	6.95/ 1	.00	6.95/ 1
Barb Chick	6.95/ 1	13.90/ 2	.00	.00	20.85/ 3
Wild Mush	.00	6.95/ 1	.00	.00	6.95/ 1
Brie	.00	.00	4.95/ 1	.00	4.95/ 1
Thai Chick	6.95/ 1	.00	.00	.00	6.95/ 1
Reuben	.00	5.95/ 1	.00	.00	5.95/ 1
Mush Pep Sau	5.95/ 1	29.75/ 5	11.90/ 2	.00	47.60/ 8
Totals	57.85	94.55	23.80	.00	176.20

Source: American Business Computers, Akron, Ohio.

Exhibit 19   Product Usage Report

Ring Off #22	—2:52 a.m.	1/06
Accumulators Cleared	—8:01 a.m.	1/05

Product Usage	Bottle Size	Ounces Poured	Bottles Emptied				
				Almond	Liter	4	
				Cacao Dark	Liter	3	
				Cacao Light	Liter	1	
Scotch	1.75 L	77	1	Menthe Green	Liter	1	
Chivas Regal	1.75 L	7		Menthe Light	Liter	15	
Cutty Sark	1.75 L	2					
Dewar's	1.75 L	82	1	Midori	Liter	2	
J&B	1.75 L	24		Peach Schnaps	1.75 L	68	1
JWalker Black	1.75 L	17		Sloe Gin	Liter	1	
				Triple Sec	1.75 L	42	1
Bourbon	1.75 L	54	1				
Jack Daniels	1.75 L	130	2	Di Saronna	1.75 L	3	
Jim Beam	1.75 L			Amorita	Liter	27	
Makers Mark	1.75 L	17		Drambuie	1.75 L	12	1
Old Granddad	1.75 L	3		Frangelico	750ml	1	
Wild Turkey	1.75 L	6		Grand Marnier	1.75 L	19	1
Canadian Club	1.75 L	64	1	Kahlua	1.75 L	4	
Crown Royal	1.75 L	17		Kamora	Liter	29	1
Irish Whiskey	1.75 L	1		Sambuca	750ml	28	1
Seagram's 7	1.75 L	60	1	Tia Maria	Liter	15	1
Seagram's VO	1.75 L	73	2				
				Chablis	1 Gal	234	1
Gin	1.75 L	43	1	Chardonnay	1 Gal	10	
Beefeater	1.75 L	6		Wht Zinfandel	1 Gal	159	1
Bombay	1.75 L	5					
Tanqueray	1.75 L	92	1	Margarita Mix	5 Gal	2	1
				Sour Mix	5 Gal	138	
Vodka	1.75 L	414	7				
Absolut	1.75 L	34	1	LemLime Syrup	1 Gal	32	
Smirnoff	1.75 L	18		Seagrams Coolr	1 Gal	7	
Stolichnaya	Liter	111	3	Cola Syrup	1 Gal	36	1
				Tonic syrup	1 Gal	40	1
Rum	1.75 L	66	1	Diet Syrup	1 Gal	9	
Bacardi	1.75 L	5					
Myers's	1.75 L			Soda	1 Gal	799	6
				Water	1 Gal	42	
Tequilla	1.75 L	15					
Cuervo Gold	1.75 L	15					
Brandy	1.75 L	15	1				
Apricot	Liter						

continued

Source: American Business Computers, Akron, Ohio.

daily sales report, a weekly sales spreadsheet report, a sales category analysis report, and a marketing category report.

The chapter stressed that while most automated food and beverage management applications sort and index data into timely and factual reports for management, menu management applications help management devise practical menu strategies. The menu engineering application was examined in detail. This application evaluates decisions regarding current and future menu pricing, design, and contents, and requires management to focus on the number of dollars a menu contributes to profit and not simply monitor cost percentages.

The chapter pointed out that one of the most common mistakes in choosing a food service computer system is deciding on computer hardware before considering software. Non-integrated applications software seldom achieves the chief objectives of data processing. Integrated software, on the other hand, can share and exchange data, reducing processing time and minimizing the number of times a piece of data must be handled. Precosting and postcosting software applications were presented as examples of how integrated software facilitates efficient data processing.

Finally, the chapter examined some of the reports produced by sophisticated automated beverage systems that enhance management's control of beverage operations.

Key Terms

chaining recipes
conversion tables
daily sales report
ingredient file
marketing category report
menu engineering
menu item file
net sales by time of day report
outstanding guest checks report
postcosting

precosting
product usage report
sales by beverage server report
sales by major beverage category
  report
sales category analysis report
sales mix by major product report
settlement methods report
sub-recipe
weekly sales spreadsheet

Discussion Questions

1. What three files does a recipe management application maintain?

2. How can other management applications use the data in recipe management files?

3. What is meant by the term "sub-recipes"? Explain how sub-recipes are used in an ingredient file of a recipe management application.

4. Why is it useful for a sales analysis application to be able to access ECR/POS system files?

5. What problems could managers encounter when the restaurant operation uses generic software applications to manage information?

6. How can managers benefit from integrated software applications?

7. What do the terms "precosting" and "postcosting" mean?

8. How are menu management applications, such as menu engineering, different from most other management applications?

9. What is the purpose of menu engineering's menu item classification report?

10. What are some of the reports produced by automated beverage systems that enhance management's control of operations?

REVIEW QUIZ

When you feel you have covered all of the material in this chapter, answer these questions. Choose the *best* answer.

Matching

1. Multiplies the number of menu items sold by standard recipe costs to determine a potential food cost amount

2. Recipes that are included as ingredients within a standard recipe record

3. A menu management application that helps managers make decisions about current and future menu pricing, design, and contents

4. Compares forecasted guest counts with standard menu item recipe costs to yield an index of expense before an actual meal period

5. Tracks ingredients (by unit and by cost) as they pass through purchasing, receiving, storing, issuing, production, and service control points

6. Indicates amounts of beverage products sold during a shift and enables managers to minimize inventory control problems

7. Contains recipes for all menu items

8. Contains data for all meal periods and menu items sold

a. chaining recipes

b. conversion tables

c. ingredient file

d. menu engineering

e. menu item file

f. postcosting

g. precosting

h. sub-recipe

i. standard recipe file

j. contribution margin

k. menu mix

l. product usage report

m. sales by beverage server report

True (T) or False (F)

T   F   9. Chaining recipes enables a computer-based restaurant management system to maintain a record for a particular menu item that requires an unusually large number of ingredients.

T   F   10. A menu engineering application focuses management's attention on food cost percentages.

T   F   11. Integrated food service software applications are cumbersome to operate because data cannot pass directly from one application to another.

T   F   12. Managers use sales mix reports to monitor product sales trends and to adjust inventory par levels when necessary.

Alternate/Multiple Choice

13. Menu engineering applications classify menu items that are high in menu mix and low in contribution margin as:

    a. puzzles.
    b. plowhorses.

14. A report produced by automated beverage systems that is useful for scheduling servers and bartenders according to expected demand is:

    a. a net sales by time of day report.
    b. a sales by beverage server report.

15. Which of the following data elements is generally *not* contained in an ingredient file of a recipe management application?

    a. purchase unit cost
    b. selling price
    c. issue unit cost
    d. recipe unit

Part IV

Other Hospitality Applications

Chapter Outline

Automation and the Hotel Sales Office
    Group Guestroom Sales
    Function and Banquet Room Sales
    Sales Filing Systems
    Sales Forecasts and Performance
       Reports
Yield Management
    Elements of Yield Management
    Using Yield Management
    Yield Management Computer Software
Food Service Catering Software Packages
    Off-Premises Catering
    Home Delivery Catering
Summary

Learning Objectives

1. Describe the benefits an automated sales office has over a non-automated sales office.

2. State the advantages of using an automated sales system to create a banquet event order.

3. Explain how computer automation facilitates sales filing systems.

4. Describe important elements of yield management.

5. Describe the types of data hotels must collect to understand how group sales affect overall room revenue.

6. Explain how hotel managers should use yield management.

7. Describe the advantages that yield management computer software offers.

8. Describe the benefits of off-premises catering software.

9. Explain the competitive advantages offered by computer-based home delivery systems.

9

Hotel Sales and Food Service Catering Applications

A TYPICAL HOTEL sales or food service catering operation generates an incredible amount of paperwork, and a great part of each day is spent managing the information collected through prospecting, selling, booking, and reporting. Today, at many properties, much of this time-consuming and costly effort is handled with computers. During the past decade, hotel sales and catering operations have begun reaping the benefits of automation, such as:

- Accomplishing tedious tasks quickly and efficiently.

- Accessing sales information instantaneously.

- Facilitating personalized mailings based on the data in electronic files.

- Reducing the risk of human error. When specific procedures are implemented, it is less likely that information will be lost or misplaced.

- Decreasing training costs for clerical personnel. Set procedures result in a faster training time and little deviation from standard practices.

- Storing information that can direct specific sales promotions or programs to prospective clients or individual guests based on zip code, desired time periods, areas of interest, and so on.

- Enhancing communication among properties, greatly facilitating the sales effort in large hotel chains.

The following sections explore the computer applications in relation to hotel sales office functions and yield management strategies, as well as off-premises and home-delivery food service catering operations.

Automation and the Hotel Sales Office

Sales records are a vital part of a sales office's communication system. They are important in establishing new accounts, servicing existing accounts, and generating repeat business. In the non-automated sales office, it is essential that salespeople familiarize themselves with sales forms, learn to complete them properly, and file them in accordance with sales office procedures. Many of these mechanical and often detailed office procedures are streamlined or eliminated in automated sales offices. Exhibit 1 summarizes a few of the differences between non-automated and automated sales office systems. The following sections compare non-automated

Exhibit 1   Non-Automated vs. Automated Sales Systems

Non-Automated	Automated
1. Account and booking information is entered on a scratch sheet.	All information is entered directly into the computer. If the account is an established one, entering the first few letters brings the name, address, contact person, and all other relevant information onto the screen. If the new booking is similar to a previous booking, the old entry can be duplicated and modified if necessary.
2. The same account and booking information is entered into the group room control log—the log is summarized manually.	The log is updated automatically; summary and forecast are calculated automatically.
3. The secretary types up group room block and function information.	The recap is automatically printed and includes all details on the group room block and the function events.
4. The same account and booking information is retyped in a confirmation letter.	Confirmation is produced automatically.
5. The same information is retyped in a contract.	Contract is produced automatically.
6. The banquet event order is typed and retyped with corrections using the same information as well as detailed menus, resource items, and comments.	Banquet event order is automatically generated by selecting menus and resources from the screen. Costs, consumption, and use at the time of the event are displayed.
7. Related follow-up correspondence is typed, referring to the same account and booking information.	Follow-up correspondence is traced and generated automatically.
8. In order to execute market research and/or telemarketing activity, a database is built by re-entering the same booking and account information.	Integrated account booking information is available for database search for marketing, telemarketing, service history, and lost business tracking.
9. Reports are created by a review of the forecast books, diaries, and booking recaps. Summary of data is entered.	Diary is automatically updated each time a booking is entered; summary and forecast are automatically calculated.
10. Salesperson booking pace and productivity reports are created through manual tabulation.	Reports are generated automatically using data in the system.
11. Tracing is done by manual entry on 3- by 5-inch cards. Traced files are delivered by secretaries to sales manager where they pile up on desks.	All activities are traced to the salesperson in accordance with a pre-developed plan. Daily trace reports remind the sales staff of such critical account and booking details as contracts due, credit checks to be done, block pick-ups, menus, and follow-up sales calls. Tentative and definite bookings are displayed and traced for follow-up. Numerous user-defined account traces and booking traces are generated for action steps.

Source: Adapted from *HSMAI Marketing Review,* Spring 1987, p. 27.

and automated sales office functions in relation to group guestroom sales, function and banquet room sales, and sales office filing systems.[1] In addition, the sections describe sales forecasts and performance reports generated by automated sales systems.

Group Guestroom Sales

In most non-automated sales offices, a guestroom control book is used to monitor the number of guestrooms committed to groups. Because front desk, reservations, and sales office employees all book guestroom business, it is important that all of these personnel be aware of group allotments and avoid overbooking.

Many properties implement yield management strategies that are designed to maximize rooms revenue by establishing a desired mix of group, tour and travel, and individual guest business for specific time periods. A later section in this chapter discusses yield management in greater detail. For the purposes of our discussion here, it is important to note that the **guestroom control book** guides guestroom booking activity by providing the sales office with the maximum number of guestrooms it can sell to groups on a given day. This quota is usually set by the general manager and the head of the marketing and sales department. The remaining guestrooms (and any unsold guestrooms allotted to groups) are available for individual guests. These guestrooms can generally be sold by front desk and reservations staff at higher rates than they could be sold to groups.

A major challenge of non-automated sales offices is maintaining an up-to-date and accurate guestroom control book. Difficulties arise during busy periods when bookings or cancellations are not recorded as soon as they occur. Therefore, before booking guestroom business, it is not unusual for a salesperson to double-check the reliability of guestroom control data by asking other sales staff members about recent activity regarding the days in question.

Automated sales offices overcome many of these problems simply because every salesperson with a computer terminal has immediate access to guestroom control information. Bookings and cancellations can be quickly processed as they occur—even as the salesperson is on the telephone with the client. This helps ensure that every salesperson has access to exactly the same information, and that "definite" and "tentative" bookings are clearly identified to prevent errors.

The computer-generated report shown in Exhibit 2 alerts the sales manager, the rooms division manager, and the general manager to the status of guestroom sales to groups. For example, assume that, for the month of January, the marketing plan for this fictional hotel establishes 225 guestrooms as a daily sales goal for group business. The report provides a summary of guestrooms currently available for sale to groups in January as well as guestrooms already committed to group business.

Columns on the left side of the exhibit show availability; columns on the right indicate actual guestrooms and parlors blocked. The "Available/Group" column on the left of the report indicates the number of unsold group guestrooms. To its right, the "Available/Total" column indicates the total number of unsold guestrooms in the hotel, including guestrooms identified for transient sales. Note that a negative number appears in the "Available/Group" column for four dates during the month. This indicates that for January 6, 11, 13, and 16, group sales will exceed the goal of 225 guestrooms. The hotel's yield management strategy will determine whether this is good news or bad news. For the purpose of this discussion, it is important to note that exceeding the group sales goal displaces transient room sales—that is, guestrooms that could be sold at a transient rate have been sold at a lower group rate.

Exhibit 2   Sample Daily Group Rooms Summary Report

```
                        THE  HOTEL  AND  TOWERS

                        Daily Group Rooms Summary
                                Page: 1

    Report for Jan  1 19XX to Jan 31 19XX


          +--------+--------+                                                          +----------+----------+
          | Available |                                                               | Definites |Tentatives |
          +--------+--------+                                                          +----------+----------+
 Day-Date | Grp |Total |SSG| 0   45   90   135  180  225  270  315  359  405          |Rooms Prlrs|Rooms Prlrs|
----------+-----+------+---+---------------------------------------------------------+----------+----------+
 Mon  1/ 1| 157 | 291  | E | DDDDDDDDDDt                        :                      |   58   0  |   10   0 |
 Tue  1/ 2| 180 | 314  | E | DDDDDDDD                           :                      |   46   0  |    0   0 |
 Wed  1/ 3| 202 | 336  | E | DDt                                :                      |   13   0  |   10   0 |
 Thu  1/ 4|  79 | 213  | E | DDDDDDDDDDDDDDDDDDDDDDDD            :                      |  146   0  |    0   0 |
 Fri  1/ 5|  13 | 147  | C | DDDDDDDDDDDDDDDDDDDDDDDDDDDDDDDDDD  :                      |  212   0  |    0   0 |
 Sat  1/ 6| -10 | 124  | A | DDDDDDDDDDDDDDDDDDDDDDDDDDDDDDDDDDDDD:DD                   |  235   0  |    0   0 |
 Sun  1/ 7|  80 | 214  | E | DDDDDDDDDDDDDDDDDDDDDD              :                      |  145   0  |    0   0 |
 Mon  1/ 8| 119 | 253  | E | DDDDDDDDDDDDDDt                     :                      |   96   0  |   10   0 |
 Tue  1/ 9|  93 | 217  | E | DDDDDDDDDDDDDDDDDDDDt               :                      |  132   0  |   10   0 |
 Wed  1/10|  81 | 215  | E | DDDDDDDDDDDDDDDDDDDDDDD             :                      |  144   0  |    0   0 |
 Thu  1/11|  -3 | 131  | C | DDDDDDDDDDDDDDDDDDDDDDDDDDDDDDDDDDD:D                      |  228   0  |    0   0 |
 Fri  1/12|  32 | 166  | C | DDDDDDDDDDDDDDDDDDDDDDDDDDDDtt      :                      |  178   0  |   15   0 |
 Sat  1/13|  -8 | 126  | A | DDDDDDDDDDDDDDDDDDDDDDDDDDDDDDtttt: :                      |  196   0  |   37   0 |
 Sun  1/14| 157 | 291  | E | DDDDDDDDDt                          :                     |   58   0  |   10   0 |
 Mon  1/15|  87 | 221  | E | DDDDDDDDDDDDDDDt                    :                      |  128   0  |   10   0 |
 Tue  1/16| -39 |  75  | A | DDDDDDDDDDDDDDDDDDDDDDDDDDDDDDDDDDDDD:DDDDDDDtt            |  264   0  |   20   0 |
 Wed  1/17| 114 | 248  | C | DDDDDDDDDDDDDDDtt                   :                      |   96   0  |   15   0 |
 Thu  1/18|  83 | 217  | B | DDDDDDDDDDDDDDDDDDt                 :                      |  132   0  |   10   0 |
 Fri  1/19| 108 | 242  | E | DDDDDDDDDDDDDDtt                    :                      |  102   0  |   15   0 |
 Sat  1/20| 135 | 269  | D | DDDDDDDDDDDDDD                      :                      |   90   0  |    0   0 |
 Sun  1/21|  57 | 191  | D | DDDDDDDDDDDDDDDDDDDDDDD              :                      |  168   0  |    0   0 |
 Mon  1/22|  38 | 172  | D | DDDDDDDDDDDDDDDDDDDDDDDDDDD          :                      |  187   0  |    0   0 |
 Tue  1/23|  25 | 159  | C | DDDDDDDDDDDDDDDDDDDDDDDDDDttt        :                      |  180   0  |   20   0 |
 Wed  1/24|  50 | 184  | D | DDDDDDDDDDDDDDDDDDDDDDDD             :                      |  155   0  |   20   0 |
 Thu  1/25|  36 | 170  | D | DDDDDDDDDDDDDDDDDDttttt              :                      |  113   0  |   35   0 |
 Fri  1/26|  58 | 192  | C | DDDDDDDDDDDDDDDDDDDDttt              :                      |  147   0  |   20   0 |
 Sat  1/27| 107 | 241  | B | DDDDDDDDDDDDDDDttt                  :                      |   98   0  |   20   0 |
 Sun  1/28| 181 | 315  | E | DDDD                                :                      |   44   0  |    0   0 |
 Mon  1/29| 157 | 291  | E | DDDDDDDDD                           :                      |   68   0  |    0   0 |
 Tue  1/30| 202 | 336  | E | DD                                  :                      |   23   0  |    0   0 |
 Wed  1/31| 148 | 282  | E | DDDDDDDDDD                          :                      |   77   0  |    0   0 |
          +-----+------+---+                                                          +----------+----------+
                                                                                      | 3959  0  |  287   0 |
```

Source: Delphi/Newmarket Software Systems, Inc., Durham, New Hampshire.

The chart displayed in the center of the report serves as a rough visual indication of sales activity. The numbers along the top of the chart represent a graded scale of the number of guestrooms in the hotel. The vertical broken line down the chart under the number 359 indicates the total number of guestrooms. The vertical line of colons down the chart under the number 225 indicates the daily group guestrooms goal as defined by the hotel's marketing plan. Definite ("D") and tentative ("t") bookings that appear to the right of a colon indicate that guestrooms protected for transient (front desk) sales have been sold at group rates.

Function and Banquet Room Sales

In non-automated properties, the key to successful function and banquet space control is the function book. This record shows the occupancies and vacancies of specific function and banquet rooms and facilitates the effective planning of functions.

Function books normally are divided into pages for each day of the year, with sections set aside for each meeting or function room. Information recorded in the function book includes the organization or group scheduling the space; the name, address, and telephone number of the group's contact person; the type of function;

the time required for the function; the total time required for preparation, break-down, and cleanup; the number of people expected; the type of setup(s) required; the rates quoted; the nature of the contract; and any pertinent remarks to help property personnel stage a successful function. Function book entries are always made in pencil because changes can occur even when a commitment seems firm. As with the guestroom control book, only one function book should be maintained to prevent mismatching of entries or double bookings.

Information from the function book and other files is eventually transcribed on a **banquet event order (BEO).** Since a BEO generally serves as a final contract for the client and as a work order for the catering department, problems arise when the function book contains inaccurate or incomplete information.

Automated sales systems build a BEO as information is gathered and input by the salesperson in the client's account file. Exhibit 3 shows a sample computer-generated BEO. Sophisticated sales and catering software packages are generally able to supplement information provided by BEOs. For example, for a specific date or range of dates, an automated sales system can produce kitchen reports (listing all menu items needed by preparation area), setup reports (listing all resource items requested on BEOs for those events), and revenue forecast reports (based on anticipated revenue from BEOs).

Problems non-automated properties encounter in maintaining the function book are similar to those they encounter in maintaining the guestroom control book. For example, consider the following scenario. A meeting planner calls and requests the best rate the hotel can offer for 50 rooms for 3 nights in April with a general session meeting room (set up classroom style with a head table for 5) and 3 break-out rooms (set up conference style). To respond to this request, the salesperson must first match April availability dates in the guestroom control book with open dates for four meeting rooms in the function book. Next, the salesperson may want to double-check the accuracy of each book's information with several members of the sales staff. Finally, the salesperson would likely have to check with the department manager before quoting a rate.

In an automated sales office, a salesperson could respond much more quickly. Availability of both group guestrooms and function room space could be checked simultaneously on a single screen of information displayed by the computer terminal. The salesperson could use a special search function of the system to match the meeting planner's needs with the hotel's offerings by providing a list of best available dates to accommodate the group (based on projected occupancy). This allows a hotel salesperson to quickly check the status of the meeting planner's preferred dates, and to suggest alternative days if the requested days are booked. If the property's yield management strategies are programmed into the system, the terminal could also provide a range of rates that the salesperson could negotiate without authorization from the department manager.

Exhibit 4 shows a sample function space profile that can be displayed on a salesperson's terminal or printed as a report to banquet and convention services departments. Each function room is listed down the left side of the report. The time periods are identified as morning (M), lunch (L), afternoon (A), and evening (E). Status letters (such as "D" for definite, "T" for tentative, and "H" for hold) appear

Exhibit 3   Sample Banquet Event Order

HOTEL AND TOWERS

GROUP NAME: AVANTUS PRODUCTIONS	BILLING INSTRUCTIONS
ADDRESS: 9568 N.W. 87th St.	Direct Bill
Suite 405	Billing Address is the same
Arcata, CA 95521	
PHONE NO: 707/592–7830	
CONTACT: Michelle A. Fleetwood	
ON SIGHT CONTACT: Robert Alaya	

==

Date	Times	Function	Room	Attendance
1/5	10:00A–2:30P	BREAKFAST	LOON II	78

==

PER PERSON		TOTAL PRICE		BEVERAGE:
MENU PRICE	$ 26.00	MENU PRICE	$2,028.00	FROM 12:00P TO 1:30P
17% GRATUITY	$ 4.42	17% GRATUITY	$ 344.76	
6% SALES TAX	$ 1.56	6% SALES TAX	$ 121.68	Mixed Drinks – Premium Brands
TOTAL	$ 31.98	LABOR FEE	$ 50.00	Imported Beer
		TOTAL	$2,544.00	Domestic Beer

BREAKFAST MENU:

From 10:00A to 2:30P

FRESH SQUEEZED ORANGE JUICE
FRESH SCRAMBLED EGGS
BACON STRIPS
FRESH BREAKFAST PASTRIES
CEREAL OF CHOICE
BUTTER, JAM, MARMALADE
COFFEE, TEA

Pour First Round on Wines and Leave One Bottle at each table.

SET UP:

  Single Bar
  Seating in Rounds of Eight
  One Reserved Table in front left of room
  Standing Podium

LINEN:

  Long Peach Tablecloths, White Overlays, and
  Mauve Napkins

AUDIOVISUAL:

  Microphone on Podium
  Hang Banner (provided by client)

GUARANTEED ATTENDANCE FIGURE IS REQUIRED TWO WORKING DAYS PRIOR TO FUNCTION. YOU WILL BE BILLED FOR GUARANTEED OR ACTUAL ATTENDANCE, WHICHEVER IS LARGER. THANK YOU.

Signature: _____   By: Virginia Ackerman   Date Issued: 1/5

Source: Delphi/Newmarket Software Systems, Inc., Durham, New Hampshire.

in each time period for which there is a room blocked. Other status letters may be unique to a specific property.

With sophisticated sales office software packages, once a booking is entered into the system, it is automatically integrated, tracked, and traced for management

Exhibit 4   Sample Function Space Profile

Report for Jan 1 19XX to Jan 31 19XX

Room Name	Time Period	Mo 1	Tu 2	We 3	Th 4	Fr 5	Sa 6	Su 7	Mo 8	Tu 9	We 10	Th 11	Fr 12	Sa 13	Su 14	Mo 15	Tu 16	We 17	Th 18	Fr 19	Sa 20	Su 21	Mo 22	Tu 23	We 24	Th 25	Fr 26	Sa 27	Su 28	Mo 29	Tu 30	We 31
PREFUNCA	M				D	D	D		D	D	D		D	T	D	T	T		D	D	T	D	D	D	D	D	D				VD	
	L			D	D		D		D	D	D		D	T	D	T	T		D	D	T		D	D	D	D	D				VD	
	A				D	D			D	D	D		D	T	D	T	T		D	D	T	D	D	D	D	VD T	D				VD T	
	E			D	DD			D	D	D	D		D	D	D	T	T				T		D T	T	VD D	VD	D				VD D	
PREFUNCB	M				H	H			D	D	D		D	D		T	T		D	D	T		h	D	D	D	T				VD D	
	L				H	H	H		D	D	D		D	D		T	T		D	D	T		D		D	D	T					
	A				H				D	D			D	D											VD D	D	D					
	E				DD		H	D																								
BALL A	M				H	H						D	D	D	D	D	D	D	D	D	D		D	D	D	D	D				VD	
	L				H	H						D	D	D	D	D	D	D	D	D	D		D	D	D	D	D					
	A				H								D	D		T																
	E				H	H															D											
BALL B	M				D	D			D	D	D	D	D	D	D	D	D	D	D	D	D		D	D	D	D	D				VD	
	L				D	D			D	D	D	D	D	D	D	D	D	D	D	D	D		D	D	D	D	D					
	A				D						D		D	D					D	D												
	E																															
BALL C	M				T	D				D	D	D	D	D	D		D	D	D	D	D		D	D	D	D	D				VD	
	L				T	D	D			D	D	D	D	D	D		D	D	D	D	D T		D	D	D	D	D					
	A																				T											
	E				T																											
BALL D	M				T	D	D			D	D	D	D	D	D			D	D	D	T		D	D	D	D	D	D	D		VD	
	L				T		D			D	D	D	D	D	D			D	D	D T	T		D	D	D	D	D	D	D			
	A																															
	E																															

Source: Delphi/Newmarket Software Systems, Inc., Durham, New Hampshire.

Exhibit 5   Sample Tickler File

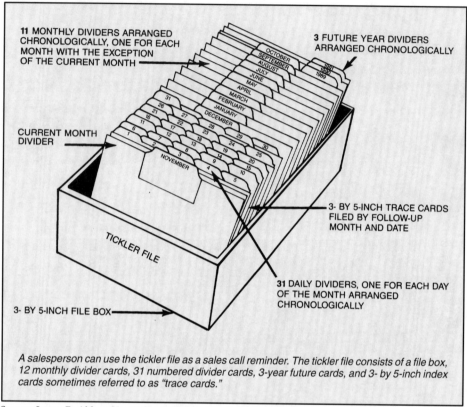

11 MONTHLY DIVIDERS ARRANGED
CHRONOLOGICALLY, ONE FOR EACH
MONTH WITH THE EXCEPTION
OF THE CURRENT MONTH

3 FUTURE YEAR DIVIDERS
ARRANGED CHRONOLOGICALLY

CURRENT MONTH
DIVIDER

3- BY 5-INCH TRACE CARDS
FILED BY FOLLOW-UP
MONTH AND DATE

TICKLER FILE

31 DAILY DIVIDERS, ONE FOR EACH DAY
OF THE MONTH ARRANGED
CHRONOLOGICALLY

3- BY 5-INCH FILE BOX

*A salesperson can use the tickler file as a sales call reminder. The tickler file consists of a file box,
12 monthly divider cards, 31 numbered divider cards, 3-year future cards, and 3- by 5-inch index
cards sometimes referred to as "trace cards."*

Source: James R. Abbey, *Hospitality Sales and Advertising,* 2d ed. (East Lansing, Mich.: Educational Institute of the American Hotel & Motel Association, 1993), p. 104.

reports, contracts, proposals, and the tediously detailed banquet event order. Incomplete information is traced for completion. Illegible information never exists.

Sales Filing Systems

For maximum efficiency in the sales office, an effective filing system is required. Up-to-date information is essential for a successful sales effort, and information must be available quickly. Most non-automated hotels use three separate files to record client information: the trace (or tickler) file, the account file, and the master card file. The contents of these files vary from property to property.

Trace Files. In non-automated sales offices a trace file (also known as a tickler file, bring-up file, or follow-up file) is used as an aid for following up accounts. A reminder note or card is filed in the tickler file by month and date; as seen in Exhibit 5, daily dividers are arranged chronologically for the current month. The system is designed to remind the user of correspondence, telephone calls, or contacts that he or she must handle on a particular date.

For example, suppose a client has reserved space for a training meeting at the property in April. The salesperson will want to contact the client no later than February 15 to finalize meeting plans, so the salesperson would slip a note or a 3 × 5 inch index card (often called a "trace card") dated February 15 into the February tickler divider. On February 1, the notes and trace cards for February would be arranged according to date, and the reminder to contact the meeting planner would be placed into the 15th slot.

This system, as long as it is updated and checked daily, works well and takes very little time to implement. However, the system also depends entirely on the accuracy, efficiency, and completeness with which individual salespersons maintain their trace files.

In automated sales offices, all traces input within the system are activated on the appropriate dates and printed for each salesperson every morning. Exhibit 6 shows a sample **trace report.** As the salesperson reads through each trace message, he or she decides whether to act on the trace or to trace it to another date. Throughout the day, the salesperson records notes on the report regarding each trace. At the end of the day, the report is handed to a staff associate who keys in the notes and updates the report for the next morning. Those traces that have been completed will no longer appear on the report, while those traces awaiting action will continue to appear on future reports until action is taken.

Account Files. In non-automated sales offices, account files are standard-size file folders holding information needed for serving the basic business needs of clients. An account file is started at the time of initial contact with a prospective client and may include programs from previous conventions or meetings the organization has held, convention bureau bulletins, and information relating to the organization that has appeared in newspapers or trade journals. Sales reports and all correspondence relating to previous efforts to secure business should also be in the file. All information in the account file should be in reverse chronological order—that is, the newest paperwork first. Account files are usually filed alphabetically and are often color-coded by geographic location or, more commonly, by market segment.

When an account file is removed, a guide card detailing the name of the group, its file number, the date of removal, and the initials of the person removing the file should be left in the file drawer in place of the file. This ensures that the sales staff will have easy access to the whereabouts of the file.

In automated sales offices, current account information is available to all authorized sales personnel with access to a computer terminal. Typically, the salesperson accessing the system determines the extent of the information displayed. Exhibit 7 shows some of the information that can be displayed at a terminal or printed as a report. This abbreviated report includes general account information, account traces, and account phone calls. General account information displays the account identification number, group name, and all salespersons (sales sources) assigned to the account, as well as contact information. The account traces list all traces attached to the account including to whom the trace is being sent, the trace message, trace date, and whether the trace has been acknowledged. Account phone calls list call reports entered into the system and logged to the specific account.

Exhibit 6   Sample Trace Report

THE HOTEL AND TOWERS
1/15

– DELPHI – **MORNING REPORT** for Ralph Johnson   – RJ   Page: 1

PICKUP TO DATE – CHECK ROOM BLOCKS

GROUP NAME	(ACCOUNT ID)	DATE	DAY	ROOM TYPE	AGREE	BLOCK	PICKUP	NEW BLOCK
SAVIOUR HOSPITAL PERSONNEL	(CLB-00000023)	2/15	Mon	Run of House	10	10	0	_____

ROOMING LIST DUE

GROUP NAME	(ACCOUNT ID)	DATE	DAY	ROOM TYPE	AGREE	BLOCK	PICKUP	NEW BLOCK
MT. SINAI DEPARTMENT OF RADIOLOGY	(DE-00000002)	2/5	Wed	Run of House	25	25	____	_____
		2/6	Thu	Run of House	25	25	____	_____
		2/7	Fri	Run of House	300	300	____	_____
SUN TOURS	(RJ-00000005)	2/16	Fri	Run of House	25	25	____	_____

DEPOSITS DUE

GROUP NAME	(ACCOUNT ID)	ARRIVAL DATE	TRACE DATE	NEW STATUS / NEW TRACE DATE
ARROW DRY CLEANING	(RJ-00000023)	3/20	1/10	____ ___/___/___

VERBAL DEFINITES – CONTRACT DUE

GROUP NAME	(ACCOUNT ID)	ARRIVAL DATE	TRACE DATE	NEW STATUS / NEW TRACE DATE
HOWARD WEDDING	(RG-00000047)	9/1	1/15	____ ___/___/___

TENTATIVES – DECISION DUE

GROUP NAME	(ACCOUNT ID)	ARRIVAL DATE	TRACE DATE	NEW STATUS / NEW TRACE DATE
SAVEMORE INSURANCE	(RJ-00000028)	3/24	11/20	____ ___/___/___
CALIFORNIA BUILDING IND. ASSOC.	(DE-00000006)	10/30	12/20	____ ___/___/___

GET HISTORY

GROUP NAME	(ACCOUNT ID)	ARRIVAL DATE	TRACE DATE	ACTION
AMERICAN WIDGET PRODUCERS ASSOC.	(BL-00000100)	7/21	12/21	____ Complete/New Trace: ___/___/___

MENU SELECTIONS/MEETING DETAILS

GROUP NAME	(ACCOUNT ID)	ARRIVAL DATE	TRACE DATE	ACTION
AMERICAN CONDUCTORS GROUP	(BL-00000123)	2/1	1/15	____ Complete/New Trace: ___/___/___

FREE FORM BOOKING TRACES

GROUP NAME	(ACCOUNT ID)	ARRIVAL DATE	TRACE DATE	ACTION
AMERICAN CONDUCTORS GROUP Trace Message: Confirm AV equipment	(BL-00000123)	2/1	1/15	____ Complete/New Trace: ___/___/___

ACCOUNT TRACES

GROUP NAME	(ACCOUNT ID)	TRACE DATE	ACTION
INDEPENDENT CITIES ASSOC. Trace Message: CALL REGARDING 199X DATES	SE-00000002	1/14	____ Complete/New Trace: ___/___/___

GENERAL TRACES

	TRACE DATE	ACTION
CHECK JUDY'S FILE FOR STATUS ON H.R.R.P. NOTES	1/15	____ Complete/New Trace: ___/___/___

Source: Delphi/Newmarket Software Systems, Inc., Durham, New Hampshire.

Exhibit 7   Sample Account Information Report

THE HOTEL AND TOWERS
12/26

Account Information Report
Page: 1

Beginning Group: A
Ending Group: AB

Listing of:

Account Information
Account Traces
Account Phone Calls

Account Information Report
Page: 2

Account ID: RG–00000025
Group Name: A.G. WARNOCK INC.
Alternate Key: WARNOCK

Group Rooms Sales Source:
Function Sales Source: RG   Ruth Gianet
Service Manager:
Outside Lead Source: CVB   Convention Bureau
Account Quality Rating:
SIC Code: Y
Market Segment: LOC   LOCAL
Geographic Code: 6   100–250 Mile Radius

Contact Name:	Mr. A.C. Warnock		Phone #:	603-944-2656 Ext:
Title:			Fax:	
Salutation:	Mr. Warnock			
Address:	1245 W. Planedale Blvd.			
City:	Camp Drum State: CA Postal Code: 94454		Country:	

Contact Name:	Ms. Kathy Witkje		Phone #:	603-943-9592 Ext.:
Title:	Acme Wedding Consultant		Fax:	603-947-4477
Salutation:	Kathy			
Address:	42777 26th. St. W			
City:	Camp Drum State: CA Postal Code: 94456		Country:	

Send To	Trace Message	Trace Date	Ack
RG	Call Warnock today.	10/14	Y
RG	Address needs to be put into system.	11/13	Y
LB	Call Kathy W. about phone numbers.	1/20	N

Call Date	Call Description
10/7	Talked with Warnock … asked me to check back next week.

Source: Delphi/Newmarket Software Systems, Inc., Durham, New Hampshire.

Master Card Files and Automated Search Routines. In non-automated sales offices, a master card (usually a 5 × 8 inch index card) contains a summary of everything needed for an effective sales effort: the organization's name, the names and titles of key executives, addresses, phone numbers, month or months in which the group meets, the size of the group, where the group has met in the past, the group's decision-maker, and other pertinent data that can help to obtain and keep that account's business. Master card files are also used to create mailing lists and quickly obtain addresses or phone numbers for additional sales efforts or follow-ups.

Master cards are often color-coded to draw attention to specific areas of consideration: geographic location, months of meetings, follow-ups required, and size of group. Some properties also arrange master cards alphabetically by market segment. For example, IBM and Xerox would be sorted alphabetically under "Corporate Business." Other properties may not separate master cards by market segment, but may use a color code system to easily identify specific market segments within the file. For example, an association account may be flagged in blue, a government account in yellow, and so on.

Some properties keep a geographic file of master cards. These cards are organized according to the geographic location of the decision-maker. This type of file enables sales personnel to quickly identify accounts in cities to which they are traveling. Salespeople can simply pull the names of the decision-makers located in the area they are visiting and call on them during the sales trip.

Master card files can easily become overloaded with data as salespeople place more and more demands on the type of information they need to prospect, book, and service clients. In automated sales offices, the functions of a master card filing system are quickly and easily performed by search routines with selection criteria defined by the salesperson's or manager's immediate needs. For example, a salesperson can call up specific information needed for an account, whether it be the names of contacts, notes on follow-up calls, or remarks that can help other members of the sales team answer questions regarding the account in the absence of the salesperson who made the call(s). In addition, a salesperson can search the data base of accounts for clients likely to fit the future booking needs of the hotel. For example, a salesperson could search for only those accounts in the northeast states that book in July for Sunday night arrival. If, on the first run, the generated list is too long or too short, the salesperson could run the search again with different criteria such as rate or space requirements.

Sales Forecasts and Performance Reports

An automated sales office system can produce reports that provide information on accounts, bookings, market segments, sales staff productivity, average room rates, occupancy, revenue, service history, lost business, and important marketing data. Many of these reports would take several hours to produce manually. The following sections describe some of these reports.

Cover Count and Revenue Summary Report. To produce a monthly catering sales forecast at a non-automated property, someone must carefully review each page for a particular month in the function book and calculate (or estimate) each day's

Exhibit 8   Sample Cover Count and Revenue Summary

THE HOTEL AND TOWERS
1/18

Cover Count and Revenue Summary
Page: 1

Report for 1/1/XX to 1/31/XX
Calculated Using Combination of Average Checks / Food & Beverage

Day-Date	Room Rental Def	Ten	Meeting Def	Ten	Reception Def	Ten	Breakfast Def	Ten	Lunch Def	Ten	Dinner Def	Ten	Break Def	Ten	Daily Revenue Summary Def	Ten	Total
Mo 1/1	1000	0	0	0	0	0	100	0	0	0	0	0	0	0	2150	000	2150
Tu 1/2	0	0	0	0	0	0	0	0	0	0	0	0	0	0	0	0	0
We 1/3	0	0	0	0	50	0	0	0	0	0	0	0	0	0	390	0	390
Th 1/4	1500	0	1170	0	230	0	0	0	305	0	190	0	150	0	21678	0	21678
Fr 1/5	300	0	450	0	150	0	0	0	240	0	0	0	150	0	8453	0	8453
Sa 1/6	0	0	75	0	150	0	0	0	0	0	200	0	0	0	7436	0	7436
Su 1/7	0	0	45	0	20	0	0	0	0	0	20	0	0	0	1036	0	1036
Mo 1/8	0	0	130	0	0	0	0	0	20	0	0	0	0	0	1206	0	1206
Tu 1/9	250	0	210	0	0	0	0	0	10	0	0	0	0	0	1832	0	1832
We 1/10	0	0	350	0	125	0	0	0	205	0	0	0	0	0	6708	0	6708
Th 1/11	0	0	157	0	150	0	0	0	137	0	0	0	0	0	4482	0	4482
Fr 1/12	0	0	540	0	0	0	0	0	365	0	0	0	0	0	9646	0	9646
Sa 1/13	500	0	327	16	820	0	0	0	287	16	820	0	0	0	37438	371	37809
Su 1/14	250	0	22	16	0	0	0	0	12	0	0	0	0	0	596	108	704
Mo 1/15	0	0	46	0	20	0	0	0	10	0	20	0	0	0	1207	0	1207
Tu 1/16	4000	0	94	0	44	0	0	0	47	0	0	0	0	0	5750	0	5750
We 1/17	0	0	985	0	0	0	0	0	0	0	0	0	0	0	6649	0	6649
Th 1/18	250	0	1030	0	250	0	25	0	520	0	0	0	0	0	17989	0	17989
Fr 1/19	600	0	555	0	0	0	25	0	115	0	0	0	0	0	6524	0	6524
Sa 1/20	800	0	280	0	420	0	140	0	0	0	520	0	0	0	22552	0	22552
Su 1/21	0	0	20	0	380	0	0	0	20	0	80	0	0	0	5732	0	5732
Mo 1/22	0	0	440	0	80	0	100	0	20	0	80	0	0	0	7377	0	7377
Tu 1/23	0	0	520	0	110	0	0	0	230	0	80	0	0	0	10453	0	10453
We 1/24	0	0	395	0	20	0	30	0	165	0	0	0	0	0	5880	0	5880
Th 1/25	0	0	160	0	110	0	0	0	40	0	110	0	0	0	5764	0	5764
Fr 1/26	0	0	380	20	590	0	0	0	310	20	540	0	0	0	27815	464	28279
Sa 1/27	0	0	50	0	360	0	0	0	0	0	360	0	0	0	13514	0	13514
Su 1/28	0	0	20	0	0	0	0	0	0	0	0	0	0	0	135	0	135
Mo 1/29	0	0	0	0	0	0	0	0	0	0	0	0	0	0	0	0	0
Tu 1/30	2500	0	1000	0	0	0	0	0	0	0	0	0	0	0	9250	0	9250
We 1/31	0	0	0	0	25	0	0	0	0	0	0	0	0	0	195	0	195

Revenue Source	Average Check	Definite Covers	Definite Revenue	Tentative Covers	Tentative Revenue	Total Revenue
Meeting	6.75	9451	63794.25	52	351.00	64145.25
Reception	7.80	4104	32011.20	0	0.00	32011.20
Breakfast	11.50	420	4830.00	0	0.00	4830.00
Lunch	16.44	3058	50273.52	36	591.84	50865.36
Dinner	28.80	3020	86976.00	0	0.00	86976.00
Break	0.00	300	0.00	0	0.00	0.00
Rental			11950.00		0.00	11950.00
Final Total			249834.97		942.84	250777.81

Source: Delphi/Newmarket Software Systems, Inc., Durham, New Hampshire.

cover count and revenue forecast. This could take several hours. Exhibit 8 shows a sample cover count and revenue summary produced in seconds by a sales software package with integrated files. The daily revenue summary figures can be calculated on the basis of estimates (such as multiplying cover counts by check

Exhibit 9   Sample Sales Performance by Market Segment Report

Sales Source Activity Report by Market Segment
Sales Performance Market Segment
Sales Activity between 12/6 and 12/21
Arrivals beginning 1/1

Booking Source: Ralph Johnson

Market Segment	Room Nights Current	(+/–)	Average Rate Current	(+/–)	Room Revenue Current	(+/–)	Food Revenue Current	(+/–)	Beverage Revenue Current	(+/–)
Corporate										
TENTATIVE:	0	0	0.00	0.00	0	0	0	0	0	0
DEFINITE:	130	130	125.00	125.00	16,250	16,250	1,150	1,150	0	0
National Association										
TENTATIVE:	435	–262	170.00	35.00	73,950	–20,145	250,000	221,851	6,100	1,420
DEFINITE:	1,267	1,267	128.80	128.80	163,195	163,195	73,149	73,149	12,680	12,680
Regional Association										
TENTATIVE:	0	0	0.00	0.00	0	0	0	0	0	0
DEFINITE::	2,225	85	134.24	2.58	298,704	16,949	41,190	0	13,845	0
SMERF										
TENTATIVE:	0	–360	0.00	–135.00	0	–48,600	0	–10,657	0	0
DEFINITE:	360	360	135.00	135.00	48,600	48,600	10,657	10,657	0	0
Social										
TENTATIVE:	0	0	0.00	0.00	0	0	0	0	0	0
DEFINITE:	0	–25	0.00	–94.00	0	–2,350	0	0	0	0
State Association										
TENTATIVE:	0	0	0.00	0.00	0	0	0	0	0	0
DEFINITE:	550	450	115.45	20.45	63,500	54,000	153,991	150,000	5,000	5,000
Tour & Travel										
TENTATIVE:	0	0	0.00	0.00	0	0	0	0	0	0
DEFINITE:	50	50	120.00	120.00	6,000	6,000	4,320	0	1,170	0
TOTAL										
TENTATIVE:	435	–622	170.00	35.00	73,950	–68,745	250,000	211,194	6,100	1,420
DEFINITE:	4,582	2,317	130.12	0.50	596,249	302,644	284,457	234,956	32,695	17,680

Source: Delphi/Newmarket Software Systems, Inc., Durham, New Hampshire.

averages for meal periods), they can represent actual revenue figures drawn from completed banquet event orders, or they can be a combination of both methods.

Sales Performance by Market Segment Report. Exhibit 9 shows a sales performance by market segment report that analyzes a salesperson's booking activity by market segment during a specified time period. Under each report heading are sub-headings labeled "cur." and "(+ / –)." "Cur." stands for "current" and shows the value of the heading at the end of the activity period. The sub-heading " + / – " shows the variation of the value during the selected activity period. This report can be used to evaluate the performance of salespersons. A summary report, combining performance data of all salespersons, can also be produced.

Sales Performance Summary Report. Exhibit 10 shows a sample performance summary report that focuses on group guestroom sales. The report helps the sales staff determine how actual sales compare to established goals. While the sample

Exhibit 10   Sample Performance Summary Report

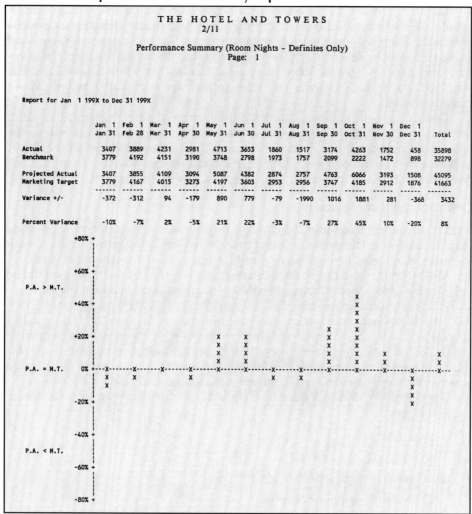

Source: Delphi/Newmarket Software Systems, Inc., Durham, New Hampshire.

report provides information on definite bookings only, similar reports can be produced for tentative bookings or for both definite and tentative bookings. Also, similarly formatted reports can be produced providing information about rates and revenue. A breakdown of sales performance by market segment can also be produced.

Yield Management

Yield management, sometimes called revenue management, is a set of demand-forecasting techniques used to determine whether prices should be raised or lowered and whether a reservation request should be accepted or rejected in order to maximize revenue. Yield management is based on supply and demand. Prices tend to rise when demand exceeds supply; prices tend to fall when supply exceeds demand. Pricing is the key to profitability. By increasing bookings on low-demand days and by selling rooms at higher prices on high-demand days, a hotel improves its profitability. In general, room rates should be higher when demand exceeds supply. They should be lower (in order to increase occupancy) when supply exceeds demand.

One of the principal computations involved in yield management is **yield,** which is the ratio of actual revenue to potential revenue. Actual revenue is the revenue generated by the number of rooms sold. Potential revenue is the amount of money that the property would receive if all of its rooms were sold at full rack rates. There are many formulas used to implement yield management strategies.[2]

Elements of Yield Management

Yield management takes into account as many of the factors influencing business trends as possible. There are various approaches to yield management. Often, each approach is modeled to meet the needs of the individual property or company.

Yield management can be used to determine whether all room rates should be raised or lowered—for example, when the hotel moves out of or into its off-season—and whether selective room rate changes are called for. Yield management becomes more complex when room rate changes are implemented on a selective rather than a general basis, and when it involves selling rooms for which there may be competing buyers. Hotels frequently offer discounts to guests falling into certain categories (for example, senior citizens or government employees). Hotels must also decide whether to accept or refuse group business at a discounted rate.

The following elements must be included in the development of a successful yield strategy:

- Group room sales
- Transient (or FIT) room sales
- Food and beverage activity
- Local and area-wide conventions
- Special events

This section focuses on group room sales.[3]

For many hotels, groups form the foundation of future business. It is common to have reservations for group sales three months to two years in advance. Some international hotels and resorts commonly book groups more than two years in advance. Therefore, understanding group booking trends and requirements can be critical to the success of yield management.

To clearly understand how group sales affect overall room revenue, the hotel should collect as much of the following types of data as possible:

- Business already on the books (reservations)
- Group booking pace (the rate at which group business is being booked)

- Business not yet on the books but likely to return

- Room booking lead time

- Displacement of transient business

Business Already on the Books. Management should determine whether the group blocks already in the reservation file should be reduced because of anticipated cancellations or overestimation of the group's size. If the group has booked at the hotel before, management can often determine this information by looking at the group's booking history. Groups often block 5 percent to 10 percent more rooms than they need to ensure that they will have sufficient space for their members. The deletion of unnecessary group rooms from the group block is called the **wash factor**.

Group Booking Pace. The rate at which group business is being booked is called the **group booking pace**. ("Booking" in this context refers to the initial agreement between the group and the hotel, not to the booking of individual rooms in the block by group members.) For example, suppose that in April of a given year, a hotel has 300 rooms in group blocks due to arrive in October of that year. If the hotel had only 250 group rooms booked for October at the same time the year before, the booking pace would be 20 percent ahead of the previous year's pace. Once a hotel has accumulated several years of operational data, it can often determine a historical trend that reveals the normal booking pace for each month of the year. While simple on the surface, this method of forecasting can become very complicated due to yearly fluctuations. Management should try to keep the method for tracking the group booking pace forecast as simple as possible.

Unbooked Business Likely to Return. Most national, regional, and state associations, as well as some corporations, have policies governing the locations of annual meetings. For example, a group may rotate among three cities, returning to each every three years. Although a contract may not yet be signed, hotel management may be quite confident that the group will return according to the cycle. In addition, tentative bookings which await final contract negotiations are normally included in the yield analysis.

Booking Lead Time. **Booking lead time** measures how far in advance bookings are made. Some hotels have average lead times of two months. For many hotels, group bookings are usually made within one year of actual arrival. Management should determine its hotel's lead time for group bookings so that a booking trend can be charted. This trend can be combined with booking pace information on a graph to illustrate the rate at which the hotel is booking business compared with historical trends (see Exhibit 11). This information can be very important when determining whether to accept an additional group and at what room rate to book the group. If the current booking pace is lower than expected or lags behind the historical trend, it may be necessary to offer a lower room rate to stimulate business through increased occupancy. On the other hand, if demand is strong and the group booking pace is ahead of anticipated or historical trends, it may not be appropriate to discount room rates to increase room revenue.

Exhibit 11   Lead Time/Booking Pace for Sample Hotel

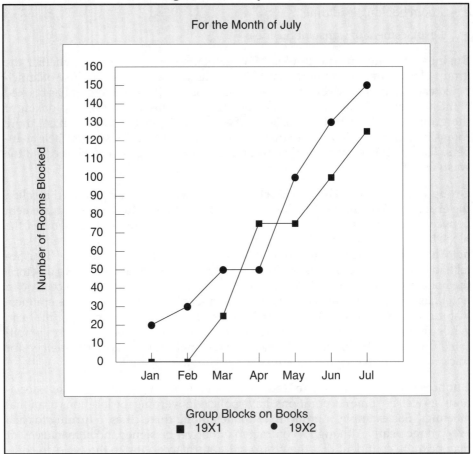

Source: Michael L. Kasavana and Richard M. Brooks, *Managing Front Office Operations,* 4th ed. (East Lansing, Mich.: Educational Institute of the American Hotel & Motel Association, 1995), p. 353.

Displacement of Transient Business. Management should consult its demand forecast when determining whether to accept group business. **Displacement** occurs when a hotel accepts group business at the expense of turning away transient guests. Transient rooms are guestrooms sold to guests who are not affiliated with a group staying at the hotel. These guests, usually called transient guests or FITs (free independent travelers), are often businesspeople or vacationers. Since transient guests often pay higher room rates than group business, any situation involving displacement should be looked at very carefully.

Assume that a 400-room hotel has a **potential average rate** of $100, an actual transient rate of $80, an actual group rate of $60, and a marginal cost (i.e., the variable cost) of $15 per room. Consider the impact of a group requesting a block of 60 rooms during the following four days:

Exhibit 12   Revenue and Yield Calculations

	Tuesday		Wednesday		Thursday		Friday	
	Without Group	With Group	Without Group	With Group	Without Group	With Group	Without Group	With Group
Gross revenue	$24,400	$28,000	$22,800	$26,400	$26,600	$27,800	$25,800	$27,800
Contribution*	19,300	22,000	18,000	20,700	21,050	21,800	20,400	21,800
Yield**	61.0%	70.0%	57.0%	66.0%	66.5%	69.5%	64.5%	69.5%

*Based on a marginal cost of $15.
**Potential revenue = $100 potential average rate × 400 rooms = $40,000.

Source: Michael L. Kasavana and Richard M. Brooks, *Managing Front Office Operations*, 4th ed. (East Lansing, Mich.: Educational Institute of the American Hotel & Motel Association, 1995), p. 354.

	Tuesday	Wednesday	Thursday	Friday
Room Nights Available	400	400	400	400
Definite Group Demand	140	140	150	150
Expected Transient Demand	200	180	220	210
Available Rooms	60	80	30	40
Suggested Group	60	60	60	60
Transient Displacement	0	0	30	20

If this group is accepted, no displacement occurs on Tuesday and Wednesday; the hotel clearly benefits on these days because it sells rooms it did not expect to sell (earning an additional $3,600 gross and $2,700 net room revenue each day). On Thursday and Friday, however, 30 and 20 transient guests, respectively, will be displaced. Still, as shown in Exhibit 12, Thursday's room revenue will rise by $1,200 gross and $750 net if the group is accepted. Friday's room revenue will rise by $2,000 gross and $1,400 net if the group is accepted. In other words, accepting the group business will increase the hotel's yield for all four days. Since it also raises the hotel's occupancy, the group business will probably increase non-room revenue as well.

Several factors help determine whether a group reservation should be accepted. As just illustrated, the hotel should first look at revenue factors. A group should probably be accepted if the expected revenue gain (including that from non-room revenue centers) offsets the transient guest revenue loss. In addition, management must consider what happens to the transient guests who cannot be accommodated. Whether they are frequent or first-time guests, they may decide not to return after the way they are treated. The transient revenue lost may not be confined simply to the nights in question if frequent guests choose not to return. Of course, turning away the group business may also reduce the chance that the group will return. Deciding whether to accept a group that forces transient displacement is more than an issue of easily identifiable numbers. Management must also consider the longer-term impact on future business.

Using Yield Management

All elements of yield management (group room sales, transient room sales, food and beverage activity, local and area-wide conventions, and special events) should be viewed together in order to make the appropriate decisions. While it is potentially complex, a failure to include relevant factors may make yield management efforts less successful than they could be.

Yield should be tracked daily. Tracking yield for past days can help reveal trends. However, to use yield management properly, management must track yield for *future* days. Calculations must be done every day for a future period, depending on how far in advance the hotel books business. If a hotel is currently at 50 percent yield for a day three weeks away, there may be plenty of time to put strategies in place to raise that number. Discounts may be opened to raise occupancy, or some discounts may be closed to raise average rate. It is the balance of occupancy and rate that achieves the highest yield. If achieving the potential room revenue is not possible (and it usually is not), the manager must decide on the best combination of rate and occupancy in order to get the highest yield.

Each piece of group business should be looked at individually. It should be compared to historical trends as well as to the budget. A hotel usually has a group sales target or budgeted figure for each month. Each group should be examined to see if it will contribute to meeting the budget. If demand is strong and the group will create low revenue, the hotel may decide not to book it. If demand is weak, the hotel may decide to accept the group simply to create revenue from rooms that would not otherwise be occupied. Using the group booking pace analysis will help management determine whether the hotel is on track for its target.

Another factor is the actual group booking pattern already on the books. For example, due to booked groups, a hotel may have two days between groups that are not busy. Management may take a lower-revenue-producing group just to fill the gap. The opposite may also occur. A group may want to come in over a period when the hotel is near filling its goal of group rooms. The group may take the hotel over its goal. While this appears to be good, it may displace higher-rated transient business. If the hotel wants the group, it may quote such a rate to the group that will help make up the lost revenue caused by the displacement of transient guests.

The same type of analysis is needed for transient business. For example, due to the discounts the hotel offers, corporate and government business may be assigned the standard category of rooms. As these standard rooms fill, the hotel may only have deluxe rooms left to sell. If demand is not strong, management may decide to sell the deluxe rooms at the standard rack rate to remain competitive. It is best to look at a combined picture (group and transient business) before making these occupancy and rate decisions.

It is important to remember that historical trends do not always apply. More recent trends must also be taken into consideration. For example, if historical trends have been strong, but recent business has been weak, it is better to plan for weak business and attempt to attract as much as possible through low rates. Likewise, if recent occupancy has been very strong, it is appropriate to follow that trend instead of a history showing lower demand.

Since the objective of yield management is to maximize revenue, tracking business by revenue source will also help management determine when to allow discounted business and when not to allow it. Some hotels may decide to allow specific types of discounted business, such as corporate business, since they are responsible for many repeat guests. As the various sources of business are determined, each should be analyzed to understand its impact on total revenue. Quite often, managers will take discounted business if it generates frequent customers, since the long-term impact is very positive.

Yield Management Computer Software

Although the individual tasks of yield management can be performed manually, doing so is very difficult and time-consuming. The most efficient means of handling data and generating yield statistics is through a computer. Sophisticated yield management software can integrate room demand and room price statistics, and project the highest revenue-generating product mix. These packages often consider what the competition is charging.

Such software does not make decisions for managers. It merely provides them with information and support for their decisions. The advantage of using a computer for yield management is that it can store, quickly retrieve, and manipulate great amounts of data on a broad range of factors influencing room revenue. Over time, yield management software can help management create models showing the probable results of decisions; these models are based on history, forecasts, and booked business.

Those industries that have applied computer-based yield management have achieved the following results:

- Continual monitoring: a computerized yield management system can track and analyze business conditions 24 hours a day, 7 days a week.

- Consistency: software can be programmed to respond to specific changes in the marketplace, according to corporate or local management rules built into the software.

- Information availability: yield management software can provide improved management information which, in turn, may help managers make more intelligent decisions more quickly.

- Performance tracking: a computer-based system is capable of analyzing sales and revenue transactions occurring within a business period to determine how well yield management goals were achieved.

Yield management software is also able to generate any number of special reports. The following reports are representative of yield management software output.

Market Segment Report. This report provides information regarding customer mix. This information is important to effective forecasting by market segment.

Calendar/Booking Graph. This graph presents room-night demands and volume of reservations on a daily basis.

Exhibit 13   Sample Overrides Report

```
┌─────────────────────────────────────────────────────────────────────────────┐
│                         THE HOTEL AND TOWERS                                  │
│                                12/26                                          │
│                                                                               │
│                       All Bookings Requiring Decisions                        │
│                                Page: 1                                        │
│                                                                               │
│  Decision                                                                     │
│   Due      Group Name                       Stat   Dates of Stay   RN's  Avg Rate   Reason      │
│                                                                               │
│   12/25    CENTER FOR HEALTH EDUCATION       D     1/9  –  1/13    270   110.00    Contribution  │
│   11/30    KINETIC SCULPTURE INC.            D     3/4  –  3/8      85   147.35    Availability   │
│   12/26    ULTIMATE TOUR AND TRAVEL INC.     D     3/6              25    94.00    Contri/Avail   │
│   11/15    ALASKA MOVING AND STORAGE ASSOC.  T     4/17 –  4/21    750   125.00    Availability   │
│   11/14    NORDIC FINANCE ASSOCIATION        D     6/16 –  6/19    773   101.48    Availability   │
│   11/30    ALPINE HILLS MEDICAL CENTER       T     6/22 –  6/23    180   150.00    Contri/Avail   │
│   11/20    EAGLE RIVER TRIAL LAWYERS ASSOC.  D     7/5  –   7/8    348   150.00    Availability   │
│   12/8     SMITH FAMILY REUNION              VD    9/1              50   120.00    Availability   │
│   12/18    SAVEMORE INSURANCE                DD    9/20 –  9/21    150   110.00    Availability   │
│   11/22    PUBLIC SAFETY EMPLOYEES ASSOCIATION T  10/13 – 10/18    965   124.33    Availability   │
│   11/20    ASSOCIATION OF COUNTY CONSERVATION T   11/6  – 11/10    372    88.00    Contri/Avail   │
│   11/20    ASSOCIATION OF COUNTY CONSERVATION T   11/6  – 11/10    281   115.00    Availability   │
│   11/16    MERRIMAC AUTOMOBILE DEALERS ASSOC. D    4/19 –  4/24     99   145.00    Contribution   │
│   11/24    STEWARD TECHNICIAN ASSOCIATION    T     5/1  –   5/5    519   142.66    Availability   │
└─────────────────────────────────────────────────────────────────────────────┘
```

Source: Delphi/Newmarket Software Systems, Inc., Durham, New Hampshire.

Booking Overrides Report. Exhibit 13 shows a sample overrides report listing all bookings that fail to meet contribution margins or availability constraints as determined by management. The report provides management with information necessary to evaluate questionable bookings before contracts are sent to clients.

Future Arrival Dates Status Report. This report furnishes demand data for each day of the week. The report contains a variety of forecasting information that allows for the discovery of occupancy trends by comparative analysis of weekdays. It can be designed to cover several future periods.

Single Arrival Date History Report. This report indicates the hotel's booking patterns (trends in reservations). The report relates to the booking graph by documenting how a specific day was constructed on the graph.

Weekly Recap Report. This report contains the sell rates for rooms and the number of rooms authorized and sold in marketing programs with special or discounted rates.

Room Statistics Tracking Sheet. This report tracks no-shows, guaranteed no-shows, walk-ins, and turn-aways. This information can be instrumental in accurate forecasting.

Since management is likely to grab a chance to enhance its revenue performance, computer-aided yield management is a welcome addition to the assortment of available hospitality industry software.

Food Service Catering Software Packages

Although considered an important growth segment in food service, catering has been a late addition to computer applications software. While catering is similar in many ways to traditional restaurant operations, there are several unique characteristics which should be addressed. There are two different types of catering for which computer applications have been developed: off-premises catering and **finished product** (or home delivery) **catering**. These are discussed in the following sections.

Off-Premises Catering

There are many details involved in the proposal, planning, and execution stages of an off-premises catering activity. Initially, the caterer suggests a standard menu or set of menus to a client for consideration. The client either selects from available offerings or requests a special meal plan. In either case, the caterer develops a proposal for the function.

Caterers are responsible for food and beverage service and may also be contracted to provide furnishings, entertainment, decorations, and the like. Before an event, the caterer typically plans for necessary purchases, personnel, production, transportation, service, and rental equipment. Generally, the caterer arrives at a catered event with all these requirements, because supplemental equipment, product replenishment, and additional staff are usually not available at the catered site. After the activity, the caterer must be sure that the client settles the account.

Catering software monitors and controls the activities associated with each stage of **off-premises catering service**. Many of the files created through the use of catering software packages perform functions similar to computer-based restaurant management applications. Typical files included in a catering software package include:

- Ingredient file
- Recipe file
- Menu item file
- Proposal/contract file
- Inventory file
- General accounting files

In addition to containing data on all purchased food and beverage products, the ingredient file includes data on such non-food items as labor, serving utensils, production equipment, rental equipment, disposable items, and entertainment options. The more complete this file, the easier it becomes for the caterer to assemble an entire catering service package.

While standard recipes for food service operations list ingredients and a set of assembly instructions, an off-premises catering recipe generally contains "ingredients" for non-food items as well. For example, a table and chairs recipe may be recorded in a recipe file to assist in determining the number of tables and chairs required for a particular catered event. A caterer who seats eight persons per table would input this as a recipe. If the caterer were planning an off-premises catering activity for 240 persons, the table and chairs recipe would state 30 tables and 240 chairs as required ingredients. In addition, the recipe file generally accesses cost

Exhibit 14   Sample Event Worksheet

```
Event:01234    Date:06/21        Start:19:30  End:21:30           Page:   1

Party:00085    Mgr:SAM

Account:GREENJ   (Cash)

Jane Green
301 Saddle River Road
Saddle River, NJ 07450
201-447-5350


Tent must be installed on Wed at 3:00pm.

          1  Buffet
         85  Crudite with Dips
         85  Assorted Cheeses
         85  Eggplant Caviar
         85  Assorted Canapes
         85  Sesame Chicken Brst
         85  Pasta Bar
         45  Assorted Pastries
          2  Chocolate Cake
          1  Ice Carving
          2  8-ft Banquet Table
         45  White Chair


Start at 14:30  for  05:00     OC:D Bert Brent     201-444-8732
         15:30  for  04:00     OC:A Andrea Andersen     201-889-8989
         15:00  for  03:50     OC:B Charles Cook    201-447-3212
```

Source: Standard Commercial Systems, Ridgewood, New Jersey.

data contained in the ingredient file and can generate the cost of supplying any number of tables and chairs. The table and chairs recipe would be used as a sub-recipe within a larger recipe. Any number of sub-recipes can be chained to produce a single recipe which contains a large number and wide range of ingredients. Cost figures for all food, beverage, and non-food ingredients can be generated for almost any recipe.

The menu item file contains meal plans for specific catered activities. Catering menu item files contain recipes for consumable as well as non-consumable items. Some catering software packages remind users to create recipes for determining required gratuities, insurance, and taxes. All of these recipes are collected within a menu item file for specific catered events.

A proposal/contract file accesses data contained in the menu item file, develops prices for menu items, and maintains a record of commitments. The inventory file and general accounting files perform the same functions as computer-based inventory and back office accounting applications.

Off-premises catering applications provide event calendars that list customer names, addresses, and notes that apply to specific events. A calendar may list events by a specific date, or it may cover a longer time period and list events assigned to a particular manager. Some applications convert information from the

Exhibit 15   Sample Cost Analysis Report

The Modern Caterer			Cost Analysis				Page 1
Jane Green				Invoice No:01234A			
301 Saddle River Road				Deliver on:06/21			
Saddle River, NJ 07450				Persons: 85			
201-447-5350							

			—Cost—		—Retail—		
Code		Qty	Price	Amount	Price	Amount	Margin
S3	Buffet @ 1.25	85			150.00	256.25	
G1	Crudite with Dips	85	.45	38.25	1.50	127.50	89.25
G2	Assorted Cheeses	85	.45	38.25	1.75	148.75	110.50
G3	Eggplant Caviar	85	.75	63.75	2.50	212.50	148.75
G4	Assorted Canapes	85	.55	46.75	1.00	85.00	38.25
G5	Sesame Chicken Brst	85	.35	29.75	.95	80.75	51.00
G6	Pasta Bar	85	.35	29.75	1.25	106.25	76.50
D2	Assorted Pastries	45	.50	22.50	2.00	90.00	67.50
D1	Chocolate Cake	2	3.00	6.00	15.00	30.00	24.00
D5	Ice Carving	1	100.00	100.00	300.00	300.00	200.00
F5	8-ft Banquet Table	2	1.00	2.00	12.00	24.00	22.00
F6	White Chair	45	.25	11.25	3.00	135.00	123.75
			107.65	388.25	490.95	1,596.00	1,207.75

Cost Per Person =   4.56   Retail Cost Per Person =   18.77

Source: Standard Commercial Systems, Ridgewood, New Jersey.

event calendars into production requirements for different preparation areas such as hot foods, cold foods, rentals, and cutlery and linen. This feature is particularly helpful because customers are likely to change the number of people expected in their party up to 24 hours before the event.

Exhibit 14 depicts a sample event worksheet. The worksheet can be used to plan an event with a customer. Also, the manager of the event uses the worksheet as a checklist to ensure that all requested items are properly prepared and readied for the event. The worksheet lists the number of people in the party, the manager in charge of the event, the employees scheduled to work the event, the customer's name and address, and all of the food, furniture, props, and other items requested.

Once entered within the system, an event worksheet can be converted into a cost analysis report. Exhibit 15 shows information a catering manager uses when pricing a particular event. If a customer requests changes, a new cost analysis is prepared for the new event worksheet. Exhibit 16 illustrates an invoice prepared from data contained in the sample event worksheet and the accompanying cost analysis.

Home Delivery Catering

The food service industry has begun adopting home delivery catering systems at an astounding rate. Much of the impetus for this current trend in food service

Exhibit 16   Sample Invoice

The Modern Caterer
1988 Main Street
Anywhere, US 12345-6789
201-447-5350

Invoice No:01234A   Event Date:06/21   7:30pm   85 Persons

Jane Green
301 Saddle River Road
Saddle River, NJ 12345
201-447-5350

1	Buffet	256.25
85	Crudite with Dips	127.50
85	Assorted Cheeses	148.75
85	Eggplant Caviar	212.50
85	Assorted Canapes	85.00
85	Sesame Chicken Brst	80.75
85	Pasta Bar	106.25
45	Assorted Pastries	90.00
2	Chocolate Cake	30.00
1	Ice Carving	300.00
2	8-ft Banquet Table	24.00
45	White Chair	135.00

Total	>>	1,596.00
Tax	>>	131.67
Less Deposit	>>	500.00
Pay this amount	>>	1,227.67

Use these two lines for advertisements,
special announcements, etc. . . . .

Source: Standard Commercial Systems, Ridgewood, New Jersey.

comes from recent computer system technology. Regardless of whether home delivery is offered by multi-unit food service chains or by single independent units, a computer-based home delivery system offers restaurateurs significant competitive advantages.

Some multi-unit food service operators have home delivery networks that are similar in design to hotel central reservation systems. The focal point of the network is an order-taking center connected to remote production and delivery stations. As orders are transmitted to remote work stations, so too is the responsibility for their fulfillment and eventual home delivery.

In the case of single independent units, the order process originates with the order-taker entering the caller's telephone number into the computer system. Entering this data automatically initiates a search through the system's customer master file.

If the customer has not placed an order before, a customer record is created as a consequence of the order-taking routine. With some systems this routine begins with the order-taker using the system's area or street index to determine whether the customer is within the establishment's delivery area. If so, the order-taker enters a

Exhibit 17   Sample Home-Delivery Order-Entry Screen

```
        F O O D M A N  –  Order-Taker  –  02/15           19:36

   1. Action:0  Telephone:447-5350        Order No:2023      Date:0125

   2. Name:  Paula Paterson              House#:345   Street:ZW
      Addr:  345 Shelton Avenue                       Del/PU:D
      Addr:  Apt 3b                                   Del by: 9:00PM
      City:  Midland Park                State:NJ     Zip:07432      Sales
        SI:  Use rear of driveway                     Brthdy:0215    $263.12

  01  │  01 │ LA  LL  LM  LR   │ Personal Pizza/Extra Cheese/Pepperoni/Mushrooms
  02  │  01 │ EL              │ Pepsi-Cola
  03  │     │ (these are menu │
  04  │     │ codes for the   │    (Line items are displayed in this section
  05  │     │ items ordered)  │     for operator verification and read-back)

  Actions:  O  =  New Order  T  =  Take–out    C  =  Change Order    Price:   6.50
            S  =  Search     N  =  Next Order  I  =  Print Invoice   Tax:      .39
            D  =  Delete     P  =  Punch-in/out Q  =  Quit           Total:   6.89
```

Source: Standard Commercial Systems, Ridgewood, New Jersey.

street code and the customer's house number and telephone number. The system then creates a customer record and automatically completes mailing information (city, state, and ZIP code) for future direct mail promotions. Some systems also add map coordinates and route information to the customer record. This information automatically appears on the receipt for the customer's order, thus helping the driver to deliver the order in a timely manner.

If the customer has placed an order at the establishment before, an electronic customer record is retrieved from the database. Exhibit 17 shows one type of order-entry screen format. Note that the screen displays the customer's total sales to date. This helps the order-taker know when he or she is talking to one of the establishment's better customers.

Many computer-based home delivery systems also provide establishments with files for scheduling employees, recording time worked by employees, analyzing sales, and recording accounts payable data. Exhibit 18 shows a special check-out screen used by delivery drivers at the end of their shifts. The system prompts the employee to enter ending mileage, coupons accepted (up to six different coupons), and any gasoline expense. The amount due from the driver is calculated. With this particular system, it is also possible to reimburse drivers who use their own cars. The compensation can be made on the basis of a percentage of the total deliveries.

Summary

This chapter compared non-automated and automated hotel sales office systems in relation to group guestroom sales, function and banquet room sales, and sales office filing systems. Automated sales office systems overcome many of the difficulties that arise in non-automated properties when a guestroom control book is used to guide booking activity. Automated systems provide every salesperson with immediate access to complete and up-to-date information about the number of guestrooms committed to groups.

Exhibit 18   Sample Home-Delivery Employee Check-Out Screen

```
                 F O O D M A N  –  Operations Manager  –  02/15    12:00

       1. Action:0                      Employee:ARD
       ──────────────────────────────────────────────────────────────────
       Press F1 to start over if you make an error
       Enter ending mileage:004534
       Enter gasoline expense:  5.00            Total Mileage:  54
                                                   Deliveries:  12   Amount: 185.76
                                                Total Coupons:  17.00
                                                Car Allowance:
                                                    Total Due: 163.76


       Enter Coupons Below:

       Code:V1      Qty:6       Code:V2     Qty:11       Code:      Qty:
       Code:        Qty:        Code:       Qty:         Code:      Qty:

       Punch-In at:16:45                    Occupation:D
       Punch-Out at:19:50 on 2/15           Total time was:03:05
```

Source: Standard Commercial Systems, Ridgewood, New Jersey.

Sophisticated sales office software packages eliminate cumbersome function books maintained by non-automated properties. Once a booking is entered into the system, it is automatically integrated, tracked, and traced for management reports, contracts, proposals, and the tediously detailed banquet event order.

Automated sales office systems eliminate trace (tickler) files, account files, and master card files maintained by non-automated sales offices. Once information is entered into the system, daily trace reports can be produced for each salesperson. Also, each salesperson can access general account information as well as detailed information, such as traces, messages, and telephone call reports related to a specific client.

Other advantages of automated sales office systems include the various reports that provide information on accounts, bookings, market segments, sales staff productivity, average room rates, occupancy revenue, service history, lost business, and important marketing data.

This chapter also examined the automation of yield management strategies. Yield management is a set of demand-forecasting techniques used to determine whether prices should be raised or lowered and whether a reservation request should be accepted or rejected in order to maximize revenue. The advantage of using a computer for yield management is that it can store, quickly retrieve, and manipulate great amounts of data on a broad range of factors influencing room revenue.

Food service catering software packages were also presented in this chapter. Off-premises catering software files include ingredient files, recipe files, menu item files, proposal/contract files, inventory files, and general accounting files. Special features of home delivery catering applications were also examined.

Endnotes

1. For more information on non-automated and automated sales offices, see James R. Abbey, *Hospitality Sales and Advertising*, 2d ed. (East Lansing, Mich.: Educational Institute of the American Hotel & Motel Association, 1993), Chapter 3.

2. For a complete discussion of these formulas, see Michael L. Kasavana and Richard M. Brooks, *Managing Front Office Operations,* 4th ed. (East Lansing, Mich.: Educational Institute of the American Hotel & Motel Association, 1995), Chapter 11.

3. For a detailed discussion of the other major elements of yield management, see Kasavana and Brooks.

Key Terms

banquet event order
booking lead time
displacement
finished product catering delivery
group booking pace
guestroom control book

off-premises catering service
potential average rate
trace report
wash factor
yield
yield management

Discussion Questions

1. What are the advantages an automated sales office has over a non-automated sales office?

2. What are the advantages of using an automated sales system to create a function book and a banquet event order?

3. How does automation facilitate trace file, account file, and master card file systems?

4. What is the goal of yield management?

5. What role does booking pace play in yield management?

6. Why is transient displacement analysis so important in determining whether to accept a group reservation?

7. What does the term "off-premises catering" mean?

8. What does "finished product catering delivery" mean?

9. What files are typically included in catering software packages?

10. What competitive advantages do computer-based home delivery systems offer?

REVIEW QUIZ

When you feel you have covered all of the material in this chapter, answer these questions. Choose the *best* answer.

Matching

1. Trace file

2. Wash factor

3. Yield

4. FITs

5. Displacement

6. Booking lead time

7. Group booking pace

8. Guestroom control book

a. Identifies number of guest-rooms available to groups on a given day

b. Also called the function book

c. Tickler file

d. Account file

e. Actual revenue divided by potential revenue

f. Measurement of how far in advance bookings are made

g. Transient guests

h. Group guests

i. Average daily rate times the occupancy percentage

j. Turning away transient guests because of group sales

k. The rate at which group business is being booked

l. A booking overrides report

m. Deletion of unnecessary rooms from a group block

True (T) or False (F)

T   F   9. A major challenge of non-automated sales offices is maintaining an accurate guestroom control book.

T   F   10. The function book shows the occupancies and vacancies of specific function and banquet rooms.

T   F   11. Among other things, a banquet event order generally serves as a work order for the catering department.

T   F   12. A market segment report charts room-night demand and reservations on a daily basis.

Alternate/Multiple Choice

13. In non-automated sales offices, the key to successful banquet space control is the:

    a. group booking pace report.
    b. function book.

14. In an automated sales office, the functions of a master card filing system are performed by automated:

    a. search routines.
    b. trace files.

15. Which of the following employees should be kept informed about group guest-room sales?

    a. front desk employees
    b. reservations agents
    c. sales office employees
    d. all of the above

Chapter Outline

Accounts Receivable Module
    Customer Master File
    Management Reports
Accounts Payable Module
    Vendor Master File
    Invoice Register File
    Check Register File
Payroll Module
    Employee Master File
    Payroll Register File
    Other Functions
Inventory Module
    Inventory Status
    Inventory Valuation
    Special Food and Beverage Concerns
Purchasing Module
    Purchase Order File
    Telecommunication of Purchase Orders
    Other Functions
Financial Reporting Module
    Chart of Accounts
    Trial Balance File
    Financial Statements
    Ratio Analysis
Summary

Learning Objectives

1. Identify functions performed by an accounts receivable module.

2. Describe files maintained by an accounts receivable module and typical reports generated for management.

3. Identify the functions performed by an accounts payable module.

4. Describe files maintained by an accounts payable module and typical reports generated for management.

5. Identify characteristics of hospitality operations that complicate the design of a back office payroll module.

6. Explain how differences among purchase units, issue units, and standard recipe units complicate the design of a back office inventory module.

7. Describe two basic ways by which a purchasing module can automatically generate purchase orders.

8. Identify functions performed by a financial reporting module.

10

Accounting Applications

Hospitality industry back office packages vary in the number of accounting applications they provide. This chapter focuses on software modules which are typically included in back office packages:

- Accounts receivable
- Accounts payable
- Payroll accounting
- Inventory accounting
- Purchasing
- Financial reporting

The specific needs and requirements of individual properties determine whether these modules are purchased and operated separately or as an integrated back office applications package. Since the greatest value (in terms of capitalizing on technology) is derived from a fully integrated package, this chapter treats each back office module as if it were part of an overall hospitality management system.

Accounts Receivable Module

The term **accounts receivable** refers to obligations owed to a lodging or food and beverage property from sales made on credit. An accounts receivable application typically performs the following functions:

- Maintains account balances
- Processes billings
- Monitors collection activities
- Generates aging of accounts receivable reports
- Produces an audit report indicating all accounts receivable transactions

Management can also set various credit limits and the module can print reports that list all accounts with balances above their established credit limit. For each account, the module can maintain a variety of credit history data. This data typically indicates the number of days elapsed between payments and the oldest invoice to which the last payment applied.

With an integrated hotel property management system, accounts receivable balances may be automatically transferred from a front office accounting module to a back office accounts receivable module during the system update routine. The **city ledger** is a subsidiary ledger listing accounts receivable balances of guests who have checked out, and other receivables as well. Data from the front office accounting module (such as balances from guest folios, non-guest accounts, bill-to accounts, credit card billings, and others) form part of the **city ledger file** of the back office accounts receivable module.

Some front office systems simplify account billing procedures by creating semi-permanent and permanent folios. Semi-permanent folios are assigned to guest or non-guest accounts designated for direct billing. Permanent folios are assigned to credit card companies and other long-term contracted credit relationships.

As payments are received or additional charges incurred, they are posted to the appropriate city ledger account. Payments or charges posted to the accounts receivable module immediately update the city ledger file, helping to ensure that all account balances are current.

Customer Master File

A **customer master file** sets up billing information. Customer data maintained in this file may include:

- Account code

- Name of guest or account

- Address

- Telephone number

- Contact person

- Type of account

- Credit limit

- Last payment date

- Last payment amount

- Credit history

Generally, management identifies the names of the various types of accounts. These accounts are not mutually exclusive and can be classified as transient, permanent, credit card company, direct billing, and so on. Accounts receivable modules automatically generate individual account invoices.

Since restaurants maintain few house accounts and accept a limited number of travel and entertainment or bank credit cards, they generally process fewer accounts receivable transactions than do hotels. Therefore, a food service accounts receivable package may be responsible for creating and maintaining a relatively small customer master file.

Management Reports

An accounts receivable module generally allows management to access data on any account stored in an accounts receivable file. Many modules maintain an

Exhibit 1   Sample Aging of Accounts Receivable Report

```
DATE:                          ACCOUNTS RECEIVABLE
                         AGED ACCOUNTS RECEIVABLE REPORT
                             01 – ABC RESTAURANT INC.
                                  Aging Date:                          PAGE: 1
```

CUSTOMER		INVOICE					
NUMBER	NAME	NUMBER	DATE DUE	CURRENT	OVER 30	OVER 60	OVER 90
1	AMERICAN EXPRESS	10577		0.00	2,442.53	0.00	0.00
1	AMERICAN EXPRESS	10776		567.71	0.00	0.00	0.00
				567.71	2,442.53	0.00	0.00
2	MASTERCARD	10578		0.00	1,676.77	0.00	0.00
2	MASTERCARD	10777		97.98	0.00	0.00	0.00
				97.98	1,676.7	0.00	0.00
10	JAMES JOHNSON	10774		122.56	0.00	0.00	0.00
10	JAMES JOHNSON	10775		165.36	0.00	0.00	0.00
				287.92	0.00	0.00	0.00

```
                       AGED ACCOUNTS RECEIVABLE TOTALS
                                 Aging Date:
```

CURRENT		OVER 30		OVER 60		OVER 90	
NO.	AMOUNT	NO.	AMOUNT	NO.	AMOUNT	NO.	AMOUNT
3	953.61	2	4119.30	0	0.00	1	0.00

Source: Datachecker Systems Inc., a subsidiary of National Semiconductor Corporation, Santa Clara, California.

accounts aging file, containing data that can be formatted into a variety of aging reports. An **aging of accounts receivable schedule** breaks down each account in the accounts aging file according to the date of the initial charge. Exhibit 1 illustrates a sample aging of accounts receivable report produced by a restaurant back office accounting system.

Although aging schedules can be printed on demand, they are routinely generated during month-end file updates. In addition, an accounts receivable module can automatically print (on letter-head stationery) a series of standard dunning letters for all accounts in 30-day and over delinquent payment categories. A dunning letter is a request for payment of an outstanding balance.

An accounts receivable module can streamline reports for specific users. Much of the detailed information in an aging schedule may not be necessary for some accounting functions. In these cases, data maintained in the accounts aging file can be selected according to the user's specific needs for customized aging reports. In addition, a summary aging of accounts receivable report may be produced for management.

For security, some accounts receivable modules issue an audit report showing accounts receivable transactions. An audit report usually charts each account by account code, account name, invoice number(s) and amount(s), and the types of transactions processed over a specified time period.

Accounts Payable Module

The term **accounts payable** refers to liabilities incurred for merchandise, equipment, or other goods and services purchased by the hospitality operation on account. The accounts payable module can be a stand-alone system or it can work with other modules of an automated accounting system. When this module is part of an accounting system, it maintains current payables records through on-line automatic posting of transactions to the financial reporting (or general ledger) module. This helps prevent duplicate entries of invoices and gives management up-to-date information on invoices and vendors.

An accounts payable application maintains a vendor master file, an invoice register file, and a check register file, and typically performs the following functions:

- Posts purveyor invoices

- Monitors vendor payment discount periods

- Determines amounts due

- Produces checks for payment

- Facilitates the reconciliation of cleared checks

- Generates numerous management reports

With a fully integrated hotel property management system, an accounts payable module can also access travel agent commission data from the front office reservations module to print travel agent commission checks. Along with each check, the module can print a voucher which lists guest name, arrival date, and other reservations data. Alternatively, accounts payable modules without access to reservations data require staff to hand-process commission checks, treating them as typical accounts payable invoices.

Additional reports that can be produced from data in accounts payable module files are payables aging reports, vendor status reports, vendor activity reports, and monthly check registers. A **check register** is a printout of the checks written during a specified time period. The checks can be sorted by vendor or by the invoice due date. An **accounts payable aging report** can contain several aging columns and list invoices by vendor number, vendor name, invoice number, and invoice date. Generally, this report can be printed on demand and streamlined to meet the needs of users. A **monthly check register** provides a hard copy audit trail of payments made to vendors. This report also identifies checks which have not been accounted for. Exhibit 2 shows a sample vendor status report.

Vendor Master File

The **vendor master file** maintains records of all current vendors. Data contained in this file may include:

Exhibit 2 Sample Vendor Status Report

Vendor	Vendor Name	Balance Accruals	MTD Payments	MTD Accruals	YTD Payments	YTD
		VENDOR STATUS REPORT BY VENDOR NUMBER				
		ECI HOTEL PROPERTIES, INC.				
051462	Spunky's Produce	150.00	150.00	143.36	603.36	453.36
051562	Upton's Fish Market	0.00	−159.63	−159.63	0.00	0.00
051662	Cory Cow's Dairy Farm	0.00	0.00	101.92	101.92	101.92
051762	Capital Dry Goods	0.00	0.00	65.00	65.00	65.00
051862	Dolly Madison Bakery			0.00	0.00	
051962	Miltons Meat Market	0.00	0.00	269.00	269.00	269.00
052062	Amy's Amenities	0.00	0.00	500.00	500.00	500.00
052162	Denmark Data Forms	0.00	0.00	2500.00	2500.00	2500.00
052262	Suttons Pool Supplies			0.00	0.00	
121213	Carmen's Cleaning Service	92.00	92.00	0.00	92.00	
121214	S&S Quality Produce	1500.00	0.00	500.00	2000.00	500.00
121215	G&G Produce			0.00	0.00	
121217	Sounds of Music	0.00	0.00	890.00	890.00	890.00
121231	Coors Dist.	0.00	0.00	1300.30	1300.30	1300.30
121235	Nordic Princess Cheesecak			0.00	0.00	
121313	Southwest Laund	125.00	248.00	123.00	248.00	123.00
171717	Southern California			0.00	0.00	
1000000	ABC Lumber					
1212121	Pacific Bell	500.00	500.00	1000.00	1500.00	1000.00
1212129	Artistic Florist	0.00	0.00	175.00	175.00	175.00
1234698	Keenan's Uniform Supplies	0.00	0.00	15069.69	33659.02	33659.02
1256153	Martins Flower Shop	0.00	0.00	0.00	300.00	300.00
3249874	Eat Um Up Food Service	0.00	0.00	10002.38	10002.38	10002.38
4151265	Pacific Gas Company			0.00	0.00	
5261235	Bostonian Federal			0.00	0.00	
5468923	Halp Company			0.00	0.00	
6587463	Liquid Refreshment Inc.	0.00	0.00	2253.68	2253.68	2253.68
7878787	First Intermedian Bank	526.34	526.34	526.34	1052.68	526.34
8585858	Tony's Seafood			0.00	0.00	
9999999	Onetime Vendor	0.00	250.00	350.00	350.00	350.00
		2893.34	1606.71	35610.04	57862.34	54969.00

[405] 30 Items Listed.

Source: ECI, EECO Computer Inc., Santa Ana, California.

- Vendor number
- Vendor name
- Contact name
- Address
- Telephone number
- Vendor payment priority
- Discount terms
- Discount account number
- Invoice description
- Payment date
- Year-to-date purchases

A **vendor status report**, such as that shown in Exhibit 2, presents summary accounts payable information. A **vendor activity report** can list gross amount invoiced, discounts taken, number of invoices, and other vendor data.

Invoice Register File

An **invoice register file** keeps a list of all invoices currently outstanding and payable. The accounts payable module can select invoices for payment by due date or by payment discount date. The **payment discount date** is the last day on which it is possible for the operation to take advantage of a cash payment discount offered by a vendor. Many vendors offer a discount on the invoice amount if payment is made within a specified time frame. For example, the terms of an invoice could be stated as: 2/10 net 30 days, meaning that the buyer applies a 2 percent discount to the invoice amount if payment is made within 10 days of the date on which the invoice was issued; if the discount period elapses, full payment is expected within 30 days of the original invoice date. Tracking discount payment dates is often a tedious and time-consuming task in non-automated hotel or restaurant properties. The accounts payable module lets employees perform more productive tasks and lets management take advantage of significant savings monitored by this module.

Although accounts payable modules can automatically select invoices for payment, they typically allow management to override selected invoices. **Override options** give management complete control over cash disbursements before engaging the check writing feature of the accounts payable module. Options which management may wish to exercise include:

- Selecting invoices for payment which are not yet due

- Making partial payments of certain invoices

- Suspending payments of certain invoices

- Adding reference data to invoices (to be printed on check stubs)

After management has exercised its options, a **cash requirements report** can be printed. This report lists all invoices selected for payment and the corresponding cash requirements. These reports can be prepared by vendor number, vendor name, due date, item or group code. They typically include vendor number, vendor name, invoice number, due date, balance due, and amount to be paid. Exhibit 3 shows a sample cash requirements report prepared by vendor number. Most accounts payable modules can print a cash requirements report at any time, basing it on a list of all open invoices.

Check Register File

The **check register file** monitors the calculation and printing of bank checks for payments of selected invoices. After printing checks, the accounts payable module deletes paid invoices from the invoice register file, preventing the possibility of double payments. With a fully integrated property management system, the check writing routine updates account balances maintained by the general ledger module. After the checks have been written, the accounts payable module prints a

Exhibit 3   Sample Cash Requirements Report

		CASH REQUIREMENTS REPORT BY VENDOR NUMBER									
		ECI HOTEL PROPERTIES, INC.									
Vendor	Vendor Name	Invoice	D/Due	Gross	07/15	07/22	07/29	08/05	08/12	08/19	Future
051462	Spunky's Produce	12312	06/15	150.00	150.00						
				150.00	150.00	0.00	0.00	0.00	0.00	0.00	0.00
121213	Carmen's Cleaning Serv	98798		25.00	25.00						
		1–6766	07/10	52.00	52.00						
		111	07/20	40.00	40.00						
				117.00	117.00	0.00	0.00	0.00	0.00	0.00	0.00
121214	S&S Quality Produce	121214	03/15	1500.00	1500.00						
				1500.00	1500.00	0.00	0.00	0.00	0.00	0.00	0.00
121313	Southwest Laundry	99998	08/10	125.00				125.00			
				125.00	0.00	0.00	0.00	125.00	0.00	0.00	0.00
1212121	Pacific Bell	12	07/20	500.00	500.00						
				500.00	500.00	0.00	0.00	0.00	0.00	0.00	0.00
7878787	First Intermedian Bank	1–6766	07/10	526.34	526.34						
				526.34	526.34	0.00	0.00	0.00	0.00	0.00	0.00
	Total for 6 Vendors			2918.34	2793.34	0.00	0.00	125.00	0.00	0.00	0.00

Source: ECI, EECO Computer Inc., Santa Ana, California.

check register by check number, which also may be sorted by vendor or by invoice due date.

Accounts payable modules can process hand-written checks and voided checks as well. Once hand-written checks are posted, the entire system is updated. Generally, the checks which are input as hand-written are highlighted on the check register printout. When a voided check is entered in the accounts payable module, the accounting system is also updated. The invoice is added back to the invoice register file, and the voided check is highlighted on the check register printout. Highlighting hand-written and voided checks on the printout enhances management's internal control.

After all entries have been made for hand-written and voided checks, the accounts payable module may print an **outstanding checks list**. This list details all checks that have been issued but remain outstanding. The outstanding checks list can be used to reconcile checks issued against canceled checks appearing on bank statements. While actual procedures for **check reconciliation** vary from one system to another, the procedure could prompt the user to enter check numbers and amounts from a bank statement. As each check is entered, the accounts payable module verifies the entry and removes (clears) the check from the outstanding checks list. When all checks have been reconciled, the system can print a **reconciliation audit report**. This report balances the total of checks removed from the outstanding checks list with the total of cleared checks appearing on the bank statement. After a check reconciliation routine, the accounts payable module typi-cally prints an updated list of all checks still outstanding.

Payroll Module

Calculating each employee's pay, developing the accounting records, and prepar-ing the necessary reports required by federal, state, and local governments are re-current tasks carried out by a hotel's accounting department. Payroll accounting can be time-consuming in non-automated properties. Not only do pay rates vary with job classifications, but, in the hospitality industry, a single employee could also work at different tasks over a number of workshifts, each of which could call for a different pay rate. Unlike many other accounting functions, payroll system require-ments are defined by sources other than property management officials. Govern-ment agencies, unions, pension trust funds, credit unions, banks, and employees themselves often have input into how payroll information is stored and reported.

A back office payroll module must be flexible enough to meet all the demands placed on it with a minimum of programming changes. Often a module utility pro-gram allows a property to define its own pay period (daily, weekly, biweekly, or monthly). Payroll modules generally perform the following functions:

- Maintain an employee master file
- Calculate gross and net pay for salaried and hourly employees
- Print paychecks
- Produce payroll tax registers and reports
- Prepare labor cost reports for use by management

Employee Master File

An employee master file maintains payroll and personnel data on each employee. Data contained in this file may include:

- Company employee number
- Name of employee
- Address of employee
- Social security number
- Job classification code(s)
- Wage rate code(s)
- Withholdings
- Deductions

This file can be extensive. Appropriate deductions and withholding amounts are subtracted from each employee's gross pay to arrive at net pay. **Withholdings** are for income and social security taxes. Since federal tax regulations frequently change and since state withholdings vary across the country, many payroll modules are designed so that the user can make the necessary programming adjustments.

Exhibit 4   Sample Payroll Withholdings and Deductions

TAXES

- Federal, state, and city withholding amounts for income taxes
- Federal Insurance Contribution Act tax (Social Security tax)
- State unemployment compensation (selected states)

OTHER

- Savings bonds
- Medical insurance
- Life insurance
- Retirement contribution
- Charitable contribution
- Capital stock purchase plan
- Savings plan, credit union
- Charge for meals
- Payroll advance
- Garnishment of wages
- Union dues

Deductions are usually voluntary and depend on the types of benefits available from the employer. Exhibit 4 lists some of the subtractions made from the gross pay of hospitality industry employees.

Payroll Register File

In order to calculate gross and net pay for hourly employees, the payroll module relies on a **payroll register file** to access the number of hours each employee worked during the pay period and other data that can require special tax calculations, such as:

- Sick leave pay
- Bonus pay
- Tips
- Expense reimbursements

In some properties, a **computerized time-clock system** records time in and time out for employees. Exhibit 5 depicts a time card produced by a computerized time-clock system. When a time-clock system is interfaced to a host computer system, data may be transferred each day to the back office payroll module and the previous day's pay calculated for each employee.

As noted earlier, the payroll module must be flexible enough to handle several pay categories per employee and several non-tax deductions (which may be required on either a fixed or a variable basis). Payroll modules typically provide override options with which management can adjust pay.

Exhibit 5   Sample Time Card from a Computerized Time-Clock System

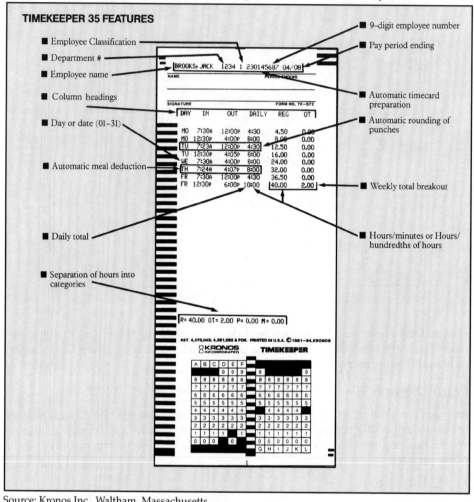

Source: Kronos Inc., Waltham, Massachusetts.

Other Functions

A payroll module can also print paychecks, paycheck registers, payroll detail registers, and deduction registers. This module generally maintains a government reporting file for quarter-to-date and year-to-date federal and state tax histories. Deduction reports can be produced with year-to-date computations. Exhibit 6 shows a sample payroll check register produced by a food and beverage back office accounting system. The check register summarizes payroll information for each employee.

Like the accounts payable module, a back office payroll module can accommodate hand-written payroll checks and voided payroll checks. The module reconciles outstanding paychecks (checks which have been issued) with paychecks that have

Exhibit 6   Sample Payroll Check Register

```
DATE 09–08                    PAYROLL CHECK REGISTER                    PAGE 1
                               01 – ABC RESTAURANT INC
```

Employee	EARNINGS			DEDUCTIONS	
	Category	Hours	Amount	Category	Amount
10	Salary	50.00	500.00	Federal	59.99
Jones, Henry				FICA	35.75
				State	13.12
				Meals	17.50
				Add'n Fed'l	12.00
				Insurance	5.00
Check Number 125					
Hours Worked 50.00					
** Gross Pay 500.00					
**** Net Pay 356.64					
20	Tipped Wages	40.00	80.40	Federal	36.61
Williamson, Johnny	Overtime	10.00	50.30	FICA	26.04
	Rptd Tips		233.50	State	6.50
	Gross Rcpts		2918.75	Uniforms	4.00
	Tip Credit		53.60	Meals	17.50
				Add'n Fed'l	7.32
Check Number 126					
Hours Worked 50.00					
** Gross Pay 130.70					
**** Net Pay 32.73					

```
***** END OF COMPANY SUMMARY *****
```

	EARNINGS			DEDUCTIONS	
01	Salary	50.00	500.00	Federal	96.60
ABC RESTAURANT INC	Tipped Wages	40.00	80.40	FICA	61.79
	Overtime	10.00	50.30	State	19.62
	Rptd Tips		233.50	Uniforms	4.00
	Gross Repts		2918.75	Meals	35.00
	Tip Credit		53.60	Add'n Fed'l	19.32
				Insurance	5.00
No of Checks 2					
Hours Worked 100.00					
** Gross Pay 630.70					
**** Net Pay 389.37					

```
***** EMPLOYER TAXES *****
Matching FICA       (630.7    +       53.60)      *      7.15% =      48.93
FUI Requirements                       0.00       *      2.00% =       0.00
SUI Requirements                     130.70       *      2.00% =       2.61
                                                                    ------
                                                                      2.61

- - - - - - - - - - - - - - - - - - - - - - - - - - - - - - - - - - - - - - -
***** STATE TAX TABLE TOTALS *****
                       GA

                    19.62
```

Source: Datachecker Systems Inc., a subsidiary of National Semiconductor Corporation, Santa Clara, California.

cleared the bank and appear on bank statements. Generally, at the end of a check reconciliation routine, the payroll module prints an updated list of outstanding checks.

In addition to printing paychecks, payroll modules can calculate sick leave and vacation hours accrued (earned) by employees in one of several ways: accrual each pay period, accrual periodically (for example, on the first pay period of the month), or accrual yearly on the basis of the employee's anniversary date.

With each employee's hourly rate (which is previously stored in the system) and calculations of pay for salaried employees, payroll modules can determine departmental labor costs. A **payroll cost report**, by department or job classification, may also be prepared for management.

Inventory Module

An accounting system may use an inventory module for internal control. Internal control is essential to efficient hospitality industry operations. Basic inventory data is stored in an **inventory master file**, which typically holds the following information:

- Item name
- Item description (brief)
- Inventory code number
- Storeroom location code
- Item purchase unit
- Purchase unit price
- Item issue unit
- Product group code
- Vendor identification number
- Order lead time
- Minimum-maximum stock levels
- Date of last purchase

With this data, a back office inventory module can address three of the most common inventory concerns: inventory status, inventory variance, and inventory valuation.

Inventory Status

Inventory status is an account of how much of each item is in storage. Inventory status may be determined by a physical inventory or a perpetual inventory, or both. With a **physical inventory system**, property staff periodically observe and count items in storage. With a **perpetual inventory system**, a back office inventory module maintains an **inventory status file** which keeps a running balance of the quantity of issued/stored items. In general, this module carries over the ending inventory of the prior period as the beginning inventory of the current period and adds all newly purchased items as they enter storage areas and subtracts all quantities issued from storage to production areas. Exhibit 7 shows a sample inventory status report produced from data in an inventory status file.

When management uses a perpetual inventory system, a physical inventory is still taken at the end of each accounting period to verify the accuracy of inventory balances tracked by the inventory module. The term **inventory variance** refers to differences between a physical count of an item and the balance maintained by the

Exhibit 7   Sample Inventory Status Report

```
                            REPORT # IP8790                    RUN DATE   5/16  10.22.24
                          INVENTORY STOCK STATUS                                 PAGE: 20
INVENTORY BALANCES FOR PERIOD: 6 ENDING: 6/30
GROUP:  B BEVERAGE                       MAJOR: 101 LIQUOR         STOCKROOM:12 LOBBY BAR
ITEM# * * * * * ITEM DESCRIPTION * * * * *   LOCN  U/M BEGIN  RECVD PUR ADJ INV ADJ  ISSUES ON HAND  ALLOC ON ORD$ ONHAND
   39  SCOTCH BELLS 12 YR OLD  750ML       BBAB01 TEN   60     0     0     0      0     60      0      0      72.90
   40  SCOTCH DEWARS 12 750ML/CSE          BBAB02 TEN   30     0     0     0      0     30      0      0      29.30
   41  GIN TANQUERY  12 750ML/CSE          BBAB03 TEN   40     0     0     0      0     40      0      0      43.20
   42  VODKA FINLANDIA 750ML               BBAB04 TEN   80     0     0     0      0     80      0      0      83.33
   43  BOURBON VIRGINIA GENTLEMAN 750ML    BBAB05 TEN   22     0     0     0      0     22      0      0      21.00
    *  MINOR $ TOTALS:                                                                                      249.73
   **  MAJOR $ TOTALS:                                                                                      249.73

                            REPORT # IP8790                    RUN DATE   5/16  10.22.24
                          INVENTORY STOCK STATUS                                 PAGE: 21
INVENTORY BALANCES FOR PERIOD: 6 ENDING: 6/30
GROUP:  B BEVERAGE                       MAJOR: 102 BEER          STOCKROOM:12 LOBBY BAR
ITEM# * * * * * ITEM DESCRIPTION * * * * *   LOCN  U/M BEGIN  RECVD PUR ADJ INV ADJ  ISSUES ON HAND  ALLOC ON ORD$ ONHAND
   44  BEER URQUELL PILSNER 4 6PK / CSE    BBAB06 EA    24     0     0     0      0     24      0      0      22.54
    *  MINOR $ TOTALS:                                                                                       22.54
   **  MAJOR $ TOTALS:                                                                                       22.54

                            REPORT # IP8790                    RUN DATE   5/16  10.22.24
                          INVENTORY STOCK STATUS                                 PAGE: 22
INVENTORY BALANCES FOR PERIOD: 6 ENDING: 6/30
GROUP:  B BEVERAGE                       MAJOR: 103 WINE          STOCKROOM:12 LOBBY BAR
ITEM# * * * * * ITEM DESCRIPTION * * * * *   LOCN  U/M BEGIN  RECVD PUR ADJ INV ADJ  ISSUES ON HAND  ALLOC ON ORD$ ONHAND
   31  WINE CHAT ST. JEAN GEWURZT 375ML    BBBB05 TEM  100     0     0     0      0    100      0      0      59.95
   32  WINE WHITE CHAT ST. JEAN FUME 750   BBBB06 TEM  100     0     0     0      0    100      0      0     108.83
    *  MINOR $ TOTALS:                                                                                      168.78
   **  MAJOR $ TOTALS:                                                                                      168.78
  ***  GROUP $ TOTALS:                                                                                      441.05
 ****  STOCKROOM $ TOTALS:                                                                                  441.05
***** CORPORATION TOTALS:                                                                                 21005.14
####   47 RECORDS PRINTED FOR REPORT:  IP8790
```

Source: Hotel Information Systems, Inc., Pleasant Hill, California.

perpetual inventory system. Significant variances may indicate control problems requiring investigation and correction.

Inventory Valuation

The term **inventory valuation** refers to the value of items in inventory. An **inventory valuation file** is used to determine the cost of goods sold and/or the replacement cost of items listed in the inventory master file. Since methods of inventory valuation vary, management must be careful to clarify which methods a particular food service inventory package should support.

An inventory valuation file tracks the value of items in inventory by any of the four generally accepted methods of inventory valuation:

- First in, first out (FIFO)

- Last in, first out (LIFO)

- Actual cost

- Weighted average

When a **first in, first out (FIFO)** method of inventory valuation is used, the products in storage areas are valued at the level of the most recently purchased items in storage. With a **last in, first out (LIFO)** method, the inventory value is assumed to be represented by the cost of items which were placed in storage the earliest. The **actual cost** approach values inventory only in relation to actual costs of items stored. The value of stored products is, then, the value represented by individual unit costs. The **weighted average** method values inventory by considering the quantity of products purchased at different unit costs. This method "weights" the prices to be averaged based on the quantity of products in storage at each price. Note that the method of valuation does not relate to the actual flow of items through storerooms.

Special Food and Beverage Concerns

From the point of view of food and beverage managers, an inventory application is perhaps the most important part of a back office package. But inventory applications tend to be the least uniform of all food service software. They vary widely with respect to file capacity and design. The usefulness of inventory reports produced by the system depends on the details within file records and the aptness of the formulas used.

The creation of a food and beverage ingredient file and subsequent file updates (daily, weekly, monthly, etc.) can be overwhelming tasks for some food service operations. Also, if errors are made when initially entering data, all subsequent processing will be unreliable and system reports will be relatively worthless. And applications that do not support integrated files can be cumbersome because users must re-input data from several files in order to run a program.

Some inventory applications provide file space for more than one ingredient designation, such as item file code number, inventory sequence number, internal customer code, and so on. The ability to work with additional designations can increase the efficiency of the inventory control system, enabling a user to print ingredients on a physical inventory worksheet according to the order in which they are shelved, for example.

Inventory is critical to a food service operation, because many ECR/POS systems cannot track an item as it passes through the control points of receiving, storing/issuing, and production. The data maintained by the inventory files of a back office package must be specific to each of these control points, because most ingredients are purchased, stored, and used in different quantities. Food and beverage inventory applications should enable users to specify tables for converting purchase units, issue units, and recipe units for individual inventory items. When conversion tables are not part of the application's design, data processing may have to be supplemented by cumbersome and time-consuming manual procedures.

Another concern is how usage is charted by the inventory application—by unit, by cost, or by both unit and cost. A system that charts items by unit might be able to report changes in stock levels, but might not provide financial data necessary for food costing. On the other hand, a system that charts items primarily by product cost may not facilitate spot-checks of items in storage. The most effective inventory applications are those which track both unit and cost. Exhibit 8 shows a sample inventory usage report that details usage in terms of both units and dollar amounts.

Exhibit 8 Sample Inventory Usage Report

Fine Restaurant

THE FOOD–TRAK (r) SYSTEM

FOOD USE REPORT

Name of Food	Inv Unit	Actual Usage (Units)	Ideal Usage (Units)	Variance in Units	Variance in Dollars	% Sales	Usage Ratio	Days Left	Beginning Inv (Units)	Purchase in Inv Units	Ending Inv (Units)	Cost per Inv Unit	Inventory Ending Value	Index
Group: 1> MEATS														
BACON	LB	158.00	111.27	46.73	$85.	0.1	1.4	12.4	100.00	150.00	92.00	$1.820	$167.44	F00212
CANADIAN-B	LB	61.30	65.25	-3.95	-$13.	-0.0	0.9	0.0	0.00	61.30	0.00	$3.190	$0.00	F00256
CANADIAN B	LB	11.50	0.00	11.50	$42.	0.1	0.0	8.9	28.00	15.50	32.00	$3.650	$116.80	F00193
CHIC LIVER	LB	351.50	120.75	230.75	$355.	0.4	2.9	0.0	327.50	96.00	72.00	$1.540	$110.88	F00200
CORN BEEF	LB	46.00	0.00	46.00	$78.	0.1	0.0	0.0	0.00	46.00	0.00	$1.690	$0.00	F00219
CUBESTEAK	LB	8.00	0.00	8.00	$18.	0.0	0.0	0.0	4.00	10.00	6.00	$2.240	$13.44	F00198
HAM	LB	94.10	101.44	-7.34	-$19.	-0.0	0.9	7.6	56.80	88.80	51.50	$2.590	$133.38	F00213
HOT DOGS	LB	9.00	0.00	9.00	$18.	0.0	0.0	0.0	5.00	10.00	6.00	$2.040	$12.24	F00196
LAMB	LB	1,155.50	1,304.84	-149.34	-$521.	-0.7	0.9	0.0	162.00	993.50	0.00	$3.490	$0.00	F00216
NEW YORK	LB	556.25	430.11	126.14	$851.	1.1	1.3	8.6	240.00	562.25	246.00	$6.750	$1,660.50	F00214
PORK LOIN	LB	50.50	0.00	50.50	$93.	0.1	0.0	0.0	0.00	57.50	7.00	$1.850	$12.95	F00188
PRIME RIB	LB	1.90	2.06	-0.16	-$0.	-0.0	0.9	0.0	4.00	5.40	0.00	$1.000	$0.00	F00279
SALAMI	LB	29.00	30.00	-1.00	-$2.	-0.0	1.0	54.5	32.00	60.00	7.50	$2.880	$21.60	F00222
SAUS LINKS	LB	20.00	0.00	20.00	$30.	0.0	0.0	31.5	0.00	20.00	63.00	$2.130	$134.19	F00201
SHOULDER	LB	707.20	758.98	-51.78	-$243.	-0.3	0.9	0.0	329.00	620.20	0.00	$1.490	$0.00	F00215
TENDER	LB	14.00	15.96	-1.96	-$5.	-0.0	0.9	4.8	38.00	0.00	242.00	$4.690	$1,134.98	F00218
TOP ROUND	LB	485.65	540.40	-54.75	-$192.	-0.2	0.9	22.6	154.75	497.90	24.00	$2.580	$61.92	F00194
TOP SIRLOIN	LB	0.00	0.00	0.00	$0.	0.0	0.0	4.6	0.00	0.00	167.00	$3.500	$584.50	F00217
VEAL	LB	0.00	0.00	0.00	$0.	0.0	0.0	0.0	16.00	0.00	0.00	$2.440	$0.00	F00197
BROCHETTE	EACH	-6.00	-6.00	0.00	$0.	0.0	1.0	15.0	0.00	0.00	6.00	$5.005	$30.03	S00024
COOK CRN B	LB	8.00	7.00	1.00	$2.	0.0	1.1	17.1	0.00	0.00	8.00	$2.253	$18.03	S00030
CB HASH	LB	148.75	24.00	124.75	$284.	0.4	6.2	15.0	172.75	0.00	24.00	$2.277	$54.64	S00026
GRAHAM CC	LB	0.00	0.00	0.00	$0.	0.0	0.0	0.0	0.00	0.00	0.00	$12.272	$0.00	S00076
GRND BEEF	LB	15.00	15.00	0.00	$4.	0.0	1.0	39.4	26.00	0.00	42.00	$7.662	$321.79	S00022
HAM 1.5 OZ	EACH	0.00	0.00	0.00	$0.	0.0	0.0	0.0	23.00	0.00	8.00	$0.243	$1.94	S00088
HAM 3 OZ	EACH	0.00	0.00	0.00	$0.	0.0	1.0	15.0	0.00	0.00	3.00	$0.486	$1.46	S00089
LAMB-TRIM	LB	0.00	0.00	0.00	$0.	0.0	1.0	46.6	189.00	0.00	143.00	$7.852	$1,122.91	S00019
LUNCH LAMB	LB	0.00	0.00	0.00	$0.	0.0	0.0	0.0	0.00	0.00	0.00	$7.852	$0.00	S00018
MEATLOAF	LB	-19.50	-19.50	0.00	$0.	0.0	0.0	0.0	0.00	0.00	0.00	$4.714	$0.00	S00023
NY – TRIM	LB	17.00	0.00	17.00	$23.	0.0	1.0	52.3	48.50	0.00	68.00	$9.000	$612.00	S00017
PRIME COOK	LB	-4.00	-4.00	0.00	$0.	0.0	1.0	0.5	17.00	0.00	0.00	$1.333	$0.00	S00097
RB 1.5 OZ 3	EACH	0.00	0.00	0.00	$0.	0.0	1.0	37.5	6.00	0.00	10.00	$0.310	$3.10	S00091
STROG MEAT	LB	-30.00	-30.00	0.00	$0.	0.0	0.0	0.0	0.00	0.00	0.00	$0.000	$0.00	S00025
TEND – TRIM	LB	-13.25	-13.25	0.00	$0.	0.0	1.0	46.0	62.00	0.00	92.00	$7.147	$657.49	S00021
TOP SIR–TM	LB	-6.00	-6.00	0.00	$0.	0.0	1.0	53.2	33.75	0.00	47.00	$6.667	$313.33	S00020
TURK 1.5 OZ	EACH	0.00	0.00	0.00	$0.	0.0	1.0	45.0	12.00	0.00	18.00	$0.245	$4.42	S00092
TURK 3 OZ	EACH	0.00	0.00	0.00	$0.	0.0	0.0	0.0	0.00	0.00	0.00	$0.491	$0.00	S00093
Group Total:		$14,563.85	$13,675.16	8.00	$889.	1.1				$13,216.91			$7,305.96	
Group: 2> SEAFOOD														
COD	LB	8.00	0.00	8.00	$16.	0.0	0.0	0.0	25.00	0.00	17.00	$1.980	$33.66	F00189
Group Total:		8.00	0.00	8.00	$16.	0.0	0.0	0.0	25.00	0.00	17.00	$1.980	$33.66	

Prepared MON 10/24/83   FOOD–TRAK is a Registered Trademark   Copyright (c) 1983 – System Concepts Inc. – All Rights Reserved

Source: System Concepts, Inc., Scottsdale, Arizona.

Management should also make clear how basic food service concepts are defined within the inventory application design. For example, is an inventory item considered "used" (for costing purposes) at the time it is received, when it is issued to the kitchen, or at the time of service? The time that is best for an operation may not be the time frame built into the application's design.

Purchasing Module

Effective purchasing methods are extremely important because cost savings directly affect bottom-line profitability—each dollar saved is an additional dollar of profit. Since a large percentage of sales income is spent on purchasing, it is critical that all procedures include effective controls. A back office purchasing module especially enhances management's control over purchase ordering and receiving practices.

Purchase Order File

Back office purchasing modules maintain a purchase order file which is typically organized by vendor and purchase order number. Although purchase orders can always be generated by hand and later entered into the purchase order file, the value of a purchasing module lies in its ability to generate purchase orders and internally update its purchase order file.

Purchase orders can be generated by a purchasing module which accesses and analyzes minimum/maximum inventory data. **Minimum/maximum inventory levels** help managers determine when products need to be purchased and how much of each product to order. For each purchase item, management sets a minimum quantity below which inventory levels should not fall and a maximum quantity above which inventory levels should not rise. The minimum level is the safety level—the number of purchase units that must always remain in inventory. The maximum level is the greatest number of purchase units permitted in storage. Using minimum/maximum inventory level data transferred from the inventory module, the purchasing module generates purchase orders based on an order point established through usage rate and lead-time factors.

The usage rate is the number of purchase units used per order period. This is an important factor for determining when more purchase units need to be ordered. In addition to usage rates, managers must also determine a lead-time quantity for each purchase item. **Lead-time quantity** refers to the anticipated number of purchase units taken from inventory between the time an order is placed and the time it is delivered. Purchase units are counted in terms of normally sized shipping containers.

The order point is the number of purchase units in stock when an order is placed. The order point is reached when the number of purchase units in inventory equals the lead-time quantity plus the safety (minimum) level. If products are ordered at the order point, the quantity in inventory will be reduced to the safety (minimum) level by the time products are received. When the order arrives, the inventory levels for the product will be brought back to the maximum level. Exhibit 9 shows a sample inventory order worksheet which may be used to determine purchasing needs based on inventory levels defined by the user.

Purchase orders can also be generated by a purchasing module which analyzes sales forecast data. This method assumes a zero-based inventory system for

Exhibit 9   Sample Inventory Order Worksheet

```
                                    REPORT #  IP8790                        RUN DATE   5/16   10.15.42
                              STOCK ORDER REVIEW WORKSHEET                     PAGE:  1
STOCKROOM:   1 MAIN STOREROOM
GROUP:  B BEVERAGE   MAJOR CLASS: 101 LIQUOR              MINOR CLASS:  002 CALL
ITEM#  * * * ITEM DESCRIPTION * * *    LOC  BIN  REORDER PAR/ORDER ON-HAND  ON-ORDER ALLOCATED  AVAILABLE REQUIRED  U/M ACT
  45    AMARETTO DE SERANO 12/CSE      A01  B03    40      100      0          0        0           0       100    TEN REV
  46    FRANGELLICO         12/CSE     A01  B03    40      100      0          0        0           0       100    TEN REV


                                    REPORT #  IP8170                        RUN DATE   5/16   10.15.42
                              STOCK ORDER REVIEW WORKSHEET                     PAGE:  2
STOCKROOM:   1 MAIN STOREROOM
GROUP:  F FOOD     MAJOR CLASS: 100 PRODUCE              MINOR CLASS:  102 VEGETABLES
ITEM#  * * * ITEM DESCRIPTION * * *    LOC  BIN  REORDER PAR/ORDER ON-HAND  ON-ORDER ALLOCATED  AVAILABLE REQUIRED  U/M ACT
   3    BROCCOLI-FRESH 10 LB CASE       A02  B22    2       5       2          2        0           4        1     CSE REV
   5    POTATOES-RED FRESH 25 LB SACK   A01  B01    2       5       4          1        0           5        0     SAK REV
   6    PARSLEY-FRESH 6 BOX CSE 10LB AVG A01 B01    2       8       2          3        0           5        3     CSE REV
  23    POTATOES-RED FRESH 50 LB SACK   A01  B01    0       0       9         10        0          19       19     SAK REV
  26    POTATOES-WHITE     25 LB SACK   A02  B17    4       8       8          1        2           7        1     SAK REV
```

Source: Hotel Information Systems, Inc., Pleasant Hill, California.

developing purchase orders. Rather than reference existing inventory levels, the purchasing module forecasts anticipated revenue, projects needed inventory items, and automatically generates the necessary purchase orders.

Regardless of the method by which purchase orders are produced, purchasing modules typically provide override options allowing management to alter items and quantities before the final preparation and distribution of purchase orders. In addition to override capabilities, computer systems can add routine purchases (furnishings, amenities, supplies, food, and the like) to purveyor orders by pre-determined date. For example, the systematic ordering of one case of bathroom cleaner each month can be added to a purchase order, eliminating the possibility of omission in ordering.

Telecommunication of Purchase Orders

A growing trend among computer system vendors and food service purveyors is to install order entry telephone lines for telecommunication of purchase orders directly from customer properties. The property must first develop its own purchase order file and then use communications software to communicate purchase orders to the purveyor's computer system.

Some purveyors allow clients to use autodial modems. An autodial modem functions without user intervention, enabling late night transmission of purchase orders for next day processing. Some sophisticated purchase order telecommunication links provide for two-way communication (duplex) between purveyor and property. This allows the operation to make on-line inquiries about current prices and stock availability at the purveyor's location, and permits the purveyor to send information about featured items, price specials, and close-out sales to the property.

Other Functions

Properties dealing with more than one purveyor may collect competitive bids and store them in a **bid specification file,** which typically contains the specific

Exhibit 10   Sample Daily Receiving Report

					REPORT # IP8230		RUN DATE	5/21	11.34.42	
					LINE ITEMS RECEIVED ON : 5/21					
P/O MBR	RCVNBR	TYP	DEPT	DUE	LINE# ITEM#	*****ITEM DESCRIPTION*****	ORDER QTY	RECEIPT QTY	U/M	UNIT PRICE
					** VENDOR: JOHN BURK ENTERPRISES					
H0000039	5555111	V	1	5/21	10 3	BROCCOLI-FRESH 10 LB CASE	3.00	3.00	CSE	14.23
H0000039	5555111	V	1	5/21	20 6	PARSLEY-FRESH 6 BOX CSE 10 LB AVG	12.00	12.00	CSE	11.25
H0000039	5555111	V	1	5/21	30 5	POTATOES-RED FRESH 25 LB SACK	12.00	12.00	SAK	22.65
					** VENDOR: COOPERS COOLERS					
H0000037	122554	V	1	5/22	10 32	WINE WHITE CHAT ST. JEAN FUME 750	6.00	6.00	CSE	125.00
H0000037	122554	V	1	5/22	20 39	SCOTCH BELLS 12 YR OLD 750ML	6.00	6.00	BTL	13.50
H0000037	122554	V	1	5/22	30 40	SCOTCH DEWARS 12 750ML/CSE	6.00	6.00	CSE	125.50
H0000037	122554	V	1	5/22	40 41	GIN TANQ 12 750ML/CSE	6.00	6.00	CSE	131.80
H0000037	122554	V	1	5/22	50 42	VODKA FINLANDIA 750ML	8.00	8.00	CSE	130.00
					** VENDOR: MEAT, MEAT, AND MORE MEAT					
H0000038	25444896	V	1	5/22	10 38	CHICKEN BRSTS BNLS 5LB PKG 5/CSE	25.00	25.00	CSE	56.35
H0000038	25444896	V	1	5/22	20 29	BEEF TENDERS 10LB AVG 10/CSE	150.00	150.00	LB	4.50
H0000038	25444896	V	1	5/22	30 30	BEEF GROUND SIRLOIN 25 LB BAG	50.00	50.00	LB	1.20
H0000038	25444896	V	1	5/22	40 33	CHICKEN WHOLE FRYERS 3LB AVG 12/CSE	150.00	150.00	CSE	82.50
####	12 RECORDS PRINTED FOR REPORT:		IP8230							

Source: Hotel Information Systems, Inc., Pleasant Hill, California.

characteristics of purchased items. Purveyors are asked to quote prices for products which meet or exceed stated specifications. Normally, a **bid specification form** can be printed at any time, upon demand. Once bids are obtained, they can be entered into the computer system, and the purchasing module may be able to sort items to be purchased by vendor and lowest bid.

Back office purchasing modules may simplify receiving practices. Receiving practices in non-automated properties can be tedious and time-consuming. Typically, a receiving clerk manually verifies shipments received by cross-checking each item against the original purchase order. The list of items received is used to make price extensions. That is, the quoted price of each purchased item is multiplied by the quantities received to yield an approximate cost of goods purchased. These price extensions are later used to scrutinize billings from purveyors. Following price extension, the quantities received are entered on an inventory worksheet alongside the name of the proper inventory item.

Purchasing modules can streamline receiving practices and simplify inventory updating. A receiving clerk may verify shipments by cross-checking items received against a list of product names and ordered quantities. Or a property may institute a blind receiving practice by supplying the receiving clerk with a list of product names (only) and require the clerk to record quantities received.

Exhibit 10 shows a sample **daily receiving report** which lists details of all items received on a given day. Once receiving is completed, amounts can be entered into the purchasing module by accessing and updating the stored purchase order. When the purchase order quantities reflect received quantities, inventory files can be instantly updated with a release to inventory function. All items and quantities on the receiving list (the updated purchase order) are added to the former perpetual inventory quantities.

The purchase price variance report, designed to notify purchasers, accounting personnel, and others when the recent price of an item exceeds the level of variance previously established by top management officials, is another popular purchasing report. This report enables management to react to price changes on a timely basis.

With a fully integrated system, data from the purchasing module can also be transferred to the accounts payable module so that updated cash requirements reports can be produced.

Financial Reporting Module

The financial reporting module, also called a general ledger module, maintains account balances and is used to prepare trial balances, financial statements, and a variety of reports for management's use. In order to assist accounting personnel in the preparation of these documents (statements and reports), the financial reporting module must have access to account balances maintained by other system modules. When the financial reporting module has limited access to data maintained by other modules or when the module serves as a stand-alone general ledger system, data may be entered directly into the module's files. Most modules can generate reports relating to individual operating departments, support centers, divisions, or entire properties (for multi-unit corporations).

Many financial reporting modules can be adapted to the needs and requirements of individual hospitality properties. Flexible codes, screen designs, and report formats allow properties to customize applications. Management may design the format of the property's financial statements by controlling headings, spacing, indentation, sub-titles, underlining, and other formatting features.

Chart of Accounts

An industry-accepted uniform system of accounts provides a logical approach to back office design because it guides accounting personnel in the preparation and presentation of financial statements by standardizing formats and account classifications.[1] This standardization permits users of financial statements to compare the financial position and operational performance of a particular hospitality property to similar types of properties in the industry. For new businesses entering the hospitality industry, a uniform system of accounts serves as a turnkey accounting system that can be quickly adapted to meet the needs of the business.

A **chart of accounts** lists general ledger accounts by type of account including account number and account title. The account names found in the **chart of accounts file** are listed in a sequence that parallels the order of their appearance on the financial statements and general ledger. The **general ledger** is the principal accounting ledger containing all of the balance sheet and statement of income accounts.

A chart of accounts shows no account balances. The main purpose of a chart of accounts is to serve as a "table of contents" to guide bookkeepers as they enter the results of business transactions in accounting records. Bookkeepers are generally not allowed to use an account unless it specifically appears on the company's chart of accounts.

For most businesses, the chart of accounts arranges accounts according to their major classification. Accounts are classified as either asset, liability, equity, revenue, or expense accounts. Asset, liability, and equity accounts form the basis for preparation of a balance sheet. Revenue or expense accounts form the basis for preparation of the statement of income. The sequence of major account classifications appearing on a chart of accounts typically is as follows:

- Asset accounts
- Liability accounts
- Equity accounts
- Revenue accounts
- Expense accounts

The use of a computer in the input (recording) phase requires that each account be assigned an account number. The account number is usually designed so that a significant digit represents one of the major account classifications (asset, liability, equity, revenue, or expense accounts). The digits which follow normally define the individual account's sequential relationship within that classification.

For example, assume that management has designed a three-digit account numbering system. Since the first major account classification is assets, the number 1 may be assigned as the first digit for all asset account numbers. The number series of 1xx will therefore include all asset accounts. Since cash is typically the first account to appear within the sequence of accounts classified as asset accounts, the three-digit account number assigned to the cash account will be 101. Since liabilities are the second major account classification, the number 2 can be assigned as the first digit for all liability accounts. Thus, the number series 2xx includes all liability accounts.

A business can use any account numbering system which meets its particular requirements. Some computerized general ledger systems accommodate up to 12-character account numbers and maintain an array of accounts for multiple corporate properties. The variety of accounts and the design of numbering systems can vary from business to business, depending on the company's size and the detail of management information desired.[2] Some businesses that use a manual accounting system may also use a variation of an account numbering system.

Trial Balance File

A **trial balance file** maintains a list of accounts with debit and credit balances. With a fully integrated hotel property management system, the daily system update is responsible for transferring data from front office and back office modules to the general ledger, ensuring that the balances held in the financial reporting module are current. A **trial balance** is prepared to test the equality of these balances (debits and credits). In a non-automated back office system, the trial balance is prepared as follows:

1. Determine the balance of each account in the ledger.
2. List the accounts and show debit balances in one column and credit balances in a separate column.
3. Add the debit balances.
4. Add the credit balances.
5. Compare the totals of the debit and credit balances.

When the total of debit balance accounts equals the total of credit balance accounts, the trial balance is said to be in balance. If debits and credits do not balance, the bookkeeper has made errors in recording the transactions, in determining the balances of each account, or in preparing the trial balance. It is important to note that a balanced trial balance is not proof that all transactions have been properly recorded. The trial balance, if correct, only indicates that debits equal credits.

Preparing a trial balance in a non-automated system can be an error-prone and time-consuming task. In an automated system, the general ledger function of the financial reporting module can generate an accurate trial balance upon demand.

The general ledger function of the financial reporting module also simplifies the closing process at the end of an accounting period. The module audits accounting files for any out-of-balance conditions. It also searches for invoices or journals that are not fully posted to the general ledger and produces a report disclosing all errors.

Some modules allow the current period to remain open while postings are made to future periods. When the current period closes, the module computes opening balances for the next accounting period. Once a period is closed, errors are generally corrected with journal entries made to the current period. Some modules can re-open previously closed periods for correcting entries.

Financial Statements

A back office financial reporting module is can access relevant data from front office and back office modules and generate balance sheets and statements of income. Most modules can also produce statements of cash flows.

The **balance sheet** provides important information on the financial position of a hospitality business by showing its assets, liabilities, and equity on a particular date. Simply stated, assets represent anything a business owns which has commercial or exchange value, liabilities represent the claims of outsiders (such as creditors) to assets, and owners' equity represents the claims of owners to assets. On every balance sheet, the total assets must always agree (that is, balance) with the combined totals of the liabilities and equity sections. In essence, the format of the balance sheet reflects the fundamental accounting equation:

$$Assets = Liabilities + Equity$$

Financial reporting modules should be able to produce balance sheets (and other financial statements) which compare current figures with those of prior periods. In addition, modules should be able to generate comparative and common-size balance sheets for managerial review.

Comparative balance sheets present two sets of figures for each balance sheet line item. One set of figures is from the current balance sheet; the other set, from the balance sheet of a previous period. Changes in amounts of line items from one period to the next are reported in both absolute and relative terms. Absolute changes show the change in dollars between two periods, while relative changes (also referred to as percentage changes) are calculated by dividing the absolute change by the amount known for the previous period. Significant changes should be brought to management's attention.

Common-size balance sheets also present two sets of figures for each balance sheet line item. One set of figures is from the current balance sheet; the other set from the balance sheet of a previous period. All amounts are reduced to percentages of their account classification. That is, the total assets on each balance sheet are set at 100%, and each asset category is reported as a percentage of the total (100%). This same procedure is followed for the total liabilities and owners' equity sections. The percentages found on the two balance sheets are then compared and significant changes are brought to management's attention.

The **statement of income** (also called the profit and loss statement) provides important financial information about the results of operations for a given period of time. The time period may be as short as one month and does not usually exceed one business year. The business year is called the **fiscal year**. Since this statement reveals the bottom line (net income for a given period of time), it should be one of the most important financial statements managers use to evaluate the success of operations. It may also be an important measure of managerial effectiveness and efficiency. Most financial reporting modules are able to generate both comparative and common-size income statements. Exhibit 11 shows a comparative income statement produced by a restaurant back office accounting system.

Financial reporting modules also produce condensed income statements comparing results of the current month with previous months, same month of previous years, and budgeted amounts. These reports may also compare year-to-date results with results of previous years.

Some financial reporting modules have extensive graphics capabilities. The phrase "a picture is worth a thousand words" certainly applies here. Although graphs do not usually provide detail, managers can track recent performance trends more easily by reviewing results through line drawings. Departmental expenses can be shown using pie charts, departmental revenue using bar charts, and so on. Charts tend to be easy to understand, and they can be used to demonstrate operational results more successfully than the traditional financial statements, which may at times appear as a confusing list of numbers.

Ratio Analysis

Hospitality industry financial statements contain a considerable amount of information. A thorough analysis of this information may require more than simply reading the reported facts and figures. Users of financial statements need to be able to interpret the contents of these documents so that critical aspects of the property's financial situation do not go unnoticed. Interpretation is often accomplished through **ratio analysis**. A **ratio** gives mathematical expression to a significant relationship between two figures. It is calculated by dividing one figure by the other.

Ratio results are meaningful only when compared against useful criteria. Useful criteria against which to compare the results of ratio analysis normally include:

- Corresponding ratios calculated for a prior period

- Corresponding ratios of other properties

- Industry averages

- Planned ratio goals

Exhibit 11   Sample Comparative Income Statement

Comparative Income and Expense
Microbilt Restaurant #10

Description	Curr Month This Year	% Of Total	Curr Month Last Year	% Of Total	Y-T-D This Year	% Of Total	Y-T-D Last Year	% Of Total
REVENUE								
Food	186,682.00	68.0	174,645.00	68.9	2,683,148.19	69.9	2,267,895.00	70.1
Beverage	86,500.00	31.5	77,880.00	30.7	1,145,800.00	29.8	959,245.00	29.7
Miscellaneous Income	1,200.00	.4	800.00	.3	7,500.00	.2	7,500.00	.2
TOTAL REVENUE	274,382.00	100.0	253,325.00	100.0	3,839,348.19	100.00	3,234,640.00	100.0
COST OF SALES								
Food	76,410.00	27.9	74,100.00	29.3	1,087,651.63	28.3	947,650.00	29.3
Beverage	750.00	.3	1,156.00	.5	11,486.00	.3	9,432.00	.3
Cost of Well Brands	7,273.00	2.7	7,191.00	2.8	95,549.00	2.5	87,750.00	2.7
Cost of Call Level 1	5,326.00	1.9	4,980.00	2.0	69,238.00	1.8	58,145.00	1.8
Cost of Call Level 2	4,547.00	1.7	4,750.00	1.9	64,111.00	1.7	58,250.00	1.8
Cost of House Wines	1,234.00	.5	679.00	.3	12,510.00	.3	10,555.00	.3
Cost of Fine Wines	554.00	.2	1,915.00	.8	12,756.00	.3	10,775.00	.3
Cost of Brandy & Liqueurs	925.00	.3	1,470.00	.6	17,523.00	.5	14,225.00	.4
Cost of Bar Garnishes	231.00	.1	182.00	.1	2,772.00	.1	2,327.00	.1
Cost of Bar Mixes	205.00	.1	224.00	.1	2,460.00	.1	2,239.00	.1
TOTAL COST OF SALES	97,455.00	35.5	96,647.00	38.2	1,376,056.63	35.8	1,201,348.00	37.1
GROSS PROFIT	176,927.00	64.5	156,678.00	61.9	2,463,291.56	64.2	2,033,292.00	62.9
OTHER INCOME								
Vending Machines	2,406.00	.9	2,145.00	.9	24,812.00	.7	22,600.00	.7
TOTAL OTHER INCOME	2,406.00	.9	2,145.00	.9	24,812.00	.7	22,600.00	.7
TOTAL INCOME	179,333.00	65.4	158,823.00	62.7	2,488,103.00	64.8	2,055,892.00	63.6
CONTROLLABLE EXPENSES								
Salaries and Wages	75,320.00	27.5	65,900.00	26.0	960,640.00	25.0	810,650.00	25.1
Employee Benefits	14,125.00	5.2	12,800.00	5.1	197,050.00	5.1	166,550.00	5.2
Direct Operating ExpeNses	17,560.00	6.4	16,995.00	6.7	258,720.00	6.7	237,220.00	7.3
Music and Entertainment	2,410.00	.9	2,240.00	.9	34,020.00	.9	28,400.00	.9
Marketing	5,130.00	1.9	4,750.00	1.9	73,960.00	1.9	62,000.00	1.9
Energy and Utility Serv's	5,600.00	2.0	5,050.00	2.0	80,200.00	2.1	67,800.00	2.1
Administrative/General	18,000.00	6.6	18,400.00	7.3	222,800.00	5.8	188,900.00	5.8
Repairs and Maintenance	4,200.00	1.5	4,710.00	1.9	58,800.00	1.5	50,100.00	1.6
TOTAL CONTROLLABLE EXPENSES	142,345.00	51.9	130,845.00	51.7	1,886,190.00	49.1	1,611,620.00	49.8
INCOME BEFORE RENT & OTHER OCCUP. COSTS	36,988.00	13.5	27,978.00	11.0	601,913.56	15.7	444,272.00	13.7
RENT & OTHER OCCUP. COSTS								
Rent And Other Occ. Costs	11,330.00	4.1	10,000.00	4.0	132,260.00	3.4	115,900.00	3.6
INCOME BEFORE Interest	25,658.00	9.4	17,978.00	7.1	469,653.56	12.2	328,372.00	10.2
INTEREST	1,850.00	.7	2,000.00	.8	25,900.00	.7	22,000.00	.7
Depreciation	4,733.00	1.7	5,000.00	2.0	66,266.00	1.7	56,950.00	1.8
TOTAL RENT & OTHER OCCUP. COSTS	17,913.00	6.5	17,000.00	6.7	224,426.00	5.9	194,850.00	6.0
INCOME BEFORE PROVISION FOR INC. TAXES	19,075.00	7.0	10,978.00	4.3	377,487.56	9.8	249,422.00	7.7
PROVISION FOR INC. TAXES								
Income Taxes	6,625.00	2.4	5,625.00	2.2	92,750.00	2.4	78,575.00	2.4
TOTAL PROVISION FOR INC. TAXES	6,625.00	2.4	5,625.00	2.2	92,750.00	2.4	78,575.00	2.4
NET INCOME	12,450.00	4.5	5,353.00	2.1	284,737.56	7.4	170,847.00	5.3

Source: MicroBilt Corporation, Atlanta, Georgia.

Ratio analysis can be extremely useful to owners, creditors, and managers in evaluating the financial condition and operation of a hotel. Users of ratio analysis must be careful when comparing two different properties because the accounting procedures of one may differ from those of another. Moreover, ratios are only indicators; they do not resolve problems or reveal what problems may exist. At best, ratios that vary significantly from past periods, budgeted standards, or industry averages indicate a reason for investigation. When problems appear to exist, considerably more analysis and investigation are necessary to determine appropriate corrective action.

Assuming that necessary financial data are stored in a computer, ratio statistics can be generated almost at will. Many ratios need not be calculated on a daily basis. In fact, if their analysis is based on too short a period of time, they may fail to provide meaningful information. It is important that management officials determine which ratios are to be calculated and how often. If all ratios were calculated daily, there could be a risk of information overload. In other words, so many statistics would be generated that the manager would not have the time—or the inclination—to search for critical information.

Operating ratios, on the other hand, may be an exception to this rule. They can be very useful when prepared on a frequent basis. For example, when a hotel's night audit is computerized, many operating ratio computations (such as average daily rate, occupancy percentage, double occupancy percentage, and others) are a by-product of the system update routine. These statistics can then be compared against budgeted goals to present management with a timely (and convenient) measure of operational success.

Summary

This chapter focused on six software modules typically included in back office accounting packages:

- Accounts receivable
- Accounts payable
- Payroll accounting
- Inventory accounting
- Purchasing
- Financial reporting

An accounts receivable module monitors outstanding balances of guest and non-guest accounts. The term accounts receivable refers to obligations owed to the property from sales made on credit. Accounts receivable balances may be automatically transferred from the front office accounting module, or may be manually posted directly into the accounts receivable module. Once they are entered into the back office accounting system, account collection begins. Account billings and aging of accounts receivable can be monitored by the hotel property management system.

The accounts payable module tracks purchases, creditor positions, and the hotel's banking status. Accounts payable activities normally consist of posting purveyor invoices, determining amounts due, and printing checks for payment.

A payroll accounting module is an important part of a back office accounting package because of the complexities involved in properly processing time and attendance records, unique employee benefits, pay rates, withholdings, deductions, and required payroll reports. The payroll accounting module must be able to handle job codes, employee meals, uniform credits, tips, taxes, and other data which affect the net pay of employees. The unique nature of payroll data dictates that special care be taken to maintain an accurate payroll register, to closely control the issuing of payroll checks, and to protect the confidentiality and propriety of payroll data.

A back office inventory module maintains an inventory master file, an inventory status file, and an inventory valuation file. This module monitors inventory status, functions as a perpetual inventory system, and may calculate the value of items in inventory by using a variety of methods, such as FIFO, LIFO, actual cost, and weighted average.

A back office purchasing module maintains a purchase order file and a bid specification file. This module enhances management's control over purchasing, ordering, and receiving practices. Using minimum/maximum inventory level data transferred from the inventory module, the purchasing module generates purchase orders based on an order point established through usage rate and lead-time factors. A purchasing module may also use a zero-based inventory system and generate purchase orders based on projected sales volume.

The use of a financial reporting module, also called a general ledger module, involves the specification of a chart of accounts (a list of financial statement accounts and their account numbers) and a systematic approach to recording transactions. The design of the general ledger module is often crucial to an effective back office system. The financial reporting module can track accounts receivable, accounts payable, cash, and adjusting entries. In addition, most financial reporting modules can access data from front office and back office modules to prepare financial statements, which include the balance sheet, the statement of income (and supporting departmental schedules), and a variety of reports for use by management.

Endnotes

1. *The Uniform System of Accounts and Expense Dictionary for Small Hotels, Motels, and Motor Hotels,* published by the Educational Institute, provides a standardized accounting system for full-service lodging properties (those with extensive food and beverage facilities) and limited-service properties (those with limited food and beverage facilities or that lease out food and beverage operations).

2. The Educational Institute has developed instructional software, titled *Hotel Financial Statements,* with which individuals can learn to properly prepare financial statements in accordance with the uniform system of accounts.

Key Terms

Accounts Receivable Module

accounts aging file

accounts receivable

aging of accounts receivable
  schedule

city ledger
city ledger file

customer master file

Accounts Payable Module

accounts payable
accounts payable aging report
cash requirements report
check reconciliation
check register
check register file
invoice register file
monthly check register

outstanding checks list
override options
payment discount date
reconciliation audit report
vendor activity report
vendor master file
vendor status report

Payroll Module

computerized time-clock system
deductions
payroll cost report

payroll register file
withholdings

Inventory Module

actual cost
first in, first out (FIFO)
inventory master file
inventory status
inventory status file
inventory valuation

inventory valuation file
inventory variance
last in, first out (LIFO)
perpetual inventory system
physical inventory system
weighted average

Purchasing Module

bid specification file
bid specification form
daily receiving report

lead-time quantity
minimum/maximum inventory
 levels

Financial Reporting Module

balance sheet
chart of accounts
chart of accounts file
common-size balance sheets
fiscal year
general ledger

ratio
ratio analysis
statement of income
trial balance
trial balance file

Discussion Questions

1. What functions are performed by an accounts receivable module?

2. How can management use an aging of accounts receivable schedule?

3. What functions does an accounts payable module perform?

4. What override options provided by accounts payable modules may be useful to management?

5. What are some uses of the cash requirements report produced by an accounts payable module?

6. What functions are performed by a payroll module?

7. What are some of the characteristics of hospitality operations that complicate the design of a back office payroll module?

8. How can differences among purchase units, issue units, and standard recipe units complicate the design of a back office inventory module?

9. What are two basic ways by which a purchasing module may automatically generate purchase orders?

10. What does a financial reporting module perform?

REVIEW QUIZ

When you feel you have covered all of the material in this chapter, answer these questions. Choose the *best* answer.

Matching

1. Liabilities incurred for merchandise, equipment, or other goods and services connected with the operation of a hospitality company that have been purchased on account

2. Maintains a vendor master file

3. A minimum quantity below which inventory levels should not fall

4. Obligations owed to a hospitality company from sales made on credit

5. Maintains an invoice register file

6. Maintains an employee master file

7. An inventory system that a purchasing module relies on when it generates purchase orders by accessing and analyzing sales forecast data

8. A computer-generated report that lists all invoices currently outstanding and payable

9. An inventory valuation method

10. Produces a cash requirements report

a. invoice register report

b. accounts receivable

c. inventory module

d. perpetual inventory system

e. general ledger module

f. accounts payable module

g. city ledger

h. actual cost

i. minimum inventory level

j. cash requirements report

k. zero-based inventory system

l. financial reporting module

m. accounts payable

n. usage rate

o. payroll module

p. maximum inventory level

True (T) or False (F)

T   F   11. Hotels generally process many more accounts receivable transactions than do restaurants.

T   F   12. A payroll module typically reconciles outstanding paychecks which have been issued with paychecks that have cleared the bank and appear on bank statements.

T   F   13. In order to efficiently maintain a perpetual inventory record, an inventory application must be able to automatically convert purchase units into issue units and recipe units.

Multiple Choice

14. Which of the following is not a function performed by an accounts receivable application?

    a. maintenance of account balances
    b. posting of purveyor invoices
    c. processing of billings
    d. monitoring of collection activities

15. Which of the following accounting applications is also referred to as a general ledger module?

    a. accounts receivable module
    b. accounts payable module
    c. inventory module
    d. financial reporting module

Part V

Management Responsibilities

Chapter Outline

Analyzing Current Information Needs
    Flowcharts
    Creating a Property Profile
Collecting Relevant Sales Information
Establishing Computer System
    Requirements
    Determining Data to Process
    Determining How to Process Data
    Determining Information Formats
Determining the Hardware Configuration
    Stand-Alone Configuration
    Distributed Configuration
    Integrated Configuration
Requesting Proposals from Vendors
Site Surveys by Vendors
Evaluating Vendor Proposals
Contract Negotiations
    Contract Provisions
    Contractual Arrangements
Installation Factors
    Training
    Site Preparation
    Design of Printed Materials
    Initial Entry of Database Elements
    Acceptance Testing
    System Conversion
    Documentation
    Contingency Planning
    Vendor Support
Summary

Learning Objectives

1. Describe the ways in which properties analyze current information needs before selecting computer systems.

2. Explain the function of a property profile.

3. Identify effective ways hospitality organizations can collect relevant sales information about computer systems.

4. Define the following terms: data identification, data collection, data entry, and data coding.

5. Describe the different types of hardware configurations.

6. Identify the function of a request for proposal and describe what it typically includes.

7. Identify indirect and hidden costs that may be involved in the installation of a computer system.

8. Describe the three basic types of contractual arrangements used in relation to hospitality computer systems.

9. Identify installation factors involved in the computer system purchase and implementation process.

10. Describe the three most important forms of documentation in relation to hospitality computer systems.

Selecting and Implementing Computer Systems

WHILE HOSPITALITY BUSINESSES have unique information needs, every business needs to minimize expenditures. Cutting expenses by failing to purchase critical hardware components or software programs can create expensive problems in the future. For example, if management purchases a central processing unit with insufficient operating capacity, the computer system will not have adequate response time, which will frustrate guests, managers, and employees alike. Likewise, if expenses are cut by purchasing relatively cheap software which eventually fails to meet the information needs of the business, modifications may be very expensive.

When management is selecting a computer system, the first steps it should take toward fiscal responsibility are these:

1. Analyze the current information needs of the business.

2. Collect relevant computer system sales literature.

3. Establish computer system requirements.

This chapter outlines how management conducts preliminary research and how the results can be used to solicit computer system proposals from vendors. The chapter also presents a multiple rating system for evaluating proposals from vendors, and addresses what management can expect when negotiating a contract for the purchase of a computer system. The final sections of the chapter focus on aspects of computer system implementation.

Analyzing Current Information Needs

The first step in analyzing the current information needs of a business is to identify the types of information which various levels of management use in the course of everyday operations. This can be accomplished by compiling samples of all reports presently prepared for management's use. These reports include the daily operations report, basic financial statements, and other reports such as those listed in Exhibit 1. Once collected, the reports can be analyzed in relation to such variables as purpose, content, users, and frequency of preparation.

This kind of analysis identifies the types of information management currently uses, but it does not necessarily reveal all the current information needs of the business. A survey should be conducted asking managers to evaluate the effectiveness of the format and content of reports they receive. The survey results

Exhibit 1   Typical Management Reports

Report	Frequency	Content	Comparisons	Who Gets It	Purpose
Daily Report of Operations	Daily, on a cumulative basis for the month, the year to date.	Occupancy, average rate, revenue by outlet, and pertinent statistics.	To operating plan for current period and to prior year results.	Top management and supervisors responsible for day to day operation.	Basis for evaluating the current health of the enterprise.
Weekly Forecasts	Weekly.	Volume in covers, occupancy.	Previous periods.	Top management and supervisory personnel.	Staffing and scheduling; promotion.
Summary Report— Flash	Monthly at end of month (prior to monthly financial statement).	Known elements of revenue and direct costs; estimated departmental indirect costs.	To operating plan; to prior year results.	Top management and supervisory personnel responsible for function reported.	Provides immediate information on financial results for rooms, food and beverages, and other.
Cash Flow Analysis	Monthly (and on a revolving 12-month basis).	Receipts and disbursements by time periods.	With cash flow plan for month and for year to date.	Top management.	Predicts availability of cash for operating needs. Provides information on interim financing requirements.
Labor Productivity Analysis	Daily. Weekly. Monthly.	Dollar cost; manpower hours expended; hours as related to sales and services (covers, rooms occupied, etc.)	To committed hours in the operating plan (standards for amount of work to prior year statistics).	Top management and supervisory personnel.	Labor cost control through informed staffing and scheduling. Helps refine forecasting.
Departmental Analysis	Monthly (early in following month).	Details on main categories of income; same on expense.	To operating plan (month and year to date) and to prior year.	Top management and supervisors by function (e.g., rooms, each food and beverage outlet, laundry, telephone, other profit centers).	Knowing where business stands, and immediate corrective actions.
Room Rate Analysis	Daily, monthly, year to date.	Actual rates compared to rack rates by rate category or type of room.	To operating plan and to prior year results.	Top management and supervisors of sales and front office operations.	If goal is not being achieved, analysis of strengths and weaknesses is prompted.
Return on Investment	Actual computation, at least twice a year. Computation based on forecast, immediately prior to plan for year ahead.	Earnings as a percentage rate of return on average investment or equity committed.	To plan for operation and to prior periods.	Top management.	If goal is not being achieved, prompt assessment of strengths and weaknesses.
Long-Range Planning	Annually.	5-year projections of revenue and expenses. Operating plan expressed in financial terms.	Prior years.	Top management.	Involves staff in success or failure of enterprise. Injects more realism into plans for property and service modifications.
Exception Reporting	Concurrent with monthly reports and financial statements.	Summary listing of line item variances from predetermined norm.	With operating budgets.	Top management and supervisors responsible for function reported.	Immediate focusing on problem before more detailed statement analysis can be made.
Guest History Analysis	At least semi-annually; quarterly or monthly is recommended.	Historical records of corporate business, travel agencies, group bookings.	With previous reports.	Top management and sales.	Give direction to marketing efforts.
Future Bookings Report	Monthly.	Analysis of reservations and bookings.	With several prior years.	Top management, sales and marketing, department management.	Provides information on changing guest profile. Exposes strong and weak points of facility. Guides (1) sales planning and (2) expansion plans.

should provide the basis for immediate improvements in the current information system and should also enable management to conduct a more in-depth analysis with flowcharts.

Exhibit 2   Common Flowchart Symbols

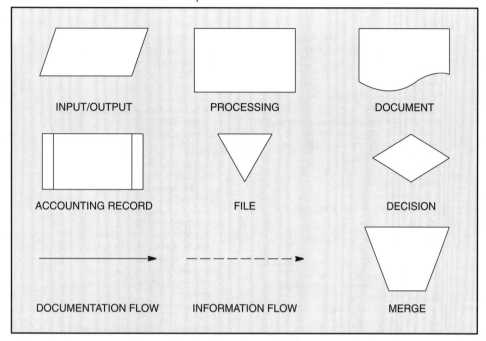

Flowcharts

Flowcharts use specially designed symbols for diagramming the flow of data and documents through an information system. Flowchart symbols have been standardized by the United States of America Standards Institute. Some of the more commonly used symbols are illustrated in Exhibit 2. Standardization is achieved by using common symbols and also by drawing flowcharts according to established procedures.

Since flowcharts reveal the origin, processing, and final disposition of each document, they are valuable techniques for evaluating the current information system of a hospitality business. Weaknesses, overlapping functions, and other redundancies can be identified, enabling management to revise and streamline current information needs which must eventually be met by the future computer system.

An alternative to detailed flowchart depictions of an information system is a series of written narrative descriptions. Written narratives are less efficient than flowcharts because they are time-consuming to write and to read. It may require a written narrative of six to eight pages to communicate the same information a detailed flowchart presents in a single page.

Creating a Property Profile

A **property profile** compiles statistics about the current information system. Exhibits 3 and 4 illustrate sample property profile formats for lodging operations

Exhibit 3   Sample Lodging Property Profile

General

___ Type of property (resort, hotel, motel, convention, condo, roadside, etc.)
___ Total number of rooms
___ Annual occupancy
___ Average room rate
___ Number of types of rooms
___ Number of suites
___ Percentage of annual occupancy from groups (tours, airlines, travel agencies, etc.)
___ Seasonal period(s); seasonal rates
___ Average length of stay
___ Number of permanent guests
___ Number of meeting rooms
___ Arrival/departure patterns
___ Number of revenue centers and locations

Reservations

___ Volume of reservation transactions (phone, telex, letter, etc.)
___ Volume of each type of reservation transaction
___ Percentage of reservations that require special handling (deposits, confirmations, etc.)
___ Hours of coverage
___ Average wage per employee
___ Annual overtime costs
___ If unionized department—will employees get raises because of automation?
___ Outside reservation services
___ Travel agent handling
___ Forecasting
___ Number of employees

Switchboard

___ Number of positions at switchboard
___ Type of equipment
___ Number of employees per shift (average/maximum)

Housekeeping

___ Number of floors
___ Number of rooms per floor (average)
___ Number of rooms or units cleaned per room attendant
___ Number of room attendants
___ Number of inspectors
___ Number of room attendants per inspector

Food and Beverage

___ Number of outlets
___ Location of outlets
___ Volume of sales
___ Number of sales
___ Number of menu items
___ Type of service

___ Number of covers
___ Average check
___ Present food and beverage registers
___ Present form of check used
___ Prechecking techniques (if applicable)
___ Inventory control methods
___ Inventory volumes
___ Percentage of sales charged to guestrooms
___ Number of employees
___ Number of function rooms

Accounting

___ Number of A/R accounts
___ Number of A/P accounts
___ Total A/R revenue handled per month (average/maximum)
___ Total A/P revenue handled per month (average/maximum)
___ Number of employees for A/R
___ Number of employees for A/P
___ Number of employees for general ledger
___ Number of employees for payroll
___ Number of employees for other accounting functions
___ Total number of employees on payroll (average/maximum)
___ Number of service bureaus presently employed
___ Cost of service bureaus
___ Number of travel agent accounts
___ Number of corporate accounts
___ Number of airline accounts
___ Number of special accounts
___ Present back office equipment
___ Cost/value/maintenance of present equipment
___ Supply cost of present equipment

Front Desk

___ Number of registration windows
___ Number of cashiering windows
___ Can registration and cashiering be done by same clerk?
___ Present equipment in use
___ Cost/value of present equipment
___ Maintenance of present equipment
___ Cost of supplies for present equipment (tapes, forms, etc.)
___ Number of employees per shift (average/maximum)
___ Average wage and benefit cost per employee
___ Number of registrants per day (average/maximum)
___ Number of check-outs per day (average/maximum)
___ Number of postings per day (average/maximum)

Exhibit 4   Sample Food Service Property Profile

FILE AND TRANSACTION VOLUMES

Sales and Cash Receipts

___ Number of seats
___ Number of covers per day
___ Number of daily menu items
___ Total number of menu items

Food Inventory

___ Number of inventory items (ingredients)
___ Daily inventory receipts (vendors)
___ Number of inventory items (classifications) per receipt
___ Daily inventory requisitions (from storeroom)
___ Number of recipes
___ Number of ingredients per recipe

Liquor Inventory

___ Number of inventory items
___ Daily storeroom requisitions (item classifications)
___ Number of recipes

Accounts Payable

___ Number of vendors
___ Invoices per day
___ Expense distributions per invoice
___ Checks (disbursements) per day

Accounts Receivable

___ Number of house accounts
___ Number of daily charges on account
___ Number of external charge media (American Express, etc.)
___ Number of daily receipts on account

Payroll and Labor Analysis

___ Number of employees
___ New hires per year
___ Number of W-2s prepared

General Ledger

___ Number of accounting periods
___ Number of accounts
___ Standard (recurring) monthly (journal entries)
___ Monthly general ledger postings (journal entries)

---

and food service operations, respectively. The types of categories and number of individual entries will vary from property to property.

A property profile proves useful when communicating information needs of the business to vendors of computer systems. The property profile allows vendors to compare the property's information system to those of similar properties which are already computerized. In addition, a property profile enables management to conduct a more informed and efficient review of computer systems sales literature.

Collecting Relevant Sales Information

After creating a property profile, management should collect sales literature on a variety of computer systems which meet the general information needs of the business by:

- Inquiring to state and national trade associations

- Attending industry trade shows

- Visiting area computer system vendors

- Making broadcast mailings to hospitality computer system vendors

State, national, and international hospitality trade associations, such as the American Hotel & Motel Association (AH&MA), the National Restaurant Association (NRA), the Club Managers Association of America (CMAA), the International Association of Conference Centers (IACC), and the International Association of Hospitality Accountants (IAHA), provide information services for their members. While these organizations will not recommend specific products, they can assist members seeking information about current computer system designs for hospitality operations.

These trade associations and other organizations regularly sponsor state, regional, and national trade shows. Attendance at these trade shows typically places management in direct contact with hospitality computer system vendors.

Management can also secure product information by visiting local computer system vendors. But this can be time-consuming, and it might not result in a representative view of the range of computer products on the market.

Perhaps the most effective approach to fact-finding is to use the information obtained through inquiries to trade associations, attendance at trade shows, and visits to local vendors to formulate a general interest letter to be mailed to all known vendors of hospitality computer systems. This broadcast mailing approach can be an efficient means of securing necessary information on various products and product lines. Management may also choose to use broadcast mailings to secure more specific information, such as:

- Hardware documentation

- Software documentation

- Lists of current product users

- Sample report formats

- Sample training materials

- Annual financial statements of the vendor's business

- Purchase/lease options

- User support and maintenance programs

Gathering this information early may prove valuable later when standardizing the form which selected vendors will use when submitting computer system proposals to top management officials. Before formulating the issues and categories of response which will appear on the proposal form, management must analyze the information needs of the business in light of the sales information collected.

Establishing Computer System Requirements

After management has analyzed the information needs of the business and collected sales literature describing relevant computer systems, the next step is to establish computer system requirements. This does not mean that hospitality managers must become experts in computer system design. Managers do not need to know the mechanics and details of electronic circuitry, but they must be able to make general determinations about what data to process, how that data is to be processed, and the formats in which processed data will be output as information.

Determining what data to process involves identifying the information tasks which can best be performed by the computer system. Determining how data is to be processed is a matter of making sure that the computer system uses management-approved formulas when performing such calculations as occupancy percentages, food cost percentages, and so on. Determining the formats in which processed data will be output as information involves decisions which may change the structure and style of current business forms, guest folios, guest checks, management reports, and other printed materials.

Determining Data to Process

Management determines which data to process through the computer system by deciding which tasks to automate. The sales literature collected during the previous fact-finding stage should help management identify tasks which are typically automated by similar operations in the hospitality industry. But just because a particular task can be automated doesn't necessarily mean that it should be. Management must carefully weigh what is to be gained through automation. Will automation improve guest services? Will it increase the efficiency of operations? Will it enhance management's effectiveness in decision-making situations?

Tasks which are performed frequently, such as front desk procedures during guest registration, are better choices for automation than tasks which are performed infrequently, such as calculating freight costs for inventory shipped from overseas.

Similarly, tasks which involve routine objective decisions are better choices for automation than are tasks which involve subjective decisions. For example, some responses to reservation requests can be made simply by comparing the types of rooms requested with rooms availability data. This task is a more likely candidate for automation than are other tasks which involve subjective evaluations. It would not be possible (or desirable) for a computer system to respond to 150 reservation requests (all received in the mail on the same day) for ocean-front rooms during the third week of March, when the property will have only 75 such rooms available. Unless programmed to use objective criteria (such as sorting the 150 requests by variables defined by management), computer systems are generally incapable of resolving such problems by making subjective judgments.

Other factors to consider when determining which data to process include the ease of identifying, collecting, entering, and coding data. These factors are essential to the timely processing and output of information.

The term **data identification** refers to the determination of elements necessary for a data processing operation. For example, in order for a computer system to calculate occupancy percentage for a given period of time, the number of rooms sold and the number of rooms available for sale during that time period must be identified. **Data collection** is the gathering of relevant data elements. In the previous example, management must determine how the number of rooms sold will be collected. Will a front desk employee count the number of rooms sold, or will these data elements be collected by the computer system?

Data entry is the physical process of inputting elements of data into the computer system. The ease with which data is entered into the computer system is an important determinant of the speed of data processing and information reporting. **Data coding** refers to techniques which enable rapid data entry, processing, and reporting. For example, it is much easier for reservationists to search for rooms available with two double beds by entering a code such as DD than it is to enter the term "double-double."

In the hospitality industry, probably the most important factor determining which data to process is how urgently the output of processed information is needed. Guest satisfaction requires that many tasks at the front desk be performed quickly and accurately; these tasks may be prime candidates for computerization. Certain tasks involved in generating timely management reports are also critical areas for computerization. In order to ensure that these reports contain reliable information, management must determine how data is to be processed by the computer system.

Determining How to Process Data

Determining how data is to be processed is a matter of making sure that the algorithmic design of the computer software programs corresponds to the actual formulas management wishes to use. The term **algorithm** refers to a prescribed set of well-defined, unambiguous rules or procedures leading to the solution of a problem. Too often, management assumes that hospitality industry jargon, such as "occupancy percentage" and "food cost percentage," means the same thing to all computer system designers. The truth is that hospitality properties themselves differ in terms of the variables going into basic calculations.

Throughout the lodging industry, occupancy percentage is calculated by dividing rooms sold by rooms available for sale. But properties may vary in their definitions of the terms "rooms sold" and "rooms available for sale." Actual occupancy percentage calculations produced by the basic formula depends on how properties take account of complimentary rooms, out-of-order rooms, no-show rooms, and other variables. Similarly, in relation to food service operations, the formulas used to calculate food cost information may vary widely. Some properties may cost food when received, others when it is issued to the kitchen, others when the food is sold, and so on.

In order to ensure that the eventual computer system will process data according to the property's standards, management must survey individual departments and compile a master list of important formulas, along with detailed explanations of how the terms within each formula are defined. This master list of formulas and the accompanying explanations identify major computer system requirements which vendors will be asked to meet as they submit proposals to top management officials.

Determining Information Formats

The information needs of the business and the format preferences of managers should dictate the choice of printing capabilities of the computer system. The sample report formats collected from various vendors during the early fact-finding stage should serve as a good starting point for management's determination of preferred formats for the property's printed materials. If the vendors solicited have installed computer systems in other hospitality operations, management should be able to secure sample designs for many kinds of printed materials, including:

- Reservation confirmation notices
- Registration cards
- Guest folios
- Billing statements
- Payroll checks

It is important that management give early attention to this area of computer system design. If management waits too long, it could lose control of the situation. When this happens, the capabilities of the computer system control management's preferences, rather than management's preferences controlling the capabilities of the computer system.

Determining the Hardware Configuration

Hardware configuration refers to the design and layout of the hardware components of a computer system. The size of a hospitality operation and the number of departments needing access to the computer system are significant factors in selecting the appropriate configuration of hardware components.

A very small hospitality operation may find that a single microcomputer work station is sufficient to meet the needs of its limited number of users. This work station would be a complete system with input/output units, a single CPU, and external storage capability.

Other hospitality operations may have a number of user groups from different departments that need access to the computer system. They can avoid spending unnecessary funds on computer equipment by selecting the particular configuration of hardware components which best meets the needs of their operations. In many cases, it is possible for users to share output devices (such as printers and external storage facilities) or the internal memory and processing capability of a central processing unit.

The advantages and disadvantages of each configuration should be considered before purchasing a computer system. The major differences among the various configurations are speed and cost. The CPU is the most expensive component in a computer system; therefore, the more CPUs a configuration requires, the greater its cost will be. The tradeoff in configuring a number of CPUs, however, is that the closer the CPU is to the I/O devices, and the fewer I/O devices making demands on the CPU, the faster the computer system will seem to operate.

The following sections discuss four basic configurations of hardware components: stand-alone configuration, distributed configuration, integrated configuration, and combined configuration.

Stand-Alone Configuration

A **stand-alone hardware configuration** creates self-sufficient work stations, each with a complete set of the same hardware components. The presence of many

Exhibit 5   Stand-Alone Hardware Configuration

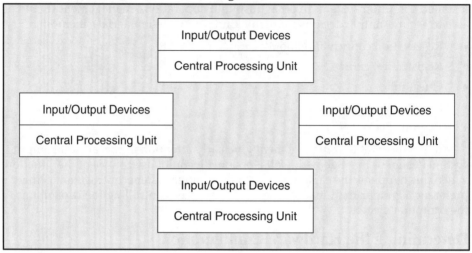

individual computers at different locations limits communication to sharing data by exchanging external storage media (disks). Exhibit 5 diagrams a stand-alone hardware configuration. The duplication of hardware components makes this a relatively expensive hardware configuration.

Distributed Configuration

The **distributed hardware configuration** is an improvement over the stand-alone configuration. Each work station is a complete computer system with an I/O device, CPU, and external storage device.

What distinguishes this configuration from the stand-alone configuration discussed previously is that the work stations are cabled together. The cabling serves as a hardware interface, creating a local area network (LAN) of individual work stations. A local area network enables users to share data, programs, and output devices (such as printers). Data sharing facilitates system-wide communications, and program sharing enables users who do not have a particular software program to benefit from its operation. From an economic perspective, device sharing is perhaps the most important benefit derived from networking. Expensive peripheral devices, such as high capacity storage devices and laser printers, can become available to all work stations cabled within the network.

Since each user group has its own computer, there is also more specialized application capability (use and storage). An additional benefit is that an individual system with operational problems does not affect other systems in the network. Exhibit 6 diagrams a distributed hardware configuration.

Integrated Configuration

An **integrated hardware configuration** creates a network of work stations dependent upon a single central processing unit and external storage capability.

Exhibit 6   Distributed Hardware Configuration

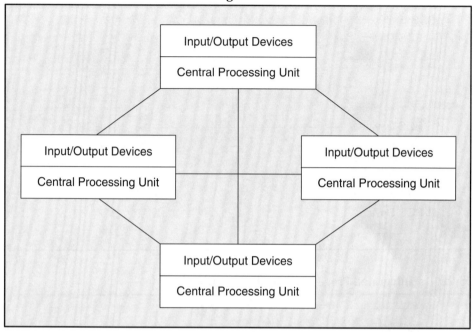

While I/O units may be distributed throughout the hospitality establishment, both the CPU and external storage capability are usually centrally located. Each I/O unit communicates with the CPU, and the CPU and external storage device work closely together. There are three basic integrated configurations: master/slave configurations, processor-based configurations, and micro-based configurations.

Master/Slave Configuration. With the **master/slave hardware configuration**, only one unit contains all the necessary components of a complete computer system. For example, an ECR may function as a master register by processing transactions entered through slave units, such as precheck or cashier terminals. Slave POS units are cabled to the ECR. Exhibit 7 diagrams a master/slave hardware configuration. Although slave units are not equipped with their own CPUs, some may possess a limited internal memory capacity.

A master/slave configuration places a heavy burden on the master unit. The ECR must not only process transactions communicated from slave units, but function as a cashier terminal and, in some cases, as a precheck terminal as well. The greatest danger associated with a master/slave configuration is that the entire system becomes inoperable if anything disrupts the master unit. This danger exists even when an ECR hosts intelligent POS terminals, because these terminals may function independently only for a limited amount of time.

Processor-Based Configuration. The **processor-based hardware configuration** is similar to the master/slave system, except that the central processing unit and external storage capacity are significantly larger and placed in a location remote

Exhibit 7   Integrated Master/Slave Configuration

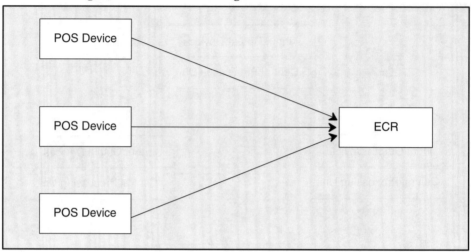

Exhibit 8   Integrated Processor-Based Configuration

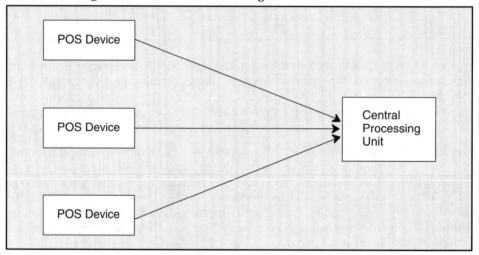

from actual restaurant operations. Exhibit 8 diagrams a processor-based configuration. This configuration enables management to monitor a wide range of transactions from a central location.

As with other integrated configurations, a processor-based system depends upon a single CPU and centralized storage capability. Should the CPU malfunction, the entire system could become inoperable or stored data could be permanently lost.

Microprocessor-Based Configuration. Recently developed microprocessor-based POS systems attempt to avoid some of the expense associated with an ECR/POS

Exhibit 9   Integrated Microprocessor-Based Configuration

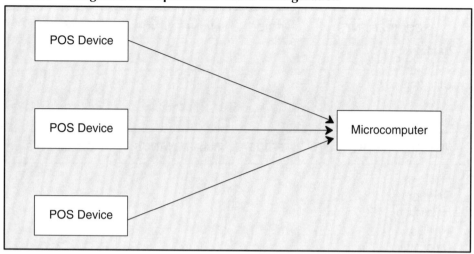

network while capitalizing on the advantages of networking. With a **microprocessor-based configuration**, a microcomputer is placed in a POS network to function as a file server and to process all system transactions. Exhibit 9 shows an integrated microprocessor-based configuration. In this type of network, each terminal relays its transactions to the microcomputer for processing. Transactions are processed in the order in which they are received. Problems may arise when several terminals relay transactions at the same time.

Requesting Proposals from Vendors

After translating information needs into computer system requirements, management is ready to request proposals from vendors. A **request for proposal** (RFP) is typically made up of three major sections. The first section tells the vendor about management's business operations; the second section establishes bidding requirements for vendor proposals; and the third section deals specifically with user application requirements.

This first section of the RFP should contain an overview of the hospitality business, list objectives and broad operational requirements for the computer system, and briefly explain the vendor's future responsibilities. This overview of the hospitality business should include a brief description of the operation and the detailed property profile management created earlier when analyzing the information needs of the business. Listing objectives and broad operational requirements for the computer system offers management the opportunity to identify particular system features as either mandatory or optional, thus assisting vendors in the preparation of their proposals. The outline of the vendor's future responsibilities should designate when the vendor's proposal must be submitted for management's consideration, and request vendors to submit as much information as possible concerning such areas as:

Exhibit 10   Sample Cost Summary Table

REQUIREMENTS	PRICE	MAINTENANCE	COMMENTS
Hardware Software Other (specify) Discount Sub-Total			
NON-RECURRING COSTS	**PRICE**	**MAINTENANCE**	**COMMENTS**
Site Prep Delivery Installation Training Other (specify) Discount Sub-Total			
Total			

- Hardware configurations
- Software descriptions
- Maintenance and support services
- Installation and training programs
- Guarantees and warranties
- Payment options
- Future expandability of the proposed system

The second section of the RFP establishes bidding requirements for vendor proposals. Allowing vendors to formulate their bids within their own chosen formats may force management to adopt a tedious and unstructured evaluation process. All proposals should be submitted on a standardized response form created by management to facilitate price and performance comparisons. Exhibit 10 shows a sample cost summary table. Note how the structured formatting enables management to make intelligent comparisons between all proposals along a common set of dimensions.

The final section of the RFP states specific computer system application requirements. Exhibit 11 shows a sample RFP form which structures vendors' responses to application requirements. Once again, note that since all vendors are asked to follow the same response format, top management officials will not waste time sifting through proposals that differ radically in both form and content.

Exhibit 11   Sample Format for Listing Applications Requirements

Instructions: Vendors are to indicate the applications they offer which are identical to those desired by the user (YES—Same), similar in function to those desired by the user (YES—Similar), function not now available but will develop (NO—Soon), or function not available (NO).

*   check appropriate column   *

FUNCTION:	YES Same	YES Similar	NO Soon	NO
Ingredient file of food items				
Recipe file of ingredients				
Menu file of recipe and subrecipes				
Inventory file of food items				
Payroll master file of employees				
Purchase order file by purveyor				
Check register of issued checks				
Daily transaction register				
Payroll register				
Accounts receivable ledger module				
Accounts payable ledger module				
General ledger module				
Income statement				
Balance sheet				

Once created, the RFP form is distributed to the vendor community for response. After receiving an RFP, most vendors will contact management and schedule a site survey.

Site Surveys by Vendors

After receiving an RFP, conscientious vendors typically schedule a visit to the property in order to conduct a **site survey**. The purpose of a site survey is to identify important factors regarding specific business operations within a property which may affect computer system design. The physical parameters of a property often determine appropriate types of hardware configurations.

During a site survey, a vendor may analyze many other characteristics specific to business operations which are important to overall computer system planning. Many details regarding the business's internal organization, policies and procedures, and daily operations directly affect the vendor's computer system proposal in relation to such areas as:

- Training programs

- Exceptional cost considerations

- System security features

- Installation schedules

- Backup system design

- Communication links

In order to secure all the information necessary to complete their proposals, vendors may require a great deal of information from different departments. This may involve the cooperation of personnel from several managerial levels within the property. To facilitate the vendor's access to necessary information and key personnel, top management officials may designate a management representative to coordinate the flow of information and help minimize disruptions to daily operations. When several vendors are scheduled to conduct site surveys at various times, it is wise to schedule the same management representative to serve as coordinator. This person may be able to provide management decision-makers with valuable information on the efficiency with which vendors conduct their surveys. Such information may become an important factor in evaluating the different proposals submitted by vendors.

Evaluating Vendor Proposals

After conducting site surveys, vendors complete their computer system proposals and submit them for management's consideration. While there are many ways to evaluate a set of proposals, a multiple rating system can be an efficient and effective method.

A **multiple rating system** uses the same criteria to judge the worth of each vendor's proposal. Generally, the criteria consist of several issues which management considers to be of critical concern in computerizing the business. Management rates each vendor's response to each issue on a scale from 1 to 100. The higher the rating, the better the proposal is judged to handle the issue. Because some issues will always be considered more important than others, simply totaling the ratings on key issues may not necessarily identify the best computer system proposal. In order to identify the best computer system proposal, management must rank the issues in the order of their importance, and assign a percentage value to each, denoting its relative importance within the overall evaluation scheme. The ratings for each issue are multiplied by their appropriate percentage values and *then* totaled to yield an overall score for each computer system proposal. The proposal receiving the highest overall score identifies the vendor with whom management should seriously consider negotiating a contract. The following example illustrates how a multiple rating system can be used to evaluate proposals from three different vendors.

Assume that a business receives three different computer system proposals, one from vendor A, one from vendor B, and one from vendor C. Assume further that top management officials have decided to evaluate each proposal on three key issues—product performance, vendor's business reputation, and cost.

The first issue focuses on product performance—how well the proposed computer system fits the information needs of the property. Each vendor's proposal is studied and given a rating from 1 to 100. For the sake of this example, assume that vendor A receives a rating of 80, vendor B a rating of 70, and vendor C a rating of 50. Furthermore, assume that management officials decide that product performance is the most important of the three issues and, accordingly, they assign this issue a relative value of 45%. Each vendor's rating on the first issue is then multiplied by 45% to arrive at a score that is relative to the entire evaluation scheme. Vendor A scores 36 points ($80 \times .45 = 36$); vendor B scores 32 points ($70 \times .45 = 32$); and vendor C scores 23 points ($50 \times .45 = 23$).

The second issue focuses on the vendor's business reputation and includes such factors as the vendor's track record in the marketplace, the degree of system support which the vendor can provide, and the financial stability of the vendor's business. In relation to this issue, management is interested in answers to such questions as:

- How long has the vendor been in the hospitality computer systems business?
- Are hospitality computer systems the vendor's principal business?
- How many installations does the vendor currently support?
- How satisfied are current users?
- Is the vendor's business financially stable?
- Is the vendor expected to remain in business?

Each vendor's proposal is studied and given a rating from 1 to 100. Vendor A receives a rating of 60, vendor B a rating of 95, and vendor C a rating of 80. Although management officials consider product performance to be their primary concern, they also consider the vendor's business reputation to be important, and, therefore, they assign this issue a relative value of 30%. Each vendor's rating on the second issue is then multiplied by 30% to arrive at a score which is relative to the entire evaluation scheme. Vendor A scores 18 points ($60 \times .30 = 18$); vendor B scores 29 points ($95 \times .30 = 29$); and vendor C scores 24 points ($80 \times .30 = 24$).

The third issue identified by management centers on economic factors such as direct, indirect, and hidden costs of purchasing the computer system. Assume that management officials were well-prepared and designed a portion of the RFP asking vendors to list the **direct costs** of individual computer system components. Avoiding a lump summary of direct expenditures enables management to:

Exhibit 12   Multiple Rating Results

	VENDORS		
CRITERIA	**A**	**B**	**C**
Product Performance	80 × .45 = 36	70 × .45 = 32	50 × .45 = 23
Vendor Reputation	60 × .30 = 18	95 × .30 = 29	80 × .30 = 24
System Cost	90 × .25 = 23	70 × .25 = 18	80 × .25 = 20
Overall Score	77	79	67

- Consider the benefits of installing the computer system in phases rather than all at once.

- Eliminate unnecessary hardware devices or software programs.

- Conduct comparative price shopping for individual system components.

Assume further that management officials researched **indirect costs** which businesses typically incur in relation to the installation, operation, and maintenance of computer systems. A portion of the RFP asked vendors to estimate such indirect costs as taxes, insurance, shipping, and other costs which may result from:

- Modifying the property's air conditioning, electrical, and telephone wiring systems

- Establishing contingency programs

- Installing uninterruptible power sources

- Maintaining an inventory of spare parts

Another portion of the RFP asked vendors to estimate additional expenses, sometimes referred to as **hidden costs**, which include costs associated with supplies, customized forms, training, overtime pay, and data conversion.

Each vendor's proposal is studied in relation to these cost factors and given a rating from 1 to 100. Vendor A receives a rating of 90, vendor B a rating of 70, and vendor C a rating of 80. Because management officials believe product performance and vendor reliability are themselves important steps toward fiscal responsibility, the cost issue is assigned a somewhat lower relative value—25%. Each vendor's rating on the third issue is then multiplied by 25% to arrive at a score which is relative to the entire evaluation scheme. Vendor A scores 23 points (90 × .25 = 23); vendor B scores 18 points (70 × .25 = 18); and vendor C scores 20 points (80 × .25 = 20).

Exhibit 12 shows the results of the multiple rating system used in this example. Vendor C's proposal will probably not receive any further consideration because it did not score well on any of the three key issues. Also, note that although vendor A offered the best computer system in terms of product performance, vendor B received the highest overall score due to its excellent reputation. However, since the overall scores of vendors A and B are so close, further analysis may be warranted before a final selection is made.

The previous example is meant only to illustrate a multiple rating system. Properties should take particular care to identify and rank key issues which relate specifically to the needs and requirements of their individual business operations. And, just as issues and their order of importance will vary from property to property, so will the relative percentage values assigned to each key issue.

Contract Negotiations

Before entering into contract negotiations with a vendor, management should secure copies of several standard contracts used by vendors of hospitality computer systems. These standard contracts are typically written in favor of the vendors and may not provide the kind of protection which the business may require. Management should examine these contracts carefully and obtain legal advice from a qualified attorney. If the attorney has no working knowledge of computer systems, management may also need assistance from an experienced computer systems consultant. In any case, the standard contract offered by a vendor serves only as the starting point for contract negotiations. Since the actual sale has not yet been made, the potential buyer may maintain a great deal of leverage in negotiating changes to the vendor's standard contract.

Contract Provisions

The general contents of hospitality computer system contracts can be divided into several areas. While some areas may be executed as separate contracts or sub-contracts, properties may find that one master contract best meets the needs of their businesses. Three basic areas of a typical computer system contract are:

- General provisions
- Hardware provisions (including maintenance)
- Software provisions (including maintenance)

General contract provisions address standard contractual terms, such as the following, which are typically covered in most purchasing contracts:

- Terms of delivery
- Terms of payment
- Survival past delivery
- Saleable product warranty
- Catastrophe remedies
- Provisions for breach of contract

Survival past delivery refers to the responsibilities of both parties once the product arrives on the buyer's premises. Saleable product warranty provides buyer assurance that the seller has a legal, marketable right to warrant the purchased product. Catastrophe remedies refer to penalties and relief in the event of a major failure of the product.

Hardware contract provisions relate to the purchase and operation of the computer equipment, including the operating system software which typically accompanies the hardware. Key areas addressed in the hardware section of a contract include:

- Specifications and performance criteria
- Delivery, installation, and testing requirements
- Costs and terms of payment
- Reliability tolerances
- Maintenance program options

Computer **software contract provisions** tend to be more difficult to negotiate because of the complex nature of software ownership. Since software programs are a compilation of ideas and processes proprietary to the seller, title is not automatically transferred to the buyer. Instead, the software often remains the property of the vendor and the buyer is granted a non-exclusive license to use the software programs. Key areas of a software contract are similar to those listed for hardware; however, the contract should demand that a copy of the source code in which the software programs are written be placed in escrow and released to the buyer should the vendor fail to carry out provisions stated within the contract.

Contractual Arrangements

In relation to hospitality computer systems, there are three basic types of contractual arrangements:

- Single-vendor contracts
- Two-vendor contracts
- Other equipment manufacturer (OEM) contracts

A **single-vendor contract** refers to an agreement to purchase hardware and software from the same vendor. In most of these cases, the vendor makes the necessary hardware and software modifications prior to system implementation. A single-vendor contract clearly identifies the vendor's responsibilities in relation to hardware and software performance and avoids the kind of confusion which may arise in other contractual arrangements when the lines of responsibility are not so clearly defined.

A **two-vendor contract** refers to an agreement to purchase hardware and software from separate sources. The hardware components may be purchased directly from the manufacturer or purchased through the software vendor, who serves as a value-added dealer or value-added remarketer. In either case, the hardware components or the accompanying operating system may require modifications by the software company in order to perform to the software's specifications.

When a business purchases (or repurchases) hardware components from one source which must be modified to perform according to specifications set by another source, confusion can arise with respect to guarantees and warranties. When a software vendor modifies hardware components in order for the system to support special application programs, guarantees and warranties offered by the hardware manufacturer could become invalid. Hardware manufacturers generally assume responsibility for product performance only in relation to designated performance specifications. Whenever hardware components have to be modified to perform according to specifications that differ from those originally designated by the hardware manufacturer, management should insist that whoever modifies the equipment backs the performance of that equipment with guarantees and warranty conditions similar to those originally provided by the hardware manufacturer.

Another area of concern in two-vendor contracts relates to trouble-shooting and maintenance. Consider the following scenario. A problem arises in the operation of the reservations module of a large hotel's computer system. The reservations staff scrambles to a manual backup operation, and management calls the hardware vendor. The hardware vendor listens to management's description of the problem and, after asking a few questions, concludes that the company can't help because the hotel's problem is really a software problem. Management then calls the software vendor. The software vendor listens to management's description of the problem and, after asking a few questions, concludes that the hotel's problem is really a hardware problem and advises management to call the hardware vendor and carefully explain the situation once again. Meanwhile, managers waste time, tempers shorten, and room sales may be lost.

Clearly, managers engaged in the daily operation of a hospitality business cannot be burdened with diagnosing a computer system problem and determining whether the hardware or software vendor is responsible for resolving the situation. When negotiating a two-vendor contract agreement, management should seek legal advice from a qualified attorney and technical assistance from an experienced computer systems consultant.

An **other equipment manufacturer (OEM) contract** refers to a situation in which a business agrees to purchase hardware components and software packages from a single source, and this single source takes full responsibility for the performance of the computer system. OEM contracts generally involve purchasing turnkey packages. In relation to hospitality computer systems, a turnkey package is a complete system which arrives at the property ready for installation. Once installed, the business "turns the key" and the system is ready to perform. This kind of contractual arrangement provides a business with the equivalent of a single-vendor contract, because all hardware and software customizing is performed by the OEM.

Installation Factors

After completing contract negotiations, management must make final decisions on such installation factors as:

- Training

- Site preparation

- Design of printed materials

- Initial entry of database elements

- Acceptance testing

- System conversion

- Documentation

- Contingency planning

- Vendor support

The following sections discuss each of these installation factors in some detail.

Training

Training should begin before installation of the computer system and continue throughout the implementation process. The primary users of the system will be those individuals responsible for data entry, report generation, and system mainte-nance. These persons should begin hands-on training with hardware components and software applications before installation. Training sessions may be conducted by the vendor or through seminars, textbooks, video, and other tutorial media.

Training conducted by the vendor can take place at the user's site or at the vendor's site. Regardless of location, management should insist that these training sessions involve hands-on experience with hardware and software identical to that being installed at the property. Although the costs of training are negotiable, the hospitality business generally assumes responsibility for any out-of-pocket ex-penses incurred by the vendor at the user's site. In addition, the hospitality busi-ness might have to bear the costs of securing any additional training equipment needed to accommodate large groups at the property.

Seminars on specific topics, ranging from the essentials of computer systems to the details of particular software programs, are often conducted by computer system experts. There has been a rapid growth in these seminars. Although the training received by individuals attending these seminars may include hands-on experience, the hardware components and software applications used during the seminar may not be identical to those which are to be installed at the property. First-time users who receive training on one kind of computer system may become very confused and frustrated when they find out that they are to work on an en-tirely different computer system.

Computer systems training through textbooks can be laborious and confusing for first-time computer users. Written materials are better suited for supplement-ing the knowledge of those who are already familiar with basic computer opera-tions. Textbooks can also be helpful for introducing experienced users to new software applications.

Video and tutorial media have proven to be highly effective training methods. Videotapes, designed to teach specific applications, generally allow a learner to progress through the materials at his or her own speed. The same is true for tutorial media (on-disk) which typically permit a learner to skip over previously mastered areas and concentrate on sessions involving applications which he or she finds more difficult.

The amount of training managers need will vary from property to property. Generally, managers are not directly involved in the daily input and processing functions of the computer system. However, since they depend on its output, it is vital that managers fully understand the system's capabilities. Since the success or failure of automating information needs often is a function of the degree of management involvement and commitment, managers must provide continual support and encouragement for personnel being trained as primary users and operators of the system.

Site Preparation

Site preparation refers to architectural or engineering changes that have to be made before the computer system can be installed. The extent of these changes depends on the size of the property and the kind of computer system which is to be installed. Depending on the circumstances, site preparation might include:

- Modifications to the property's air conditioning, electrical, and telephone systems

- Construction of individual work stations to accommodate computer hardware components and cables

- Installation of uninterruptible power sources

- Construction of a computer room

These facets of site preparation must be carefully planned and executed in order to prevent disruptions to operations during installation and later when the system is fully operational.

Design of Printed Materials

Many general questions about printed materials must already have been answered in order for a business to purchase the appropriate printing devices for the computer system. Details regarding the nature of printed materials must also be addressed before full implementation of the computer system.

Lodging properties may choose to design new formats for reservation confirmation notices, registration cards, guest folios, room key envelopes, billing statements, payroll checks, and many management reports which are prepared on a daily basis. Printed materials that may be redesigned by food service businesses include guest checks, menus, promotional materials, and various management reports.

Other questions about printed materials that must be answered include the following:

- Which forms will be printed out on single-sheet paper and which on continuous paper?

- Will different qualities of paper stock be used for different print jobs?

- Which forms and reports will use paper pre-printed with the business's logo and other artwork?

Answering these questions during site preparation will ensure smoother installation of the computer equipment and enable management to refine printed materials during acceptance testing of the computer system. In addition, appropriate personnel will be able to receive the more specific kind of training which might be necessary in order to prepare and print intricate forms and reports.

Initial Entry of Database Elements

Long before installation of the computer system, management officials and the vendor should work together to create the database elements which will meet the information needs of the business. The creation of database elements entails identifying the elements which are to be included in the business's database *and* the design specifications for each element to guide users in the input, processing, and output functions. This is a critical area of computer systems planning—once the system is installed and implemented, the content of a system's database limits and controls its potential application.

While database design specifications are usually the mutual responsibility of the vendor and management officials, the actual entering of data elements according to design specifications is the responsibility of trained property employees. Initial data entry can be a time-consuming process. For most lodging properties, initial data entry entails inputting room types, room numbers, room rates, revenue center codes, employee identification numbers, posting codes, settlement plans, sales history data, guest history files, and so on. For most food service operations, initial data entry entails inputting ingredient lists, recipe and sub-recipe codes, meal plans, menu prices, identification of house accounts, historical menu mix (sales) data, and much more. It is extremely important that initial data entry be completed within a time frame that permits extensive acceptance testing before the business converts to full automation.

Acceptance Testing

Before converting from manual procedures to computerized functions, properties generally conduct extensive **acceptance testing** of the computer system. Acceptance testing involves more than simply checking whether the computer system works. Tests should be developed to determine whether computerized operations function according to standards defined by management. Fundamental areas of acceptance testing include:

- Hardware efficiency

- Software reliability

- System integrity

Hardware efficiency refers to the ease of use of system equipment and the suspense time involved in searching for necessary data. These areas must be tested and found acceptable. Users must be able to retrieve necessary data in the timely fashion required by management.

Software reliability refers to the accuracy with which the programs process data. The reliability of applications software programs should be challenged with a set of test data. This can be done by processing a known set of data through the computer system and then comparing the system's output with calculated results generated by the previous information system. Lodging operations can input data from a previous month and process a series of statistical reports and financial statements through the computer system. These reports and statements can then be compared with the actual reports and statements prepared by the previous information system. Similarly, food service operations can input data from a prior period and test the accuracy of the applications software in calculating food cost percentages, menu counts, and payroll expenses. In any case, the use of previously processed data can be extremely helpful in verifying the new computer system's algorithmic design.

System integrity refers to the degree of software integration. Sharing data files to produce comprehensive reports is typically a major issue in the selection of one computer system over another. System testing should prove that such integration does in fact exist and that it functions according to standards defined by management.

System Conversion

System conversion is the process of switching from the current information system to the capabilities of the computerized system. System conversion within a hospitality operation can be a difficult, if not trying, experience. Two commonly used conversion strategies within the hospitality industry are parallel conversion and direct cutover conversion.

With **parallel conversion**, the property operates two different information systems simultaneously—the previous system and the newly computerized system. Both systems are maintained simultaneously for at least one complete accounting period. When comfortable with the new system's operation, management directs a complete conversion to the new computer system. While there is relatively little risk involved with parallel conversion, it has the main disadvantage of the high costs of operating two information systems simultaneously.

With **direct cutover conversion**, management chooses a date on which the property is to switch from current procedures to new computerized functions. Direct cutover is also called "going cold turkey" because it involves a complete withdrawal from the previous information system. This approach may be especially effective when the previous system is cumbersome and inadequate, or when the new computer system is perceived as something new and unique for the property. The major advantage of a direct cutover conversion is that the hospitality business is not required to operate two different information systems simultaneously. The major disadvantage is the potential risk of adopting a wholly new system without having the old processes and procedures to back it up.

There are a number of conversion strategies which combine aspects of direct cutover and parallel conversion. Lodging properties may choose to immediately convert areas such as reservations, rooms management, and guest accounting, but maintain parallel conversion procedures for a full accounting period for payroll and general ledger accounting. In food service operations, computerized cash register systems may be implemented soon after installation; but inventory records, accounts payable lists, fixed asset files, and financial statements may be generated by both information systems for some period of time.

Whatever the particular strategy management chooses to implement, costs must always be balanced against risks. Risks can often be minimized by careful attention to acceptance testing, training, and contingency planning.

Documentation

Securing adequate documentation of each computer system component is critical to the success of system operations beyond the installation period. Documentation is essential for the ongoing training of staff and for identifying underutilized system capabilities and possible weaknesses within the computer system. The three most important forms of documentation in relation to hospitality computer systems are operator's guides, technical manuals, and system flowcharts.

Operator's guides, also called user's guides, are training materials for specific application procedures. Some vendors provide a single, all-encompassing guidebook. However, the documentation for a system with extensive application options might be segmented by job functions, with a separate user's guide for cashiers, another guide for front desk employees, and so on.

Technical manuals, also called systems manuals, focus on the engineering features of the computer system. These manuals typically include schematic diagrams of electronic circuitry and list trouble-shooting hints for service and repair workers. Managers of some businesses fail to request this kind of technical documentation because they do not foresee using it themselves. However, technical manuals can be valuable resources in times of emergency.

Computer **system flowcharts** may not be part of the standard documentation package; however, management should request them because they offer users insight into the operation of the computer system. System flowcharts illustrate the input-process-output logic, file structures, program sub-routines, interprogram relationships, and the level of program integration within the system. These flowcharts provide a way to analyze the effectiveness of the computerized information system and prove invaluable when management contemplates software or hardware modifications to meet new information needs.

Contingency Planning

The purpose of **contingency planning** is to define procedures which are to be followed when, for whatever reason, the computer system is not able to function properly. Contingency planning is an important aspect of computer systems implementation. This is especially true for businesses in the hospitality industry which may operate 24 hours a day, 7 days a week. There are four basic parts to an effective contingency plan.

The first part designates an emergency team. The computer system manager (or supervisor) typically spearheads this team, which is made up of representatives from various departments. Each team member is assigned specific duties and responsibilities which may range from being able to install spare parts to troubleshooting and carrying out somewhat sophisticated diagnostic routines.

The second part of a contingency plan identifies detailed information about hardware and software configurations, suppliers, environmental requirements, and site considerations. This information is typically stored in a specific location and is made available to members of the contingency team.

The third part of the plan identifies computer backup sites (such as local service bureaus) and sources of substitute equipment.

The final section of a contingency plan details procedures for recovering damaged files and for implementing temporary non-automated operations.

Vendor Support

The quality of documentation of the user's manual provided by the vendor of an ECR/POS system can be an enormous help in coordinating service and production communications and in establishing efficient order-entry procedures. However, too often, user's manuals are outdated and fail to correspond to current system screens, parameters, protocols, prompts, keys, and commands. Poorly documented manuals can be fatal to system operations.

A vendor's continuing research and development in the area of ECR/POS systems can extend a system's useful life and operational capabilities. Restaurant managers cannot be expected to keep abreast of technological advances, software breakthroughs, and other computer-related developments. Vendors with a history of updating systems they offer are likely to provide the kind of enhancements that will keep a property's computer system current.

Summary

In order to minimize expenditures when purchasing a computer system, management must focus on long-term considerations and avoid the tempting, but potentially disastrous, policy of pursuing a short-term path of lowest cost. This chapter stressed that fiscal responsibility begins with careful research which translates the information needs of a business into computer system requirements. Before soliciting computer system proposals from vendors, management must analyze current information needs, collect relevant computer system sales literature, and then establish specific computer system requirements that identify what data to process, how data will be processed, the formats through which processed data will be output as information, and the configuration of hardware components. This information is then used to structure a request for proposal form which is distributed to selected vendors.

Structuring the format of the request for proposal document puts management in control of how vendors will submit computer system proposals. Since all vendors will be required to respond to the same set of issues, top management officials will not waste time sifting through proposals which vary widely in form and content. The chapter showed how management can use a multiple rating system to select the best proposal and suggested what management can expect when negotiating a contract with vendors.

The final sections of the chapter outlined decisions which management must make regarding such installation factors as:

- Training
- Site preparation
- Design of printed materials
- Initial entry of database elements
- Acceptance testing
- System conversion
- Documentation
- Contingency planning
- Vendor support

Key Terms

acceptance testing
algorithm
contingency planning
data coding
data collection
data entry
data identification
direct costs
direct cutover conversion
distributed hardware configuration
flowchart
general contract provisions
hardware contract provision
hidden costs
indirect costs
integrated hardware configuration
master/slave hardware
  configuration
microprocessor-based
  configuration

multiple rating system
operator's guides
other equipment manufacturer
  (OEM) contract
parallel conversion
processor-based hardware
  configuration
property profile
request for proposal
single-vendor contract
site preparation
site survey
software contract provisions
stand-alone hardware configuration
system conversion
system flowcharts
system integrity
technical manuals
two-vendor contract

Discussion Questions

1. How can management go about analyzing the current information needs of a hospitality operation? Explain how flowcharts can be used as a method of analysis.

2. What are some of the ways management can collect product literature regarding computer systems?

3. What factors must management take into account when determining computer system requirements?

4. What does the term "algorithm" mean? Explain how this term relates to management's task of determining computer system requirements.

5. What are the three major sections of a "request for proposal"? Explain why it is important for management to ask vendors to follow the same format when submitting proposals for review.

6. In relation to purchasing a computer system, what do the terms "direct costs," "indirect costs," and "hidden costs" mean? Give examples of each.

7. What are the three areas typically addressed in a contract for the purchase of a computer system?

8. What are the major differences between single-vendor, two-vendor, and other equipment manufacturer contracts? Describe the advantages and disadvantages of each.

9. Upon completing contract negotiations, what factors must management officials address regarding the installation of a computer system?

10. Why is securing adequate documentation of each computer system component critical to the success of system operations beyond the installation period? Identify the three critical forms of documentation.

REVIEW QUIZ

When you feel you have covered all of the material in this chapter, answer these questions. Choose the *best* answer.

Matching

1. Use specially designed symbols for diagramming the flow of data and documents through an information system.

2. Provides statistics about the current information system of a hospitality operation

3. A sources of sales literature on a variety of computer systems

4. The determination of elements necessary for a data processing operation

5. The physical process of inputting elements of data into a computer system

6. A prescribed set of well-defined, unambiguous rules or procedures leading to the solution of a problem

7. A system for evaluating vendor proposals that uses the same criteria to judge the worth of each vendor's proposal

8. An agreement to purchase hardware and software from the same vendor

9. Architectural or engineering changes that have to be made before the computer system can be installed

10. The process of switching from the current information system to the capabilities of a computerized system

a. property profile
b. site survey
c. two-vendor contract
d. data entry
e. parallel conversion
f. state and national trade associations
g. contingency planning
h. flowcharts
i. direct cutover conversion
j. multiple rating system
k. single-vendor contract
l. operator's manual
m. system conversion
n. site preparation
o. data identification
p. algorithm

True (T) or False (F)

T   F   11. The first step in analyzing the current information needs of a hospitality business is to identify the types of information which various levels of management use in the course of everyday operations.

T   F   12. A system conversion chart is helpful in analyzing the current information needs of a hospitality operation.

T   F   13. Hospitality managers should consult with experts in computer system design before determining the general nature of what data to process, how that data is to be processed, and the formats in which processed data will be output as information.

Multiple Choice

14. Which of the following steps in establishing computer system requirements involves management determining which tasks to automate?

    a. determining what data to process
    b. determining how to process data
    c. determining information formats
    d. determining current information needs

15. Which of the following refers to the degree of software integration?

    a. hardware efficiency
    b. software reliability
    c. system integrity
    d. hardware reliability

Chapter Outline

MIS Design and Function
    Information Processing Technology
    MIS Management
Managing Multi-Processor Environments
    Synergistic Value and Cost
        Effectiveness
    System Testing
    Past Interface Successes
    Contract Considerations
    Downtime Procedures
MIS Security Issues
    Energy Backup Systems
    Information Backup Procedures
    Information Protection
Summary

Learning Objectives

1. Identify the purpose of a management information system.

2. Describe the functions performed by information processing technology.

3. Describe the typical responsibilities of a property systems manager and a department systems supervisor.

4. Explain what a multi-processor environment is.

5. Identify the criteria that management can use to evaluate the possibility of interfacing computer systems.

6. Identify how hospitality operations can ensure data security.

7. Explain the advantages and disadvantages of these information backup procedures: redundant copy, duplicate copy, hard copy, and fault-tolerant processing.

8. Explain what a hospitality operation can do to ensure information protection.

9. Identify the term "computer virus," and explain how a virus enters and affects a computer system.

12

Managing Information Systems

THE COMPUTER SYSTEMS of automated hotels and restaurants can produce literally hundreds of reports for managers. However, simply distributing routine reports does not in itself ensure an effective information system. To achieve the full potential of an automated information system, computer functions must be integrated with management's information needs.

A **management information system (MIS)** is designed to provide managers with the necessary information needed to plan, organize, staff, direct, and control operations. An effective MIS extends the power of the computer beyond routine reporting and provides managers with the information they need to:

- Monitor progress toward achieving organizational goals

- Measure performance

- Identify trends

- Evaluate alternatives

- Support decision making

- Assist in corrective action

This chapter examines the design and functions of an MIS and describes the major responsibilities of an information systems manager in relation to multiprocessor environments and information security issues.

MIS Design and Function

The design of an effective MIS is built around the information needs of managers. As managers define and prioritize their specific information needs, an information system can be designed to organize computer applications so that they support decision-making activities at all levels within the organization.

The levels of decision-making supported by an MIS are: strategic planning, tactical decision-making, and operational decision-making. Strategic planning refers to decision-making activities through which future-oriented goals and objectives of an organization are established. Tactical decisions relate to activities required to implement strategic planning decisions. Operational decisions address specific tasks that normally follow previously established rules and patterns.

Once the information needs of managers have been identified, an MIS is designed to perform the following functions:

- Enable managers to better monitor and administer business transactions and activities.

- Provide a high level of operational and internal control over business resources.

- Produce timely and comprehensive reports formatted to the specific needs of managers.

- Reduce managerial paperwork and operational expenses by eliminating unnecessary source documents and streamlining data transfer and recording procedures.

To perform these functions effectively, an MIS uses a variety of information processing technology and decision support systems.

Information Processing Technology

Information processing technology establishes a communication process in which data are transferred from independent computer systems, such as a hotel's reservations system, front office modules, point-of-sale systems, accounting applications, or sales applications. The transferred data are processed according to pre-established decision-making rules, financial models, or other analytical methods. The processed data are then stored in information formats tailored to the needs of individual managers and printed on demand or at set intervals.

Information processing technology also includes simulation capability and the incorporation of expert systems. Decision support systems with simulation capability enable managers to explore "what if" possibilities. These systems are interactive, computer-based information systems that use decision models and a management data base to provide information customized to support specific decisions that managers face. Expert systems differ from decision support systems in that they apply specialized problem-solving expertise and are used to actually make decisions. Therefore, an expert system helps or replaces an expert to solve problems.

MIS Management

In large, fully automated hospitality properties, the MIS management staff may consist of a property systems manager and department systems supervisors. Generally, the **property systems manager** participates in the evaluation, selection, and installation of computer system hardware and is trained in the operation of software applications used throughout the property. The property systems manager provides on-premises systems support and, when necessary, functions as a software applications troubleshooter. **Department systems supervisors** are typically individuals already employed within a specific department who receive extensive training in the operation of software applications used in their departments. These supervisors train others within their departments and provide technical support services as well.

The property systems manager has a wide range of responsibilities. More often a generalist than a technician, the property systems manager must understand not only computer technology, information processing techniques, and principles of management, but also the operation and interrelations of functional areas within the property. Without this understanding, it would be difficult to direct the MIS to meet the specific information needs of managers throughout the property. Other duties of a property systems manager include:

- Planning and controlling MIS activities, which includes identifying the processing priorities within the system

- Selecting department systems managers and establishing training programs

- Managing multi-processor environments, which includes developing configuration and design alternatives in relation to the placement and processing capabilities of computer hardware and software

- Designing and implementing information security controls

The remaining sections of this chapter focus on managing multi-processor environments and dealing with MIS security issues.

Managing Multi-Processor Environments

In order to maximize the effectiveness and efficiency of their management information systems, many automated hotels are becoming multi-processor environments. A **multi-processor environment** results from interfacing independent computer processing units (CPUs), enabling them to share data, peripheral devices (such as printers), and operating systems. Important criteria by which to evaluate the possibility of interfacing computer systems include:

- Determining the synergistic value and cost-effectiveness of the planned interface

- Testing each system to be interfaced

- Investigating properties that have successfully interfaced the same computer systems

- Studying the provisions of existing contracts

- Planning alternative procedures during interface downtime

Synergistic Value and Cost Effectiveness

Synergy refers to the enhanced value of each computer system brought about through interfacing. Interfacing should create a whole (the multi-processor environment) that is perceived to be of greater value than the sum of its individual parts (the independent, stand-alone computer systems). For example, compare traditional hotel posting procedures with the synergistic value gained through an effective POS/PMS interface. A front desk employee, working without a POS/PMS interface, must manually post restaurant charge vouchers to folio accounts. This process requires the front desk employee to sort the vouchers, retrieve the appropriate folios, post the charges, and refile the folios. By contrast, the POS/PMS interface allows the restaurant charges to be electronically transmitted from points of sale to the PMS guest accounting module. Charges are posted to the proper folios without the intervention of a front desk employee.

After determining the synergistic value, management should conduct a cost/benefit study to analyze whether the benefits of the proposed interface outweigh the costs of interfacing. In the course of such an analysis, both intangible and tangible benefits should be considered. Although intangible benefits (such as improved guest service, more efficient clerical procedures, and higher employee morale) may be difficult to quantify, they should not be ignored.

System Testing

Before interfacing any stand-alone computer systems, managers must be sure that each system operates satisfactorily and adequately supports its own functions. Since the PMS serves as the host in a multi-processor environment, it is imperative that it be thoroughly tested and evaluated before any independent system is interfaced with it. Once additional applications are brought on-line, it is much more difficult to detect and correct problem areas that may be specific to PMS operations. After the PMS has been tested, the systems to be interfaced must also be analyzed as stand-alone entities.

Before interfacing a food service outlet's point-of-sale system with a hotel's property management system, the restaurant managers must be familiar enough with the POS equipment to recognize its strengths and weaknesses. If the POS system is not well understood, there is a significantly higher risk of interface failure. Thorough testing and analysis of PMS needs and POS system capabilities are essential for successful interfacing.

Consider a POS system that stores only guest check totals. This system, which may well meet the immediate needs of the restaurant's management, may create a number of problems when interfaced with a PMS. For example, a convention group may desire that food charges be posted to a master folio while beverage charges are posted to individual guest folios. Since, in this particular case, data are transferred from the POS in the form of guest check totals only, front office employees would have to manually sort through restaurant guest checks to determine food and beverage subtotals. These subtotals would then have to be manually posted to the appropriate folios. This could be a time-consuming process. No matter how well other aspects of this POS/PMS interface operate, data transferred from the restaurant will not meet the posting requirements of the hotel's guest accounting module.

Past Interface Successes

Cabling the hardware components of two computer systems is easy; getting the two systems to intelligently communicate with one another can be a formidable software challenge. The development of necessary communications software programs, specific to the interfacing systems, is critical.

It is generally easier to implement an interface that has performed successfully elsewhere than it is to research and develop a first-time interface. Management officials may obtain important information by investigating successful interfaces at other properties involving computer systems identical to those under consideration.

Contract Considerations

Before interfacing computer systems, management officials should investigate the impact of such interfaces on current computer system contracts. Questions that need to be addressed include:

- Is the user entitled to details regarding system design that he or she may need to know before implementing a successful interface?

- Does the user have the right to alter the computer system that is to be interfaced?

- Does interfacing alter existing maintenance agreements?

- To what degree will each system vendor assume responsibility for implementation and maintenance of the interfaced systems?

In addressing these questions, management officials may need the advice of an attorney. In some cases, system vendors may be reluctant to provide detailed technical information about the internal design of their systems. Issues of confidentiality, contractual license, and similar legal matters must be resolved.

Downtime Procedures

When analyzing the feasibility of an interface, it is important to determine the potential frequency and duration of downtime. The term **downtime** refers to the interval of time when the computer system is not available for interface activity or is experiencing an internal system failure. For example, problems related to a POS/PMS interface may include an inability to communicate with the PMS when it is processing its own reports, or a failure to serve as a POS system when communicating data to the PMS.

A possible solution to interface downtime involves implementing concurrent operating systems—ones that support multi-tasking. **Multi-tasking** refers to the ability of a CPU to perform more than one task at a time. Exhibit 1 attempts to diagram the simultaneous processing activity of a PMS with multi-tasking capability.

When a hotel becomes dependent on interface system capabilities, downtime can leave operations in a state of chaos. Some properties routinely simulate computer system failures and evaluate the ability of staff to continue to meet operational demands. Contingency plans should outline non-automated procedures to follow in case of system failures.

MIS Security Issues

Three important areas of MIS security involve energy backup systems, information backup procedures, and information protection. Although management often focuses on the dangers involved in a power failure or information backup procedures, unprotected information can pose a more serious threat to a hospitality operation. Consider the consequences of payroll information becoming unexpectedly available to employees, the competition gaining access to guest history files, or the

Exhibit 1   Multi-Tasking

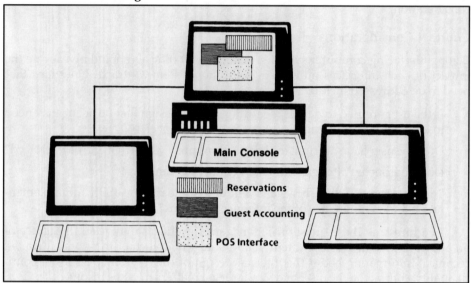

loss of the general ledger files. However, with proper care, both the energy and information problems can be avoided.

Energy Backup Systems

The loss or fluctuation of electrical power can lead to problems in computing. However, the risks involved in many energy-related computer problems can be significantly reduced through use of an **uninterruptible power supply** (UPS). The UPS is equipped with a battery pack and is placed on the computer's power line so that any fluctuation in the quality of power coming to the computer will trigger the battery pack that compensates for any energy deficiencies. This provides the computer with a continually stable energy source. In addition, many systems automatically recharge the batteries whenever the normal power source is in operation.

A preventive maintenance program is essential to protect against downtime (times during which the computer system is inoperable because of repair work). All components must be kept clean and operational to achieve optimal system productivity. There must also be a predetermined emergency maintenance plan outlining the steps to take in a crisis. For example, in addition to energy backup, there should be plans for hardware backup, such as sources for quickly obtaining needed parts or loaner equipment.

Information Backup Procedures

Backup procedures should not be left to emergency situations. Information backup should be a standard operating procedure to ensure that data are not lost at any time. There are four ways to back up information:

Exhibit 2 Redundant Copy

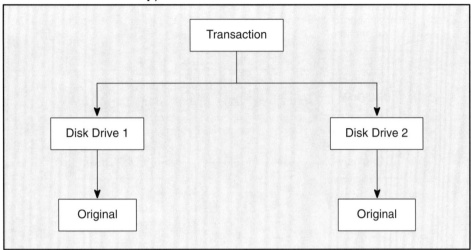

- Redundant copy
- Duplicate copy
- Hard copy
- Fault-tolerant processing

While many computer manufacturers advocate using more than just a single backup procedure, management must ensure that at least one procedure is used regularly. The following sections describe each of these information backup procedures.

Redundant Copy. Redundant copy requires two storage devices that work simultaneously. Exhibit 2 shows that, as transactions occur, they are saved to two external storage devices. Assuming that a food service system employs a disk drive as a base for one external storage device, a second disk drive is required. As data are input, they are sent to both drives for storage on their respective disks. This can be an expensive hardware configuration and requires more attention than other backup methods. It is analogous to recording a theatrical performance on two tape recorders simultaneously. Many people believe that it is more efficient to concentrate on producing one superior recording and duplicating it at a later point in time. Two recordings are still obtained, but through duplication, not redundancy.

Duplicate Copy. Duplicate copy is the most popular and efficient means of accomplishing information backup. This backup strategy is illustrated in Exhibit 3. In the case of **duplicate copy**, the computer system writes to only one storage device, so a second disk drive is not needed. A copy of the data on the single drive can be made later. It can be duplicated on the same device with a blank disk or can be placed onto magnetic tape. Due to its sequential access characteristics, magnetic tape is

Exhibit 3   Duplicate Copy

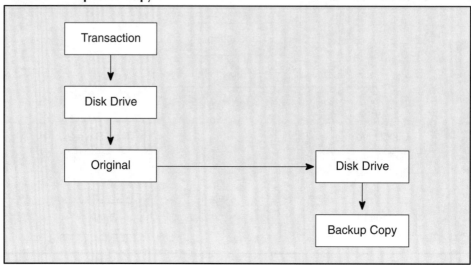

not an efficient storage medium for day-to-day operations. However, since the backup tapes are stored and used only in case of a disk error or failure, the sequential access to data does not severely reduce a property's ability to maintain efficient computer operations.

Hard Copy. Exhibit 4 illustrates the hard copy backup technique. **Hard copy** (printouts from disk files) should be used as a backup technique only in conjunction with redundant or duplicate copy procedures. The user who relies solely on hard copy information backup will encounter an avalanche of work should data files need to be reconstructed. In this case, all information stored on hard copy must be manually re-entered to recreate the system's database. When used to supplement one of the other two approaches, hard copy backup provides a means for troubleshooting any missing or incorrect transactional recordings. Should a mishap occur that affects only a small section of a disk, that area of the disk can be compared with the most current hard copy to recover any information that may have been lost.

Fault-Tolerant Processing. A more recently adopted on-line verification procedure is termed fault-tolerant processing. **Fault-tolerant processing** is capable of adjusting (or at least continuing) operations after one or more components have stopped functioning. In essence, the system disregards the device that, for whatever reason, goes out of synchronization. In comparison to a redundant system, which requires the user to purchase two disk drives that operate simultaneously, fault-tolerant designs employ a variety of devices in unique on-line configurations.

One approach to fault-tolerant processing is termed switched backup. In a switched backup design there are two central processors; one is used for processing data, while the second is activated upon the failure of the first. Obviously, in

Exhibit 4   Hard Copy

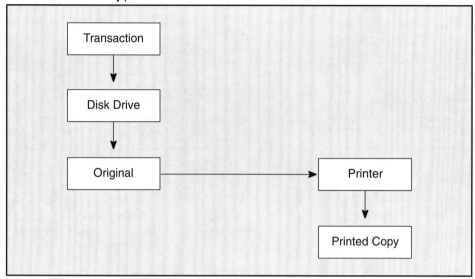

this case, one processor sits idle until a failure occurs. It is for this reason that switched backup is usually perceived as an inefficient backup procedure.

Triple modular redundancy is an alternative approach that involves triplicate hardware components. For most hospitality operations, this fault-tolerant processing design is not cost justifiable.

Perhaps the best current fault-tolerant approach for the hospitality industry is comparison logic, which is illustrated in Exhibit 5. In a comparison logic design, there are two paired processors actively working at all times. Data processed by the first pair of processors (A and B) are compared with the data processed by the second pair of processors (C and D). If data processed by the first pair of processors match the output from the second pair, processed data go forward as information output. A failure of any one of the paired processing units presents no problem to the system, since its work is a duplicate of the other three.

Information Protection

Information protection is much more complicated than energy backup procedures or information backup procedures, and should involve the following strategic considerations:

- *F*unctional division of duties
- *R*ecovery
- *A*voidance of tampering
- *U*nauthorized access prevention
- *D*etection and correction

Exhibit 5   Fault-Tolerant Processing—Comparison Logic

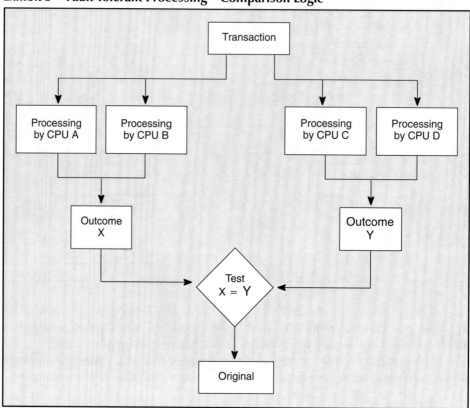

Functional Division of Duties. In the past, separation of duties involved, for example, ensuring that the person who received cash did not record it. In a computerized environment, this type of separation is often not possible or cost justified. It is important, however, to consider separating programmers from users so that the system is not easily manipulated by dishonest employees.

Recovery. There are procedures to minimize the damage that may result from the loss of data. These will be addressed in the final section of this chapter, which discusses information backup techniques.

Avoidance of Tampering. Security is enhanced by protecting assets from potential threats. This includes not only keeping the computer room and data files locked, but also ensuring that important files are kept in fire-proof areas, that the equipment is protected from environmental dangers, and so on.

Unauthorized Access Prevention. Unauthorized use of the computer can be avoided by restricting access to the computer through passwords, locked systems, file access codes, and other measures.

Detection and Correction. If a problem is detected early, its impact on operations can be minimized, and it will be easier to correct. One method of ensuring the early detection of problems related to data security is the use of error logs. Many computer systems generate error logs every time an unusual request is made to the system; this log may be examined by supervisors who can deal promptly with any potential problem.

If these factors are considered when managers plan and design a computerized information system, they should protect the operation from unauthorized acquisition, modification, or destruction of information. They are (note the first letter of each strategy) set up to prevent FRAUD!

A relatively new problem in relation to preventing unauthorized access is the phenomenon of computer viruses.

Computer Viruses. A **computer virus** is any unauthorized programmed code that attaches itself to other programs. Viruses usually enter computer systems through external programs or files. The user unknowingly brings these infected programs into the computer system by:

- Downloading programs or files from electronic bulletin boards

- Using disks or files that were created on someone else's computer system

- Using tampered-with shared public domain software

Typical symptoms displayed by a system infected by a computer virus include:

- Disappearing disk space or files

- Files increasing in size on their own

- Suspicious "out of memory" errors

- Unwanted/strange screen messages

- Unwarranted printer problems

- Slowed computer operations

- Non-requested disk accessing

Computer viruses can be benign or malignant in nature. A benign computer virus (termed a "firecracker") is one that erupts without any specific destructive purpose or intent. Benign viruses typically cause a computer to display unwanted messages or to beep, and they can cause other minor distractions as well. A benign computer virus may replicate itself, but does not intentionally cause serious problems for a computer system. However, unchecked replication can eventually lead to "disk full" messages or to an overloaded network.

A malignant computer virus (called a "bomb") is created with a specific target in mind. Malignant computer viruses are also called directed viruses. In addition to replicating themselves, malignant computer viruses may also destroy data and programs, interfere with computer use, and crash (halt) a computer network.

While computer virus detection software is available, the best protection against infection is to limit access to the computer system to authorized personnel only and to prohibit the use of disks or programs that are external to the property's system.

Summary

This chapter described the function of a management information system (MIS) as providing managers with the necessary information needed to plan, organize, staff, direct, and control operations. An effective MIS extends the power of the computer beyond routine reporting and provides managers with the information they need for strategic planning, tactical decision making, and operational decision making.

An MIS accomplishes these functions through information processing technology that includes decision support systems and incorporates expert systems. This technology establishes a communication process in which data are transferred from independent computer systems; processed according to pre-established decision-making rules, financial models, or other analytical methods; and stored in information formats tailored to the needs of individual managers.

The chapter also described characteristics of multi-processor environments. In order to maximize the effectiveness and efficiency of property management systems, many automated hotels are interfacing independent computer processors (CPUs), enabling them to share data, peripheral devices, and operating systems. Important criteria by which to evaluate the possibility of interfacing computer systems include: determining the synergistic value and cost-effectiveness of the planned interface, testing each system to be interfaced, investigating properties that have successfully interfaced the same computer systems, studying the provisions of existing contracts, and planning alternative procedures during interface downtime.

Three major areas of management concern in relation to data security are energy backup systems, information backup procedures, and information protection. Since a loss or fluctuation of electrical power can cause problems in computer operation, an uninterruptible power supply is necessary to compensate for any energy deficiencies. Data security measures, a preventive maintenance program, and an emergency maintenance plan should be carefully considered when designing a computerized information system.

To ensure that data are not lost at any time, information backup methods should be standard operating procedures. Information backup procedures include redundant copy, duplicate copy, hard copy, and fault-tolerant processing.

Information protection involves safeguarding data and files by preventing unauthorized access either by individuals or computer viruses.

Key Terms

computer virus
department systems supervisor
downtime
duplicate copy

fault-tolerant processing
hard copy
information processing technology
management information system (MIS)

multi-processor environment
multi-tasking
property systems manager

redundant copy
uninterruptible power supply

Discussion Questions

1. What is the purpose of a management information system?

2. What functions are performed by information processing technology?

3. What are the typical duties and responsibilities of a property systems manager? of a department systems supervisor?

4. What does the term "multi-processor environment" mean?

5. How can multi-tasking prevent potential interface problems?

6. What criteria can management use to evaluate the possibility of interfacing computer systems?

7. What does the term "data security" mean? Identify steps that hospitality operations can take to ensure data security.

8. How do "redundant copy," "duplicate copy," and "hard copy" differ as information backup techniques? Explain the advantages and disadvantages of each for hospitality operations.

9. How does "fault-tolerant processing" differ from other information backup procedures? Explain how a comparison logic design operates.

10. How can computer viruses enter a computer system? What symptoms are displayed by a system infected by a computer virus?

REVIEW QUIZ

When you feel you have covered all of the material in this chapter, answer these questions. Choose the *best* answer.

Matching

1. Computer virus

2. Downtime

3. Comparison logic

4. Multi-tasking

5. Redundant copy

6. Hard copy

7. Multi-processor environment

8. Uninterruptible power supply

a. Interfaced CPUs sharing data, peripherals, and operating systems

b. A type of fault-tolerant processing

c. An energy backup system

d. Also called duplicate copy

e. Should be used only in conjunction with other backup methods

f. Also called switched backup

g. A type of triple modular redundancy

h. Period when a computer is not available for interfacing

i. Password

j. The ability of a CPU to perform more than one task at a time

k. Requires two storage devices that work simultaneously

l. Synergy

m. An unauthorized programmed code that attaches itself to other programs

True (T) or False (F)

T F 9. Duplicate copy is the most popular and efficient means of backing up files.

T F 10. Fault-tolerant processing is designed to stop all computer operations immediately when one or more components have stopped functioning.

T F 11. Malignant computer viruses replicate themselves and may destroy data and programs on a computer system.

T F 12. A preventive maintenance program is essential to protect against computer downtime.

Alternate/Multiple Choice

13. Redundant copy requires _____ attention than other backup methods.

    a. more
    b. less

14. Information protection is much _____ complicated than energy backup procedures.

    a. more
    b. less

15. Which of the following does not restrict access to files within a computer system?

    a. passwords
    b. file access codes
    c. locked systems
    d. multi-tasking

Glossary

A

ACCEPTANCE TESTING

Before converting from manual procedures to computerized functions, properties generally conduct extensive acceptance testing of the computer system. Tests should be developed to determine whether computerized operations function according to standards defined by management.

ACCOUNTS AGING FILE

Contains accounts receivable data that can be formatted into a variety of aging reports that segment accounts in the file according to the date the charge originated.

ACCOUNTS PAYABLE

Liabilities incurred for merchandise, equipment, or other goods and services that have been purchased on account.

ACCOUNTS PAYABLE AGING REPORT

Contains several columns listing invoices by vendor number, vendor name, invoice number, and invoice date.

ACCOUNTS RECEIVABLE

Obligations owed an organization from sales made on credit.

ACTIVE CALL ACCOUNTING SYSTEM

Enables a hotel to take control over local and long-distance services and apply a markup to switchboard operations. Call accounting systems are capable of placing and pricing local and long-distance calls. Passive call accounting systems do not employ an automatic route selection switch with a least-cost routing device.

ACTIVITY REPORT

A report generated by automated systems providing an in-depth analysis of sales transactions and actual labor hours during selected time periods.

ACTUAL COST

A method of inventory valuation. Values inventory only in relation to actual costs of items stored. The value of stored products is, then, the value represented by the sum of individual unit costs.

ACTUAL DEPARTURES REPORT

Lists the names of guests who have checked out, and their room numbers, billing addresses, and folio numbers.

AFFILIATE RESERVATION SYSTEM

A hotel chain's reservation system in which all participating properties are contractually related. Each property is represented in the computer system database and is required to provide room availability data to the reservations center on a timely basis.

AGING OF ACCOUNTS RECEIVABLE SCHEDULE

Segments each account in the accounts aging file according to the date the charge originated.

ALGORITHM

A prescribed set of well-defined, unambiguous rules or procedures leading to the solution of a problem.

ALPHA DATA

A type of electronic data consisting only of letters of the alphabet.

ALPHANUMERIC DATA

A type of electronic data consisting of both letters and numbers.

ANTENNA UNITS

Part of a system that supports the use of wireless, hand-held server terminals. Antenna units relay signals from hand-held terminals to a radio base station.

AUTODIAL/AUTO-ANSWER

In electronic communications, sophisticated modems can be programmed to place a call to a specified phone number at an exact time, or they can be programmed to be in a ready state to receive incoming calls.

AUTOMATIC FORM NUMBER READER (AFNR)

A feature of a guest check printer that facilitates order entry; instead of a server manually inputting a guest check's serial number to access the account, a bar code imprinted on the guest check presents the check's serial number in a machine-readable format.

AUTOMATIC IDENTIFICATION OF OUTWARD DIALING

A feature of a call accounting system that immediately identifies the extension from which an outgoing call is placed.

AUTOMATIC ROOM/RATE ASSIGNMENT

Computerized assignment made through algorithms formulated according to parameters specified by hotel management officials. Rooms may be selected according to predetermined floor zones (similar to the way in which guests are seated in a dining room) or according to an index of room usage and depreciation.

AUTOMATIC ROUTE SELECTION

A feature of a call accounting system that provides the capability of connecting with a variety of common carriers.

AUTOMATIC SLIP FEED (ASF)

A feature of a guest check printer that prevents overprinting of items and amounts on guest checks.

AUTOMATIC SPELL CHECK

A computer program that helps users proofread documents by automatically checking for spelling errors. The words in the document are electronically compared to entries in the spell checker's dictionary. When a word appears in the document which does not appear in the program's dictionary, it is generally highlighted on the display screen so the operator can correct it.

B

BALANCE SHEET

Provides important information on the financial position of a hospitality business by showing its assets, liabilities, and equity on a particular date.

BANQUET EVENT ORDER (BEO)

Information from the function book and other files is eventually transcribed on a banquet event order (BEO). A BEO generally serves as a final contract for the client and as a work order for the catering department.

BAR CODE TERMINAL

A terminal activated by hand-held, pen-like bar code readers that servers use to enter orders at service station terminals from a laminated bar coded menu.

BAUD RATE

In electronic communications, the rate of modulation or the number of times the carrier signal is modulated per second. Baud is a measure of the speed with which data is transferred, approximately the number of data bits sent in one second. The higher the baud rate, the faster the transfer.

BID SPECIFICATION FILE

Contains the specific characteristics of purchased items. Purveyors are asked to quote prices for products that meet or exceed stated specifications.

BID SPECIFICATION FORM

Submitted to vendors to obtain item quotations.

BIDIRECTIONAL PRINTING

A feature of some electronic printers that moves the print head from left to right only on every other line. On the alternate lines, it reverses everything and prints right to left, saving time.

BINARY CODE

A counting system based on only two digits, zero and one. This is the easiest way for a computer to handle data because electronic circuits have two natural states: "on," usually represented by the binary digit one; and "off," represented by the binary digit zero.

BIT

The smallest unit of electronic data. The term is short for *BI*nary digi*T* (which is either zero or one). All characters (letters, numbers, and symbols) are represented by a special sequence of binary digits.

BOILERPLATE FILE

Standard textual material stored on floppy disks. The standard content stored in a boilerplate file can be retrieved and automatically inserted into appropriate documents as needed. This eliminates retyping and ensures consistency of content.

BOLDFACING

A word processing formatting technique used to emphasize words, phrases, titles, or formulas by making them stand out from the rest of the text. The item headers listed in this glossary are all boldfaced.

BOOKING LEAD TIME

A measurement of how far in advance bookings are made.

BUS SYSTEM

The electronic circuitry over which power, data, and other signals travel; three buses within a computer system are the data bus (transports data), the address bus (directs operations), and the control bus (transmits instructions).

BYTE

A special sequence of bits (electronic data) representing a single character. A byte is a group of adjacent bits that work, or are operated on, as a unit. Theoretically, a byte may be any length, but the most common length for a byte is eight bits, with some computers using seven.

C

CABLE

A device used to interface (connect) separate hardware components of a computer system.

CALCULATOR FEATURE

A feature of some advanced database management software packages that is capable of carrying out basic arithmetical and statistical operations.

CALL RECORD

Hard copy documentation containing essential transactional support data for individually placed telephone calls.

CALL RECORD FILE

Monitors details regarding calls processed by a call accounting system; includes such data as: date, guestroom extension number, telephone number dialed, time call was placed, duration of call, cost of call, and tax and markup charges.

CASH REQUIREMENTS REPORT

Lists all invoices selected for payment and the corresponding cash requirement totals; prepared by vendor number, vendor name, due date, item, or group code and typically including vendor number, vendor name, invoice number, due date, balance due, and amount to be paid.

CELL ADDRESS

In electronic spreadsheet programs, the coordinates of a cell (the particular column letter and row number).

CELL RANGE

In electronic spreadsheet programs, a group of adjacent cells.

CELLS

In electronic spreadsheet programs, cells are formed by the intersection of rows and columns.

CENTRAL PROCESSING UNIT

The control center of a computer system. Inside are the circuits and mechanisms that process and store information and send instructions to the other components of the system.

CENTRAL RESERVATION OFFICE

Typically deals directly with the public, advertises a central telephone number, provides participating properties with necessary communications equipment, and bills properties for handling reservations.

CENTRAL RESERVATION SYSTEM

An external reservation network. *See also* **AFFILIATE RESERVATION SYSTEM** and **NON-AFFILIATE RESERVATION SYSTEM.**

CHAINING RECIPES

Including sub-recipes as ingredients for a particular standard recipe. This enables the computer-based restaurant management system to maintain a record for a particular menu item that requires an unusually large number of ingredients.

CHART OF ACCOUNTS

Lists general ledger accounts by type of account including account number and account title.

CHART OF ACCOUNTS FILE

Lists the names of accounts in a sequence that parallels the order of their appearance on the financial statements and general ledger.

CHECK RECONCILIATION

Balancing the total of checks removed from the outstanding checks list with the total of cleared checks appearing on the bank statement.

CHECK REGISTER

After the check writing routine, the accounts payable module prints a check register by check number. The check register also may be sorted by vendor or by invoice due date.

CHECK REGISTER FILE

Monitors the calculation and printing of bank checks for payments of selected invoices.

CITY LEDGER

A subsidiary ledger listing accounts receivable balances of guests who have checked out, and other receivables as well.

CITY LEDGER FILE

Contains data from the front office guest accounting module, such as balances from guest folios, non-guest accounts, bill-to accounts, credit card billings, and others.

COMMISSION AGENT REPORT

Delineates reservation transactions and commissions payable, by agent.

COMMON CARRIER

Any recognized entity that transmits messages or other communication for general use at accepted rates.

COMMON-SIZE BALANCE SHEETS

Present two sets of figures for each balance sheet line item. One set of figures is from the current balance sheet; the other set is from the balance sheet of a previous period. All amounts are reduced to percentages of their account classification.

COMMUNICATIONS CONTROLLER

Part of an electronic communications setup responsible for sending data to (or receiving data from) its connector and the cable.

COMMUNICATIONS PARAMETERS

Electronic communications settings, such as baud rate and how data will flow through the communication channel. Both the sending and receiving modems must be set to the same parameters.

COMPATIBILITY

In electronic communications, compatibility between modems is determined by manufacturing design and by operating characteristics (also called communications parameters), which are defined by communications software programs.

COMPUTER

A managerial tool capable of processing large quantities of data more quickly and accurately than any other data processing method. It can perform arithmetic operations such as addition, subtraction, multiplication, and division, and logical functions as well, such as ranking, sorting, and assembling operations. It can also store and retrieve tremendous amounts of information, and thereby allows managers to exercise control over procedures that might otherwise be overlooked.

COMPUTER PROGRAM

A sequence of instructions that commands a computer system to perform a useful task.

COMPUTER VIRUS

Any unauthorized programmed code that attaches itself to other programs.

COMPUTERIZED TIME-CLOCK SYSTEM

Records time in and time out for employees.

CONTINGENCY PLANNING

Defining procedures to be followed when, for whatever reason, the computer system is not able to function properly.

CONTROL FOLIO

Constructed for each revenue center and used to track all transactions posted to other folios (individual, master, non-guest, or employee). Control folios provide a basis for double entry accounting and for cross-checking the balances of all electronic folios.

CONVERSION TABLES

Track ingredients (by unit and by cost) as they pass through purchasing/receiving, storing/issuing, and production/service control points.

CREDIT MONITORING ROUTINE

Compares a guest's current folio balance with a credit limit (also called a house limit) that is predetermined by management officials.

CRITERIA AREA SPECIFICATIONS

Most database management programs support a query language that enables a user to make requests through the keyboard. Criteria area specifications define the necessary sequence of keystrokes.

CRT UNIT

An acronym for cathode ray tube. A CRT unit is composed of a television-like video screen and a keyboard that is similar to a typewriter keyboard. Data entered through the keyboard can be displayed on the screen. The CRT operator can edit and verify the on-screen input before sending it for processing.

CURRENT CELL

In electronic spreadsheet programs, the cell that contains the pointer at any particular time.

CURSOR

A flashing marker on a computer display screen that indicates where the next character to be entered will appear.

CUSTOMER DISPLAY UNIT

A display screen that may rest atop, inside, or alongside the ECR/POS device.

CUSTOMER MASTER FILE

Sets up billing information. Customer data maintained in this file includes: account code, name of guest or account, address, telephone number, contact person, type of account, credit limit, last payment date, last payment amount, and credit history.

D

DAILY LABOR REPORT

A report generated by automated systems listing the names, employee numbers, hours worked, wages earned, and wages declared for each employee on a given workday.

DAILY RECEIVING REPORT

Lists details of all items received on a given day.

DAILY SALES REPORT

Summarizes all sales revenue activity for a day. Revenue is itemized by the following categories: net sales, tax, number of guest checks, number of covers, dollars per check, dollars per cover, sales category, day-part totals. Affected general ledger accounts are listed, and associated food costs and sales percentage statistics are noted.

DAILY TELEPHONE REVENUE REPORT

Also called a daily profit report. It sorts traffic transaction data by type of call and records the cost, price, and gross profit earned for each call processed by a call accounting system.

DAILY TRANSACTIONS REPORT

A report generated by automated food and beverage systems providing an in-depth analysis of sales transactions by individual server.

DAISYWHEEL PRINTER

An electronic printer that uses solid type (also called preformed characters), not dots, and produces a higher quality print than dot matrix printers. A daisy wheel is a circular printing head with characters mounted on the ends of spokes radiating from the wheel's center.

DATA

Facts or figures to be processed into useful information. Three types of data are alpha data, numeric data, and alphanumeric data.

DATA CODING

Techniques that enable rapid data entry, processing, and reporting.

DATA COLLECTION

Gathering data elements relevant to an application.

DATA ENTRY
The physical process of inputting elements of data into a computer system.

DATA IDENTIFICATION
The determination of elements necessary for a data processing operation.

DATA PROCESSING
The transformation of raw facts and isolated figures into timely, accurate, and useful information.

DATA PROCESSING CYCLE
A cycle of events identified as input, process, and output in which data is converted into information.

DATABASE
A collection of related facts and figures designed to serve a specific purpose.

DATABASE FIELDS
The detailed facts or figures contained in database records.

DATABASE FILES
A collection of database records and fields.

DATABASE RECORDS
A collection of database fields.

DEBIT CARD
These differ from credit cards in that the cardholder must deposit money in order to give the card value. The cardholder deposits money in advance of purchases through a debit card center or an electronic debit posting machine. As purchases are made, the balance on the debit card falls.

DEDUCTIONS
Subtractions from gross pay that are usually voluntary and depend on the types of benefits available from the employer.

DEFAULT SETTING
Preset controls of computer software programs. For example, with word processing, the margins of a document are usually already set to conform to the requirements of typical typing tasks.

DELIVERY NETWORK
Part of an automated beverage control unit that transports beverage item ingredients from storage areas to dispensing units.

DEMAND CONTROL
A feature of an energy management system that maintains usage levels below a given limit by shedding energy loads in an orderly fashion.

DEPARTMENT CODE

In relation to POS terminals, the menu category to which an item on a preset key belongs.

DEPARTMENT SYSTEMS SUPERVISOR

An individual already employed within a specific department who receives extensive training in the operation of the department's software applications, and afterward conducts training sessions for others and provides some technical support services.

DESCRIPTOR

The abbreviated description of a menu item, such as "SHRMPCKT" for shrimp cocktail or "PRIME" for prime rib.

DIRECT COSTS

In relation to the purchase of a computer system, the costs of individual computer system components.

DIRECT CUTOVER CONVERSION

In relation to the implementation of a computer system, management chooses a date on which there is to be a complete switch from current procedures to new computerized functions. Direct cutover is also called "going cold turkey" because it involves a complete withdrawal from the previous information system.

DISK DRIVE

A computer system component that holds the jacket of a floppy disk still and spins the disk, reading information from (or writing information to) the disk surface through an opening in the jacket called a head slot.

DISPLACEMENT

The turning away of transient guests for lack of rooms due to the acceptance of group business.

DISPLAY SCREEN

An output device of a computer system that is usually capable of displaying both text and graphics (e.g., graphs, pie charts, etc.) in soft copy. Also, these output units may be programmed to various foreground and background color combinations while operating many software applications.

DISTRIBUTED HARDWARE CONFIGURATION

Each work station is a complete computer system. The presence of an I/O device, CPU, and external storage device at each location provides a multiprocessor environment. In the case of an ECR/POS system, a distributed system is similar to a stand-alone configuration. Each register of a distributed configuration possesses all the hardware components necessary for a complete computer system, but the ECRs are cabled together.

DOT MATRIX PRINTER

An electronic impact printer that forms characters by firing a vertical line of pins through an inked ribbon onto paper. Each time a pin is fired, it strikes the inked ribbon and presses it against the paper to produce a dot; a pattern of dots forms a character.

DOWNTIME

The interval of time when a computer system is unavailable for interface activity or is experiencing an internal system failure.

DUNNING LETTER

A request for payment of an outstanding balance (account receivable) owed by a guest or non-guest to an operation.

DUPLICATE COPY

An information backup technique in which a computer system writes to only one storage device, and a duplicate of the information is made later.

DUTY CYCLING

A feature of an energy management system that turns off equipment on a sequential basis for a given period of time each hour.

E

ELECTRONIC CASH REGISTER

Normally defined as an independent, stand-alone computer system. The ECR frame houses all the necessary components of a computer system: an input/output device, a central processing unit, and storage (memory) capacity.

ELECTRONIC DATA PROCESSING

Automates the input, process, and output events within the basic data processing cycle; the addition of a memory unit allows for the storage of data or instructions for more reliable and thorough processing; transforms data into timely, accurate, and useful information by reducing turnaround time, streamlining output, and minimizing the handling of data.

ELECTRONIC MAILBOX

In relation to telecommunications, involves reserving an addressable storage location on a rental company's disk. The sender then telephones the rental company (instead of the receiver) and transmits the document to the pre-specified mailbox.

EMPLOYEE FOLIO

Used to track employee purchases, compute discounts, monitor expense account activity, and separate authorized business charges from personal expenditures.

EMPTY BOTTLE SENSOR

Can be part of an automated beverage control unit; relays a signal to the order-entry device.

EXPANDED MEMORY

The additional memory capacity that resides outside the computer's basic memory. It can be accessed in revolving blocks, and is available as add-on boards that are inserted into one of the computer's expansion slots.

EXPECTED ARRIVAL/DEPARTURE REPORT

A daily report showing the number and names of guests expected to arrive with reservations, as well as the number and names of guests expected to depart.

EXPECTED ARRIVALS LIST

A daily report showing the number of guests and the names of guests expected to arrive with reservations.

EXPECTED DEPARTURES LIST

A daily report showing the number of guests expected to depart, the number of stay-overs (the difference between arrivals and departures), and the names of guests associated with each transaction.

EXTENDED MEMORY

Memory that reaches beyond a computer system's basic limits; usually required for advanced multi-tasking (running several applications simultaneously).

F

FAULT-TOLERANT PROCESSING

An on-line verification procedure capable of adjusting (or at least continuing) operations after one or more components have stopped functioning. In essence, the system disregards the device, which, for whatever reason, falls out of synchronization.

FAX BOARD

Allows a computer user to send and receive electronic documents; prepares data files for transmission and then, using an internal modem, places a telephone call to the destination computer for transmission (FAX is an abbreviation of Facsimile).

FIND COMMAND

In database management software, the find command normally functions more quickly than the locate command. It generally works only with files that have been indexed in terms of the specific field category for which the user is searching.

FINISHED PRODUCT CATERING DELIVERY

Home delivery catering services.

FIRST IN, FIRST OUT (FIFO)

A method of valuing inventory; the products in storage areas are valued at the level of the most recently purchased items to be placed in inventory.

FISCAL YEAR

Twelve consecutive months that define a business year.

FLOPPY DISKS

External storage media of computer systems, also called diskettes, frequently used for shipping data and programs from one location to another. They are made of thin, flexible plastic protected by a jacket. The plastic is coated with a magnetized oxide compound designed to hold electronic information. The size of the floppy disk (eight inch, five and one-quarter inch, or three and one-half inch) depends on the type of computer system used.

FLOWCHART

In relation to computer systems, uses specifically designed symbols to diagram the flow of data and documents through an information system.

FORMATTING

A process that creates the tracks and sectors of a floppy disk on which the computer system is able to read and write information.

FORMULA PREFIX

In electronic spreadsheet programs, a symbol used to alert the program that the input involves either a formula, a label, or a numeric value.

FORMULAS

In electronic spreadsheet programs, formulas instruct the computer to carry out specific calculations, such as adding all numbers in a certain range of cells. The cells in which formulas are entered will display the results of the calculations. If any of the amounts entered in the range of cells change, a formula is able to immediately recalculate the amounts and place the new result in the same designated cell.

FULL-DUPLEX CONNECTION

In relation to telecommunications, allows simultaneous two-way communication across two communications channels, one going in each direction. A telephone conversation is an example of full-duplex communication between two persons at the same time.

FUNCTION KEYS

When part of an ECR/POS system terminal, function keys help the user process transactions; they are important for error correction (clear and void), legitimate price alteration (discount), and proper cash handling (no-sale).

G

GENERAL CONTRACT PROVISIONS

Address standard contractual terms typically covered in most purchasing contracts, such as terms of delivery, terms of payment, survival past delivery, saleable product warranty, catastrophe remedies, and provisions for breach of contract.

GENERAL LEDGER

The principal accounting ledger containing all of the balance sheet and statement of income accounts.

GIGABYTE

Often abbreviated as "GB," equal to 1,073,741,834 bytes, and commonly used to describe computer memory capacity.

GLASS SENSOR

Part of an automated beverage control unit, an electronic mechanism located in a bar dispensing unit that will not permit liquid to flow from the dispensing unit unless there is a glass positioned to catch the liquid below the dispensing head.

GLOBAL RESERVATION SYSTEM

Provide access to travel and tourism inventories through direct linkage with the reservation systems of hotel, airline, car rental, and travel agency companies on a world-wide basis.

GROUP BOOKING PACE

The rate at which group business is being booked.

GUEST CHECK CONTROL REPORT

Compares guest checks used in revenue outlets, such as in food and beverage outlets, with source documents to identify discrepancies.

GUEST CHECK PRINTER

An ECR/POS on-board printing device that is sometimes called a slip printer. A sophisticated guest check printer may be equipped with an automatic form number reader and may possess automatic slip feed capabilities.

GUEST CHECK SENSOR

Part of an automated beverage control unit preventing the system from fulfilling beverage orders unless they are first recorded on a guest check.

GUEST DISCREPANCIES

Charges disputed by guests.

GUEST INFORMATION SERVICES

These automated information devices in public hotel areas allow guests to inquire about in-house events and local activities.

GUESTROOM CONTROL BOOK

Guides guestroom booking activity by providing the sales office with the maximum number of guestrooms it can sell to groups on a given day. The remaining guestrooms (and any unsold guestrooms allotted to groups) are available for individual guests.

H

HALF-DUPLEX CONNECTION

In relation to telecommunications, permits an alternating two-way communication over a single channel. A CB radio is an example of half-duplex communication, because only one person is permitted to communicate at a time. In half-duplex data communication systems, data cannot be simultaneously transmitted and received.

HAND-HELD TERMINAL

Wireless server terminal, also called a portable server terminal; performs most of the functions of a precheck terminal and enables servers to enter orders at tableside.

HARD COPY

A printed paper copy of computer-processed information.

HARD KEYS

Keys on an ECR/POS system terminal dedicated to specific functions programmed by the manufacturer.

HARDWARE

A computer systems term referring to the physical equipment of a system. Computer hardware is visible, movable, and easy to identify. In order to have a computer system, three hardware components are required: an input/output (I/O) unit, a central processing unit (CPU), and an external storage device.

HARDWARE CONTRACT PROVISION

Relates to the purchase and operation of computer equipment, including the operating system software that typically accompanies the hardware. Key areas addressed in the hardware section of a contract include specifications and performance criteria, delivery, installation, and testing requirements, costs and terms of payment, reliability tolerances, and maintenance program options.

HARD-WIRED ELECTRONIC LOCKING SYSTEM

An electronic locking system that operates through a centralized master code console that is interfaced to every controlled guestroom door.

HEADER/FOOTER

Word processing formatting techniques. A header is information placed at the top of each page above the regular textual material of the document. A footer is information placed at the bottom of each page below the regular textual material of the document.

HEADER INFORMATION

Data elements needed to create a folio, such as guest name, address, room number, and folio number.

HIDDEN COSTS

In relation to the purchase of computer equipment, costs associated with supplies, customized forms, training, overtime pay, and data conversion normally not included in the system purchase price.

HIERARCHICAL DATABASE STRUCTURE

In database management software, arranges data files, records, and fields into formations which resemble the structure of the roots of a tree.

HIGH-LEVEL PROGRAMMING LANGUAGE

A category of computer programming languages that are made up of familiar words and symbols; they are the most sophisticated programming languages, because a relatively simple command instructs the computer to perform complex procedures that involve a number of different operations.

HOBIC SYSTEM

Acronym for Hotel Billing Information Center, a service supplied by a telephone company that provides a means to record time and charges on each long-distance call that guests make.

HOUSE LIMIT

A credit limit predetermined by management officials.

HOUSEKEEPER ASSIGNMENT REPORT

Used to assign floor and room numbers to room attendants and to list room status. This report may also provide space for special messages from the housekeeping department.

HOUSEKEEPER PRODUCTIVITY REPORT

Provides a relative productivity index for each housekeeper by listing the number of rooms cleaned and the amount of time taken to clean each room.

I

IDENTIFICATION CODE

Generally, the first few letters of a guest's last name. An identification code enables the guest accounting module to process a charge to the correct folio when two separate accounts exist under the same room number.

IMPACT PRINTER

An electronic printer, such as a dot matrix or daisywheel printer, that prints character by character and line by line.

INDEX COMMAND

In database management software, this command does not rearrange the records of a database file. Instead, it provides a limited working file that identifies records containing certain data, somewhat as the index of a textbook identifies page numbers containing certain types of information.

INDIRECT COSTS

In relation to the purchase of a computer system, these costs include taxes, insurance, shipping, and other costs that may result from: modifying the property's air conditioning, electrical, and telephone wiring systems; establishing contingency programs; installing uninterruptible power sources; and maintaining an inventory of spare parts.

INDIVIDUAL FOLIO

Assigned to an in-house guest for the purpose of charting the guest's financial transactions with the hotel.

INFORMATION

The end result of data processing and electronic data processing in which pieces of data are organized or manipulated into significant output.

INFORMATION PROCESSING TECHNOLOGY

Technology that establishes a communication process in which data are transferred from independent computer systems; processed according to pre-established decision-making rules, financial models, or other analytical methods; and stored in information formats tailored to the needs of individual managers. Includes decision support systems and the incorporation of expert systems.

INGREDIENT FILE

Contains important data on each purchased ingredient, such as ingredient code number, ingredient description, purchase unit, purchase unit cost, issue unit, issue unit cost, recipe unit, and recipe unit cost.

INK JET PRINTER

An electronic non-impact printer that works by spraying a minute and finely controlled jet of ink onto paper. The ink (carbon) is electrically charged as it is sprayed onto the paper. Once charged, the jet of ink can be moved around by electric fields in much the same way that an electron beam is used to produce a picture on a television set.

INPUT AREA SPECIFICATIONS

In database management software, these define data entry procedures. Screen templates can be designed to guide users with data input responsibilities. For example, the display screen at the front desk of a hotel may guide front desk employees in entering specific data regarding guests during check-in.

IN-ROOM BEVERAGE SERVICE SYSTEM

A system capable of monitoring sales transactions and determining inventory replenishment quantities. Two popular in-room beverage service systems are non-automated honor bars and microprocessor-based vending machines.

IN-ROOM CHECK-OUT

When in-room computers are interfaced with a computer-based property management system's guest accounting module, they are able to access folio data and provide guests with a way to approve and settle their accounts.

IN-ROOM MOVIE SYSTEM

When interfaced with a computer-based hotel property management system, an in-room movie system provides guestroom entertainment through a dedicated television pay channel.

INTEGRATED HARDWARE CONFIGURATION

A network of work stations that is dependent upon a single central processing unit and external storage capability. Each I/O unit communicates with the CPU, and the CPU and external storage device work closely together. Three types of integrated configurations used by ECR/POS systems are: master/slave configurations, processor-based configurations, and microprocessor-based configurations.

INTEGRATING SPREADSHEETS

Electronic spreadsheets that can be integrated with other software applications, such as word processing systems, database management programs, and electronic cash register systems.

INTERACTIVE ROOM AND RATE ASSIGNMENT

A rooms management program that gives front desk personnel direction in decision-making while increasing their control over actual room assignments. For example, in a property with 800 rooms, a front desk employee can narrow the search routine by clarifying the guest's needs through a series of room and rate category queries. In addition, the front desk employee may use the rooms management module to display an abbreviated list of available rooms selected by type and rate.

INTERFACE BOARD

Also called an interface card; a series of microchips on a printed circuit board placed into an available expansion slot inside the computer; the interface board connects to the CPU and allows communications between the CPU and an input/output device.

INTERSELL AGENCY

A reservation network that handles more than one product line. Intersell agencies typically handle reservations for airline flights, car rentals, and hotel rooms.

INVENTORY MASTER FILE

Maintains basic inventory data, such as item name, item description (brief), inventory code number, storeroom location code, item purchase unit, purchase unit price, item issue unit, product group code, vendor identification number, order lead time, minimum-maximum stock levels, and date of last purchase.

INVENTORY STATUS

An account of how much of each item is in storage. Inventory status may be determined by a physical inventory or a perpetual inventory.

INVENTORY STATUS FILE

In a perpetual inventory system, keeps a running balance of the quantity of issued/stored items.

INVENTORY VALUATION

The value of items in inventory.

INVENTORY VALUATION FILE

Contains data for determining the cost of goods sold and the replacement cost of items listed in the inventory master file.

INVENTORY VARIANCE

Differences between a physical count of an item and the balance maintained by the perpetual inventory system.

INVENTORY VARIANCE REPORT

Lists differences between a physical count of an inventory item and the balance maintained by the perpetual inventory system.

INVOICE REGISTER FILE

Maintains a complete list of all invoices currently outstanding and payable.

J

JOURNAL PRINTER

A remote printing device of an ECR/POS system that produces a continuous detailed record of all transactions entered anywhere in the system. Hard copy is produced on narrow register tape (usually 20 columns wide) and provides management with a thorough system audit. In addition to providing an audit trail, journal printers are capable of printing a variety of management reports.

K

KEYBOARD

The most common input device of a computer system; the number, positioning, and function of the keys on any particular keyboard will depend on the type of computer system used as well as on the needs of the individual user.

KILOBYTE

Often abbreviated as "K" or "KB," equal to 1,024 bytes, and commonly used to describe computer memory capacity.

KITCHEN MONITOR

Video display units capable of displaying several orders on a single screen. An accompanying cursor control keypad enables kitchen employees to easily review previously submitted orders by scrolling full screens at a time.

L

LABEL

The term for alpha data entered into an electronic spreadsheet program.

LABOR MASTER FILE

A file maintained by sophisticated ECR/POS systems containing one record for each employee; it typically maintains the following data: employee name, employee number, social security number, authorized job codes, and corresponding hourly wage rates. This file may also contain data required to produce labor reports for management.

LABOR MASTER REPORT

A file maintained by sophisticated ECR/POS systems containing general data maintained by the labor master file; it is commonly used to verify an employee's hourly rate(s), job code(s), or social security number.

LASER PRINTER

A high-speed electronic non-impact printer similar in appearance to desktop photocopying machines. While other printers print one character at a time, laser technology enables these devices to print an entire page all at once.

LAST IN, FIRST OUT (LIFO)

An inventory valuation method that assumes that the products that are most recently purchased are used first. The inventory value is assumed to be represented by the cost of items placed in storage the earliest.

LATE CHARGES

Charged purchases made by guests that are posted to folios after guests have settled their accounts.

LEAD-TIME QUANTITY

The anticipated number of purchase units withdrawn from inventory between the time an order is placed and the time it is delivered.

LEAST-COST ROUTING

A feature of an active call accounting system that directs calls over the least-cost available line, regardless of carrier.

LEDGER SUMMARY REPORT

Presents guest, non-guest, and credit card activity by beginning balance, cumulative charges, and credits.

LINE-PRINTING TERMINAL

An electronic impact printer that prints one line of type at a time.

LINKING SPREADSHEETS

A technique that enables electronic spreadsheet users to work with smaller spreadsheets and achieve the same results they would with a single extensive spreadsheet. This technique permits users to link spreadsheets in such a way that they share data and can interact to perform functions that none of them could perform individually.

LOCAL AREA NETWORK

Often abbreviated LAN; a distributed hardware configuration that enables users to share data, programs, and output devices (such as printers).

LOCATE COMMAND

In database management software, functions by matching file entries with the character string for which the user is searching. Searches issued by the locate command tend to be less efficient than searches issued by the find command, especially when large database files are involved.

LOW-LEVEL PROGRAMMING LANGUAGE

A category of computer programming languages that are sometimes called machine languages, because the computer can directly understand their instructions.

M

MACHINE LANGUAGES

Computer programming languages that can be directly understood by a computer system. Machine languages typically vary from one computer manufacturer to another; also, they may vary among the different models offered by the same manufacturer.

MACRO COMMANDS

Sophisticated electronic spreadsheet software packages that enable a user to create macro commands that minimize key strokes, thus permitting faster data entry, consolidation, and reporting.

MAGNETIC STRIP READER

Optional input device that connects to a ECR/POS system register or terminal capable of collecting data stored on a magnetized film strip typically located on the back of a credit card or house account card.

MAGNETIC TAPE

An external storage medium used with computer systems. It is made from polyester base material coated with an oxide compound.

MAIL MERGE

A word processing technique used to personalize form letters. The technique involves the use of two files: a primary file and a secondary file. The primary file contains the standard textual material that the user wishes to distribute. The secondary file contains variable textual material, such as a mailing list consisting of individual names and addresses.

MANAGEMENT INFORMATION SYSTEM (MIS)

A system designed to provide managers with the necessary information needed to plan, organize, staff, direct, and control operations.

MARKETING CATEGORY REPORT

Compiles weekly totals summarizing the revenue earned by food and beverage departments (or categories).

MASTER FOLIO

Generally applies to more than one guest or room and contains a record of transactions that are not posted to individual folios. Master folios are commonly created to provide the kind of billing service required by most groups and conventions.

MASTER/SLAVE HARDWARE CONFIGURATION

An integrated ECR/POS system configuration with one register containing all the necessary components of a complete computer system. This ECR functions as the master register by processing transactions entered through slave units, such as precheck or cashier terminals. Slave POS units are cabled to the ECR.

MEGABYTE

Often abbreviated as "MB," equal to 1,048,576 bytes, and commonly used to describe computer memory capacity.

MEGAHERTZ (MHz)

A unit of electrical frequency equal to one million cycles per second; used to measure the speed of a computer system's central processing unit.

MENU BOARD

A keyboard overlay for an ECR/POS system terminal that identifies the function performed by each key during a specific meal period.

MENU ENGINEERING

A menu management application for evaluating decisions regarding current and future menu pricing, design, and contents. This application requires that management focus on the number of dollars a menu contributes to profit and not simply monitor cost percentages.

MENU ITEM FILE

A file maintained by sophisticated ECR/POS systems containing data for all meal periods and menu items sold. Important data maintained by this file may include: identification number, descriptor, recipe code number, selling price, ingredient quantities for inventory reporting, and sales totals.

MICRO-BASED POS SYSTEM

Recent POS system designs that place a microprocessor at each POS terminal location. These microprocessors are networked to form a complete POS system that functions without a large, remote CPU.

MICROCOMPUTER

Also called a personal computer; despite its relatively small size, it contains the same types of components as larger machines and may also have additional options, such as hard disks, color monitors, graphics capability, and others.

MICRO-FITTED ELECTRONIC LOCKING SYSTEM

An electronic locking system that operates as a stand-alone unit. Each door has its own microprocessor which contains a unique, predetermined sequence of codes. A master console at the front desk contains a record of all code sequences for each door.

MICROPROCESSOR

The central processing unit of a microcomputer; an integrated circuit package containing a complete electronic circuit or group of circuits. It controls the computer, carries out calculations, directs the flow of data, and performs many other functions.

MICROPROCESSOR-BASED HARDWARE CONFIGURATION

Recent POS system designs that place a microprocessor at each POS terminal location. These microprocessors are networked to form a complete POS system that functions without a large, remote CPU.

MICROPROCESSOR-BASED VENDING MACHINE

Vending machine which contains beverage items in see-through closed compartments. The compartment doors may be equipped with fiber optic sensors that record the removal of stored products. Once triggered, the sensors relay the transaction to a built-in microprocessor for recording. Individual room microprocessors are typically cabled to a large CPU, which stores recorded transactions.

MINICOMPUTER

A slower, less powerful, but smaller and cheaper alternative to the mainframe computer. It is generally more powerful than a microcomputer.

MINIMUM/MAXIMUM INVENTORY LEVELS

Help managers determine when products need to be purchased and how much of each product to order. For each purchase item, management sets a minimum quantity below which inventory levels should not fall and a maximum quantity above which inventory levels should not rise.

MODEM

In relation to telecommunications, a modem performs both the modulator and demodulator functions. The word *MODEM* is a contraction of *MOdulate/DEMo-dulate.*

MODIFIER KEYS

Parts of an ECR/POS system keyboard used in combination with preset and price look-up keys to detail preparation instructions (such as rare, medium, and well-done) for food production areas; also used to alter prices according to designated portion sizes (such as small, medium, and large).

MONTHLY CHECK REGISTER

Provides a hard copy audit trail of payments made to vendors. This report also identifies checks that have not yet been accounted for.

MOUSE

A small manual input unit used in place of, or with, a computer keyboard. Designed to fit comfortably under a user's hand, it controls the cursor or pointer on the display screen. It can also be used to choose commands, move text and icons, and perform a number of operations.

MULTIPLE GUEST SPLITS

Charges that are to be divided among a group of guests.

MULTIPLE RATING SYSTEM

In relation to the purchase of a computer system, a technique used to judge the worth of each vendor's proposal by applying the same criteria to each. Generally, the criteria consist of several key issues that management considers to be of critical concern in computerizing the business.

MULTIPLE SEARCHES

In database management software, a technique used to retrieve information. The first search indexes the database file in terms of a primary key field, which is the broadest field category involved in the search. Subsequent searches focus on secondary keys, which order and limit the primary key field.

MULTIPLE WINDOWING

A feature of sophisticated spreadsheet programs that enables a user to split the display screen (vertically, horizontally, or both) and view separate areas of a spreadsheet simultaneously.

MULTI-PROCESSOR ENVIRONMENT

Results from interfacing independent computer processing units (CPUs), enabling them to share data, peripheral devices (such as printers), and operating systems.

MULTI-TASKING

Refers to the ability of a CPU to perform more than one task at a time.

N

NET SALES BY TIME OF DAY REPORT

A report produced by sophisticated automated beverage systems indicating hourly sales; the report is useful for forecasting sales and scheduling servers and bartenders according to expected demand.

NON-AFFILIATE RESERVATION SYSTEM

A subscription system linking independent properties. A hotel subscribes to the system's services and takes responsibility for updating the system with accurate room availability data.

NON-AUTOMATED HONOR BAR

Typically involves stocks of items that are held in dry and cold storage areas within a guestroom. Changes in the bar's beginning inventory level are noted either by housekeeping room attendants during their normal rounds or by designated room service employees.

NON-GUEST FOLIO

Created for an individual who has in-house charge privileges but is not registered as a guest in the hotel. Individuals with non- guest folios may include health club members, corporate clients, special club members, political leaders, or local celebrities.

NON-IMPACT PRINTER

A category of electronic printers which includes thermal, ink jet, and laser printers.

NON-VOLATILE MEMORY

A computer systems term describing ROM (Read Only Memory); programs stored in ROM are not lost when the computer is turned off or otherwise loses electrical power.

NUMERIC DATA

A type of electronic data consisting only of numbers.

NUMERIC VALUES

Numeric data entered into cells of an electronic spreadsheet program from a keyboard's numeric keypad. Spreadsheet software programs are normally able to immediately distinguish data input as labels from data input as numeric values.

O

OFF-PREMISES CATERING SERVICE

A catering service that typically requires the caterer to be responsible for food and beverage production and service and possibly for providing furnishings, entertainment, decorations, and the like.

OPEN CHECK FILE

A file maintained by sophisticated ECR/POS systems that maintains current data for all open guest checks; it is accessed to monitor items on a guest check, add items to a guest check after initial order entry, and close a guest check at the time of settlement.

OPERATING SYSTEM

Responsible for orchestrating the hardware and the software within the computer system. It establishes the system's priorities and directs its resources to accomplish desired tasks.

OPERATOR DISPLAY SCREEN

Part of an ECR/POS system terminal enabling the operator to review and edit transaction entries.

OPERATORS' GUIDES

Also called users' guides; written training materials for specific application procedures on computer systems.

OPTICAL CHARACTER RECOGNITION

Often abbreviated OCR; automates the time-consuming input stage of word processing by scanning typed copy produced by ordinary typewriters or electronic printers and converting it into an electronic form that can be entered into the word processing system.

OTHER EQUIPMENT MANUFACTURER (OEM) CONTRACT

In relation to the purchase of a computer system, a contract in which a business agrees to purchase hardware components and software packages from a single source, and this single source takes full responsibility for the performance of the computer system. An OEM contract generally involves purchasing turnkey packages.

OUTPUT AREA SPECIFICATIONS

In database management software, these control the generation and formatting of reports. Since data stored in a database are independent of their applications, database management programs are able to separate related information and generate a variety of report formats.

OUTSTANDING CHECKS LIST

Details all checks that have been issued but remain outstanding; can be used to reconcile checks issued against canceled checks appearing on bank statements.

OUTSTANDING CHECKS REPORT

A report produced by automated point-of-sale equipment that lists all guest checks (by server) that have not been settled; information may include: the guest check number, server identification number, time at which the guest check was opened, number of guests, table number, and guest check total.

OUTSTANDING GUEST CHECKS REPORT

A report produced by sophisticated automated beverage systems to resolve any discrepancy existing between the sales by major beverage category report and the sales by beverage server report.

OVERRIDE OPTIONS

Provide management with complete control over cash disbursements before engaging the automatic check writing feature of the accounts payable module.

OVERRUN FACILITY

A hotel property selected to receive reservation requests after chain properties have exhausted room availabilities in a geographic region.

P

PARALLEL CONVERSION

In relation to the implementation of a computer system, a property operates two different information systems simultaneously: the previous system and the newly computerized system. Both systems are maintained for at least one complete accounting period. Once comfortable with the new system's operation, management directs a complete conversion to the new computer system.

PARALLEL TRANSMISSION
In relation to telecommunications, uses multiple channels to transmit several bits of data simultaneously. In this type of data transfer, the bits that encode a character travel as a single pulse along a set of wires within the communications cable.

PASSIVE CALL ACCOUNTING SYSTEM
Under this system, no options are available to the call distribution network. Selection of a route is based on convenience rather than on minimizing expense.

PAYMENT DISCOUNT DATE
The last day on which it is possible for a lodging operation to take advantage of a cash payment discount that may be offered by a specific vendor.

PAYROLL COST REPORT
Shows labor costs by department or job classifications.

PAYROLL REGISTER FILE
Maintains the number of hours each employee worked during a pay period and other data that may require special tax calculations, such as sick leave pay, bonus pay, tips, and expense reimbursements.

PERIOD LABOR REPORT
A report generated by automated systems listing hour and wage information for each employee who worked during a period specified by management.

PERPETUAL INVENTORY SYSTEM
An inventory system that keeps records up-to-date by tracking all additions to and subtractions from stock.

PHYSICAL INVENTORY SYSTEM
An inventory system in which property employees periodically observe and count items in storage.

POINTER
In electronic spreadsheet software, the flashing cursor that appears in a cell on the display screen.

POINT-OF-SALE TERMINAL
Contains its own input/output component and may even possess a small storage (memory) capacity, but usually does not contain its own central processing unit.

PORT
A plug on a computer hardware device into which a cable is inserted for interfacing capability.

POSTCOSTING
Postcosting multiplies the number of menu items sold by standard recipe costs to determine a potential food cost amount. When actual recipe costs are known, these figures are multiplied by the number of menu items sold to produce an actual cost figure.

POTENTIAL AVERAGE RATE

A collective statistic that effectively combines the potential average single and double rates, multiple occupancy percentage, and rate spread to produce the average rate that would apply if all rooms were sold at their full rack rates.

POWER PLATFORM

Consolidates electronic communications between a hospitality establishment and a credit card authorization center. Power platforms can capture credit card authorizations in three seconds or less. This swift data retrieval helps reduce the time, cost, and risk associated with credit card transactions. An ECR/POS power platform connects all ECR/POS terminals to a single processor for transaction settlement. This eliminates the need for individual telephone lines at each ECR/POS cashier terminal.

PRECHECK TERMINAL

An ECR/POS system terminal without a cash drawer; used to enter orders, not to settle accounts.

PRECOSTING

A special type of forecasting which compares forecasted guest counts with standard menu item recipe costs to yield an index of expense before an actual meal period.

PRESET KEY

Part of an ECR/POS system keyboard programmed to maintain the price, descriptor, department, tax, and inventory status of a menu item.

PRICE LOOK-UP (PLU) KEY

Part of an ECR/POS system keyboard that operates like a preset key, except that it requires the user to identify a menu item by its reference code number (up to five digits) rather than by its name or descriptor.

PRIMARY KEY FIELD

In database management software, the first search of a multiple search routine, which looks for the broadest field category involved in the search.

PRINTER CONTROLLER

Part of an ECR/POS system that coordinates communications between cashier or precheck terminals and work station printers or kitchen monitors, while ensuring that servers need enter their orders only once. Also called a network controller.

PROCESSOR-BASED CONFIGURATION

An integrated ECR/POS system configuration similar to the master/slave system, except that the central processing unit and external storage capacity are significantly larger and are placed in a location remote from actual restaurant operations.

PRODUCT USAGE REPORT

A report produced by sophisticated automated beverage systems indicating amounts of beverage products sold during a shift; the report enables managers to minimize inventory control problems.

PRODUCTIVITY REPORTS

In relation to automated food and beverage systems, reports that detail sales activity for all assigned server sales records; may be generated for each server and cashier in terms of guest count, total sales, and average sales.

PROPERTY PROFILE

Compiles statistics about aspects of the current information system; useful when communicating information needs of the business to vendors of computer systems.

PROPERTY SYSTEMS MANAGER

A manager who participates in the evaluation, selection, and installation of computer system hardware and is trained in the operation of software applications used throughout a property. Also provides on-premises systems support and, when necessary, functions as a software applications troubleshooter.

R

RADIO BASE STATION

Part of a wireless system supporting the use of hand-held server terminals that relays signals received from antenna units to a digital computer's processing unit.

RANDOM ACCESS MEDIUM

A characteristic of an external storage medium of computer systems (such as floppy disks) permitting data to be stored in any available location on the disk. Since the tracks and sectors of the disk are numbered, the computer system allows a user to access stored data quickly and easily.

RANDOM ACCESS MEMORY

Often abbreviated as RAM, a portion of a computer's internal memory that holds a temporary version of the programs or data which users are processing.

RATIO

Gives mathematical expression to a significant relationship between two figures. It is calculated by dividing one figure by the other.

RATIO ANALYSIS

Analysis of financial statements and operating results through the use of ratios.

READ ONLY MEMORY

Often abbreviated as ROM, a portion of the internal memory of a computer that holds a permanent record of information that the computer needs to use each time it is turned on.

READ/WRITE

A computer is said to "read" when it takes data in for processing and "write" when it sends processed data out as information. RAM is often described as read/write memory; the user can both read from RAM (retrieve data) and write to RAM (store data).

REAL TIME CAPABILITY

Refers to simultaneous processing. For example, real time capability enables a reservationist to receive necessary feedback from the system immediately in order to respond to a caller's requests during a telephone call.

RECALCULATION

A feature of electronic spreadsheet packages that offers managers opportunities to explore "what if" possibilities. The cells in which formulas are entered will display the results of calculations. If any of the amounts entered in the range of cells change, a formula is able to immediately recalculate the amounts and place the new result in the same designated cell.

RECEIPT PRINTER

On-board printing devices that produce hard copy on narrow register tape.

RECONCILIATION AUDIT REPORT

Balances the total of checks removed from the outstanding checks list with the total of cleared checks appearing on the bank statement.

REDUNDANT COPY

An information backup technique that requires two storage devices working simultaneously. As transactions occur, they are written to two external storage devices.

REFERENCE CODE

Generally, the serial number of a departmental source document.

REGISTER

An ECR/POS device that is connected to a cash drawer.

REGISTRATION PROGRESS REPORT

Provides the rooms department with a summary of current house information; may list present check-ins, number of occupied rooms, names of guests who have reservations but are not yet registered, and the number of rooms available for sale; may also profile room status, rooms revenue, and average room rate.

RELATIONAL DATABASE STRUCTURE

A database structure in which the data files are formatted as rectangular tables of rows and columns and are similar in appearance to electronic spreadsheets.

REMOTE PRINT SITE

In relation to telecommunications, a means through which a computer may communicate with a computerless receiver. Documents are transmitted to a designated remote print site for immediate hard copy dissemination to a computerless receiver.

REMOVABLE HARD DISK

A backup data storage method.

REQUEST FOR PROPOSAL

In relation to the purchase of a computer system, a three-part document prepared by management. The first section orients the vendor to management's business operations; the second section establishes bidding requirements for vendor proposals; and the third section deals specifically with user application requirements.

RESERVATION INQUIRY

A reservation request is formulated into a reservation inquiry by the reservationist. This inquiry typically collects the following data: date of arrival, type and number of rooms requested, number of room nights, room rate code (standard, special, package, etc.), and number of persons in party.

RESERVATION RECORD

The reservationist's initial inquiry procedures create a reservation record that initiates the hotel guest cycle. Reservation records identify guests and their needs before guests arrive at the property; such records enable the hotel to personalize guest service and appropriately schedule needed personnel.

RESERVATION TRANSACTION RECORD

Provides a daily summary of reservation records that were created, modified, or canceled.

REVENUE CENTER REPORT

Shows cash, charge, and paid-out totals by department and serves as a macro-analysis of departmental transactions.

REVENUE FORECAST REPORT

Projects future revenue by multiplying predicted occupancies by current house rates.

RINGBACK MECHANISM

A feature of a call accounting system that ensures that a guest is charged only for calls that are answered.

ROOM OCCUPANCY SENSORS

Sensors that use either infrared light or ultrasonic waves to register the physical occupancy of a room.

ROOM STATUS

Information about current availability is absolutely essential in order for front desk employees to properly assign rooms to guests at the time of check-in. Housekeeping's description of the current status of a room is crucial to the immediate, short-run selling position of that room. Common housekeeping descriptions of a room's status include: on-makeup, on-change, out-of-order, clean, and ready for inspection.

ROOM STATUS DISCREPANCY

A situation in which the housekeeping department's description of a room's status differs from the room status information that guides front desk employees in assigning rooms to guests. Discrepancies can seriously affect a property's ability to satisfy guests and maximize rooms revenue.

ROOMS ACTIVITY FORECAST

Provides information on anticipated arrivals, departures, stay-overs, and vacancies. This report assists managers in staffing front desk and housekeeping areas.

ROOMS ALLOTMENT REPORT

Summarizes rooms committed (booked or blocked), by future date.

ROOMS AVAILABILITY REPORT

Lists, by room type, the number of rooms that are available each day (net remaining rooms in each category).

ROOMS DISCREPANCY REPORT

Signals to management the specific rooms whose status must be investigated to avoid sleepers. The report notes any variances between front desk and housekeeping room status updates.

ROOMS HISTORY REPORT

Depicts the revenue history and use of each room by room type. This report is especially useful to those properties employing an automatic room assignment function.

ROOMS PRODUCTIVITY REPORT

Ranks room types by percentage of occupancy and/or by percentage of total rooms revenue.

ROOMS STATUS REPORT

Indicates the current status of rooms according to housekeeping designations, such as: on-makeup, on-change, out-of-order, clean, and ready for inspection.

S

SALES ANALYSIS REPORT

A report generated by automated food and beverage systems that enables management to measure the sales performance of individual menu items by department or product category over various time intervals.

SALES AND PAYMENT SUMMARY REPORT

A report generated by automated food and beverage systems providing managers with a complete statement of daily or monthly sales (by shift or broken down by food and beverage categories) and a listing of settlement methods.

SALES BY BEVERAGE SERVER REPORT

A report produced by sophisticated automated beverage systems indicating the total sales of each beverage server during a shift.

SALES BY MAJOR BEVERAGE CATEGORY REPORT

A report produced by sophisticated automated beverage systems indicating the expected beverage income by major beverage category (liquor, beer, wine, etc.).

SALES BY TIME OF DAY REPORT

A report generated by automated food and beverage systems enabling managers to measure the sales performance of individual menu items by department or product category within certain time intervals.

SALES CATEGORY ANALYSIS REPORT

Shows relationships between amounts sold by sales category and day-parts defined by management; enables management to view at a glance which menu items sell and when they sell.

SALES MIX BY MAJOR PRODUCT REPORT

A report produced by sophisticated automated beverage systems indicating how much of each beverage product was sold during a shift; the report is useful for monitoring product sales trends and adjusting par inventory levels when necessary.

SCANNERS

A computer system input device capable of translating a page of text into a machine readable format by converting the images on a page into digitized information that the computer can recognize.

SCROLL

A word processing keyboard technique for moving through soft copy. Special keys and key combinations of applications software programs permit a user to move through a document a full page at a time. As the user types the appropriate keys, the document is displayed on the screen in a rolling manner, similar to the way in which a very long sheet of paper would roll through a typewriter's carriage. As lines successively disappear at the top of the screen, new lines appear at the bottom.

SECONDARY KEYS

Part of a multiple search routine of database management software that orders and limits the primary key field.

SECTOR

A computer systems term referring to characteristics of an external storage medium. The surface of a floppy disk is divided into tracks, which are invisible concentric rings of magnetic zones. Each track contains a number of sectors.

SELF CHECK-IN/CHECK-OUT TERMINALS

Typically located in the lobbies of fully automated hotels, some resemble automatic bank teller machines, while others are unique in design and may possess both video and audio capability.

SELF-RESERVATION SYSTEM

Allows users with telecommunications equipment to retrieve computer-stored reservation packages and view them on their television screens or display monitors.

SEQUENTIAL ACCESS MEDIUM

A computer systems term referring to an external storage medium, such as a magnetic tape, which stores data in chronological sequence.

SERIAL TRANSMISSION

In relation to telecommunications, uses a single channel to transmit data bit by bit. In this type of data transfer, the data bits travel as a sequence of pulses over a single wire. Eight bits encode a single character. Data flow is coordinated by start and stop bits that are transformed into pulses that precede and follow each character.

SETTLEMENT KEYS

Part of an ECR/POS system keyboard used to record the methods with which accounts are settled: cash, credit card, house account, charge transfer, or other payment.

SETTLEMENT METHODS REPORT

A report produced by sophisticated automated beverage systems indicating the amounts due in the form of cash, credit card vouchers, and house account charges for sales made during a shift.

SILICON CHIPS

Pieces of semiconductor material onto which electronic circuitry is etched.

SIMPLEX CONNECTION

In relation to telecommunications, carries data in only one direction. Television and radio use simplex communication.

SINGLE-VENDOR CONTRACT

In relation to the purchase of a computer system, an agreement to purchase hardware and software from the same vendor. In most of these cases, the vendor makes the necessary hardware and software modifications before system implementation.

SITE PREPARATION

In relation to the implementation of a computer system, architectural or engineering changes that must be made before the computer system can be installed.

SITE SURVEY

In relation to the purchase of a computer system, visits by vendors to identify important factors regarding specific business operations within a property that may affect computer system design.

SLEEPER

A vacant room that is believed to be occupied because the room rack slip or registration card was not removed from the rack when the guest departed.

SMART CARD

Smart cards are made of plastic and are about the same size as credit cards. Microchips embedded in them store information that can be accessed by a specially designed card reader. Smart cards can store information in several files that are accessed for different functions, such as a person's vital health statistics, dietary restrictions, credit card number, and bank balance. The security of information stored in smart cards is controlled because a personal identification number (PIN) must be used to access files.

SOFT COPY

A computer systems term referring to output on a display screen that cannot be handled by the operator or removed from the computer system.

SOFT KEYS

Parts of an ECR/POS system keyboard that can be programmed by users to meet the specific needs of their restaurant operations.

SOFTWARE

A computer systems term referring to a set of programs that instructs or controls the operation of the hardware components of a computer system. Software programs tell the computer what to do, how to do it, and when to do it.

SOFTWARE CONTRACT PROVISIONS

Software programs are a compilation of ideas and processes proprietary to the seller; title is not automatically transferred to the buyer. Instead, the software often remains the property of the vendor, and the buyer is granted a non-exclusive license to use the software programs. Key areas of a software contract are similar to those for hardware; however, the contract should stipulate that a copy of the source code in which the software programs are written be placed in escrow and released to the buyer should the vendor fail to carry out provisions stated within the contract.

SORT COMMAND

In database management software, when a database file is retrieved and the sort command issued, a new database file is created which is equal in size and content to the original (source) file. However, the sort command changes the order of the records in the source file according to a field category designated by the user.

SOURCE DOCUMENT

A printed voucher, usually serially numbered for internal control purposes, from a revenue-producing department showing an amount that is charged to a folio.

STAND-ALONE HARDWARE CONFIGURATION

Creates self-sufficient work stations, each with a set of hardware components necessary for a complete computer system. A stand-alone configuration for a restaurant ECR/POS system is made up of a series of independent electronic cash registers.

STATEMENT OF INCOME

Also called the profit and loss statement, provides important financial information about the results of operations for a given period of time.

STATION MESSAGE DETAIL RECORD

A feature of a call accounting system that charts and monitors telephone traffic.

STREAMLINING

An electronic data processing practice of generating only those reports that are requested by staff members who will actually use the information.

STYLE SHEET

A word processing technique; a predesigned form, also called a format, for a typical document processed by a particular business.

SUB-RECIPE

Recipes that are included as ingredients within a standard recipe record.

SYSTEM CONVERSION

The process of switching from the current information system to the capabilities of a computerized system.

SYSTEM FLOWCHARTS

Illustrate the input-process-output logic, file structures, program sub-routines, interprogram relationships, and the level of program integration within the system. These flowcharts provide a basis on which to analyze the effectiveness of the computerized information system, and prove invaluable when management contemplates software or hardware modifications to meet new information needs.

SYSTEM UPDATE

Performs many of the same functions performed by the night audit routine in non-automated properties. System updates are run daily to allow for report production, system file reorganization, and system maintenance, and to provide an end-of-day time frame.

SYSTEMS SOFTWARE

A computer systems term referring to the mechanism that controls the interactions between hardware components of a computer system and software application programs. Although applications software tells the computer how to manipulate data to yield desired results, each set of these programs depends on systems software for its instructions to be carried out correctly.

T

TAPE STREAMERS

An external storage medium for computer systems. A magnetic tape cartridge containing seven track tape and a large storage capacity; permits rapid copying of all data stored on even the largest of hard disk formats.

TECHNICAL MANUALS

Also called systems manuals; they focus on the engineering features of the computer system.

TELETYPE TERMINAL

Often abbreviated as TTY; an electronic input/output device that used to be common in the hospitality industry. Input is entered through a keyboard and printed out on a roll of paper. As the operator enters data into the system, a printed report can be made at the TTY console. The entered data is then communicated to a remote unit for processing. After processing, the information is sent back to the TTY and printed out on the paper.

TEMPLATES

Preformatted electronic spreadsheet programs that enable the user to simply enter data into predefined data cells.

THERMAL PRINTER

Also called an electrothermal printer; works by burning a protective layer off specially treated paper to reveal ink.

TIMEOUT FEATURE

A feature of a call accounting system that ensures that callers begin paying for calls only after a predetermined amount of time, thus allowing for wrong numbers.

TOUCH-SCREEN TERMINAL

Contains a unique kind of cathode ray tube (CRT) screen and a special microprocessor to control it. The self-contained microprocessor is programmed to display data on areas of the screen that are sensitive to touch. Touching one of the sensitized areas produces an electronic charge, which is translated into digital signals indicating what area was touched for transmission to the microprocessor.

TRACE REPORT

In automated sales offices, all traces input within the system are activated on the appropriate dates and printed in a report for each salesperson every morning. As the salesperson reads through each trace message, he or she decides whether to act on the trace or to trace it to another date.

TRACK

A computer systems term referring to characteristics of an external storage medium. The surface of a floppy disk is divided into tracks, which are invisible concentric rings of magnetic zones. Each track contains a number of sectors. The tracks and sectors are numbered, enabling the computer to store information on the disk at specific locations.

TRAFFIC TRANSACTION FILE

Part of a call accounting system that maintains data necessary for generating reports for management.

TRANSFER REPORT
Shows transfers to non-guest (city) ledgers from guest accounts.

TRIAL BALANCE
Tests the equality of debit and credit account balances.

TRIAL BALANCE FILE
Maintains a list of accounts with debit and credit balances.

TURNAROUND TIME
An electronic data processing term referring to the time that elapses between data input and information output.

TURNAWAY REPORT
Also called a refusal report, tracks the number of room nights refused because rooms were not available for sale. This report is especially helpful to hotels with expansion plans.

TWO-VENDOR CONTRACT
In relation to the purchase of a computer system, an agreement to purchase hardware and software from separate sources.

U

UNDERLINING
A word processing formatting technique used to emphasize words, phrase, titles, or formulas by underlining them, thus making them stand out from the rest of the text.

UNINTERRUPTIBLE POWER SUPPLY
A power supply that is equipped with a battery pack and is placed on the computer's power line so that any fluctuation in the quality of incoming power will trigger the battery pack, which compensates for any energy deficiencies. This provides the computer with a continually stable energy source.

V

VENDOR ACTIVITY REPORT
Lists gross amount invoiced, discounts taken, number of invoices, and other vendor data.

VENDOR MASTER FILE
Maintains records of all current vendors. Data contained in this file includes: vendor number, vendor name, contact name, address, telephone number, vendor payment priority, discount terms, discount account number, invoice description, payment date, and year-to-date purchases.

VENDOR STATUS REPORT
Presents summary accounts payable information.

VERBAL RECOGNITION/SYNTHESIS
Recent technology associated with the development of talking computers.

VOICE RECOGNITION SYSTEMS
Recent technology associated with the development of computers that can respond to a set of instructions given by human voice; these systems directly convert spoken data into electronic form suitable for entry into a computer system.

VOLATILE MEMORY
A computer systems term used to describe random access memory (RAM); when the computer loses electrical power, or is deliberately turned off, all user data stored in RAM is lost. In order to save data stored in RAM for future use, the user must instruct the computer to save it on some type of external storage device.

W

WASH FACTOR
The deletion of unnecessary group rooms from a group block.

WEEKLY LABOR REPORT
A report generated by automated food and beverage systems listing the names, employee numbers, hours worked, wages earned, and wages declared for each employee on a given workday; may be useful for determining which employees are approaching overtime pay rates.

WEEKLY SALES SPREADSHEET
Provides a weekly summary of all information reported by relevant daily sales reports.

WEIGHTED AVERAGE
An inventory valuation method that considers the quantity of products purchased at different unit costs. This method "weights" the prices to be averaged based on the quantity of products in storage at each price.

WINDOWS
Divisions of a computer system's display screen; special keystroke commands of some applications software packages split the display screen into any number of desired sections. This permits a user to view more than one document at a time on the computer's display screen.

WITHHOLDINGS
Subtractions from gross pay for income and social security taxes.

WORK STATION PRINTER
Remote printing devices usually placed at kitchen preparation areas and service bars.

Y

YIELD
The ratio of actual revenue to potential revenue.

YIELD MANAGEMENT
A technique based on supply and demand used to maximize revenues by lowering prices to increase sales during periods of low demand and by raising prices during periods of high demand.

Index

A

acceptance testing, 288–289
account files, 213, 215
account settlement, 113–114
accounts
    aging file, 237
    chart of, 253–254
    payable aging report, 238
    payable module, 18–19,
        238–242
    receivable module, 18,
        235–238
actual departures report,
    107–108
add-ons, 39–41
affiliate reservation system,
    83
AIOD, 125
algorithm, 272
applications
    accounting, 18–20, 235–259
    catering, 17–18, 226–231
    F&B management, 179–202
    F&B pre/postcosting,
        193–194
    F&B service, 145–176
    management, 17
    sales, 17–18, 205–226
    service, 16
    software, 11, 51–76
ARS, 125
automated search routines,
    216
automatic route selection, 125
auxiliary guest service
        devices, 16, 132–133

B

backup procedures, 300–303
balance sheet, 255–256
banquet event order, 209, 210
bar code terminals, 165
BASIC, 45
baud rate, 75
beverage control systems,
    169–174
    management reports,
        194–199

beverage dispensing units,
    173–174
bid specification, 251–252
bidirectional printing, 28
binary code, 7
bit, 7
boilerplate files, 56
booking lead time, 221, 222
bring-up file, 212–213
bundled tower unit, 174
bus system, 37–39
byte, 7

C

C, 45
call accounting systems, 13,
    123–128
call record file, 126–127
CAS, 13, 123–128
cash requirements report, 240,
    241
catering software, 226–231
cathode ray tube, 26, 30–31
cells, 58, 59
central processing unit, 25,
    31–34
    speed, 37
chaining recipes, 184
chart of accounts, 253–254
check register, 238
    file, 19, 240–242
city ledger file, 236
COBOL, 45
commission agent reports, 94
communications, electronic,
    71–76
    network, 72–73
comparison logic, 303, 304
computer system
    conversion, 289–290
    installation, 285–291
    mainframe, 8–9
    microcomputer, 9–10
    minicomputer, 9
    needs analysis, 265–269
    selecting/implementing,
        265–292
    types of, 8–10
    viruses, 305–306
configuration, 16

hardware, 273–277
confirmation letters, 91–92
console faucet, 174
contingency planning,
    290–291
contracts with vendors,
    283–285
control folios, 111
cover count and revenue
        summary report,
        216–218
CPU, 25, 31–34
    speed, 37
credit limits, 112
credit monitoring routine, 112
CRT, 26, 30–31
cursor, 26
customer master file, 236

D

daily receiving report, 252
daily transaction report, 162,
    163
daisywheel printers, 29
data collection, 271
data identification, 271
data processing, 4–7
    cycle, 4–5
    electronic, 5–7
data, types of, 6–7
database, 64
    files, records, fields, 65–66
    management, 64–71
    structures, 67–68
debit cards, 169
delivery network (beverage),
    171–174
demand control, 132
desktop publishing, 57–58
direct cutover conversion, 289
disk drive, 36
diskettes, 34–36
disks, 34–36
displacement, 222–223
display screens, 27–28,
    150–151
distributed configuration,
    274, 275
documentation, system, 290
DOS, 42

dot matrix printers, 28
downtime, 299
dunning letter, 114
duplicate copy, 301–302
duty cycling, 132

E

electronic
   cash register, 16
   data processing, 5–7
   locking systems, 13–14,
      129–131
   mail, 76
email, 76
employee folios, 111
employee master file, 242–243
empty bottle sensor, 170
energy backup systems, 300
energy management systems,
     14–16, 131–132
expected arrival and
     departure lists, 94,
     106–107
external storage devices,
     34–36

F

fault-tolerant processing,
     302–304
FAX board, 40
FIFO valuation, 247–248
financial reporting module,
     19, 253–258
financial statements, 255–256
firecracker, 305
fiscal year, 256
floppy disks, 34–36
flowcharts, 267, 290
folio types, 109–111
follow-up file, 212–213
footers, 55
formatting, 34–36
FORTRAN, 45
four-box analysis, 189–190
front office applications,
     11–13
full-duplex connection, 76
function keys, 26, 149

G

gigabyte, 7
glass sensor, 170

global reservation systems,
     88–89
graphics, spreadsheet, 58,
     62–63
group booking pace, 221, 222
guest accounting module, 13,
     108–114
   reports, 114
guest check, 156–157
   printers, 151
   sensors, 170
guest information services,
     139–140
guest-operated devices,
     133–140
guestroom control book, 207

H

half-duplex connection, 75–76
hand-held terminals, 165–166,
     168
hard copy, 31, 302
hard disks, 36
hardware, 25
   configurations, 273–277
   F&B ECR/POS, 145–156
   telecommunications, 73–74
headers, 55
HHTs, 165–166, 168
hidden costs, 282
hierarchical database, 67
high-level programming
     languages, 45–46
HOBIC, 123–125
honor bars, 137–138
hose and gun device, 173–174
house limits, 112
housekeeper reports, 108
housekeeping, 106

I

identification code, 112
impact printer, 28
income statement, 256, 257
in-room beverage service
     systems, 137–139
in-room check-out, 136
in-room movie systems,
     136–137
individual folios, 109
information processing
     technology, 296
ingredient file, 179–181
ink jet printers, 30
input/output units, 25–31

integrated configuration,
     274–277
interface board, 41
intersell agencies, 87–88
inventory
   file, 160–161
   module, 19, 246–250
   status, 246–247
   usage report, 248–249
   valuation, 247–248
invoice register file, 19, 240

J

journal printers, 152

K

keyboards, 25–26
   F&B, 146–150
kilobyte, 7

L

labor master file, 159–160
labor reports, 159–160
laser printers, 30
late charges, 114
LCR, 125–126
lead-time quantity, 250
least-cost routing, 125–126
ledger summary reports, 114
LIFO valuation, 248
line-printing terminal, 28
local area network, 72
locking systems, 129–131
   hard-wired, 129
   micro-fitted, 129–130
low-level programming
     languages, 44–45
LPT, 28

M

machine languages, 44–45
macro commands, 64
magnetic strip readers,
     167–169
magnetic tape, 34
mail merge, 56–57
mainframe computer, 8–9
management information
     systems, 295–307
management reports, 266
master card files, 216

master folios, 109–110
master/slave configuration, 275, 276
memory
  expanded, 40
  extended, 40
  RAM/ROM, 32–34
menu
  board, 146–147
  engineering, 187–193
  item file, 158–159, 184
  management, 185–191
  summary sheet, 190–191
message-waiting systems, 133
micro-based POS systems, 120
microcomputer, 9–10, 36–41
microprocessor, 9–10, 37
microprocessor-based configuration, 276–277
minicomputer, 9
minimum/maximum inventory, 250
mini-tower pedestal, 174
MIS, 295–307
  security, 299–306
modem, 40, 73–74
modifier keys, 150
monitors, 27–28, 150–151
mouse, 27
multiple rating system, 280–283
multi-processor environments, 297–299
multi-tasking, 43, 299

N

net sales by time of day report, 198, 199
night audit, 113
non-affiliate reservation system, 83–84
non-guest folios, 111
non-impact printers, 28
no-show report, 96
non-volatile memory, 33

O

OCR, 52
operating system, 32, 41–46
operator's guides, 290
optical character recognition, 52
OS/2, 43

outstanding checks report, 157
outstanding guest checks report, 196, 197

P

parallel conversion, 289
parallel transmission, 72
PASCAL, 45
payment discount date, 240
payroll module, 19, 242–246
payroll register file, 243
personal computer, 8
PL/1, 45
PLU keys, 148–149
point-of-sale systems, 13, 16, 119–123
ports, 72
postcosting, 194, 195
power platform, 167
precheck terminal, 146
precosting, 193–194
preset keys, 148
preventive maintenance, 300
price look-up keys, 148–149
printers, 28–30
  F&B, 151–156
processor-based configuration, 275–276
product usage report, 199, 201
profit and loss statement, 256, 257
programming languages, 44–46
property management system, 11–16, 81–142
  interfaces, 13–16, 119–142
property profile, 267–269
purchase order file, 250
purchasing module, 19, 250–253

Q

query, 68

R

RAM, 32, 33–34
random access medium, 36
random access memory, 32, 33–34
rate assignment, 104–105
ratio analysis, 256, 258
read only memory, 32–33

read/write memory, 33–34
real time capability, 90
receipt printers, 152
recipe management, 179–184
redundant copy, 301
reference code, 112
registration progress report, 106–107
relational database, 67–68
reports, consolidated, 161–162
request for proposal, 277–279
reservation inquiry, 89–90
reservation record, 89, 90–92
reservation systems, 83–98
  central, 83–89
reservation transaction record, 93–94, 96
reservations module, 11–12, 89–94
restaurant management systems, 16–17, 143–202
revenue center reports, 114
revenue forecast report, 92, 95
revenue management, 18, 219–226
ringback mechanism, 126
ROM, 32–33
room assignment, 104–105
room occupancy sensors, 132
rooms activity forecast, 107
rooms allotment report, 106
rooms availability report, 92, 94
rooms discrepancy report, 104
rooms management module, 12, 101–108
  reports, 106–108
rooms management module
rooms status report, 102–104

S

sales, 205–226
  analysis, 184–186
  and payment summary report, 161
  by beverage server report, 196, 197
  by major beverage category report, 196
  by time of day report, 161–162
  filing systems, 212–216
  function/banquet, 208–212
  group, 207–208
  mix by major product report, 199, 200

performance by market
    segment report, 218
performance summary
    report, 218–219
scanner, 27
sectors, 34
security, information system,
    299–306
self check-in/check-out
    systems, 134–136
self-reservation, 95
sequential access medium, 34
serial transmission, 72
settlement keys, 150
settlement methods report,
    196, 198–199
silicon chips, 8
simplex connection 75
site preparation, 287
site survey, 279–280
smart cards, 168–169
smart switch, 88–89
soft copy, 31, 52–53
software, 41, 51–76
software applications, 11,
    51–76
    catering, 18, 226–231
    database management,
        64–71
    electronic communications,
        74–76
    F&B ECR/POS, 157–162
    food service, 191–194
    spreadsheet, 58–64
    word processing, 51–58
    yield management,
        225–226
spell check, 55–56
spreadsheets, 58–64
    linking, 64
stand-alone configuration,
    273–274

standard recipe file, 181–184
statement of income, 256, 257
station message detail record,
    126
streamlining, 6
style sheet, 56
switched backup, 302–303
synergy, 297
system conversion, 289–290
system testing, 298
system update, 113

T

tape streamers, 36
technical manuals, 290
telephone call accounting
    systems, 13, 123–128
teletype terminal, 31
testing, system, 298
thermal printers, 29–30
tickler files, 212–213
time clock system, 243–244
timeout feature, 126
touch-bar faucet, 173
touch-screen terminals, 26,
    163–165
trace files, 212–213
trace report, 213, 214
tracks, 34
traffic transaction report, 127
training, computer system,
    286–287
transfer reports, 114
trial balance file, 254–255
triple modular redundancy,
    303
TTY, 31
tube tower unit, 174
turnaround time, 6
turnaway reports, 94

U

uninterruptible power supply,
    300
UNIX, 42–43
user's guides, 290

V

vending machines, 138–139
vendor master file, 19,
    238–240
vendors, 277–285
    evaluating, 280–283
    negotiation with, 283–285
    support, 291
viruses, computer, 305–306
voice mailboxes, 133
voice recognition systems, 27
volatile memory, 34

W

wake-up calls, 133
wash factor, 221
window environments, 44
wireless terminals, 165–167
word processing, 51–58
work station printers, 152

Y

yield management, 18,
    219–226

HOSPITALITY INDUSTRY COMPUTER SYSTEMS

REVIEW QUIZ ANSWER KEY

The numbers in parentheses refer to the page(s) where the answer may be found.

Chapter 1	Chapter 2	Chapter 3	Chapter 4
1. b (7)	1. f (31)	1. e (59)	1. m (89)
2. f (7)	2. c (28)	2. i (62)	2. l (96)
3. e (3)	3. i (33)	3. l (72)	3. g (84)
4. a (9)	4. h (36)	4. j (64)	4. f (87)
5. h (7)	5. b (33)	5. k (68)	5. c (92)
6. j (18)	6. k (34, 36)	6. b (54)	6. b (88–89)
7. m (8)	7. d (26)	7. d (55)	7. e (94)
8. c (9)	8. a (32)	8. f (59)	8. i (92)
9. T (4)	9. T (26)	9. T (52)	9. T (84)
10. T (6)	10. T (27–28)	10. T (56)	10. T (91)
11. F (6–7)	11. F (30)	11. F (64)	11. T (92)
12. F (7)	12. F (34)	12. T (75)	12. F (94)
13. a (11)	13. a (26)	13. b (54)	13. b (89)
14. b (3)	14. b (40)	14. a (58)	14. c (89)
15. c (19)	15. d (29)	15. b (56)	15. d (93)

Chapter 5	Chapter 6	Chapter 7	Chapter 8
1. g (107)	1. e (119)	1. c (146)	1. f (194)
2. j (109)	2. l (125)	2. g (167)	2. h (184)
3. l (108)	3. k (124)	3. l (146)	3. d (187)
4. c (113)	4. c (125)	4 m (169)	4. g (193)
5. h (112)	5. m (125)	5. i (169)	5. b (181)
6. a (112)	6. a (127)	6. e (159)	6. l (199)
7. f (104)	7. b (129)	7. k (146)	7. i (181)
8. b (114)	8. i (132)	8. b (146)	8. e (184)
9. T (104)	9. T (120)	9. T (149)	9. T (184)
10. T (105)	10. T (123)	10 F (152)	10. F (187)
11. F (106)	11. T (125)	11. F (170)	11. F (193)
12. F (109)	12. F (126)	12. F (171)	12. T (199)
13. a (113)	13. a (132)	13. b (151)	13. b (187)
14. d (101)	14. b (138)	14. d (149)	14. a (199)
15. b (106)	15. c (133)	15. b (156–157)	15. b (179–180)

Chapter 9	Chapter 10	Chapter 11	Chapter 12
1. c (212)	1. m (238)	1. h (267)	1. m (305)
2. m (221)	2. f (238)	2. a (267, 269)	2. h (299)
3. e (220)	3. i (250)	3. f (270)	3. b (303)
4. g (222)	4. b (235)	4. o (271)	4. j (299)
5. j (222)	5. f (238)	5. d (272)	5. k (301)
6. f (221)	6. o (242)	6. p (272)	6. e (302)
7. k (221)	7. k (250-251)	7. j (280)	7. a (297)
8. a (207)	8. a (240)	8. k (284)	8. c (300)
9. T (207)	9. h (247-248)	9. n (287)	9. T (301)
10. T (208)	10. f (240)	10. m (289)	10. F (302)
11. T (209)	11. T (236)	11. T (265)	11. T (305)
12. F (225)	12. T (244-245)	12. F (267, 269)	12. T (300)
13. b (208)	13. T (248)	13. F (270-271)	13. a (301)
14. a (216)	14. b (235)	14. a (271)	14. a (303)
15. d (207)	15. d (253)	15. c (289)	15. d (304)

The

Educational Institute Board of Trustees

The Educational Institute of the American Hotel & Motel Association is fortunate to have both industry and academic leaders, as well as allied members, on its Board of Trustees. Individually and collectively, the following persons play leading roles in supporting the Institute and determining the directions of its programs.

Richard M. Kelleher, CHA
Chairman of the Board
President & CEO
Doubletree Hotels Corporation
Phoenix, Arizona

Jack J. Vaughn, CHA
Secretary
President
Opryland Hospitality and
Attractions Group
Nashville, Tennessee

Philip Pistilli, CHA, CHE
Vice Chairman—Industry
Chairman
Raphael Hotel Group
Kansas City, Missouri

**Anthony G. Marshall, Ph.D.,
CHA, CHE**
Assistant Treasurer
Dean
School of Hospitality
Management
Florida International
University
North Miami, Florida

**Ronald F. Cichy, Ph.D., CHA,
CFBE, CHE**
Vice Chairman—Academia
Director
The School of Hospitality
Business
Michigan State University
East Lansing, Michigan

Ronald A. Evans, CHA
Assistant Secretary
President & CEO
Best Western
International, Inc.
Phoenix, Arizona

**W. Anthony "Tony" Farris,
CHA**
Treasurer
President & CEO
Quorum Hotels and Resorts
Dallas, Texas

Robert T. Foley
President
President & CEO
Educational Institute of
AH&MA
East Lansing, Michigan

Steven J. Belmonte, CHA
President & COO
Ramada Franchise
  Systems, Inc.
Parsippany, New Jersey

John Q. Hammons
Chairman & CEO
John Q. Hammons
  Hotels, Inc.
Springfield, Missouri

David J. Christianson, Ph.D.
Dean
William F. Harrah College of
  Hotel Administration
University of Nevada,
  Las Vegas
Las Vegas, Nevada

Arnold J. Hewes, CAE
Executive Vice President
Minnesota Hotel & Lodging
  Association
St. Paul, Minnesota

Caroline A. Cooper, CHA
Dean
The Hospitality College
Johnson & Wales University
Providence, Rhode Island

S. Kirk Kinsell
President—Franchise
ITT Sheraton World
  Headquarters
Atlanta, Georgia

Edouard P.O. Dandrieux, CHA
Director
H.I.M., Hotel Institute,
  Montreux
Montreux, Switzerland

Donald J. Landry, CHA
President
Choice Hotels International
Silver Spring, Maryland

Valerie C. Ferguson
General Manager
Ritz-Carlton Atlanta
Atlanta, Georgia

Georges LeMener
President & CEO
Motel 6, L.P.
Dallas, Texas

Douglas G. Geoga
President
Hyatt Hotels Corporation
Chicago, Illinois

Jerry R. Manion, CHA
President
Manion Investments
Paradise Valley, Arizona

Joseph A. McInerney, CHA
President & CEO
Forte Hotels, Inc.
El Cajon, California

William R. Tiefel
President
Marriott Lodging
Washington, D.C.

John L. Sharpe, CHA
President & COO
Four Seasons-Regent Hotels
 and Resorts
Toronto, Ontario, Canada

Jonathan M. Tisch
President & CEO
Loews Hotels
New York, New York

Paul J. Sistare, CHA
President & CEO
Richfield Hospitality Services
Englewood, Colorado

Paul E. Wise, CHA
Professor & Director
Hotel, Restaurant &
 Institutional Management
University of Delaware
Newark, Delaware

Thomas W. Staed, CHA
President
Oceans Eleven Resorts, Inc.
Daytona Beach Shores, Florida

Ted Wright, CHA
Vice President/Managing
 Director
The Cloister Hotel
Sea Island, Georgia

Thomas G. Stauffer, CHA
President & CFO
Americas Region
Renaissance Hotels
 International, Inc.
Cleveland, Ohio